SEE JANE WIN

SEE JANE WIN

*The Rimm Report on
How 1,000 Girls Became
Successful Women*

SYLVIA RIMM, PH.D.

with Sara Rimm-Kaufman, Ph.D.,
and Ilonna Rimm, M.D., Ph.D.

Three Rivers Press

NEW YORK

OUR BOOK IS DEDICATED TO OUR FAMILIES,
WHO HAVE ALWAYS BEEN SO SUPPORTIVE,
AND ESPECIALLY TO
OUR MOTHERS, DAUGHTERS, SISTERS, SISTERS-IN-LAW,
AND GRANDDAUGHTERS

Published by Three Rivers Press, New York, New York.
Member of the Crown Publishing Group.

Originally published in hardcover by Crown Publishers in 1999.

Random House, Inc. New York, Toronto, London, Sydney, Auckland
www.randomhouse.com

THREE RIVERS PRESS is a registered trademark of Random House, Inc.

Design by Susan Hood
Printed in the United States of America

Library of Congress Cataloging-in-Publication Data
Rimm, Sylvia B., 1935–
    See Jane Win : the Rimm report on how 1,000 girls became
successful women / Sylvia Rimm with Sara Rimm-Kaufman
and Ilonna Rimm.
    1. Parent and teenager.   2. Teenage girls—Psychology.   3. Self-
perception in adolescence.   4. Self-esteem in adolescence.
5. Success—Psychological aspects.   6. Achievement motivation in
women.   I. Rimm-Kaufman, Sara.   II. Rimm, Ilonna Jane.
III. Title.
HQ799.15.R56   1999
155.5'33—dc21   98-55295
                                                                      CIP
                        ISBN 0-609-80560-6

            10   9   8   7   6   5   4   3   2   1
                    First Paperback Edition

CONTENTS

*Actual name, used with permission.

Introduction

The feminist movement has opened doors for women to achieve equality in many new leadership positions. The women who enter through those doors and rise to new career heights, often combining their careers with parenting, are, in effect, explorers and adventurers. Opportunities that women of earlier generations never even dared to imagine are now available to them. Surely the parents, teachers, and mentors who influenced and encouraged today's women were not given guidance on how to raise them for today's careers. Yet it is certain that genetics alone does not select girls for new opportunities; genetic differences have always been with us. It is the increase in opportunities that permits women to enter those new frontiers, and the childhood home and school environments that encourage girls to pioneer and explore careers that their mothers and grandmothers were prevented from entering.

For the first time in our country's history, women work and lead alongside men in major business enterprises. They are directors and administrators in school districts, hospitals, and major community agencies; they lead worship services in churches and synagogues; they are elected to political office at the local, state, and national levels; they play in symphony orchestras and exhibit their art in major museums; they direct laboratories and conduct major research projects; they are included in the ranks of physicians and attorneys; they staff major radio and television networks, edit important magazines and newspapers, and report and make news throughout the world; they continue to be the mainstays of the traditional helping professions in schools, hospitals, and mental health clinics; and a small percentage of them elect to be full-time homemakers to raise their own children the way they were raised.

As our society gradually equalizes opportunities for women (perhaps too gradually, as you will ascertain when you read about our group of women), a better understanding of the parenting and educational techniques that will guide girls to strive for these opportunities is needed. To date, the research on raising girls for equality has come from comparisons of how boys and girls are treated at home and in classrooms. A major report published by the American Association of University Women focused on how girls are shortchanged in school.[1] The assumption has been that if girls are raised similarly to boys and the same educational opportunities are provided, girls and boys will become equally successful. It is also assumed that if girls are given the same opportunities as boys, they will become as fulfilled as boys. These assumptions may in fact be correct, and certainly we have learned from these research comparisons. However, they assume sameness rather than equality, and biology tells us that men and women are surely not the same. Gender differences need to be addressed.

Although the study of the different early environments of girls and boys may give us important clues about raising girls for equal opportunities, it is the study of the childhood paths of successful and fulfilled women that can yield tangible information, resulting in concrete advice that can be passed on to parents and teachers. Our research studies the childhood influences of women who have successfully entered careers that were previously reserved for men and that often continue to be male-dominated. It also examines childhood influences on women who entered some of the careers that have been traditional for women. The goal of our research was to identify the essential childhood elements that encouraged these women to achieve fulfilling careers. However, most parents and teachers would agree that it is not enough just to raise girls to pursue prestigious and fulfilling careers. Therefore, the women in our study were asked to participate only if their personal and family lives were reasonably happy as well.

It is not the desire to understand eminence that motivates our research, because only a few can reach eminence. Instead, we wanted to gain a better understanding of the motivating factors in the lives of successful, happy women so that parents and educators might apply those factors to raising and educating their daughters and female students. In short, we want to know what has *worked* and what real-life ingredients have influenced women to combine interesting careers with happy personal lives. We hope girls and young women who read this book can also be inspired by the stories of successful women. These stories are about both the American dream and the feminist dream.

While there are a great number of male-dominated career fields we could have explored, we initially selected eight career areas in which women are presently only beginning to participate: science and technology, media, orchestral music, visual arts, business administration, medicine, law, and government office. Once our research began, it became clear that the leadership roles in business administration seemed to divide naturally into two categories: for-profit business and not-for-profit organizations. These nine areas are sufficiently different from each other to provide valuable comparisons and are a manageable number to explore.

All these areas historically had few women; although presently there are many women training for careers in these areas, they are only in the pipeline and often are not yet represented in leadership positions. Studying the childhoods of the successful and fulfilled women in these areas thus provides a laboratory for discovery.

Although it was our original intention to research the childhood influences of women in only nontraditional careers, in our published search for volunteers we attracted a hue and cry from successful and happy women in careers in which women have historically been heavily represented. They reminded us that women should have choices and that many women are both fulfilled and making important contributions in more traditional careers. Furthermore, it seemed important to know if there were differences in how they were parented and taught. Of course, women have had a long history of leadership opportunities as teachers, nurses, social workers, executive secretaries, community volunteers, and homemakers. We didn't want to diminish the value of these or any other traditional career paths. In fact, we agree that we need to encourage both women and men to continue their contributions in all these areas.

We heard the voices of these women in traditional careers and heeded their requests by extending our study to include four career areas traditional to women: education, mental health, allied health, and homemakers–community volunteers. We requested that women in these areas who wished to participate in our research be happy with their career choice and not wish they had chosen a different career with more status or more salary. Our research reveals the similarities and the differences in raising girls for both typical and atypical careers.

The research and writing of this book have taken approximately three and a half years to complete. We advertised for volunteers for our study through more than seventy professional newsletters and another hundred national weekly and daily newspapers. We also sent mailings to women in specific career categories and advertised for candidates on public radio, television, and the Internet. We also invited volunteers through university contacts at Harvard Medical School, Yale Medical School, Massachusetts Institute of Technology, Johns Hopkins Medical School, Case Western Reserve University School of Medicine, Wellesley College, University of Virginia, and Douglass College. The group may not be random but is at least representative of many talented women.

We gathered our information with an extensive twenty-three-page questionnaire, which was initially piloted by twenty-five women and finally completed by more than fourteen hundred successful women from all over the United States. Our actual questionnaire response rate was 23 percent. Many women commented that the questionnaires were time-consuming and sometimes psychologically difficult to complete. Others commented that the actual completion of the questionnaire was rewarding and permitted an important self-assessment for them. They often wrote long notes and indicated appreciation for the opportunity to participate and express their concerns.

We eliminated from the study those who considered themselves neutral or unhappy in their work, leaving us with 1,236 questionnaires for analysis. The average age of our respondents was forty-four, and the range in age was between twenty-nine and eighty-five. We followed up the questionnaires by interviewing 120 of these women. Questionnaires provided the detailed data that helped us to understand the important formative environments that impacted on the raising and educating of these women, and interviews provided the fascinating stories that will give parents, educators, and young women an in-depth understanding of the essential principles needed to bring up girls for the twenty-first century.

Our book is designed for at least four groups of readers. First and foremost, we hope that parents will find in this book good, commonsense research-based advice for raising their daughters. Teachers and mentors will also benefit by understanding the positive difference they make by encouraging girls. A third audience should be women who might like to compare their stories to those of successful women in order to better understand themselves. Finally, we're hoping that preadolescents, teens, and young adult women will find inspiration and guidance in the stories of these successful women.

The main findings of our research are summarized in Chapter 1. Each success summary is accompanied by advice based on those findings. Chapter 1 also includes profiles of the five main career groups. The thirteen actual careers researched are categorized as (1) power brokers, (2) healers and discoverers, (3) communicators, (4) artists and musicians, and (5) nurturers. Brief descriptions of each category provide themes typical of the category as well as the differences between careers within the category.

The remainder of the book elaborates on the findings and provides stories of and quotations from the women (actual names used with permission are denoted with asterisks). We describe commonalities and differences among the career paths as well as themes that seem to run through the childhoods of successful women in most careers. Some differences between the older (over forty-four) and younger (under forty-four) women in our study are also described. If you are interested in viewing a copy of the survey, please write to Dr. Sylvia Rimm, Educational Assessment Service, Inc., W6050 Apple Road, Watertown, WI 53098-3937.

Each chapter is followed by case stories. Each story was chosen because it seemed a particularly good match for the theme of that chapter. Some of the childhood stories included are of individual women, while others provide a blend of the childhoods of more than one woman.

CHAPTER 1

ONE THOUSAND
SUCCESSFUL WOMEN

Twenty Guidelines for Raising
Your Daughters

Here are the twenty most important findings of our research and the resulting guidelines for raising girls for success.

Research Finding #1

Both the American dream and the feminist dream are alive and well for the successful women who participated in our study. They have outperformed both their mothers and fathers in their educational attainments. Although less than a third of their mothers and less than half of their fathers completed college, almost all of the women had at least college degrees. A third had master's degrees, and another third had doctorates in the arts and sciences or a professional degree in medicine or law. The women in our study were not only successful but happy in their families and social relationships.

GUIDELINE #1 *Set high educational expectations for your daughters. Expect them to complete college and beyond, whether or not you did. Discuss careers with them, and expect them to have careers. Teach them that educational attainment is of the highest priority.*

Research Finding #2

About 70 percent of the women believed that *both* their parents had high expectations for them. More than a third of the women indicated they felt pressure from parents, teachers, peers, and themselves, although for the most part they liked the pressure or at least didn't seem to mind it.

GUIDELINE #2 *Don't be too quick to back off if your daughters have to cope with some pressure. It's all part of learning resilience. Expect much from your daughters, and they will expect much of themselves. Coach them for success. Expectations are much more effective if both parents agree (whether or not they're married to each other). If you can't agree, having one parent who sets high expectations is much better than neither doing so. However, too much pressure can cause serious problems. Don't set unrealistically high expectations. If your daughter is experiencing symptoms of pressure, help her to make decisions about how to manage her time better or which activities to eliminate. If she reports too much pressure or begins to show physical symptoms, get professional help.*

Research Finding #3

Although most of the successful women in the study were highly intelligent according to various measures, many described themselves as above average or even average in intellectual abilities. Most of the women invested considerable time in study and homework while in school. Motivation seemed at least as critical as ability.

GUIDELINE #3 *Help your daughters to understand that they don't need to be the smartest to feel smart, but assure them that you believe they are intelligent and that "airheads" don't make it but "brains" do. Studying does pay off. Help them to develop good study habits. Even perfectionism, if not too extreme, can lead to production and achievement. Assure your daughters that they won't wear their IQ score on their foreheads, and for the most part, they should not consider their IQ score a limitation as long as they are interested, motivated, and willing to persevere.*

Research Finding #4

In choosing words to describe themselves as they were growing up, the women of the study chose "smart," "hard worker," and "independent" most often. Those descriptors were also chosen most by the women to describe their perceptions of how others saw them. "Happy," "mature," "adultlike," "creative," and "good little girl" were also mentioned frequently. There were various descriptors used by women in some careers, but "smart" and "hardworking" were constants for all careers.

GUIDELINE #4 *View your daughters as intelligent, good thinkers, and problem solvers. Value work. Be positive about your own work. Have family work projects. A work ethic and a love of accomplishment underlie motivation. Doing chores around the house, baby-sitting, running small businesses (such as lemonade stands), tutoring or teaching others, and working on creative projects will all build a sense of personal competence.*

Research Finding #5

Many successful women described themselves as "sensitive," "kind," "shy," "emotional," "perfectionistic," and "self-critical." Very few used terms such as "troublemaker," "manipulative," "problem child," "rebellious," or even "fashion leader."

GUIDELINE #5 *Characteristics that are gender-stereotyped as female characteristics don't necessarily interfere with success. Assertiveness can be learned. On the other hand, if your daughter is having behavior or learning problems in school, take it seriously. Get the kind of professional assistance that will help her view herself as hardworking, smart, and independent.*

Research Finding #6

Most of the successful women in our study, 79 percent, were educated in public schools; 16 percent attended parochial schools, and 5 percent went to independent schools. Comparable figures for the general population are 89 percent in public schools, 9 percent in parochial schools, and 2 percent in independent schools. Approximately twice as many of our successful women attended parochial and independent schools as do children in the overall population.

Attendance at same-gender schools and colleges was viewed favorably and positively by the women who attended those schools. Ten percent of the women attended all-female high schools. Thirteen percent attended women's colleges. Approximately 20 percent of the successful women admitted that boys and social life adversely affected their seriousness about school and learning during their middle- and high-school years. Specific teachers were frequently mentioned by these women as inspiring regardless of whether they attended public or private schools.

GUIDELINE #6 *Your daughters can be successful at public schools; however, there may be some advantages to parochial, independent, and all-girls schools. Consider the quality of the particular school, and carefully review your own economic priorities as well as your daughters' interests and needs when planning for your daughters' educational opportunities. The middle-school and high-school years may be a more important time than the elementary years to choose a special school if finances are limited. On the other hand, it may not be worth a financial sacrifice if your daughters are doing well at good public schools. Search for schools with dedicated and inspiring teachers. They may make a great difference for your daughters.*

Research Finding #7

The best academic subjects of these women as early as elementary school may have at least partially predicted many of their career directions. (Because this is a retrospective study, their memories may be prejudiced by their current interests.) The women in medicine, science, and the allied health professions were best at science. Best in math were the physicians, scientists, and executives in business. More women in media were best at reading and English, and many loved writing and were fascinated with the use of words. More women in government and law performed best in social studies and history. The women's strengths became more pronounced as they matured. The overall best subject for the total group of women was English, which should delight English teachers and reaffirm findings that women tend to have strong verbal skills. It's unlikely we'd find that a best subject among many successful men.

GUIDELINE #7 *Encourage your daughters to develop math and science skills. Counting, measuring, and experimenting can begin during the preschool years. Encourage girls to play with toys that involve spatial relationships, such as puzzles and blocks. The future will offer your daughters more opportunities if they are comfortable with math.*

Reading is a very high priority. Begin reading to your daughters during infancy. Don't worry if your daughter is a bookworm. There were many bookworms among the women of the study in every successful career category. Read to and with your daughters, and let them see you enjoy reading. Encourage their love of history and social studies as well. Girls who are truly interested in learning have a better chance of success.

Research Finding #8

Middle-school math decline is real for many women, even for some successful women. Although as many women indicated that confidence in math and science improved as indicated it declined, excellent math and science grades provided the threshold for the women who entered scientific professions. Thus, if they were not good at math, doors to most science careers were closed. Math was also important for the women in business. Also, the percentage of women who took advanced math and science courses was directly related to the numbers that went into careers that required math and science. The most important reason given by women for taking advanced courses was their personal interest. The second and third reasons were teacher and parent advice.

GUIDELINE #8 *Whether you liked or feared math, encourage your daughters to enjoy the subject. Your daughters will have more choices if they conquer advanced math. If they're struggling, arrange for tutoring. Encourage them to take advanced courses even if it means getting a B or C rather than the A they and you hoped for. They may need you to say things like "We admire the way you take on challenges" or "We're glad you're taking the hard courses." Don't hesitate to advise your daughters to take advanced math, even if it was difficult for you. If possible, encourage their teachers to offer the same advice. If you have a choice, find a school that encourages girls to take math and science. All-girls schools often take pride in their math and science emphasis. Encourage your public schools to offer all-girls math and science classes.*

On the other hand, if after real effort, your daughters truly have no interest in math, there are many verbal and creative careers available to them (traditional and nontraditional) despite the fact that some of these careers are very competitive or less financially satisfying.

Research Finding #9

A quarter of the women skipped subjects and 15 percent skipped grades during elementary and secondary school. These percentages varied by career group. Grade and subject skipping seemed to build intellectual self-confidence and may have been important experiences in learning to cope with challenge. Furthermore, the time saved by the skipping and acceleration was valued and reassuring for the women who pursued many years of postgraduate education. There was no indication that grade skipping had an adverse effect on social adjustment.

GUIDELINE #9   *If your daughters are not challenged academically, evaluate with professionals the possibility of shortening their education by grade or subject skipping.*

Research Finding #10

The successful women in our group talked and read early. The attorneys talked and read earliest of all. The women in the study were very actively involved during childhood and adolescence. Reading was a favorite childhood activity, followed by music and involvement in Girl Scouts. Many women said they were motivated by reading biographies of successful women. Athletics and student government became increasingly important as they moved from elementary to high school. There were three times as many women in sports as in cheerleading during high school. Half the women indicated that spending time alone had been important during their childhood. Most women watched two hours or less of television daily.

GUIDELINE #10   *Extracurricular activities are important—music, art, dance, Scouts, band, orchestra, chorus, drama, religious groups, and sports. It's worth the effort and time to drive your daughters to meetings and practices. Learning to manage busy schedules teaches girls to handle complexity and ambiguity when they become adults. Teach them organizational and planning skills. However, also insist on some quiet time*

alone for girls to learn to entertain themselves, cultivate their imagina-
tions, and read. Encourage girls to read about successful women. Televi-
sion watching should be minimized.

Research Finding #11

Many of our successful women listed "winning in competition" as an
important positive experience for them. The third, fourth, and fifth
most frequently chosen positive experiences were "award in a talent
field," "exhibition of work at school," and "school-elected office." These
are all competitive experiences. It seems that winning is motivating. In
light of the controversial effort by many schools to eliminate or minimize competition in education, this finding is enlightening. Coping with
winning and losing in competition builds resiliency.

GUIDELINE #11   *Girls often feel competitive, but they may not admit it. It*
is almost as if they believe that "good little girls" aren't supposed to be
competitive. Furthermore, girls sometimes avoid competitive activities
unless they are certain they'll be winners. Encourage them to enter music
contests, art shows, debates, science fairs, 4-H exhibits, math competitions,
and creative problem-solving meets.

Obviously, your daughters don't have to enter all competitions, but
there are many from which they can choose. Winning builds confidence;
losing builds character. If girls are to be successful and take risks in a
competitive society, they will have to experience both winning and losing,
and entering a variety of contests will provide some winning experiences
they will never forget as well as some losing ones from which they will
undoubtedly benefit without even remembering them.

Research Finding #12

The second most frequently chosen positive experience for women at
all developmental levels and in all career groups was travel. Travel with
their families was viewed as enriching and adventurous. It also provided family bonding. Independent travel built self-confidence.

GUIDELINE #12   *Plan to travel with your family, and encourage your*
daughters to travel independently when they're old enough. Also, plan

*twosome trips (mother-daughter, father-daughter) to encourage close-
ness and bonding; as a bonus, this type of trip is not as complex to plan.
Although family travel arrangements can sometimes be difficult, children don't seem to remember the hassles—only the fun, learning, family
togetherness, adventure, and independence.*

Research Finding #13

The negative experience most frequently mentioned by the women in
the study was "isolation from peers." Although about a quarter of the
women considered themselves more social than others their age, by
high school 40 percent of the women considered themselves to have
been less social than typical. The women of some professions were considerably more social, including those in media, education, government,
and business.

The women in all careers tended to have friends during their childhood and adolescence who were achievement-oriented and cared
about learning. Although some had a mixture of friends, almost none
had mainly negative friends who were rebellious and did not care about
success in school.

GUIDELINE #13 *Let your daughters know that popularity is not important even if it feels important to them. Be careful to avoid pressuring
them to have lots of friends. Set limits. Negative friends may spell trouble
for them, although even some of the successful women had negative
associations during high school. They should value independence from
their peers. If you let your daughters know they can be different, they
may not wish to be part of a particular crowd. They can move between
groups and may enjoy the freedom to do so. They may even be able to
form their own crowd.*

*Loneliness can be difficult during adolescence. Loneliness can also be
difficult for successful executives, scientists, attorneys, writers, and artists.
Consider this another important step in teaching resilience. If teens
understand that many others experience loneliness, they'll feel less isolated. During lonely times, compensate by planning fun family activities.
If having friends is hard for your daughters, allow them to invite a friend
along on family outings. On the other hand, if your daughters are already
too social, keep family activities for family members only, to build family
bonds.*

Research Finding #14

Tobacco, alcohol, and drugs were used minimally by our successful women. Many went through college during the late sixties and early seventies, and experimented with drugs. Younger women in the study used more drugs in college than the older women. Older women used more tobacco than the younger women while in college. Alcohol use was similar for both groups. There were very few women who indicated they were substance abusers.

GUIDELINE #14 *If you used drugs, drank too much, or smoked when you were young, don't glorify your own experimentations. You survived, but you probably remember some peers who didn't. The drugs of today are more potent than the ones that were available twenty years ago, and there is more research that proves drugs, even marijuana, to be harmful. Tell your daughters about the friends who lost out and whom you lost, and make it clear that you expect them not to smoke, drink illegally, or use illegal drugs. Be realistic. If they experiment, don't give up on them. Don't condone it, or they may take it one step further than is good for them.*

Research Finding #15

Although there were some women in every career group who had been rebellious adolescents, most of the women got along well with their parents most of the time. There weren't as many "excellent" ratings for relationships with parents during adolescence as in childhood, but the women mainly considered their relationships with both their parents to be quite good. Relationships with parents were most problematic for those women who became mental health professionals. Also, more of the parents of mental health professionals were not firm disciplinarians. The women attorneys indicated more conflict with their mothers during their high-school years than women in other careers, although that was not the case for them during their elementary or middle-school years.

GUIDELINE #15 *You are your daughters' best supporters. Remind them you're their ally and definitely not their enemy. Be a coach, not a judge. Give adolescent girls enough freedom to explore their world, but don't accept rebellion. Set firm limits for your teens and stay as positive as pos-*

sible. Avoid overpunishment. Encourage them to choose positive activities, and don't take their positive activities away from them as punishments if you're angry or if they've misbehaved. Their positive activities and relationships are the source of their identity building. Don't reward them for good behavior with activities or possessions that you believe will be harmful, even if they'd like to have them.

Research Finding #16

Our study showed that all careers had women of all birth orders. Nonetheless, certain birth orders seemed to give women some advantage in some careers. There were many more firstborns in all of the nontraditional career groups and in education, followed by middle and then youngest children. In the other three career groups traditional to women, there were differences in predominating birth orders. The homemakers' category had the most middle children; the mental health professionals had the most youngest children; and the allied health professional group had as many middle children as oldest.

GUIDELINE #16 *While birth order is important, it is not the major factor for success. Be sure that your daughters get leadership opportunities and responsibilities regardless of birth order. Don't baby the youngest daughter. Be sure middle children also receive individual attention. Don't label your children "the scholarly one," "the creative one," "the athlete," and so on. Your daughters can be part of a whole smart family and creative and athletic without having to be the smartest, the most creative, or the best athlete in the family.*

Research Finding #17

Although 83 percent of our successful women had mothers who were full-time homemakers when the women were preschoolers, many had careers or returned to school after their children's preschool years. By the women's high-school years, almost two-thirds of their mothers had careers outside of home. More women in traditional occupations had mothers who remained homemakers and didn't continue their education.

Approximately half of the successful women identified with their mothers; a quarter identified with their fathers. Some women identified with their mothers early and then shifted that identification to their fathers or teachers as they matured. Some women identified with other people or no one. Parents were these women's most frequent role models.

GUIDELINE #17 *As mothers, don't hesitate about fulfilling your own life dreams by returning to school or entering a career. Your daughters are watching you. If you achieve, they see you as competent and are more likely to believe that they, too, can be competent. As fathers, be supportive of your wives' achievement goals. Your daughters are likely to benefit even more than if your wives stayed at home. You are both important to your daughters' self-confidence.*

Research Finding #18

Successful women learned resilience. Sixty-two percent described times in their education when they experienced great difficulty or "hit a wall." Many changed majors, underachieved, or even dropped out of college temporarily. Many more experienced anxiety or depression. The most frequently reported survival skill was perseverance.

GUIDELINE #18 *Expect ups and downs for your daughters. Don't assume their setbacks are permanent. Believe in their survival skills, and let them know that they too can persevere. Don't overprotect them because they're girls, difficult as that may feel.*

Research Finding #19

The three most common reasons the women of our study chose for recommending their careers to others were that the career was "challenging," "makes a contribution," and is "creative." "Financially satisfying" was not chosen by a large number of women, nor did many women complain about financial dissatisfaction.

GUIDELINE #19 *Teach your daughters to value the three C's: challenge, contribution, and creativity. If they are afraid to try new experiences, problem-solve with them on how to be daring and courageous. Role-play the skills they will require for new challenges and experiences.*

Making a contribution to society should be valued as important. Society needs the intellect and skills of women and making a positive difference should be valued by families. However, girls should grow up to expect equivalent remuneration to that of men in similar positions rather than settling for inequality. Girls should learn to insist on equal treatment.

Encourage your daughters' creative thinking. If they have unusual ideas, hear them out. Listening and encouraging their creativity does not prevent your setting reasonable limits but will permit them to think beyond compliance.

Research Finding #20

Your daughters may wish to have families and careers. Our successful women struggled and sacrificed to balance the roles of mother, wife, and professional. They sometimes experienced fertility problems related to delayed childbearing. A mothering metamorphosis often took place after the birth of the first child. Many redirected their careers or took time off. As a result, they often coped with penalties in their careers because of their parenting commitments. Women in some careers commented on "glass ceilings" and "sticky floors"; promotion opportunities sometimes seemed unfair. For many others, careers followed alternating sequences (explained further in Chapter 10), and, indeed, their stairways to success were circuitous. In our study the women in the traditional careers—homemakers, educators, allied health workers, and mental health professionals—more frequently rated their family lives as excellent.

GUIDELINE #20 *Talk about the wonderful metamorphosis that takes place for new mothers, although your daughters will have to experience it to believe it. Your daughters can have choices in the way they would like to balance or sequence career and family.*

If your daughters plan to marry, encourage them to select partners who are willing to share power and parenting responsibilities. If your daughters wish to have careers, they should choose husbands who will respect their choices.

Don't disdain the option of a traditional career. Educators, allied health professionals, mental health professionals, and homemakers make important and creative contributions to our society. If your daughters want to be full-time homemakers, they should make a commitment to volunteer in the community in order to contribute to society and build personal self-confidence. Furthermore, even if homemaking is their first choice, they should be expected to have an education for a career so they'll be prepared for emergencies and self-sufficiency should the need present itself.

Your daughters may wish to postpone or slow career growth in order to devote more time to family, or they may prefer a full commitment to their careers and share the family responsibilities with child-care providers. Give them the freedom to set their own sequences without encumbering them with your own preferences.

Main Childhood Characteristics of Each Career Category

THE POWER BROKERS

Women were almost entirely absent in the power-broker professions a generation ago. These careers have in common involvement in leadership and assertiveness with people. They include for-profit and not-for-profit business, government, and law.

Included in the women in government were state senators and representatives; judges at state, county, and local levels; government appointees; state attorney generals and assistant attorney generals; health commissioners; and mayors of cities and small communities. The for-profit businesswomen included CEOs, presidents, and vice presidents in small, medium, and large businesses as well as consultants and entrepreneurs who began their own successful businesses. The women in not-for-profit business included administrators of foundations and nonprofit charitable organizations; school district and college deans and other administrators; clergy; and hospital administrators. Most of the attorneys were associates or partners in law firms; a few were professors of law. Many of the women in government were trained as attorneys but were differentiated for this study because they considered their primary career to be in government at this time.

All three of these professional groups included women who were quite social during childhood. The only group that tended to be somewhat less social were the attorneys. The women in government were the most social and the most directly involved in school politics, although almost all of the power-broker women had plenty of school involvement. More of the women in for-profit business and law tended to be rebellious during adolescence, although their relationships with their parents were generally favorable.

Many of the attorneys and women in government were involved in debate and forensics during their school years. Many of the women in for-profit business were entrepreneurs as children. The women in both business groups and government said they were most frequently described by others as "leaders" throughout their school years. Compared to the other three groups, the attorneys were described as "leaders" least often. Instead, "brainy" was much more frequently used to describe their perceptions of how others viewed them. Furthermore, the attorneys tended to rank higher academically in their graduating classes than the women in any of the other three groups, although many women in all four groups were considered to be very smart. The subjects most favored by the women in government, law, and nonprofit business were social studies and history, but mathematics topped the list for the women in for-profit business. Higher percentages of power-broker women in all four categories went to women's colleges and held leadership positions during college.

Although women in all four careers were mainly happy in their careers, the women in for-profit business and law indicated the most financial satisfaction, and those in nonprofit business and government had larger percentages that indicated financial dissatisfaction. Again, home lives were mainly satisfactory for the women of all groups, but fewer of the women in business indicated the "very happy" category for their home satisfaction. The women in for-profit business also had slightly higher divorce rates than those in the other three categories. In contrast, the women attorneys and politicians had more frequent complaints about their jobs taking too much time from their families than the other two groups.

THE HEALERS AND DISCOVERERS

Women are now prominently involved in many areas of science and medicine, although they continue to be a very small minority within some specialties. Only a generation ago, very few women were part of these scientifically oriented professions.

The women in science and medicine share strong backgrounds in science and mathematics that were thresholds to entering their professions. Almost all of the women in these careers have earned advanced degrees, including Ph.D.'s , M.D.'s, and veterinary and dentistry doctoral degrees. A few of the engineers have bachelor's or master's degrees in engineering. Many of these women are involved in the practice of medicine or related specialties. Although more of the physicians are involved in pediatrics and obstetrics than any other specialty, there are also surgeons, orthopedic surgeons, internists, family practitioners, urologists, psychiatrists, cardiologists, radiologists, and dermatologists. Among the researchers are quite a few who are conducting biological, biochemical, or psychological research, and a fair number who are engineers.

The physicians and scientists tended to be somewhat less social as children, particularly in middle and high school, although they were very active in extracurricular activities and often assumed leadership roles in those activities. They had more than typical involvement on sports teams and tended to enjoy other competitive activities as well. They also tended to be more involved in outdoor activities and had high Girl Scout participation. As children, they also participated in music more often than the women in most other careers.

The physicians and scientists enjoyed and mastered science and mathematics from elementary school on, much more so than all other groups. In general, very few of them experienced mathematics, science, or general grade decline during middle or high school. Actually, many of these women increased in academic confidence as they moved through adolescence. They were less distracted by boys during those crucial teen years and had smoother adolescent relationships with their parents than some of the other career groups. Although more of them identified with their mothers than their fathers, when these groups were compared to other career groups, larger percentages identified with their fathers. Many of their mothers returned to school to continue their education while they were growing up.

The women in this category were frequently considered "brainy" by others, although—as with most of the successful women in our study—"smart," "hardworking," and "independent" were very frequent descriptors. "Creative" was mentioned as a somewhat more frequent descriptor about the scientists than the physicians, and "athletic" somewhat more by the physicians than the scientists. More of these women went to parochial schools for their elementary education, and fewer of them went to women's colleges compared to other career groups.

These women were mainly happy with their career choice, although more women in medicine expressed mixed feelings about their career. They indicated more time spent on their job than all other career groups, with more than half indicating they worked over fifty hours per week. Both the physicians and scientists expressed concerns that their careers took too much time from their families. Some scientists commented that their careers involved too much competition. More of the physicians indicated that their job was financially satisfying, and both career groups credited their careers as being challenging and making a contribution. More of the scientists than the physicians liked the creativity involved in their careers.

THE COMMUNICATORS

The women in media and mental health have almost as many differences as similarities, but their emphasis on verbal communication and the fact that these careers are semitraditional bind them together. There have always been some women in media, but traditionally producers, executives, and the most important radio and television news anchors had been men. Presently there are as many women news anchors as men and at least as many if not more women producers. Even some of the technical crew are women. Executive producers continue to be mainly men, but more women are making inroads there as well. Many more women have become involved in print media, although editorial positions in non–women's magazines continue to be held most frequently by men. There remain semipervious glass ceilings, of course, but media is a career area in which women have made early inroads.

The same holds true for the field of mental health. Although social work has always been considered a traditionally female profession, psychologists were rarely women. Now there are probably as many if not more women in the practice of psychology than men. (Psychology researchers were not included among the communicators, but were considered in the research scientist category.)

Most of the mental health professionals were psychologists, although some were social workers or counselors. Among the media women were a great range of radio and television producers, news anchors, and program hosts at the national and local levels. Those involved in print media included editors, reporters, and publicists on local and national levels.

Both these groups of communicating women described themselves as emotional and sensitive during their childhood more frequently than the women in other careers, although their main descriptors also included "smart," "hardworking," and "independent," which were frequent descriptors for women in other career groups as well.

Although the women in both media and mental health professions were similar in their IQ distribution, the mental health professionals achieved better academic performance in school than the media women. The women in media seemed to study less than almost any other group and experienced more decline in grades in middle and high school. Both groups were strong in English and writing, but the mental health professionals also indicated special strength and interest in social studies. Math and science were not strong areas for the women in either group.

Other differences existed between the two career groups. The women in the media group were more typically oldest children, while more of the women in mental health were youngest in birth order. Although they were about equal in social involvement in elementary school, the women in media were more social in high school than the mental health professionals. Both groups indicated that the influence of boys caused grade decline for them in middle school. Both groups took fewer advanced math and science courses in high school, and both showed grade improvement in high school compared to middle school, perhaps related to their lesser enrollment in advanced courses.

Parents of the mental health professionals tended to be less firm with them as they were growing up, and they were actually the most rebellious with their parents during adolescence. Although the media women's parents were similar in firmness to the total group, some of these women had difficulty with their parents during adolescence as well.

Both groups mainly enjoyed their careers but also commented on the financial disappointment and the overcompetitiveness of those careers. While the mental health professions indicated more frequently that "makes a contribution" was a most important reason for recommending their careers, more of the women in media suggested "creative" as their most important reason. More mental health professionals were divorced than media women; however, more media women were single despite the higher divorce rate of their parents. Their younger-than-average age may account for their fewer divorces.

THE ARTISTS AND MUSICIANS

The visual artists and orchestral musicians were grouped together because from early in their childhood they were recognized by others mainly for their talents and their creativity. Although they were also considered smart, hardworking, independent, and "good little girls," their more frequently mentioned traits were related to their specialized talent and interest.

Most of the women in the orchestral musician category played in major symphony orchestras throughout the country. A few played in opera or ballet orchestras or were on the teaching faculties of music departments of universities or music conservatories. These women were eager participants in the study in that we received a fairly immediate response from them to our questionnaire, and many offered to participate in interviews. The visual artists tended to be more difficult to locate and somewhat more reluctant to participate in the study, perhaps because of the necessary criterion that they be happy with their work. Although many defined themselves by their artwork, even those who said they were happy in their work seemed frustrated by issues of financial reward. A great variety of visual arts were represented in the study, including but not limited to photography, sculpture, graphic arts, painting, jewelry, and pottery making.

These particular artistic careers are indeed pioneering professions. There were almost no women to be found in symphony orchestras a generation ago, and if there, they usually sat behind a harp or piano. Some of the women in our study were the first women in their orchestras, and some were the only women for a long time. Some of the women commented that they no longer feel like pioneers because there are presently many more women in orchestras, but others reminded the authors of continued glass ceilings in the area of music. Female orchestral conductors are still rare, although our study does include one, and there are definitely particular instruments that are infrequently played by women—for example, the brass instruments and bass violins.

There continues to be fewer women than men in the visual and graphic arts. Because it can be so difficult to earn a living through the arts, some of our artists began their careers in other fields until they could afford to work in their beloved arts. Others acknowledged they could afford to be engaged in their sculpting or painting only because they were financially secure through their spouses.

A slightly larger percentage of both musicians and artists were only children. There were more oldest children in both career groups. If not oldest children, more of the visual artists, like the total group, were middle children, and more of the musicians were youngest children. Also, family size tended to be smaller for the musicians. Perhaps birth order and smaller families were advantages for the musicians because of the financial and time investment necessary for the development of their skills.

Although more visual artists identified with their mothers than their fathers, more of these women identified with their fathers compared to the total group. Also compared to the total group, both the visual artists and musicians had larger percentages that identified with someone other than their parents, namely, their music or art teachers.

The musicians were similar to the total group in their developmental milestones, but the visual artists had fewer women who were very early talkers or readers and more that were somewhat late in their verbal skills. The visual artists seemed to struggle more with their schoolwork despite reported high IQ scores. They also reported more middle-school decline in grades and confidence. The orchestral women were mainly excellent students, and very few of them reported drops in grades or in academic confidence. By high school, however, fewer of both groups took advanced math and science classes despite the fact that some of the musicians were very involved in math; some even majored in math in college. By high school both these groups of women were immersed in their specialty areas, practicing for many hours, and teaching their skills to younger children who shared their special talent. Both groups spent considerable time alone as well. Despite that, by high school more of the visual artists socialized with other high-school students, and more of the orchestral women socialized less and found their social opportunities within their orchestra and among music camp comrades.

The women of both groups found English to be their best subject. However, while the musicians often were strong in math and science in middle school, the visual artists tended not to be. By high school artists mentioned writing as their best subject next to English, and orchestral musicians chose foreign language. The orchestral musicians tended to be excellent students and graduated high in their class, while the visual artists tended to do somewhat less well in their academic subjects. Both these groups indicated higher-than-typical frequencies of grade skipping.

Although the artists and musicians often defined themselves by their talents early, more women in both these career groups were hesitant about recommending their careers to other young women. Almost a third of both groups indicated financial disappointment as the reason for not recommending their careers. The legendary "starving artists" are not only legendary. In addition, many of the orchestral women commented on the too-competitive nature of orchestral music as well as the great amount of time taken from their families and relationships. "Challenging," "creative," and "fulfilling" were indicated most frequently as why these women would recommend their careers.

THE NURTURERS

The educators, allied health professionals, and homemakers are described together not only because they establish nurturing others as a priority, but also because those careers enable sufficient time for parenting and family relationships. They are indeed the most traditional careers selected by women, the careers that, from the start, have allowed and invited women to join. Today they remain careers that are primarily filled by women; indeed, men make up only a small minority within them.

Because one of the criteria for inclusion in the study was satisfaction in the career chosen, women who were unhappy with their traditional career were eliminated. Actually, a considerable number of women in the allied health professions submitted questionnaires indicating they were not happy with their careers, and thus they were not included in the tabulation. It's possible that their unhappiness may be related to national changes in the structure of health care provision at this time, but unhappiness was not typical of any other of the selected careers. Also, full-time homemakers who intended to return to a career once their children were in school were not included in this study. Some homemakers did work part time outside their homes and planned a career for after their children were grown.

The educators were mainly teaching at the elementary level, although some were at the middle- and high-school levels. Some taught classes for special groups such as learning-disabled or gifted children. A few taught teachers at the college level. Those respondents at the college level were primarily teachers rather than researchers. College-level education department faculty who had important research responsibilities were classified as scientists.

Among the allied health professionals, respondents were typically registered nurses who functioned in nursing or nursing administration. There were also some physical and occupational therapists. No practical nurses or nursing aides were included in this study. Most of the nurses had bachelor's degrees, and some had master's degrees and doctorates as well.

Although there were a few homemakers whose children were grown, most respondents had very young children at home. A few also held part-time jobs outside the home but considered their homemaking and child-rearing responsibilities primary and expected that to continue despite earlier career training. Some acknowledged that they had little commitment to the career for which they were trained and expected to change their career direction after their children were grown. Others, particularly those trained as educators, expected to return to that career at a future date, sometimes even as their mothers had.

Perhaps to no one's surprise, more of the women in all three groups were married; fewer were single or divorced. More of them reported their family lives as very happy, homemakers most of all. The average ages of two of the groups were slightly different from that of the total group, with the homemakers being younger and the teachers older. The birth order distribution was somewhat different for the three groups. Among the educators, more were oldest children in the family and fewer were youngest children compared to the total group. More of the allied health professionals and homemakers were middle children, and more came from larger families. The large size of their families could explain the large number of middle children.

Highest on the list of this group's perceptions of how they were viewed by others were "smart," "hardworking," and "good little girl," but slightly higher on the list of frequently mentioned descriptors compared to other groups were "happy" and "kind." These women tended to have good relationships with their parents, but better relationships with their mothers than fathers. More of them identified with their mothers than did other career groups, and fewer of their mothers had returned to school or careers while they were growing up. Fewer of these women in traditional careers identified with their fathers compared to other career groups.

Although just as many began as excellent students in elementary school, by middle school fewer described themselves as excellent students and more as only good students. They tended not to study as much by middle and high school and did not rank as high at graduation. They experienced more general grade decline and more math and science decline during middle and high school. The exception was the allied health professional category, which experienced decline in math confidence but not in science. The allied health professionals' best subject tended to be science from the start, and they continued to be strong in it throughout high school. The best subjects for the educators tended to be reading, English, and writing. English and writing ranked first for the homemakers. Fewer women in all three groups took advanced and AP courses in high school, and fewer of them skipped grades or subjects.

Slightly fewer women in all three categories were involved in music, but more of the educators and allied health professionals were involved with sports. The homemakers did considerably more television viewing than the other two groups and, for that matter, any other career category. All three of these career categories tended to be more social than many of the other career groups.

When the nurturers were asked why they recommended their careers, the most frequently mentioned reason for the allied health professionals and educators was "makes a contribution" and the second most frequently mentioned was "challenging." One hundred percent of the homemakers indicated they thought what they were doing was "worthwhile," and the next most frequently mentioned reason was "fulfilling." Educators also frequently indicated that they considered their careers to be "creative."

TURNING ROADBLOCKS AND REVERSALS INTO OPPORTUNITIES

Dr. Janice Douglas*
Medical Researcher

Turning Roadblocks and Reversals into Opportunities" is the title Dr. Janice Douglas used for an address she presented, but we borrowed it with her permission because it so appropriately describes her story. Despite the roadblocks, Janice considers her career path to have been easy by comparison to the obstacles that her mother, grandmother, and great-grandmother had to face.

Janice is proud to acknowledge four generations of educated, professional women in her family dating back to slavery. Her great-grandmother taught school after being freed from slavery and had a wet nurse to take care of her two children. Janice's grandmother taught English at Langston University in Langston, Oklahoma, after having received degrees in English and music from that same institution. Janice's mother, Dr. Electa Green, practiced dentistry for more than thirty years and continued her career as a faculty member at Meharry Dental School. Janice's current position is professor of medicine and physiology and biophysics at Case Western Reserve University School of Medicine. She was the first female to be appointed professor of medicine at that institution. She was also the first woman to head a major division in the Department of Medicine and also the first to be appointed vice chair of a department. She is internationally renowned for her studies on cellular and molecular mechanisms of blood pressure regulation and has received more than $20 million in grants to support her research during her career.

Less than 3 percent of both women and men in academic medicine are African-Americans. Although Case Western Reserve presently has approximately a hundred African-American medical school students enrolled, ironically Janice herself was rejected by this university years ago despite her perfect 4.0 average, excellent test scores, and Phi Beta Kappa membership. She was told by the dean of admissions in the mid-sixties that she should go to a minority school. Despite that statement, she believes her rejection was related more to her gender than to her race; Dr. David Satcher, the current surgeon general of the United States, who had told her himself that his record was not as impressive as hers, was accepted into the same class for which she applied. Not being accepted into an M.D./Ph.D. program at the time was only one of the very critical roadblocks for Janice as she determinedly moved ahead to become a significant medical researcher in the field of hypertension.

Janice and her sister, who was fourteen months older, lived with Janice's maternal grandmother until they were in kindergarten because Janice's parents were just beginning their medical and dental education. They couldn't manage both their education and parenting, so Janice's grandmother volunteered to care for them instead. Janice's parents would come to be with them only during the summers. Her grandmother had been widowed, and they lived on a farm in Tast, Oklahoma, one of the few all-black towns in Oklahoma. Janice remembers it as a wonderful place to live and visit. Her home holds many fond childhood memories for Janice, including the poetry reading her grandmother did with the girls, an abundance of outdoor activities, and the very special relationship Janice had with her grandmother.

Janice tended to push limits and was often in trouble. Her mother describes Janice as always a challenging child, and Janice recalls receiving more than her fair share of spankings, sometimes daily. Janice remembers stories of her "spunkiness" from her preschool years. If her grandmother would say not to do something, she would think she had to try it—just out of curiosity. For example, she remembers that she was told not to go into the chicken coop because her grandmother didn't want the girls to mess up their clothes. So Janice took off her clothes and went in, pointing out that indeed she had heard her grandmother's message not to mess up those clothes. Another time, while at church, her grandmother told her not to go outside with her good shoes on, so

Janice took off her good shoes and climbed out of the window, again creatively disobeying.

Janice's sister was quieter and less assertive than Janice, even though she was older. Janice recalls that her sister was afraid of the dark and shadows. Their house cast a large shadow at the end of the day, and Janice would tease her sister by taking a toy from her and then running around in the shade with it. Her sister would be too fearful to follow her into the shade to get her toy back.

The difference in their temperaments remained constant. Janice would always tease her sister that if she could have a new car or a new stove, her sister would pick the stove and Janice would pick the car. Janice meant that she would want a new car to get out and do things while her sister would be contented to stay home, cook, and be a homemaker. Actually, Janice's sister trained to become an accountant, but married an Episcopal priest and has always enjoyed her homemaker status. Although Janice identifies with her mother's side of the family, she thinks her sister identified with the women on her father's side of the family. They tended to be homemakers, while her own dentist mother wished to avoid cleaning the house at almost any cost and would hire someone to do the household chores. Housecleaning is not Janice's favorite task, either.

Janice began school at a segregated Catholic school in Birmingham, Alabama. Her family was Episcopalian, but her parents thought this particular school was better. They worried, however, that the school might convert the children to Catholicism; thus, after that first year, Janice's parents moved the children to the public schools, which were also segregated at the time.

In grade school, Janice was always at the top of her class. She recalls, however, that she provoked many of the teachers because she would always ask "too many" questions and challenge them. If teachers said something that she didn't think was correct, she would check the facts out. She remembers an episode from second grade when a teacher commented that in the summer the sun was closest to the earth and in the winter it was just the opposite, which Janice knew wasn't true. She had her parents help her look it up in the encyclopedia. When she found out the teacher was wrong, she unhesitatingly and assertively corrected the teacher, though the teacher did not particularly appreciate it.

Janice also remembers winning many spelling bees in elementary school and thought of herself as the "best" speller. When she was in grade school, she lived near her four male cousins. She and one of her cousins were extraordinarily competitive. He was the second brother in his family and was closest to her in age. They would vie to be first at everything. Sometimes she would beat him, and other times he would beat her. They were both especially good at math. The competition never interfered with their close friendship.

Janice's favorite subjects were math and science. Janice's love of science began with all their outdoor activities on the farm. She remembers planting vegetables and picking fruit. Her love of the outdoors continued through her many Girl Scout and camping activities. She also wrote quite creatively. For many years she sent her writing to her grandmother, who would correct it and send it back to her; there was an ongoing learning relationship between her grandmother and her. Janice learned early to accept helpful criticism.

Janice began taking piano lessons in kindergarten. She rarely had to be urged to practice and thought she was born with self-discipline and a love of music. She continued those lessons as well as her independent, motivated practice throughout high school.

When Janice was a little girl, she always assumed she would be a dentist and that the dental profession was women's work and the medical profession was men's work. Her mother had some female friends who were also dentists, and Janice was probably ten or eleven years old before she realized that most dentists were men, not women. She didn't know any male dentists or female doctors. Janice was very interested in dentistry, and in high school she would spend the summer working in her mother's dental office and in labs where they prepared false teeth and dental work.

Janice clearly remembers her segregated junior high in Birmingham, Alabama. It was located in what was known as the "annex to the high school"—rows of dilapidated houses with potbellied stoves. The electrical wiring was inadequate and dangerous, but despite the awful quarters, their classes were small and the teachers were good. They taught only the basics, but they were strict, and there was no question that Janice was receiving a good education. The students were expected to work especially hard because the teachers were preparing them for the school integration that was expected to come in the late 1960s.

Integration was beginning in Birmingham, and the atmosphere was tense. Janice and her classmates were riding on buses (in the back) when Rosa Parks refused to sit at the back of the bus in nearby Montgomery, Alabama. In Birmingham, crowds assembled in the streets and threw rocks at the buses. Janice was not only confused but also terrified and not at all sure she would arrive home safely.

Meanwhile, Janice's doctor father was a leader in trying to integrate the Birmingham hospitals and golf courses. Janice's family was in the news and was a target of violence. She recalled one night when a white man was looking in the back window while she and her sister were alone in their home. She was terrified, and she didn't know what was going on. Janice's parents feared for their children. Neighbors had already been hurt, and some had moved. Her parents finally decided they, too, must move to be safe.

The family's move from Birmingham to Shaker Heights, Ohio, was difficult, and Janice recalls the strange adjustment to the January cold and icy snow. She was in the second half of ninth grade and first attended Woodbury Junior High School. Her parents were told that both she and her sister should be put back a grade, but their parents wouldn't agree to that. Both girls had skipped a grade in Birmingham. Janice recalled that smart children in the South skipped grades because there were no gifted programs. As a matter of fact, Janice and her sister had no trouble keeping up academically. Janice proved she didn't need to be held back by earning the highest score in her Ohio class on the ninth-grade mathematics achievement test.

Janice remembers studying very hard at Shaker Heights High School. She'd work on projects until 1 or 2 A.M. and routinely did four hours of homework nightly. The high school was highly competitive, and almost all of its graduates went on to fine colleges and universities. At age sixteen Janice was the youngest graduate of the 585 students in her class. She never earned below a B. She was always in the top quarter of her class and had no trouble at all keeping up with honors classes in all her subjects.

In high school, a science teacher, Mr. Hendrix, taught Janice chemistry, and she recalls participating in some exciting projects. In one, she took X rays of hamsters at her mother's office to determine the effect of vitamin D deficiency on the hamsters' bones. Her science project was so good it was entered in the state competition, and there she won honorable mention. She also recalls with laughter that one of those hamsters got loose in the house, and they had a rather wild time searching for the missing hamster in their huge, old four-story home.

There were only five African-American students in Janice's Ohio high-school class, and none was in honors classes with her. Because Janice had lived through it in Birmingham, she was very vocal in her explanations of the reality of desegregation during history classes. The other students assumed that the schools were separate but equal. She set them straight on how terribly unequal blacks' education had been.

As Janice thinks about her parents' relationship with each other, she doesn't ever recall hearing them argue. They were very busy, but they had an idyllic kind of relationship. She always knew they really liked each other. "You couldn't just push them into an emergency" when she was a teenager. She'd try to get them to make a snap decision, and they would "just drive her up a wall." They'd say they had to sit down and talk about it. They were always very thoughtful, and they were definitely united. Her mother would prepare the breakfast they ate together every morning, and they always had dinner together at night as well. Her parents' office hours were arranged around their dinner hour.

Janice's parents were very careful about her social activities and were very strict. She could talk on the phone only a little while. She was "allowed to smile at kids at school and be friendly," but other social activities, such as parties or dating, were prohibited. African-Americans did not date Caucasians in those days. She was in ninth grade before a boy was allowed to come to the house to visit her. Her parents encouraged a social life through a national organization sponsored by the African-American community called Jack and Jill. The Jack and Jill group would have parties, dances, and national conventions especially for African-American young people who were mainly from upper-middle-class professional families. Her mother made sure that Janice had a disciplined and structured social life. Janice had her first date at age fourteen. She recalls walking with her friend to a movie at Shaker Square and returning home to find that a surprise party had been planned for her.

Janice did not make the decision about what college she would attend. Her mother chose Fisk University for her because it had a wonderful academic reputation, and her mother thought that after Shaker Heights High School, where there were so very few African-Americans, Janice needed more socialization with other African-Americans. Her mother wanted Janice to meet young people who could become her lifelong friends. Fisk is officially a coed school, but women predominated in the enrollment at that time. Janice's first year in college was "a breeze" for her. She declared math as her major initially, and then took a lot of math and science courses because she liked them. She knew she would probably not major in math, but if she declared herself a math major, she could earn good money tutoring math to other students. She enjoyed both the tutoring and the extra earnings.

Janice views her decision to go to medical school as accidental. Janice had majored in chemistry and minored in French and wanted to continue to study for a Ph.D. in chemistry. It was too late to apply to graduate school because she hadn't taken the Graduate Record Examination (GRE). Because she had been considering medical school earlier and had already taken the medical school entrance exam (MCAT), she decided to try to apply to medical school instead. She applied to Case Western Reserve, Ohio State, and Meharry (an African-American medical school with an emphasis on training primary-care physicians). As mentioned earlier, the admissions officer at Case Western Reserve told her that in spite of her perfect average, he did not think she would do well there. Even at Meharry, Janice's interest in a medical education was suspect. Very few women attended medical school in those days, and it was inferred that she was just looking for a doctor husband.

Janice was married the day she finished college. Her husband (they later divorced) was a biology major she met during her last year of college. He encouraged her to go into medicine; they viewed her parents as role models for their plan to go to medical school despite the fact that they were a family. Janice's husband was accepted to Meharry Medical College before Janice, even though her academic record was considerably better than his.

Janice's daughter was born in her last year of medical school. Janice was very careful not to use her family as an excuse for not carrying out the full responsibilities of medical school. Nevertheless, she thought that some professors and students resented her having a child. During her last year, she slipped from first to second in her rank in her graduating class. Her son was born during her medical residency. Janice managed to complete her residency with two small children, but they needed much child-care support. In addition, an "aunt," who was actually a good friend of her mother's from college, lived across the street and would often help out if there was an emergency.

The research Janice began doing during medical school led to her long-term career path. She worked on projects during the weekends and had publications when she graduated. She then decided to do a residency in internal medicine and established a relationship with Dr. Grant Little, who was chairman of medicine and head of endocrinology at nearby Vanderbilt University.

After Janice's husband completed his service in Vietnam, it was necessary for them to relocate for his orthopedic surgery residency and her fellowship. They moved to the Washington area, where she was able to attain a new research position while her husband did his residency. They were in the Washington area for three years, but they were never able to adjust their marriage to the change. Janice didn't know whether to attribute the problems to her husband's difficult period spent in Vietnam or to her independence while her husband was away, but it seemed to her that he wanted her to become more dependent on him. He also didn't like the fact that they had live-in help. At the time that he was a resident, Janice was in a very senior research position, attending national meetings and presenting her research. With Janice becoming increasingly successful, competitive issues arose between them.

Janice had a number of mentors, none of whom was female. There simply were no women medical researchers available for her to emulate. Her first male mentor was Dr. Grant Little. He provided leadership for many research opportunities. Although he was extraordinarily busy and very famous, he was always there to give her advice. At one point, when her husband was in Vietnam and she had car trouble, Dr. Little took the time to pick her up on his way to work, drive her daughter to kindergarten, and then make sure her daughter was picked up from school and driven safely home. Despite the fact that Janice feels very indebted to him and appreciative of his professional and personal contribution to her life, she can also remember some strange but sexist comments like "What have you done this week besides go to the beauty parlor?" Janice learned to laugh these off, but they hurt.

Dr. Robert Brown, known as "Red" because of his ruddy complexion, was another medical school mentor for Janice. He set the tone for all the residents and interns. He insisted that the indigents their inner-city hospital treated be given the best possible medical care. He explained that just because they were a minority medical school, they didn't want to be perceived as "selling spoiled meat at a ghetto store." His message always stayed with Janice. She learned to give people the very best care no matter who they were or where they came from. Before she finished her residency with Dr. Brown, he died suddenly of a cerebral hemorrhage, while still in his mid-thirties. His stroke was associated with severe hypertension, and his death distressed Janice greatly. Janice's sadness further motivated her to work in the area of hypertension.

One of Janice's favorite adages is Dr. Martin Luther King Jr.'s statement "You should be the best at whatever you are. If you cannot be a tree on the top of a hill than be a shrub in the valley, but be the best little shrub that you can be." She hopes that women who may begin as "shrubs in the valley" will become "trees at the top of the hill" eventually. Janice mentors many young women who are interested in medical research, in the hopes of encouraging their academic development.

Janice sees the field of medicine as now open to women, and she is always happy to mentor them. She believes, however, that women who have families can't find the "protected time" to invest in the research that will permit promotions. Furthermore, there is presently more pressure in medicine to do additional clinical work. If there is no time for getting grants, publishing, and becoming nationally and internationally prominent, women will be limited to the lower levels of academic medicine and not have the training to invest in the research that would propel their careers to higher rungs of the academic ladder.

Despite the fact that Janice's success story was one of drive, resilience, and optimism, she modestly emphasized chance in her own description: "Everything has been rather serendipitous. None of what I've described to you was planned. Opportunity came as there were changes in directions in my life, and I was able to get good positions and good things just happened."

A RENEWED IDENTITY—MOUNTAINS TO CLIMB

Suzanne Daniels
State Senator

Although Suzanne Daniels never anticipated going into politics as a child, she was recently elected to the state senate after a career that included science education, full-time homemaking, public relations, and journalism. She thoroughly enjoys her senate seat. She talks about liking variety in her work, and perhaps that's part of the reason she's successful in politics. She savors her time working quietly at a desk, writing and accomplishing, but she also especially values activity and being around people. She says, "I'm so achievement-oriented, I have to keep going, and when I get tired I just vary what I'm working on." Suzanne is fifty-one and is in a second marriage. She credits her husband with providing important support and encouragement in her new career. She has two grown sons.

Suzanne was the oldest of four children in a close family. Her father was a reporter when Suzanne was younger, but he moved into public relations work when she was in middle school. Her mother was a full-time homemaker. Suzanne recalls, "We didn't have much money when we were growing up, so we didn't have a lot of experiences that many kids have today. I think raising four kids was a struggle." As a result, Suzanne and her siblings spent a lot of time playing with neighborhood kids or doing things together as a family. Suzanne does remember going shopping with just her mom. Even though in retrospect Suzanne realizes that money was a problem, as a child she felt she had everything she needed and felt very secure and loved.

Suzanne mainly identified with her mother but was "quieter in personality," like her father. Suzanne remembers her mother trying to bring her out socially. She was very shy and reserved and didn't develop her social skills until she was older. Specifically, her mother's message to the family was, "Let them know you're there. Speak out. Make your presence known." Apparently her mother's message was heeded. Suzanne's careers have always given her the opportunity to speak out, whether in the classroom, through her writing, or with her service in the senate. Suzanne's father was also probably an important model to her through his career, since one of her arenas for speaking out was journalism, the same career her dad had followed initially.

Suzanne's parents always had high academic expectations for her. They considered school "to be everything." Despite that, Suzanne says, her parents mainly projected marriage and a family for Suzanne's future, not a career. She says, "My parents were 'with it.' It was just typical of the times." Suzanne was expected to marry and be a support person to her husband. Suzanne considers both parents to have been firm in their parenting approach, and her relationship with both parents was excellent for the most part, although in high school, she admitted, it was "a little stormy at times." She also had a very close relationship with her siblings, but, as the oldest girl, she surely did her share of mothering them.

Although Suzanne was an excellent student in elementary school, her grades "took a slight dip" in seventh and eighth grade as she became engrossed in social life. Her friends were always nice kids, but they were more important, at least temporarily, than her grades. In high school her grades improved again and she felt more confident, although her social life and friendships continued to be a priority. She took advanced and challenging science and math classes mainly because her parents, teachers, and peers encouraged her to, although she never found math particularly interesting. Suzanne recalls her mathematics experience in high school: "I always took the most advanced math courses, and by twelfth grade very few girls were in my class. The tests were all take-home tests, and the boys always helped me with mine. Girls weren't expected to understand math. I got A's, but by the end I didn't have a clue about what was going on. I had total math phobia in college. As a result, I avoided taking any math classes at college."

In comparison to others, Suzanne considers herself to have been very social all during her years in school. She was a cheerleader and was always elected to and active in student government during high school. However, to her disappointment, she always lost her elections for student government office. She ran for secretary because in those days "girls didn't run for president." She says she always lost to those "cute little girls with turned-up noses," whereas she was more studious. To see the exceptionally pretty Senator Suzanne Daniels today makes one believe that she must have been every bit as cute as those other girls. Perhaps her peer problem was only that she was more studious. Even though Suzanne never won an election, her parents always encouraged her to run for student government. Her courage to run for office may date back to those high-school days.

Suzanne majored in botany at Smith College and easily adjusted academically. She had almost all A's and even managed to avoid taking any mathematics courses. She admits her social adjustment to Smith wasn't quite as easy—the only time during her schooling when she viewed her social life as less active than average. Of course, she was at a women's college, so perhaps the absence of men in her classes discouraged some of her socializing and may even have been conducive to her superb academic performance.

Although Suzanne's botany studies were very important to her, she spent only two career years in science education. She returned to graduate school several times for medicine, business, and journalism, but discontinued her graduate education each time due to the "competing needs of her marriage and family." She never felt supported by either her husband or her parents and always felt guilty about taking time from her family. She was afraid she wouldn't be able to "get a hot meal on the table" and felt she wasn't living up to the expectations of her family (mostly her parents and her husband). Suzanne struggled and vacillated for ten years trying to determine her direction. She recalls feeling "stuck" at those times. Like many women of her generation, finding her identity came later in adulthood, and only after choosing journalism did she finally feel "unstuck."

Suzanne admits that she now resents the times in which she was raised. Girls were taught to get married and support their husbands in their careers. She was guided to take practical courses such as typing instead of substantial academic courses. Suzanne never found mentors or knew of any women who were successful in their careers. She saw absolutely no role models for combining career and family. She describes the period of life when she shifted from one school program to another as one in which she felt victimized, and she recalls it as a very frustrating time in her life. Her neighbors, she remembers, thought it was terrible when she would have someone else care for her children because she was working. Her mother tolerated it, and her sister-in-law was critical of it. Suzanne remembers hearing only discouraging "negative feedback," which made her feel the world was "unfair" to women. Everyone seemed to be accusing her of being a "bad mother."

When Suzanne's career as a journalist took off, she was excited, enthusiastic, and finally felt she had found herself. Unfortunately, she also discovered that she was outgrowing her first husband, and she decided to leave him. She acknowledged that a large part of her decision was his lack of support for her independent accomplishments. She had such a strong internal drive to achieve and so thoroughly enjoyed her journalism career that she simply couldn't trade personal accomplishment for the more traditional homemaker's role he would have wanted.

A few years ago a very close, longtime, and trusted friend suggested to Suzanne that she run for the state senate. She had never considered politics prior to this but was very actively involved in the community. Because she enjoys people, she saw politics as providing her the opportunity to balance her essentially solitary writing career with a more people-oriented, social career. Suzanne thought that even if she didn't win, at least her campaign would open other doors for her and she'd meet some interesting people. She concluded she had absolutely nothing to lose and that it would be fun. She explained she was really willing at that point in her life to take a risk, even if it was a very public one. Because her children were out of the house, she would be free to work "every single second," and that was exciting to her. Suzanne emphasizes that she loved being a mother but missed terribly the freedom of independent work. She never wanted to "hit the end of the road" and was always looking toward "new mountains to climb." The state senate seemed like a reasonable challenge.

Suzanne, like many of the women of our study, attributes much of her success to luck: "Coming across the right people who are kind is really critically important to becoming successful."

Suzanne recommends to parents of daughters that they provide them with a family environment that promotes interests in current events, community involvement, and the arts. She also suggests they advise their daughters not to marry too early; instead, she believes, parents should encourage their daughters to search for the excitement of "new and higher mountains to climb."

CHAPTER 2

THE AMERICAN DREAM FOR YOUR DAUGHTERS

Be a Coach, Not a Judge

Part 1: Findings

Most women of past generations could only marry the American dream; they didn't dare to have such high expectations for themselves. Most of the women in our study, however, are living the American dream through their own achievements. As a group, they have outperformed both their mothers and fathers in economic and educational attainments. Figures 2.1 and 2.2 dramatically compare the education levels of 1,236 women in our study to those of their mothers and fathers. Almost all of the women in the study had earned college degrees, compared to less than a third of their mothers and less than half of their fathers. Approximately a third of the women had earned master's degrees, and another third had doctorates in the arts and sciences or professional degrees in medicine or law, compared to fewer than 1 percent of their mothers and very few of their fathers. Although some of the women in the study were raised in families where both parents had college degrees, most (about two-thirds) were not. Thirteen percent had at least one parent who was an immigrant.

Our data should not be interpreted to mean that parents who do not have college degrees have an advantage in motivating their daughters to success. In fact, parents' higher education is an important motivator

FIGURE 2.1

The American Dream:

Educational Attainment of Successful Women Compared to Their Fathers

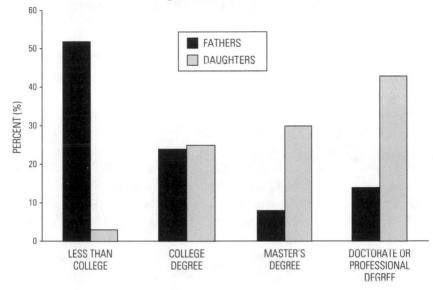

The Feminist Dream:

Educational Attainment of Successful Women Compared to Their Mothers

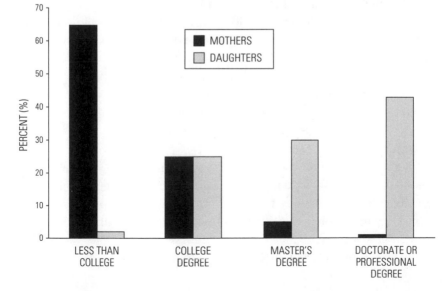

for their children.[1] The successful women in our study were at least five times more likely than women in the general population to come from homes in which mothers had a college education, and also five times more likely to come from homes in which fathers had a college or professional education. Most important, however, our findings confirm that the American dream is possible for girls whose parents do not have higher education.

HIGH EXPECTATIONS

Although true equality for women has not yet arrived in our nation, your daughters can pass through doors that women never dared to dream of entering only a generation ago.

Parents' high expectations were a major factor in the success of the women who participated in our study, and examining their childhoods can teach you how to set high expectations for your daughters. Ninety-eight percent of the successful women had at least one parent who set high expectations for them. Most of those women believed that both parents expected them to be successful. Parents expressed those expectations in a variety of ways, and sometimes the expectations were different for the women than for their brothers, but the expectations were clearly expressed and motivating to the women.

Dr. Janet Smith, who is now retired, was chair of the Department of Pediatrics at a major northeastern children's hospital for many years at a time when there were almost no women chairing medical departments. While growing up, Janet worked alongside her blind father and became his eyes in his tent-making business as well as on his fishing expeditions. Although her dad didn't have even a high-school education, he would only half laughingly say that Janet could be president of the United States.

Janet's mother, who had attended normal school and been a teacher and a principal, gave up her career to care for her two daughters. Although she was a loving mother, she was often bored because she no longer worked outside the home. As a result, she encouraged her daughters to have careers.

Janet's parents were "too proud" to borrow money or even to accept scholarships for their daughters' education. They had sufficient resources to pay, and they thought it wrong to accept other people's help. They urged their daughters to seek admission to the colleges of their choice. Although Janet's parents tended to laugh at her interest in medicine because they knew of so few women who were doctors, they did encourage her to get a quality education. Janet attended Johns Hopkins Medical School, one of the first universities in the country that supported women who chose to enter medicine.

When Janet was offered her first excellent medical position and reported her salary to her parents with great pride, her father's response—again with some laughter—was, "Is that all? You're worth much more than that." Janet's parents' high expectations were often delivered with humor but revealed a solid belief in her potential.

Dr. Mary Alice Cox, a thirty-four-year-old radiation oncologist, had a dad who did exactly what psychologists tell parents not to do: He told her he expected all A's and that they were the only acceptable grades. He told her further that she was smarter than her brothers. Mary Alice indicated that she admired her dad so much she wanted only to please him, so she worked hard and experienced some pressure to deliver those A's. Had her father not set such high goals for her, Mary Alice thinks she might otherwise have been distracted by her love of music and art, and especially her interest in boys.

Rabbi Miriam Kane has a similar story, except her dad was even more extreme in his expectations. She recalls bringing her straight-A report card to him. After reviewing it, he told her he was proud of her, but then asked her why she didn't have some A+'s. She understood that her dad was joking, but she accepted the challenge. The next semester Miriam brought home A+'s. She was motivated to work harder to prove to the dad she so admired that she could meet his challenge. She graduated at the top of her class.

Moriah Epstein's father also set high expectations. Moriah is a successful entrepreneur and owns a fashionable women's clothing store. She explained, "Dad regretted not having finished college. Although he had only daughters, and it was before the women's movement, he valued intelligence and education. He brought us up with love and was strict about boys and dating. Some of his favorite sayings were: 'The legal age for marriage on our street is thirty-two'; 'Everyone in this house will go to college and finish before any weddings are discussed'; and finally, 'No matter where you are or what you've done, you can always call me, and I'll come and get you.'" Moriah felt she would never dare to disappoint a dad who believed in her so strongly.

Mary Alice, Miriam, and Moriah may be unusual examples and shouldn't necessarily guide parents to these extremes; nevertheless, they show that even demanding parents can motivate girls provided the girls feel able to meet such high expectations.

Judge Katherine Logan recalled that her parents always emphasized that the better things in life are available only if you have an education and a career. Her mother always wanted her to be independent; marrying the right man was never considered a viable means to the end. Education meant freedom, and that was interpreted by Katherine to mean that "education could never be pointless." "My parents both had a good education and had good careers and demonstrated by their lives the importance of their message to me."

Jody Hill, vice president for economic development, recalls that her own mother, an Episcopalian priest, emphasized high expectations in terms of self-fulfillment. Jody's mother explained that people with talents don't feel satisfied unless they use all their talents, and the more talent they have, the more they are called upon to do; thus Jody's talents carried with them both obligation and motivation for fulfillment.

Among the parents of the older women in the study, expectations were typically different than for the younger women. These parents often expected high academic attainment with no real career goals and traditional marriage goals instead.

State Senator Suzanne Daniels recalls that her college-educated parents expected their children to be excellent students, to take honors classes, to be leaders in extracurricular activities, and to go to prestigious colleges. Thereafter, as was typical of the times, they assumed their daughters would marry and raise children and their sons would have careers.

Not all the successful women in our group were fortunate enough to have two parents in their home throughout childhood. Fourteen percent had parents who were divorced while they were growing up, and 9 percent had one or the other parent die during their childhood. Single parents often set high expectations for the women, and even memories of deceased parents' expectations guided some of the women in the study.

Attorney Leslie Hanna remembers watching her mother, who, without a high-school diploma, found work, cared for her and her brother, managed the house, and never lost her sense of humor. Leslie believed from her observations of her mother that she, too, could do well in any endeavor she chose to undertake.

Artist Sandra Sheets was inspired to read and learn by memories of her father's love of learning. When she was desperate, she would think of her dad, who had died early; her memory of him would keep her motivated.

Some women remembered their parents' expectations as subtle and unclear. Although a few women found the absence of clear parental expectations to be motivating and liberating, others cited the uncertainty of their parents' expectations as the reason they accomplished less than they might have.

Although guidance counselor Karly Rheam graduated in the top 10 percent of her high-school class, she never felt particularly smart or scholarly. Her parents encouraged her to be a good student, but their expectations were only that their children would do their best. This kind of expectation would be supported as appropriate by most educators and psychologists. Somehow, despite high grades, Karly never believed she was doing very well. When she got a 97 on a test, she thought it wasn't good enough and wondered why she hadn't been able to get a 100. Perhaps she even realized that she "wasn't doing her best." However, she didn't put in the extra effort to get those three extra points.

Although she took honors classes in high school, she never did much homework—only half an hour a night, much less than most women in our study. Math came easily to her. She remembers carelessly completing it, thus receiving only B's for her work. She recalls a math teacher who, while reviewing Karly's SAT math score of 680, leaned over to her and said, "You know all this work, don't you?" For that brief moment Karly realized she might be intelligent, but during junior and senior high school "boys and sex just seemed more interesting than mathematics and vocabulary."

Karly majored in education in college, married young, and had two children. She divorced after seventeen years of marriage. It wasn't until many years later, as she completed her master's degree in counseling, that she realized she could have been a scholar. Although Karly enjoys her work as a school counselor and has been self-sufficient because, according to her, "working in schools has always facilitated child care," she believes her career would have been much more interesting had she become a researcher, and that she could have accomplished that goal if she and others had set higher expectations for her.

Not all parents helped girls to set their goals higher. Pediatrician Dr. Mary Murphy* recalls that when she told her dad she wanted to be a doctor, he recommended she become a nurse. When he realized how serious she was about her intentions, he tried to steer her toward dentistry so that she would have more time for her family. Now that she has a family, she realizes how correct he was about the difficult time commitment. Nevertheless, she has no regrets, and although she works full time, she has managed to do that in a four-day week, which at least permits her a little more time with her children.

PRESSURES

As you would expect with such high expectations placed upon them during their childhood, some of these women felt pressured during middle school and high school. It is perhaps surprising that most of them did *not* feel pressured despite the high expectations. Approximately a third remembered pressure in middle school, and slightly less than half remembered it in high school. These women recall that the pressures emanated approximately equally from parents, teachers, siblings, and themselves. Again, surprisingly, most of the women enjoyed or at least didn't mind the pressure. A small percentage of the women didn't like it, and a very small percentage (about 2 percent) acknowledged that they hated the pressure they felt.

More women in media than in any other career group noted that they felt pressured. More of these women were social in middle and high school and more of them experienced decline in grades and confidence in science and math than women in some of the other career groups. Together these factors could provide more reasons for feeling pressure. For the most part, however, despite their feelings of pressure, these women liked or at least didn't mind the pressure.

Fewer of the women in the traditional career groups (teaching, allied health, mental health, and homemaking) felt pressured as adolescents. Perhaps being unaccustomed to pressure was one of the factors, although obviously not the only one, that directed them toward careers that would also mean less pressure on them. Entering nontraditional careers was risky and required a willingness to cope with extreme pressure in the process of being accepted. Although there are obviously other important reasons for women to enter traditional careers, a willingness to tolerate the pioneering stress of being different and having to prove oneself requires a special resilience.

FOLLOW YOUR DREAM

Some women in all career areas heard the message to "follow your dream" from either their mothers or fathers. Many parents went to great pains to be supportive of their daughters, taxiing them to lessons, providing expensive teachers, attending concerts and recitals, paying for attendance at special classes or schools and camps, purchasing specialized equipment, and investing themselves personally as well as financially in their daughters' dreams. Sometimes these women's paths led them to successful careers. Unfortunately, others' dreams were destroyed by the reality of the intense competitiveness of their fields. Despite their talent and dedication, there simply were no opportunities for them. Those who found success were appreciative of the message to follow their dreams. For those who did not achieve their dreams, there was a sense of disappointment and emptiness even though they now have what would be described by most people as successful careers.

Barbara Blair's dream was to be a solo violinist. After one year at college in a very fine music department she failed her coursework, became depressed, gave up the violin, and told herself she would never hold an instrument again. She found it impossible even to listen to symphonic music without pain. She said that hearing a violin caused her to relive the many hours of stress and practice and the feelings of failure. Later she returned to college, attended medical school, and finally adjusted to a new career goal, although she does not yet feel she can enjoy music.

Ann Dobbs had set her sights on becoming a cancer researcher at a prestigious university. She leaped obstacles successfully to become an assistant professor who led her own laboratory. She even managed to combine her successful career with marriage and family. The time pressure was horrendous, and the available grant money diminished, as did tenure opportunities. She knew she would have to abandon the academic cancer research career she'd dreamed of since childhood. She wondered to herself, "Is it me, or is it that so few women—and almost none with families—have made it in my field?"

Denise Dennison dreamed of becoming a dancer with the New York City Ballet. Talented, focused, and dedicated to her ballet, she sacrificed a high-school diploma and settled for a GED in order to study ballet in New York. Five years later she had managed to dance professionally with a modern dance company, but repeated injuries prevented her from continuing with her beloved dance career. Returning to college and passing the high-level mathematics courses without the prerequisite math and science she would have had from high school required even more dedication and discipline than she had devoted to dancing. Four years later she graduated from a prestigious technical institute, ninth in her class. Her college years as a returning adult were stressful, and she recalls the tears, the pressure, and the horrible fear of failure.

Successfully employed in national television production, Denise wishes nostalgically for what could have been. She acknowledges she will probably forever mourn the loss. When asked if she would advise her talented young daughter to pursue dance, an immediate no emphasized how horrendously difficult it had been for her to follow her dream, despite her parents' encouragement.

Generally, when the women were encouraged by their parents to follow their dreams and those dreams were realistic—that is, to be doctors, attorneys, or educators—they felt fulfilled and were pleased with their parents' messages. However, when those dreams were for highly competitive careers, some very talented women were unable to achieve the high goal they dreamed of.

For the most part, the shattered dreams belonged to women who had high goals in the arts, media, or highly competitive science positions. Some regrouped and eventually became reasonably contented. Others believed they would never feel contentment; for still others it is too soon to tell.

UNITED EXPECTATIONS

Parents were not always united in the follow-your-dream message. For some of the women, that sometimes felt like lack of support from the parent who tried to be more realistic. Denise Dennison remembers thinking that her mother didn't believe she was capable enough because she tried to protect Denise from the harsh world of dance. She wonders if her mother's reserve may have actually adversely affected her personal confidence in dance. Because she had selected such a challenging dream, she believed she could succeed only with the total confidence of both parents. It is difficult to separate out what effect her mother's slight caution truly had on Denise's dream, because it was such a competitive one to realize.

For the most part, when both parents were in the home, they supported each other in giving messages of high expectations. Even when one parent set irrationally high expectations, the second parent rarely contradicted the other, although they may have been more moderate in their own expectations. More mothers than fathers tended to be moderate in their expectations for their daughters, but many of the successful women recall being inspired by the more extreme expectations, which is a pattern that is very different from what I see in my clinical work with bright, underachieving students. Unlike these talented, achieving women, underachievers often lack confidence and thus believe they are not capable of fulfilling the extreme expectations of the parent who expects more, and instead they look to the parent who expects less for an easy way out of the challenge. Thus, the difference in parental expectations encourages their underachievement instead of spurring them on to new heights.

When women were unable to fulfill their dreams, they did not tend to blame their parents for setting expectations too high. However, some women wished their parents could have known more and guided them better.

Norah Barnes, flutist for a large city opera orchestra, explained her feelings of disappointment: "I often wished my parents could have given me more guidance. I'm not sure I would have selected music if they could have given me the big picture of how competitive music really is."

SETTING SIGHTS HIGHER

Several women in the study were encouraged by their parents to set their sights higher in order to get past gender stereotypes. Dr. Janelle Stein recalls, "When I was in third grade, we drew pictures about what we wanted to be when we grew up. I brought home a picture of a nurse. My mother said if I was interested in medicine, I should consider all medical fields. She made sure I knew I could be a doctor and didn't have to be a nurse just because all current doctors in my life were males and nurses were females." Attorney Terri Arkins recalls, "My father always expected me to get a professional degree, i.e., graduate school, in whatever field I chose, and rise to the top of it. I considered nursing and physician assistant training, and he was shocked and stated clearly that he expected me to get an M.D. if I chose a health field." Terri chose law, not medicine, but did hear the communication from her dad to aspire to a high-level professional career.

Paula Sands, an author who lives in Oregon, remembers that her mother always said, "You'll be the first woman rabbi." Paula's family practiced no religion, and there were no women rabbis at the time. Paula interpreted her mother's message as "I could be whatever I chose even if there were no women in the field."

PRESSURE FOR HOMEMAKING

None of the women in the study noted that they were pressured by their parents to follow a specific career path just because it was a parent's career, as was perhaps typical in past generations for males (for example, a son becoming a doctor because his father was a doctor). There were women like medical researcher Dr. Janice Douglas,* who assumed she would become a dentist like her mother, but it was never an expectation stated to her by either parent. There were also women, however, who felt pressured specifically by both mothers and fathers *not* to take on challenging careers because they would interfere with family life, or were pressured to spend more time parenting instead of devoting themselves to their careers. Some of the women sometimes felt angered and misunderstood; however, the pressure did not deter most of these successful women from pursuing their careers. It can be assumed, however, that many other women were prevented from taking on challenging careers because of the pressure placed on them by parents, friends, and even from personal feelings of guilt about hurting their families if they attempted to establish a career.

Some of the women were also cautioned by their parents or others not to go to medical school or graduate school because they would "educate themselves out of finding a husband." However, these successful women disregarded that advice.

Attorney Jane Summers, a retired partner of a law firm in Washington, D.C., reported: "My mother, who was also a graduate of Wellesley, was—and still is, at age ninety-five—very supportive of my educational and career aspirations but very concerned I have a 'normal' life with marriage and children. My father's doubts emerged when I started law school. Wellesley helped me to value women, but even in the 1940s, society's expectations for family life dominated much of the scene."

Teacher and homemaker Nancy Collier felt pressure not to leave her small community and go to college. Most young people from her hometown simply graduated from high school, married, and raised families.

Certainly homemaker and community volunteer Roberta Baldwin,* with her high IQ (145) and excellent college grades in the sciences, could have had her choice of careers, but in her time, being a homemaker and leader in the community and supporting her physician husband were hailed as personal fulfillment, and Roberta did indeed feel good about her role in life. Now in her sixties, Roberta works more than twenty hours a week, although she doesn't earn anything for her voluntary contribution. She believes she's made a difference for hundreds of people, and she loves helping others. Perhaps, she admits, in this generation she would have chosen to be an attorney, but she wonders how our country will manage without community volunteers.

The younger women in our study felt much less pressure to choose between career and family than did their mothers. Most of their mothers gave up their career goals in order to be homemakers and parents. In some cases it was because the women's fathers absolutely objected to their wives having careers. In other cases the women's mothers voluntarily decided their priorities needed to be their families.

Part 2: Advice

We culled some obvious advice from the stories of our successful women, but some of their stories contradict the conclusions of other educational and psychological research. We will begin with the clearest findings and discuss how the more controversial findings apply to parenting daughters.

GENDER EQUITY

Parents need to set equally high expectations for their children regardless of gender. That is easier for this generation than it was for previous generations because there are many more opportunities for women and because society has become more accepting of women having careers. Girls of today have encountered women doctors and have seen women in government and law on television. However, parents still need to be aware of subtle (and not-so-subtle) gender stereotypes in their families and communities, in children's literature, in movies, and on television in order to correct them and let their daughters (and sons) know that all career options are available to them regardless of gender stereotypes.

Challenge your preadolescents to think of careers that do not include members of both genders. If their response is "president of the United States," remind them they are only temporarily correct, and if they are girls, you may wish to issue them the challenge to be the first one. Women in our study remembered and were inspired by challenges given to them during their childhoods in this lighthearted way.

DELIVERING A POWERFUL MESSAGE
ABOUT THE IMPORTANCE OF EDUCATION

The unflinching belief that education is the highest priority is very motivating for children. It prevents children from viewing school as irrelevant almost regardless of the quality of their education. Thus parents who didn't go on to higher education but wish they had are in a powerful position to inspire the American dream in their children; so are parents who valued their own excellent education. However, inspiring your children is much more difficult for parents who didn't consider education valuable in their own lives or who have unpleasant memories of their own school experiences. Therefore, if you didn't like school as a child, even if you had an excellent educational background, there is a risk that you might deemphasize the value of school to your children. You may too easily buy into your daughters' arguments about the irrelevance of school and thus unconsciously blunt their motivation to learn in school. Because in our society education is tied to greater economic opportunity, and the salaries of women in almost every profession are coming closer to those of men in the same careers, your daughters' futures are directly related to their success in school.

HIGH EXPECTATIONS VERSUS
TOO-HIGH EXPECTATIONS

Although most of the successful women's parents expected hard work and good grades, many of their expectations were quite extreme. Expectations varied from being president of the United States to discovering the cure for cancer to being a solo violinist to being a Supreme Court justice. Some parents set high grade standards, such as expecting all A's or even A+'s; others placed little emphasis on grades. Why did extreme expectations work so well for many of these women without causing undue pressure? These women not only remember those high expectations but obviously valued them. Furthermore, they were motivated to work harder to achieve whatever goals were set before them. No challenge seemed too great.

Parents' unrealistic expectations would be considered bad form, bad psychology, or at least politically incorrect by most of today's educators and psychologists. Teachers constantly report that parents pressure their children too much or expect all A's. From teachers' points of view, such pressure is almost always considered negative, either preventing kids from having fun or causing them to be tense and anxious. Often teachers blame parents' high expectations for their children's underachievement in school. From a medical or psychological point of view, when children report headaches, stomachaches, or generalized anxiety, they are almost always attributed to the pressures parents (mainly mothers) placed on their children, and teenagers often complain to professionals that their parents or teachers expect too much of them. How can we reconcile these points of view?

It is possible for you to set high expectations for your daughters and build their confidence without placing debilitating pressure on them. Praise is the most frequently used tool for communicating expectations, and it is an important technique for helping your daughters build self-esteem. If you praise your daughters, they will assume you are pleased with them, but those words also convey that you value or expect the qualities you've praised. You will have to know your daughters well, however, for this to work. In order for girls to value praise without feeling it as pressure, they must believe that the praise is warranted. They require academic and personal self-confidence; then and only then, apparently, can they thrive on high expectations. They also must believe you are an ally and that you believe in them. On the other hand, if they feel inadequate or believe your goals are unrealistically high, if they don't have good study habits, if they expect punishments if they can't achieve the goals, or if they view your goals as different from their own, they will be angry at you or defy you. They will feel pressured and show symptoms of stress. They may even become very rebellious or underachieve simply by not doing their assignments or studying.

Because it is so hard to determine why some high praise inspires success and why other high praise produces uncomfortable pressure, we'll give you examples of what kind of praise can cause problems for your daughters and how you can determine if you've gone too far.

- Extreme praise given early in a child's life is probably riskier than praise given later that is related to actual performance. Although young children always enjoy the praise, it is difficult to determine whether they will be able to accomplish what appears likely when they are quite young. If they are not able to fulfill expectations set by praise, the high praise will cause them to feel pressured.
- Praise should convey meaningful, potentially realizable expectations. For example, "smart" is more realistic praise than "brilliant." If girls see the praise as too high, the pressure they feel may increase and even cause them to become angry at the one who praises.
- When praise is given and taken with humor, its message is tempered and may convey less pressure.
- The person who praises must be viewed as an ally by the girl being

praised, or she will not accept the praise and may consider it manipulation. If she views it as manipulation, she may feel anger.

EARLY PRAISE

When you hold that wonderful infant daughter in your arms, whatever
spectacular descriptive words emerge from your lips will make little
difference for your daughter's future. Whether you call her "brilliant,"
"miraculous," "perfect," or "gorgeous," the warm love you share tran-
scends whatever words you might use because she doesn't yet understand your words. When preschoolers become verbal, however, the
meaning of words you use for praise will begin to convey to them the
expectations you have for them. Not only are your expectations conveyed, but the values and expectations of society are communicated
when other adults make comments about children either directly to
them or indirectly to others within their hearing. Because setting expectations begins early, parents should think carefully about the characteristics and behaviors they'd like to emphasize. The talk will take place,
consciously or unconsciously. It's better to be deliberate in your choice
of words and sensitive to how those words affect your children.

In a later chapter, we'll discuss the words that describe how the
successful women in our study viewed themselves as children and adolescents. These words provide us with some important clues about how
to set the expectations that will be internalized by your daughters as
self-expectations. High on the list of descriptors chosen by these
women were "smart," "hardworking," "independent," "mature," "good
little girl," and "sensitive." It would seem to be important to look for
opportunities to comment on and praise these qualities in your daughters. We would suggest you not go overboard with your praise. There's
no reason to use "smartest," "brilliant," "perfect," or "gifted" when
they're preschoolers. It is important for you to be able to tune your
appreciation of your daughter's terrific qualities to her development so
that she can live up to high expectations in the future. If not, you may
have a teenager who is perfectionistic and who feels pressured and
inadequate.

BEAUTIFUL VERSUS SMART,
HARDWORKING, AND INDEPENDENT

As parents, you may wonder how to handle the controversial issue of
beauty. Every little girl and every woman in the world would enjoy
being considered beautiful, but we hope the feminist movement has at

least taken us beyond valuing women only for their appearance and attractiveness to men. Only a very small percentage of the women in our study believed they were considered beautiful by others, and most of those were in media and arts careers. Considering that it's hard to know if your beautiful toddler will become a stunning teenager or adult, you could be setting your daughters up for extreme pressure, and even eating disorders, by emphasizing beauty too much. They will believe that you and the world, and especially boys and men, will value them only if they are beautiful. Many child models have suffered through adolescence and adulthood because they have not lived up to early expectations of attractiveness, and thousands of adolescent girls and young women struggle with wanting to be beautiful; they search for a way to please boys and men and lose themselves in the process. Following are some cases from my clinical experience that will help to emphasize the nature of the problem.

Six-year-old Molly was an absolutely beautiful child. Her flowing red hair attracted attention wherever she went. Furthermore, both her parents believed they had not been praised sufficiently when they were children, so they put much energy into telling Molly how smart and beautiful she was.

My meeting with Molly was fun. She was verbal and expressive. When asked how she liked first grade, her response was, "It's all right, but the teacher doesn't give me enough attention." Her mother reported to me later that Molly's first words to her after leaving my office were, "Dr. Rimm didn't tell me how beautiful I was."

Eight-year-old Janine, an only child, hated to go to school. She said she felt ugly and wanted to shave her legs so the other girls would think she was pretty and would like her. (Yes, you did read that age correctly.) Pressure to be beautiful can happen very early.

Thirteen-year-old Ariel, with tears rolling down her cheeks, explained that she only wanted to be pretty so she would be popular. She wanted to have her hair dyed, and her parents weren't about to spend the $80 to have it done. She was equally sure she needed to wear makeup to be popular and pretty.

Ariel's older sister had been a child model, and her grandmother watched soap operas regularly with Ariel and referred to the cast of the soaps as "the beautiful people." Ariel's mother reassured her constantly that she was a very beautiful girl. She was neither unattractive nor especially pretty. On the other hand, the high value her family (and society) placed on beauty was obvious and omnipresent. The more her mother told her she was beautiful, the more she cried and the angrier she felt.

There's nothing in the world wrong with letting your daughter know once in a while how pretty, how attractive, and even how absolutely ravishing she is. However, it's important that she not define herself only by her appearance. If she thinks her beauty is what you admire most about her because you praise her appearance constantly, she will primp continuously, be overly fashion-conscious, and will not believe that you have other, more important expectations for her. She may lose confidence in herself entirely if her appearance during adolescence and adulthood doesn't measure up to society's definition of beauty. Although extreme beauty may lead to popularity in high school and even to a beauty-based career, there are great, even possibly lethal risks to her self-esteem if she can't fulfill the expectations for beauty she has internalized. If she tends to be overweight, eating disorders are likely. She will have many more opportunities available to her if she's smart, hardworking, and independent and can control all three of those characteristics healthfully.

SHE CAN GET ALL A'S . . . OR CAN SHE?

The statement "You can get all A's," particularly from fathers of our successful women, seemed to be a positive challenge to many of them because they believed they could accomplish their dads' expectations. That same message given by parents to girls who don't believe all A's are possible causes some girls to feel sad, even depressed, while others become very angry. That probably holds true for the statement "You will be president of the United States" (or editor of the *New York Times,* another Picasso, or discoverer of the cure for cancer). Humor may help, but it may also backfire if your daughters are not already excellent students.

Too much emphasis on A's may cause your daughters to avoid taking challenging courses, or could tempt them to cheat on tests to get those A's. Furthermore, your daughters could become too anxious about their grades and possibly even study too much in their attempt to please you.

If your daughters are underachieving and you are frustrated with their lack of effort, I would strongly recommend that you not say, "You could get all A's if only you'd do your work." Underachieving girls hardly ever truly believe they could get all A's even if they did their work. Sometimes they don't even believe they could get B's. Because they imagine the expectation of A's to be unrealizable, their safest alternative is to do as little work as they can get away with. That permits them to build an excuse for their poor grades. They can say the work is boring or irrelevant instead of coping with the more troublesome worry of not being as smart as they believe everyone expects them to be.

As you already know, most of the women in our study were hard workers. If you teach your daughters to be hard workers, then you can be delighted and astonished about all the good work they can accomplish. Once they are working, you'll have a better sense of how extravagant your praise can be while still avoiding putting impossible pressure on them.

It's not a good idea to continuously tell your daughters or students what a great job they've done when they haven't put forth much effort. If you want them to be workers, they should do some real work before they're praised for it. If you praise kids for halfhearted attempts, they'll see no reason to put forth more effort. Not only that, your praise seems insincere, and they really don't believe they've accomplished much. Karly Rheam explained it this way: "What really built my confidence was when people expected me to do a challenging task. They gave me no-nonsense feedback and sometimes tough criticism, and then let me know, sometimes even gruffly, that I had done the job well. That told me more about what I could truly accomplish than high grades and frequent compliments."

BE A COACH, NOT A JUDGE

Watch your daughters' gymnastic or swim team coaches. Observe a good Little League coach. They're enthusiastic, positive, demanding, and often very specific in their suggestions. They convey a sense that they believe in the kids they coach. When you're a coach, you want your daughters to win, and they know it. You can criticize, you can expect a lot, and they'll accept all that in the spirit of learning. Now imagine the judges who are portrayed in courtrooms on television. Their job is to determine if a person is guilty or innocent. When you're a judge, you're looking for your daughters' mistakes and are ready to mete out punishments. When you're a coach, you can overexpect and even overpredict a bit, and your daughters will love it and feel you believe in them. However, when you're a judge, to your daughters high praise means only, "*Now* what do you want me to do?" or "What will the punishment be if I don't meet the high standard?" Your daughters will feel like you're manipulating or threatening them.

Sometimes your daughters will be angry even if you say the right thing. It's tricky, because obviously your daughters must learn to accept criticism. If they're going to be successful, they'll have to learn to accept a lot of it. Specific criticism about how to correct an error or how to perfect a skill is easier for people to handle when it comes from a coach. You've rarely heard a coach tell a player they're just no good. Coaches can be powerful team leaders. Judges require the power of the law to get people to follow their orders.

Whatever psychologists and teachers say about expectations that are too high seems to be modified when girls view their parents as coaches. It is also clear that these same expectations are harmful when they come from parents who place themselves in the role of judges.

UNITED COACHING AND POWER

When both parents are coaches and neither are judges, you'll have the most effective team for setting high but realistic expectations for your daughters. The power of praise is multiplied if your daughters believe that you're both powerful people. If you demean the parent who praises, the praise will not seem as important to your children. If you demean yourselves, your expectations of your daughters will not be as meaningful to them. Rabbi Miriam Kane's mother realized that later in life. She wondered why mothers of smart daughters so often tell the daughters they're like their fathers. In a sense, she sabotaged her own relationship with her daughter during her daughter's teen years by demeaning herself.

Mothers who are full-time homemakers and who set high expectations for their daughters are effective only if it's clear that their more powerful career-oriented spouses respect their roles as homemakers. Otherwise, teenage daughters in our society today tend to ignore messages from homemaker mothers. They say to their moms, "Get a life." Successful mothers in high-status careers are more likely to be heard by their daughters, unless, of course, fathers resent their wives' work and demean them for it. If you as a mother don't feel very powerful at home, take your daughter to work; she is likely to regard you with new respect when she sees how you are valued in the workplace. Also, don't apologize for yourself; let your daughter know your strengths. It's best if your husband will reinforce those strengths. It is good for girls to believe they have wise and intelligent mothers and fathers. Too often women identified only with their fathers because their mothers were so modest about their own abilities and accomplishments.

THE AMERICAN DREAM FOR YOUR DAUGHTERS

You can help your daughters to achieve the American dream by expecting them to accomplish, to learn, to perform in school and at home, and to prepare for a challenging career. High expectations by parents have always been critical for achievement. You will have to be sensitive to your daughters' abilities, temperament, and interests so that you don't make the mistake of setting expectations that will cause them to feel pressured and lose confidence. If you have successful careers, you needn't worry too much about your children having to surpass you to fulfill the American dream. You can be a wonderful role model of success for your daughters instead.

SHE LEARNED THAT WOMEN ARE STRONG

Margaret Karnes
Executive of a Mining Company

When Grandma was anywhere around, there was no question about who was in charge." No one argued with Margaret's grandmother. She was a strong person—tall, with big, peasant-type hands—and no one challenged her position in the family. When her husband died, in his fifties, she independently turned her home into a boardinghouse to support herself and her children.

Margaret described her mother as strong, too, but she was strong in a quiet way. She was almost shy, but she was also very controlled and calm. Both Margaret's mother and aunt helped her dad build their business from the ground up, and although Margaret's dad was known by all to be absolutely in charge, he tended to be volatile, adventuresome, and even sentimental. Margaret's mother was the steadying force in the business, and Margaret sensed her mother's strength in the partnership. She watched her parents build their successful mining and concrete businesses together from almost nothing to an American success story. She recalls her parents in some heated arguments about the business. Her dad was a visionary; he looked to the future with an uncanny optimism. Her mother kept him grounded. She was always his strong partner.

Margaret's childhood was a strange paradox of being inspired by her father to believe the sky was her limit, but then being expected by the entire family, including her father, to have as her primary destiny marriage and family. Her brother, John, who was five years older than she, was declared crown prince and heir apparent, as the family, in its typically European way, believed that only men direct businesses. He was being prepared to lead the family's growing kingdom.

Margaret's childhood of self-motivation, ambition, achievement, hard work, accomplishment, and internalized pressure was supposed to have the dual function of propelling her toward unlimited success as well as toward becoming a contented, full-time homemaker and mother. As energetic, organized, and goal-directed as she was, she was never included in the family's business plans.

It was perhaps the contradictory messages Margaret received that caused her to give up college after a year, become pregnant, and marry the father of her child, who made her feel temporarily secure. The marriage was quickly followed by divorce and a startling learning experience that destroyed Margaret's naïveté forever. The sadness, humiliation, rejection, and emotional hurt from those experiences taught Margaret painful lessons she has never forgotten, and although the experiences stole from her a "princess" status, they also strengthened her. She explained that her tragedy "leveled the playing field," and she knew she would have to deal much more carefully and defensively with people the rest of her life. Her near disaster gave her a full dose of learning about people that has made her more cautious and smarter in all her business dealings—a heavy burden for a nineteen-year-old, but one that stood her in good stead for her future as a business leader.

As a child, Margaret mainly remembers concentrating on how to be a "good little girl." Surrounded by parents, grandparents, aunts, and uncles who were all immigrants who spoke English with a German accent, and who lived within the cultural traditions of their Hungarian-German heritage, Margaret felt, again paradoxically, both secure and insecure. Within her family, there was warmth, laughter, music, good food, good fun, and tradition. She felt totally loved and even adored. Weekends at the lake, boating, outdoor activities, sports, and then brief winter vacations together in the Florida Keys provided balance for an ambitious family that worked tirelessly together to build an extraordinary business. Outside of her family, however, in her school and neighborhood, Margaret felt alone and very different. She was ashamed to bring her friends to her home because of her parents' strange accent and different food. Furthermore, she couldn't explain to her family or her friends about how important it was for her to feel American and not be associated with her heritage. She was both so proud of her loving family and yet so ashamed of their not being American. In some ways, she admitted, her difference and uniqueness made her feel stronger. It also made her feel like an objective outsider constantly observing the interactions of people.

Margaret spent much time alone during her childhood. Her mother and aunt were busy working in the family business. She initiated her own activities, did a job when she saw it needed doing, and went outside to play if she wanted to pal around with her friends. She recalls, "I learned to think for myself and function on my own. When I went out to the playground, I learned to lock the door behind me. No one had to remind me of my responsibilities. I would clean up the kitchen and scrub the bathroom faucets. I wasn't asked to do things. I just took pride in our home, but I do have to admit I ducked the laundry. I just hated and avoided it even when I knew it had to be done."

Margaret always completed her homework and practiced her organ lessons on her own. She played sports, was an outdoor kid, and skated skillfully on the pond in winter. Although her parents hardly ever picked up a book, and no one ever encouraged her to, she loved to read. She read everything, but especially adventure and travel books. She lived the adventures in those books vicariously, and was never satiated.

Girl Scouts was very special to Margaret. She earned every badge she could, setting her own goals and organizing a plan to complete the requirements for each badge, one after another. Her mother led her Girl Scout troop, which gave her special time with her mother and also a personal path for becoming the "good little girl" her mother expected. It was a path not open to her brother.

Margaret recounted her feelings about Girl Scouts: "Not only did I value my mother's time, but she had the most wonderful craft ideas and was so very creative. After she would introduce the crafts projects in Scouts and everyone loved them, I felt so proud that she was my mother. Because we would take the leftover materials home, I could also work on the projects at home afterward. I would make gifts for all my relatives and adult neighbors, making friends with all the neighbors I gave the gifts to. I never created just one project. I continually made them and was so proud of my increasingly improved craft projects."

Margaret looked forward to Girl Scout cookie sales, which developed her entrepreneurial skills. She prided herself on selling the most cookies in the troop every single year. She was the first one out on the street when cookie sales began, and she loved knocking on doors to persuade people to buy cookies from her. If they didn't buy, that never stopped her. She'd try to figure out a way to sell to them the next year. She actually kept lists of people who hadn't bought from her in earlier years, and before Girl Scout cookie sales would begin, she would visit the people on the list early to remind them cookie sales were coming soon. Because they hadn't bought from her the previous year, she would politely ask them to save their purchases for her that year. Each year she sold more cookies, and each year she set her goal higher.

Margaret was asked about her competitiveness and if winning in competition had been important in her childhood: "I don't think I was really so competitive, except perhaps in selling Girl Scout cookies. It was more that I competed with myself, constantly setting higher goals and showing myself that I could do better."

Margaret's mother was clearly in charge of Margaret's life, but she was not generous with her praise, and Margaret tried very hard to please her. Margaret identified more with her adventurous father and was inspired to accomplish much because he believed she could. Margaret often worked in her parents' business. Even though her job was to put things in alphabetical and numerical order and to process "hundreds and hundreds and hundreds of tickets," she would also be watching, always observing, absorbing the operation of the business "like a sponge." Margaret studied her parents' interactions, and they became a blueprint for her own future—a business to provide adventure and challenge, plus a close family to balance intense work with love and laughter.

Margaret attended a public school for only a few years before she transferred to a small Lutheran school. She worked hard but described herself as an average student. By middle school, her math and science confidence and skills declined. She avoided difficult math and science classes for fear they would lower her grades, but she loved social studies and English and was absolutely fascinated by her religion classes. "Marvelous" Mr. Schmidt, who was both principal and teacher, led her through the Bible. She still owns and reveres the tattered and dogeared copy of the King James Bible she used in eighth grade. She loved the stories, the ethical discussions, and the values she was taught. Margaret remembers her teacher explaining about the importance of honesty. His voice and his words have been a guiding force through the years. Although her family is not presently active in church life, the ethical values she learned in school have guided her throughout her life and are the foundations of her business dealings today.

The small Lutheran school that Margaret so enjoyed had only four teachers for eight grades, and she acknowledged that the emphasis on religion and ethics may have stolen time from other academic subjects. She did not really feel prepared for the large Lutheran high school she attended in ninth grade. She worked hard and was a good student, but she felt isolated and intimidated in the larger school. She hated classes, and she was fearful about the new dating scene. She felt surrounded by strangers and found herself becoming sick to her stomach every morning before school.

In the meantime, her parents' business had improved dramatically. The family moved to an elegant suburban neighborhood where most of their neighbors were doctors and lawyers. Margaret recalled: "The girls in the neighborhood dressed perfectly, with matching hats and gloves and beautiful dresses. They all read *Seventeen* magazine, and I didn't have the clothes that were shown in *Seventeen.* Although we had a beautiful home, I was more embarrassed than ever about my family. One of my aunts who had a very heavy accent cleaned our house, and I was always afraid if my girlfriends came in they would hear her, and I would be mortified. Sometimes she'd be cooking Hungarian or German foods, and because they smelled so different from what I smelled at other people's homes, I would run around opening windows to get rid of the smell in case my friends should decide to visit. I tried to go to their homes rather than invite them to ours, but there was always the fear and embarrassment that they might stop by to see me."

One Sunday Margaret had seen a large ad in the newspaper for a private girls' school. She studied the ad all day; in the evening she showed it to her dad and announced that she wanted to attend the school. He promptly agreed to visit and told Margaret to make the necessary appointment. Together they entered the beautiful and sophisticated brick school building, observing the parquet floors, high ceilings, elegant furnishings, and refined, almost silent, atmosphere. Margaret feared she didn't have the background for this impressive school, but quietly said to her father, "I want to go here." He whispered back, "Are you sure?" They sat down in the dignified setting of the director's office. She recalls, "There was my very rough workingman father in this very strange, sophisticated setting. You could hear a pin drop." The director prepared to describe the school, and Margaret's father interrupted with one simple question: "How much does it cost?" The director told him what the tuition was, and Margaret's father got up to walk away, adding that his wife would send a check and that Margaret could take care of the rest. The director attempted to discuss admission criteria, but Margaret's dad was already on his way out of the office. Margaret was left to handle the details and admission tests.

Thus Margaret became the token immigrant student from the west side of town at a very exclusive girls' high school comprised largely of wealthy east siders. All the other girls had grown up together and knew each other well. They spoke the same, had special nicknames for each other, and wore knee-highs, pleated plaid skirts, and identical blazers. They were very competitive in academics and sports. Margaret was an absolute oddity; however, she assessed the situation and prepared to adjust and become accepted. She liked this school.

At Margaret's request, her mother took her to shop for the "right" clothes to help her to fit in. She studied hard in her classes but avoided the advanced math and science courses, again for fear they would make her feel dumb. She joined the field hockey team and was a good team player, and she visited her friends on the "right" side of town. Although she never did entirely fit in with the rest of the girls, she was accepted not only as a member of the class but also, rather quickly, as a social leader—even though her family was considered "new money," and she was therefore the only student who couldn't be a debutante. She remembered her terrible disappointment about that. The irony came many years later, when she eagerly suggested to her daughter that she might like to make her debut, but her daughter had no interest in "such nonsense."

Perhaps it was Margaret's independence that won her immediate acceptance; perhaps it was her handsome older brother and all of his friends she could introduce the other girls to. She had a busy social life, but except for sneaking a few mugs of beer, Margaret continued to be the "good little girl" her parents expected her to be.

Margaret's brother, John, continued in his private military school. The whole family went to view him each Sunday in his elegant military regalia and sat around talking about his successes. He was simply the pride and joy of the family. Margaret says that she was a part of his isn't-he-wonderful club but also admits that once she went off to college and he was put into the business at her father's side, jealousy really affected her. She realized that her family had left no place for her and that all the expectations about the sky being the limit were directed at John. Margaret was expected only to be a homemaker.

Although Margaret had in her freshman year tried both a small college and a large one, neither had been a good fit for her. It was then that she turned to the man who became the father of her child for security and solace, or even perhaps out of anger. When her husband turned out to be a bad fit, too, Margaret was left with only depression and vulnerability.

In retrospect, she admires her parents' wisdom at that difficult time of her life. They invited her and her baby home to live with them, never showing any anger at Margaret's unexpected pregnancy, but wisely enough understanding that dependency would not give her back her confidence. Her mother decided it was time to semiretire from the business and take the role that her own mother had played for her, to help with her daughter's first child and permit that daughter to establish her own identity. Margaret's father presented Margaret with a small travel agency he had purchased at a bargain price—though what he explained to Margaret was that he had won the business and a piano at a poker game, and she could choose the one she wanted. She, in turn, suggested that he give her sister-in-law the first choice. Her sister-in-law chose the piano, leaving Margaret with the travel agency to develop. Margaret assumes her father must have manipulated that entire arrangement to get her involved and provide her with a way to rebuild her confidence.

Margaret had no idea of where to begin, but having for so long observed her father's model of learning from his environment, she began learning the travel business. She assessed her needs, found the experts to teach her, and turned the small agency into a thriving success. Margaret's confidence soared, and she felt independent and strong again.

Family summers on the lake continued to be memorable for Margaret, but the summer she met Don, her second husband, changed her life. Unlike her first husband, Don was dependable, loving, generous, thoughtful, and patient. He was also wonderful to Margaret's little girl. He seemed a good and natural match, and indeed, the marriage has been a good one for more than thirty years.

Eventually Margaret sold her successful travel business to establish a goal initially set for her by her parents: to be a full-time homemaker for her family and to serve her community. Margaret's internship in community service went far beyond that of the typical volunteer. Although she was committed to Scout leadership, PTA, and school board activities, she also sat on boards of directors where no woman had ventured before, and coordinated local, state, and national political campaigns. As with the travel agency, Margaret learned to lead from observation. She became well known for her leadership and organizational skills in political campaigns. While parenting her three children and being a wonderful wife and hostess were primary, her secondary community leadership was primary to others, and indeed she helped candidates win many elections. Confident at age forty, she knew she could continue her volunteer leadership, but she also recognized it was not enough for an ambitious, vigorous woman such as herself. Margaret was an executive in her heart and soul.

At the time it was difficult for Margaret to change the tradition of male-dominated business. Her brother was to inherit all the family's business enterprises, and she would get some sort of fair financial inheritance. However, money wasn't the issue; Margaret needed more than that. She thirsted for leadership and ownership. She wanted the exhilaration of reaching for the limitless sky. With Don at her side, she petitioned her father to let her take over the mining business, which had been earmarked for her brother. It was not, she explained, for her husband; he already had his own business. She wanted this because, as a woman, she knew she could lead, expand, and drive this business. Her father, whom she always adored, did not disappoint his "princess." He hesitantly made the business hers on a trial basis, provided she would take the time to learn to administer it. So Margaret gradually took over this successful male-dominated business where previously the only female employees had been the secretaries and bookkeepers. Again, as was her style, she assessed the situation and delivered the charisma required to expand a business traditionally considered "a man's world."

Margaret's volunteer and political efforts never flagged, nor did her commitment to reproduce the family warmth, closeness, fun, and tradition that provided her childhood security. Now, at age fifty-five, all her children are married, and she has two grandchildren. She will never forget her immigrant parents, whose fervor, energy, hard work, and reaching for the sky permitted them and her to live the American dream.

NO ONE EVER TOLD HER WHAT SHE COULDN'T DO

Dr. Ana Casa
Cardiothoracic Surgeon

Dr. Ana Casa doesn't exactly know how her path led to cardiothoracic surgery. Perhaps, she speculates, it's simply because no one ever told her what she couldn't do, so she assumed she could do whatever she chose.

In many ways Ana's life pattern does not fit that of most female physicians. She grew up in New York City in an ethnically mixed neighborhood. She was three when she emigrated from the Dominican Republic to the United States with her mother, who was twenty-four. Ana's father, who was an accountant, had died when Ana was two, and her mother remarried three years later. Ana spoke only Spanish until she entered school, which she did early so she could learn English, and she recalls in preschool not being certain whether she was speaking in English or Spanish. She learned English quickly, accommodated to American culture, and quickly came to feel that it was her culture. She recalls a photograph of her and her best friends in kindergarten and notes that two were African-American and one was Caucasian. They were all hugging each other, and she doesn't remember being aware of any ethnic differences at that age. She doesn't believe her Hispanic background had any special impact on her. She thinks that perhaps the facts that her stepfather was Italian and that her neighborhood was so diverse contributed to her lack of Hispanic identity.

When Ana discovered reading, she read constantly, and in second or third grade, when a friend took her to the neighborhood public library, it opened up a whole new world of books for her. She read voraciously all through school, as many as four or five books a week. The library became Ana's second home. She has memories of loving school from the start. She was an outstanding student and always felt she was the smartest student in her class. Teachers frequently praised her for being an excellent student, and school became the only place she received so much support and recognition. Support at home was almost nonexistent. Ana believes her ability to learn more quickly than others and her love of reading caused her to feel different and isolated from others both at home and at school. Ana describes an incident that illustrates how her unusual abilities seemed to set her apart from her family: "Because my mother always worked in the garment industry and sometimes brought work home, she had an industrial-type sewing machine at home. One day my mother walked in to see me (at age seven) sitting at the machine in deep concentration making doll clothes, even though I had never been taught how to use a sewing machine. Although my mother was astonished, she said nothing to me, most likely, I think, out of fear that if she broke my concentration, I might hurt myself with the machine. However, my mother's awareness of my ability to accomplish almost anything I chose to do probably also served as a reason not to interrupt. Because no one told me I couldn't sew, I assumed I could, and my mother, too, came to wonder at my ability to do everything I attempted with extraordinary success."

Ana is most aware of the differences between her and her mother and the lack of communication between them. She doesn't remember ever feeling close to her mother. In Ana's words, "My mother was brought up in a different culture and a different time." Her mother had barely a grade-school education, and although she is literate, she continues to speak mainly Spanish. Ana acknowledges that her mother may have felt intimidated and somewhat awed by her gifted, fluent-in-English daughter. She views her mother as strong in many ways—she worked very hard and coped with many difficulties—but she sees her also as too dependent and uncomfortable about making decisions. The emotional distance between them, according to Ana, came about because Ana was perceived as not fitting within the family. If Ana received a grade of 98, her mother would ask, "Why didn't you get 100?" She would also—awkwardly for Ana—say to Ana's brother, "Why can't you get good grades like Ana?" So Ana felt early on as if she was the smartest in the family. Perhaps her unusual height added to her sense of power, but early on Ana felt as if she knew more than the rest of her family.

Ana doesn't remember her biological father (although she wonders if she inherited his height and his intelligence). She never got along well with her stepfather and truly feared him. She remembers having been physically abused by him, yet she also recalls that he was able to explain adult matters in an understandable and interesting manner. Their relationship was emotionally distant but intellectually close. She remembers one of her stepfather's explanations that seemed especially meaningful and influential to her. His mother had died, and Ana was mystified by the cause of her death. Her stepfather patiently explained to Ana how his mother's blood could no longer flow to her heart and why her heart had stopped. Ana believes his explanation may have planted the seed for her interest in medicine, specifically medicine related to the heart. It is ironic that despite Ana's fearful relationship with her stepdad, he had a subtle but very powerful influence on her.

Ana believes her mother expected a lot of her and was firm with her, but she never felt as if either of her parents was supportive of her. It seemed to her that they resented her intelligence. She always felt far more intelligent than her brother and sister but believes her brother and sister received much more attention than she did. However, she admits that her siblings also felt they weren't given as much attention. Ana explained that each sibling had a separate designation of special-ness. Ana was the firstborn of the extended family, including all her cousins; her brother was in the revered position of being the first and only boy in the extended family; and her younger sister had the special place of being the baby of the family.

Ana attended elementary school first at a public school and later at a Catholic school. She was involved in few extracurricular activities except piano lessons. She was an avid reader and watched a lot of tele-vision. She was a loner in her elementary school as well as in the Catholic boarding school to which she was sent after sixth grade. She skipped seventh grade. Even after that, the schoolwork seemed easy to her. She didn't fit in socially, but that was nothing new; she never had. She liked her first year at the school, but resented the rigidity and regi-mentation. She wanted to leave the school for ninth grade, but her sib-lings and cousins were also enrolled at the school. They were separated by age and gender, so she really didn't see much of them during the school day, yet her mother insisted she stay another year because she expected her to set an example for the other children in the family. She was disappointed but "took on the burden and stopped complaining." She continued to feel socially isolated and lonely, although she always had a few good friends. Her grades were always high, and she did well in everything, including math and science. She reminded her inter-viewer, "No one ever told me I couldn't do math, so I assumed I could." She studied and, of course, she always completed her homework, but she never viewed either as a burden.

Ana attended an all-girls Catholic high school where, again, she never felt she fit in. She was not involved in any extracurricular activi-ties and spent most of her time alone, either reading or watching televi-sion, as she had when she was younger. Although her mother rarely gave her overt encouragement, she could tell by hearing her mother talk to her aunts and uncles about her, and from comments she made after teacher conferences, that she was proud of Ana's academic accomplishments. She received more feedback from other kids' parents, who let her know frequently that they would have traded her report card for those of their own children.

Although Ana assumed she'd grow up having both marriage and a career, her career choices fluctuated daily between such typical childhood wishes as teacher, fireman, nun, doctor, and astronaut. At first her mother expected only marriage and family for her bright daughter, but by junior high she realized that Ana would also have a career. There were no doctors in Ana's extended family and no college graduates among the adults; therefore, there were no family role models for a professional career of any kind. Ana was the first in her family even to consider going on to college.

Ana chuckled as she remembers a meeting with her guidance counselor, who told her she probably wouldn't go to college and recommended she take typing. Ana said that she thought this advice might have been devastating for another student, but Ana, who was so confident in her academic achievement in all honors classes, left the office and only laughed. She said she would never have been assertive enough to contradict the nun. She simply assumed the counselor had looked at the wrong file, so she ignored her advice. She wondered if "the nun had told some other kid who couldn't read to go to Harvard by mistake." It was only years later that she even considered that the counselor's advice could have been inspired by prejudice. Not many Hispanic girls in the school went on to college.

Teachers were always important in Ana's life. It was a female French teacher in high school who befriended Ana and inspired her to go on to college. The teacher was interesting, enthusiastic, and always gave her positive feedback and academic encouragement. With her support and inspiration, Ana was a Regents Scholar at graduation and prepared to attend the City College of New York.

At seventeen Ana left home to attend college and has never been close to her parents since. She has renewed efforts recently to befriend her brother and sister, but even that seems strained. Neither of them has a college education, and both have families of their own. A small circle of friends has always been Ana's support group. Ana did well academically in college but was unhappy socially. She felt more isolated than ever. She also couldn't decide on a major, so she left after two years to try to determine some direction for her life. She worked for a while and then just woke up one morning and said, "I think I'll go to medical school." Again, during her interview, Ana added laughingly, "No one told me I couldn't do medicine, so I just assumed that I could." She has no idea where the decision actually came from, and the only related inspiration she could recall was that earlier discussion with her stepfather.

A chance encounter after she applied to medical school had a tremendous impact on Ana's future. She had sent in her application and had not received any response after a long period of time. Finally, after many calls to the admissions office, she discovered her file had been lost. She simply didn't know what to do, and it would have meant waiting another whole year to reapply. She had given up when she coincidentally met a woman counselor at a social event who was active in minority affairs. They were chatting casually, and Ana blurted out the story of her lost file. The woman immediately put in a call to the appropriate office, gathered all of Ana's scores and information, and delivered them to the right person and "pushed the whole process through" for her. She remembers hearing the woman talking on the telephone to the admissions office, saying, "I don't care if you lost her folder. You'll have to make up a letter for her." Ana credits this woman for getting her into medicine. Furthermore, the woman left an indelible example of making the right connections to accomplish what needs to be done. She was a very impressive role model of assertiveness for Ana; from her Ana learned never to let obstacles get in the way of achieving her goals.

Ana never dreamed of becoming a surgeon, and in her first encounters with surgeons she thought they were pompous and arrogant, but when she did her surgical rotation and was suited up for the first time in gown and surgical gloves, she suddenly felt "at home." She loved surgery, but a friend in medical school was determined to talk her out of her decision. Ana also had many doubts about the time commitment involved. However, the more the friend raised doubts and the more she warned Ana against going into surgery, the more Ana felt convinced it was her only choice. The debate helped Ana to become more comfortable about her final decision. She has never regretted the decision or the special friendship that emerged from this close, questioning relationship. She followed her interests, and they took her into cardiovascular surgery, a pioneering area in which there are even now very few women.

When Ana chose surgery, she recognized it was a male-dominated field. Furthermore, the residency was referred to as pyramidal, meaning that each year some residents who couldn't meet the high standards would be dropped. She was one of two females in the first year of surgery. Ana knew the other woman had political connections and was afraid she might be the one to be "weeded out." As it turned out, both women were successful. However, after the second year, Ana felt she desperately needed a break from the pressures of her surgical residency. She applied for a two-year program at the National Heart Institute to do clinical work and research and was accepted. She returned after two years, revitalized to complete three more years of residency, which were followed by two more years within her specialty at another hospital.

With ten years of training beyond undergraduate and medical schools, it seemed logical to ask Ana how that long eighteen-year training period fit with any expectations of marriage and family. She said she had considered that extensively before making her decision about surgery, but in a sense, she explained, marriage and family wasn't a choice she could logically make. There was no special person in her life when she started, and for her to take a different, less interesting route in the hope that the right person would come along, when in fact surgery was exactly what she wanted to do, seemed "silly" to her. She tried to talk herself into doing something else, but she absolutely loved surgery. Although Ana feels discouraged about the climate for physicians in our country at this time, she continues to consider her surgical work as "great." Despite the fact that Ana loves the challenge and fulfillment of her work and feels good about making a contribution to society, she says that if young women were to ask her for advice, she would not recommend the field of surgery because of the long training, the lack of female mentors, and the time required away from family and relationships. On the other hand, she acknowledged that if this is what a woman really wants, none of those disadvantages need get in her way.

Ironically, Ana, who had so few friends as a child and was so isolated, finds her friends to be her main support group. Ana, now in her mid-forties, is not married and is not close to her mother or siblings. Ana defines her friendship network as her family. She says she is not a doctor first, and her friends, many of whom are not in the medical field, help her to keep her life in perspective with the rest of the world. Paradoxically, a lonely childhood, during which Ana defined herself mainly by her achievement, has led her to an achieving lifestyle in which her friendships have become central to the personal definition of herself.

Ana denies any family influence on her achievements and successful career. In light of our research, which finds parental influence to be so important for success, perhaps one can interpret Ana's denial of influence as related to an unconscious wish to disassociate herself from her lower-socioeconomic-status immigrant mother, who worked so many hours in a factory but nevertheless managed to find the tuition to send Ana and her siblings to private schools and even private boarding school. It is not unusual for children of immigrants to feel ashamed of their parents' accents or their lack of education. Generation gaps are often greater between immigrants and their Americanized children. Although children of immigrants often live out their parents' American dream, it may cause a great gulf between generations. One wonders about the difficult price that uneducated immigrant parents often pay as their children climb to the higher socioeconomic status that may well have motivated them to immigrate.

CHAPTER 3

GOOD LITTLE GIRLS
AREN'T SO BAD

Part 1: Findings

The women in the study were given the opportunity to list their self-perceptions as well as how they believed they were perceived by others. Figures 3.1 and 3.2 include the twenty most frequently selected descriptors chosen by the total group. Although there were some differences on the lists for the various careers, "smart," "hardworking," and "independent" were at or very near the top of the list of self-perceptions for every career group. These women were mainly viewed as "good little girls" from the start. In the words of Kathleen Olds,* former editor in chief of *Glamour* magazine, "I was just born good." Susan Widham,* president of Beech-Nut Nutritional Corporation, recalls that as a child she simply concentrated on being good. Her case study follows this chapter.

Some of the other words the women used to describe themselves included "sensitive," "brainy," "kind," "teacher's pet," "mature," "leader," "happy," "persistent," "bookworm," and "adultlike." All of them seem to fit with the concept of what most people would consider "good little girls."

"Creative" was selected often by the women in media, orchestral music, and art, and fairly frequently by those in quite a few other

FIGURE 3.1

Top Twenty Self-Perceptions During Elementary, Middle, and High School

Elementary School	Middle School	High School
Smart 53	Smart 50	Hard worker 54
Hard worker 51	Sensitive 47	Smart 50
Loved 51	Hard worker 45	Independent 49
Sensitive 46	*Self-critical 40	Sensitive 48
Happy 42	Independent 38	Self-critical 46
Independent 39	Loved 37	Adultlike 45
Kind 38	Kind 34	Mature 40
Good little girl 37	*Different 33	Different 37
Shy 35	Strong-willed 32	Loved 36
*Self-critical 35	Shy 31	Creative 36
*Different 33	Adultlike 30	Kind 35
Bookworm 32	Insecure 30	Happy 32
Creative 32	Happy 30	Leader 30
Talented 31	Creative 30	*Insecure 30
*Tomboy 31	Mature 30	Perfectionistic 30
Leader 26	*Perfectionistic 28	Shy 30
*Perfectionistic 26	Bookworm 28	Confident 29
*Insecure 26	Good little girl 27	Talented 28
Adultlike 25	Brainy 27	Brainy 27
Mature 25	*Lonely 25	*Lonely 24

*Characteristics not on top twenty list of perceptions by others

careers. "Gifted" and "talented" were high on the list for the musicians and artists but not as high for most other career fields. "Outgoing" and "popular" were selected frequently by the women in the two business groups, government, media, and the visual arts, as well as the traditional groups, including educators, homemakers, and mental health professionals. The women in medicine, nursing, and teaching recalled themselves as "athletic."

"Strong-willed" was on the list for women in all the nontraditional careers, while "compliant" and "quiet" were frequently listed for those in the traditional careers. Perhaps surprisingly, "compliant" was also checked frequently by the physicians. The artists, media women, and mental health professionals described themselves as "emotional." The mental health professionals also described themselves as "sad" or

FIGURE 3.2

Top Twenty
Perceptions by Others During
Elementary, Middle, and High School

Elementary School	Middle School	High School
Smart 65	Smart 58	Smart 70
Good little girl 54	Brainy 43	Hard worker 52
Hard worker 51	Hard worker 37	Adultlike 46
Adultlike 41	Adultlike 37	Confident 43
Happy 37	Good little girl 35	Brainy 43
Mature 34	Mature 33	Mature 41
Kind 34	Talented 32	Independent 40
Independent 34	Strong-willed 31	Leader 40
* Teacher's pet 33	* Confident 31	Talented 39
Leader 33	Independent 30	Creative 34
Talented 32	* Leader 30	Kind 33
Loved 31	Kind 29	Happy 31
Creative 31	Creative 28	* Good little girl 27
* Confident 30	Happy 27	Loved 24
Bookworm 30	Bookworm 27	Bookworm 23
* Gifted 29	Loved 23	Sensitive 21
* Strong-willed 28	Sensitive 22	Different 20
Sensitive 27	Shy 19	Perfectionistic 19
Shy 23	* Athletic 19	* Beautiful 18
* Chatterbox 22	* Beautiful 18	Shy 15

*Characteristics not on top twenty list of women's perceptions of themselves

"unhappy" with some frequency, which perhaps feeds the assumption that learning to cope with one's own unhappiness may in part attract women to careers where they can help others who struggle with emotional issues.

There were some important differences in how women believed they were viewed by others compared to how they perceived themselves. Characteristics such as "self-critical," "different," "perfectionistic," "tomboy," "insecure," and "lonely" were selected quite frequently as self-perceptions, but not as perceptions by others. Thus, many women coped with insecurities even though they believed that they hid them from others.

THE INTELLIGENCE OF THE WOMEN IN THE STUDY

Our questionnaire requested information about a great many measures of the intellectual achievements of the women in the study. Some women reported their IQ scores, their Scholastic Aptitude Test (SAT) scores, their rank in their high-school graduating classes, awards received at graduation, and grade-point averages in college and graduate school. Although there were many women who indicated they did not know some of their scores or had never even been tested, the data we collected suggests there were many highly intelligent women in the study. Figure 3.3 shows the average IQ scores and the range of scores for the women in each career group. Only one-third of the total group actually identified their IQ scores on the questionnaire. Furthermore, the scores may be biased because the reported scores were more likely those of either younger or highly intelligent women who were more likely to have been tested during their school years. The figure also shows readers that many women in the study had average and above-average abilities.

For those who may not be familiar with IQ scores, an average score is considered to be 100. The average range is between 90 and 109. Above-average scores fall between 110 and 119. The superior range is usually considered to be from 120 to 129, and 130 and above is considered very

FIGURE 3.3

Average IQ and IQ Range of Successful Women

	Average	*Range*
For-profit Business	137	104–196
Nonprofit Business	128	103–148
Government	134	120–162
Law	139	115–172
Media	140	114–185
Medicine	143	115–184
Music	140	125–178
Science	143	110–180
Arts	135	110–158
Allied Health	127	120–140
Education	128	100–156
Homemaking	131	115–145
Mental Health	134	114–160

superior or gifted. There is considerable variability among IQ tests, and it is assumed these women were tested with a variety of different tests.

Although IQ tests don't measure abilities, such as creativity or social and emotional skills, they are the best available predictors of school success. You can see by the test scores that there was good reason for many of these women to feel smart. However, you can just as readily conclude that many women felt smart despite the fact that their IQ scores might not have predicted their intellectual self-confidence. Motivation and the resulting good grades also build intellectual self-confidence.

FEELING SMART

Most of the women commented on feeling smart during much of their childhood. They identified their smartness by comparing themselves to other students in their classes, taking into consideration their better grades. Sometimes they thought of themselves as smart because they were in special or honors classes.

Dr. Anne Caroles believes she was smart because she was good at math and science. She recalls, "It was the *Sputnik* age, and because the country was falling behind Russia and needed to catch up, anybody who was smart in math and science was really encouraged." She considered her sister to be every bit as bright in writing and English, and she even thought her sister was probably more creative, but her sister wasn't considered as bright by her family because she didn't do as well in math and science.

Anne summarized her intellectual confidence: "If someone said I was unattractive or was difficult to get along with, I would believe them, and they could drag me down with those statements; but if someone told me I was dumb, I would just look at them as if they were crazy."

Some women identified their intelligence by their love of reading or enjoyment of school. Quite a few women who did not feel accepted or valued at home found school a shelter, often the only place they felt valued.

Although many of the women in the arts were excellent students, they frequently commented that music practice, artistic involvement, or writing helped them to feel smart in a special way and served as an escape from competition in other arenas with their siblings or friends.

Norah Barnes remembers closing her door with great relief to practice her flute for hours, a way of escaping the competition she felt with her sister (who later became a scientist). Norah was a very good student, but her sense of being "smarter" was related to her abilities in playing the flute. Her music also protected her from feeling less intellectually competent than her sister.

Denise Dennison remembers her older sister as being "very hard on her," but in her world of dance, she knew she was better, and her sister very quickly retreated from dance lessons and any competition related to dance. Denise's dancing became her specialty area for "feeling smart" within her family.

Rhonda Baker's sixth-grade science teacher discovered her artistic talent and for years afterward would invite Rhonda back to the elementary school to teach art projects to his students. Rhonda used her art in her English classes as well as her art classes, helping her to feel smart as well as an artist in all her schoolwork, not only in her art classes.

For Martha Frank, who had a serious reading disability, it was her father's patient work with her and his insistence that she was indeed very smart despite her difficulties with reading that helped her to believe in herself, persevere, and finally complete her college degree. She now directs a large animal laboratory in a major research center and has no doubt that her dyslexia did not mean that she wasn't smart.

It is true that many of the women in the study did not feel equally smart in all subjects. For those who lost confidence in math and science and did not take advanced courses in those areas, their success in other subjects seemed to reinforce their confidence in their intelligence.

A WORK ETHIC

The best explanation for the intellectual self-confidence expressed by so many of the women was their work ethic. For the most part, they perceived themselves as hard workers at home, school, and in their adult workplaces. Madeleine Lane, a violist, remembers the message her parents passed on to her while growing up: "The one really positive message I got from my mom and dad was that anything you want to do, you could do. If you want it, you can get it. They *were* the Protestant work ethic. The harder you work, the more talented you are."

Dr. Catherine Burns, an engineer, prides herself on her hard work as well and recalls both her parents' messages about the importance of hard work, but most especially her dad saying, "You can do anything you want if you work hard" and "Nothing comes for free."

As adults, many of the women attributed their success to their willingness to work harder than others. The successful and highly intelligent medical researcher Dr. Alyssa Gaines insists that she is probably less smart than many other scientists but is successful because she's learned to work longer and harder than others.

HOMEWORK AND STUDY

For the most part, the successful women in the study spent considerable time studying and doing homework. In elementary school, the average time remembered was forty-five minutes a day. By middle school that increased to one and a half hours, and by high school, two hours. All career groups were similar for amount of study time in elementary school. By middle and high school, the women in media were studying considerably less than the women in other groups. Women in medicine, science, and music studied more in the upper grades than other career groups. Dr. Melissa Sparks,* an assistant chief medical nursing director, shares her memories of homework: "I think I always had a fair amount of academic confidence. I think that it was sort of humming along; I never felt myself at the top of the class, but I never really had any major problems because I studied very hard. I used to study from the time I got home till it was time to go to bed. You wanted to do well, you were expected to do well, and you knew you could do well, but it just meant putting the effort into it."

Some women studied and did homework as an escape from loneliness. Psychologist Dr. Karen Brooks remembered, "I really didn't date at all in high school and was kind of a loner even though I did have some girlfriends. I certainly was not a popular kid, but I was salutatorian of my high-school class because the only source for my self-esteem was making good grades. I studied like a dog and never made anything below an A in all of junior or senior high school. I received only one B in my whole undergraduate career and only one B in graduate school."

Not all of the women were hard workers at school. Some were underachievers and remembered being told they could do better if they would only work harder. Some even manipulated parents into doing work for them:

Sally Sahn, a sports publicist, recalls that when her math would get hard, she'd ask her dad for help. He would soon become impatient with her and lose his temper. That would permit her to go to her mother for assistance, and she and her sister both knew that when their mother assisted, she actually completed most of the work for them. Sally paid for that underachievement later with a very difficult academic adjustment to college.

State Senator Suzanne Daniels took advanced math classes mostly with boys. She could always get the boys to help her with the take-home exams and therefore got excellent grades. Perhaps she realized that seeming not so smart to boys was a social advantage. However, she admitted learning little and recalls suffering from math anxiety thereafter.

Jane Southern, who loves being a full-time homemaker but acknowledges not feeling totally successful during school, remembers: "I wish my parents had given me study habit kinds of things to do. I don't remember anyone ever saying, 'Have you done your homework?' or 'That's an interesting topic; tell me more about it,' or anything like that. Maybe it was the negative attention. I hated going to school. I hated it because I had such butterflies; I was never prepared, and I knew a lot of other people who were like that."

CHORES, RESPONSIBILITIES, AND JOBS

Almost all of the women remembered having responsibilities for chores around the house, and almost half also had outdoor chores. A quarter of them ran small businesses; not surprisingly, the women in business careers were more entrepreneurial when they were growing up than were women in other groups. Almost half of the women worked for others doing baby-sitting, housecleaning, tutoring, and so on. Quite a number of women, especially those in the fields of music and art, gave lessons to other children. By high school, only a small percentage didn't have jobs outside their home. Several of the women recalled that when they asked if they could get an outside job while in high school, their parents' response was, "Your job is school." The women interpreted this to mean that high grades were expected, and they were not disappointed by their parents' redirection. They placed their energy toward further study instead of jobs.

About a third of the women indicated that their childhood jobs influenced their careers. Musicians and artists often received payment for their teaching or performances while they were in high school. Jane Summers did clerical work in her dad's accounting office and, as a result, determined she would probably go into some kind of business when she grew up. Dr. Diane Butler* remembered positive experiences baby-sitting that helped her select pediatrics as a medical specialty. Actually teachers, homemakers, and child psychologists alike remembered baby-sitting as an important influence in selecting a career that involved children.

Susan Widham,* president of Beech-Nut Nutritional Corporation, was motivated to earn money for the maintenance of her horses, and her positive work experience helped her to establish confidence in her adult career.

INDEPENDENCE

The women in the study remembered themselves as independent, mature, and often adultlike. The women in the nontraditional careers often referred to themselves as strong-willed, but the term seemed to be used to describe positive attributes of believing in themselves, being purposeful, and persevering rather than a need to fight adult authority.

Denise Dennison recalls leading her entire middle-school class in a protest action against the school board because she didn't think it was fair that girls were not allowed to take shop classes. Her leadership and assertiveness changed the school policy for girls thereafter. She recalls that she never did like the shop course, but it was a matter of fairness and her determination to stand up for what was right. She was strong-willed when she saw an important purpose, particularly if it was related to fairness.

Judge Edna Conway recalls that when people would tell her what couldn't be done, she'd quietly assess the challenge and decide she could rise above the challenge. She recalls that she might have experienced setbacks and failures, but she'd just stay focused on the task until the job was done. Her attitude was "You just gotta keep going," and she simply didn't quit. Not even peer pressure adversely affected her.

The stories of independence driven by purposefulness and higher goals are dramatic among these women and provide strong evidence that parents need to encourage independence in their daughters.

Part 2: Advice

When the successful women in our study were little girls, for the most part they fell within the stereotypical category of "good little girls" who pleased others and were "kind," "sensitive," and "persistent." There were also many "bookworms" and "tomboys." Furthermore, many of them perceived themselves as "perfectionistic," "self-critical," "insecure," and "different." As you try to build self-esteem in your daughters, you may notice they are anxious to please others (as in "good little girls"). It's important to realize that this is a normal part of childhood for little girls—and, perhaps to a lesser extent, for little boys. Therefore, this wish to please others shouldn't be defined as unhealthy. Sometimes parents refuse to give guidance because they fear that their daughters are not assertive enough. These parents are hoping that the girls will discover within themselves a personal direction. When parents tell their daughters to do what they want and refuse to advise them, the girls become confused. They're not sure whether to do what they think their parents would like or whether they would please their parents more if they didn't do the expected. They may resolve their confusion by following their peers. Such little girls may define independence as the opposite of what most parents expect. Both parents and girls often feel guilty when the girls wish to please others. Attempts to force girls into establishing that identity before they are developmentally ready is akin to rushing maturity and accidentally teaching oppositional and rebellious behavior to them. Girls sometimes become arguers for the sake of arguing instead of being directed by purposefulness and a search for identity.

Because children want to please parents and teachers during early and middle childhood, they gain competencies and learn skills that will permit them to make more and more choices as they mature. Self-esteem emerges gradually for children as they discover that they're good at accomplishing in many areas. The most powerful tool for building skills is the confidence that comes when girls discover they can have many interests and learn much from them. Those developed intrinsic interests will assist them in navigating adolescence. To some extent, insecurity, feeling different, and being self-critical during adolescence should be considered normal for your daughters. During a time when too many girls sit around worrying about how to please boys, the best diversion for building self-esteem may indeed be activities that are begun and become more specialized and developed during adolescence. For example, music, art, drama, speech, computers, athletic activities, and academic skills help girls feel competent. Social acceptance by boys may also cause girls to feel competent, but if it becomes their only goal, it will distract them from developing their sense of self and lead them to be entirely dependent on male approval.

Self-esteem, or liking oneself, should perhaps be defined as a continuous process of exploration, learning, and growing during childhood and adolescence. Social learning is surely part of that exploration, but for building true self-esteem, it can never be allowed to be the only measure. Daughters need to begin developing their interests and getting involved in activities early but gradually.

INTELLIGENCE AND IQ TESTS

High IQ test scores communicate to teachers and parents that a child is highly intelligent. However, that's not a reason to run out and get your daughter tested by a psychologist. On the other hand, if your daughter is very verbal early or is a spontaneous reader, it's probably a worthwhile investment to have her tested early. If her score is unusually high, it will help you to communicate to her school about her need for challenge. If the subscores within the test vary considerably, a psychologist may be able to give you some tips on how to improve your daughter's weak areas. For example, very verbal girls sometimes don't have the strong spatial skills they will require for higher math. There is considerable research that indicates that early intervention during the preschool years, when brain growth is most rapid, may have the effect of improving spatial skills. Although the research is still preliminary, singing, listening to classical music, and learning to play the piano (or another keyboard instrument) have resulted in positive gains in spatial skills for preschool children. Playing with puzzles and spatial games seems to improve spatial skills for many young children.

A few cautions about arranging for early testing of your daughter. Children's behavior is quite unreliable at young ages, and so are their test scores. For example, a very young child may not find the task interesting enough to pay attention, or a shy child may be hesitant about answering a question even if she knows the answer. It's not a good idea to assume that an IQ score obtained before age seven or eight is a reliable indicator of your child's aptitude. However, if you use it as a guide for early decision making, it can be helpful. For example, you may wish to use the score to make a decision as to whether your daughter should enter school early.

Another important consideration is that your daughter not feel like some sort of brilliant "freak" if she scores unusually high. Of course, she doesn't need to know her numerical score, and she doesn't even need to be labeled as gifted. Regardless of the score, she should be told she's a smart kid. Remember, "smart" does not mean "smartest" or "genius" or "brilliant," even if a psychologist says her IQ score is over 155.

PROBLEM-SOLVING OPPORTUNITIES

An excellent way to help your daughters feel smart is to give them opportunities to solve problems; for example, "What do you think we can do about keeping the kitty from scratching the furniture?" or "How do you think we could build a playhouse in our tree?" Help your daughters feel like girls with good, practical, commonsense ideas. Tell them they're good thinkers, and certainly don't save all the problem solving for their brothers. Ask your daughters such questions when they are alone so that an older sibling or more assertive brother doesn't respond before they've had time to think of some smart answers. Try not to tie their smartness to being right or wrong, but more to trying many solutions. This will prevent them from becoming defensive when they make mistakes, and it will enhance their creativity. Too many little girls think of themselves as smart only when the smart is attached to receiving an A or being right, and feel dumb if they're criticized or make mistakes. From the start, it's good to view mistakes as a vehicle for learning and to be able to laugh at them. This concept can help your daughters avoid extreme perfectionism and will encourage them to take the risks they'll need to grow intellectually and emotionally.

WHEN GIRLS DON'T FEEL SMART

We know that children compare themselves to others to determine if they're perceived as smart. If your daughter doesn't feel smart, you may need to explain why she is. For example, if she says, "Stacy is smart and I'm not," you may wish to say something like, "Stacy may indeed be smarter and may even get better test grades, but there can be lots of smart kids in the class, and you can be one, too, even if your grades aren't the best." You can also explain how important it is to love to learn and work hard, which will always make her feel smarter, even though it may never help her to feel smartest.

Depending on your daughter's age, you may wish to talk about the many different ways to be smart, and explain that some people are smarter than others in some ways and not as smart in other ways. Be sure to remind your daughter, and yourself, that neither kids nor adults walk around with IQ scores on their foreheads. What will count in her life will be attitude, initiative, and application of her abilities to the problems she'll face. A positive attitude, creativity, and resilience will go a long way toward stretching her intelligence for lifelong applications.

Some of the women in our study described situations in which they felt dumb, or at least less smart temporarily. Denise Dennison read early and skipped kindergarten. Despite the skip, she recalls that she was one of the smartest kids in the class in her urban school. The family moved after first grade to a prestigious suburban area. She attended second grade in a new school. Although her mother recalls that the teacher assured her that Denise had made an excellent adjustment and was a very good student, Denise never felt like an excellent student again. Perhaps not being the best student was sufficient to cause Denise to lose confidence in her intelligence.

Barbara Parker entered an independent school from a public school. She had always been an A student and had not had to put forth much effort. In her new school she could not earn a single A, and even had a few C's on her report card. Even after some serious effort, her grades did not improve. She felt anxious and paralyzed and lost confidence in her ability. Her grades decreased further, and she entered college with little confidence. However, in college her grades improved, as did her motivation. Her confidence in her intelligence varied with her surroundings and her grades.

Being sensitive to potential threats to your daughter's intellectual confidence will help you to help her interpret her feelings. Helping her understand the comparisons by which she evaluates herself will teach her lifelong resilience.

On the other hand, if your daughter gets into a poor-me routine of coming to you saying she isn't smart and nobody likes her, don't fall into the pattern of giving her too much sympathy. You're trying to help your daughter build resilience, and your pity based on a constant litany of woes will not assist her in becoming strong. It will only teach her a habit of lifelong complaining.

After you've listened, suggest some study or social skills, depending on your daughter's concern. Then encourage her to use them and discontinue her constant complaining. If you feel unable to teach her study skills, you can find a good tutor to do it. If you feel unable to teach her social skills, you can probably find a therapist who conducts specific training in social skills. Remind her, too, of the importance of being strong and independent.

INDEPENDENT STUDY AND ENRICHMENT

Encouraging girls to use good study habits is easy while they're in elementary school. Many girls want to please teachers, and so homework may be welcomed by girls at that age.

Many girls' diligent efforts evaporate by middle school, but there's a much better chance of keeping your daughters interested in schoolwork if they develop good habits when they're younger.[1]

During middle and high school, when some girls feel less interested in study—either because their interest is diverted to boys or because they feel less confident about their intelligence—parents can help motivate their daughters by showing special interest in what their daughters are learning. This is a good time for independent learning projects that extend their schoolwork. Thus, you can encourage your daughter to enjoy a science project by taking a family outing related to botany or any other topic she is studying in school. Discuss what she's learned in history class, or talk about the news you've watched on television together. Bring out a globe or encyclopedia, or search the Internet together for further information. If your daughter isn't already too social, it's a good idea to include a friend who may join her in presenting a completed project to the class. The family and peer support will allow her to enjoy her interests without feeling totally isolated.

This is also an excellent time for girls to participate in organized enrichment programs on weekends or during the summer. Attending a program where peers share interests with your daughter can be very motivating. Furthermore, she'll make new friends in an environment that doesn't penalize her for being a good student. Foreign language, computer science, art, music, creative writing, science, nature, and math camps can engage your daughter's interest and help her to understand that there are many other teens who value intelligent pursuits.

TEACHING A WORK ETHIC
AND VALUING WORK

Chores Most parents expect children to do chores, and many parents find the teaching process difficult. Sometimes it's easier to do the work yourself. Here are some tips that can help you to encourage your children to be workers.

• Start early. By age two children can perceive themselves as helpers and workers. They'll need you to join them, and don't expect either consistent willingness or efficiency. There will definitely be stops and starts, and girls will go through stages when they are more or less willing workers. New tasks may be harder to accomplish than tried and true ones.

• Be persistent and flexible. Although it is important to teach children to carry a job through to the end and to do it with pride and quality, don't set standards too high and do make exceptions if your busy children have other legitimate activities.

• Learning a new task works better in partnership with an adult. You become their role model and can give your daughter attention when you work together.

• Don't teach only gender-stereotyped chores. Even if you and your spouse are accustomed to doing gender-stereotyped work, encourage your daughters to take turns with each of you. They can mow the lawn and take the trash out as well as your sons, and cooking and setting the table doesn't have to be reserved for daughters. Girls can do outdoor work and will enjoy the challenge. Moms and daughters can do construction projects. If you, the mom, are hesitant about doing it alone, do it as a whole family. That way, you, too, can learn by example.

• Putting siblings together to share jobs can backfire. They may take on the roles of worker and shirker. It would be better not to have a shirker in your family. You can pair your kids later as they all become more efficient.

• Reserve payment for special tasks. Children shouldn't be paid for everything they do. Special tasks such as washing the car or painting a room both deserve incentives and build risk-taking skills and confidence.

Developing a Positive Work Attitude A positive attitude toward work develops when kids have been praised as good workers, when they observe their parents enjoying and taking pride in their work, and when they derive a sense of accomplishment in doing something worthwhile.

Praising kids for being good workers is relatively easy. "Good job" is a familiar term in both homes and classrooms. You only need to be sure that girls hear it as frequently as boys. Sometimes their usual good work is taken for granted, with "good job" reserved only for improvement.

Your own positive work attitude is harder to monitor. Your daughters should not only visit your workplace from time to time but should hear positive comments about your day when you walk in the door.

Your daughters' sense of accomplishment is easier to boost when they're younger and when setting the table for the family brings positive observations from the whole family. Planning and preparing a meal, if the results are successful, can also be satisfying, but the really big projects are often delegated to the boys in the family. With just a little rethinking, laying a new patio, hauling wood for the fireplace, building a tree house, and baling hay can become projects for the whole family. Of course, some of these projects may be more suitable in rural areas and suburbs. City dwellers, and even suburbanites, can run out of major work projects that build true respect for work. Consider toy and furniture construction that can be done by a parent-daughter team or by the whole family. If you've run out of projects or don't have the know-how yourself, join church or community groups that take families to impoverished areas to work. Pitch in with residents who are sand-bagging their city to prevent flooding, or take your daughters with you to hammer nails and saw wood for Habitat for Humanity. This country needs volunteers, and volunteering as a family provides a double reward—helping others and family bonding. Even one such experience is enough to change an anti-work girl into an effective and confident worker. She will never forget her pride of accomplishment.

Responsible baby-sitting, doing errands, reading to or caring for the elderly in the neighborhood, and teaching or tutoring others are all important jobs that build confidence and pride in work. Be sure to coach your daughter first in how to handle these responsibilities. Not every girl automatically knows how to manage children or the elderly. Help your daughter learn the skills that will make these truly satisfying work experiences. Encourage her to enroll in classes when they're available.

Getting a Real Job Neighborhood responsibilities may quickly expand to real jobs when your daughter is competent. You'll have to help her to determine which jobs are valuable in terms of experience and which will take too much away from her education. A potential musician can gain much from teaching two or three students or performing at an occasional wedding. However, the demands for her teaching can easily squeeze her time, and practice and schoolwork may fall by the wayside.

The local fast-food restaurant may be happy to pay your daughter for thirty hours a week of her efficiency, and the sudden inflow of money can entice her to be a new kind of shopper. She may be tempted by the glamour and financial independence to believe that her educa-tion can be put on hold. For example, because she doesn't pay you for the use of your home, food, or electricity, she imagines that $6 per hour is enough to move in with her boyfriend and forget about college. Some early planning can help her to avoid such short-term, dead-end think-ing. State the educational expectations clearly and prevent too many hours of work. Ten to fifteen hours a week is more than enough work time for a full-time high-school student during the school year. If she works too many hours, she'll be tired and inattentive in school. Her homework and study will slip, and so will her grades. Research shows that students who work more than twenty hours a week tend to disengage from home and school and spend their money on big-ticket items such as expensive clothes, cars, stereos, and—unfortunately—alcohol and drugs.[2]

There are at least three aspects of jobs to be considered. First and foremost, your daughter must receive the clear message from you that her first job is her education.

The second consideration is money. Part of your daughter's earnings should be set aside for her education (whether or not she will need it). We would also recommend that she donate some to charity. Furthermore, let her know that R-rated movies, even if she can sneak in, don't fit with your values even if she's spending her own money. You may also veto inappropriate CDs or clothing, and obviously drugs are a no-no. You can give your daughter some freedom to spend, but don't give all control away. She's not an adult yet, and you continue to provide most of her support. If she understands her discretionary spending limits from the start, she'll enjoy her financial freedom without squandering her money—or at least she'll do only a little squandering.

The third consideration is the learning experience. Your daughter can take jobs to earn money, but she can also take jobs to explore careers. There is a big payoff when her work helps her to find something she loves to do. Working as an orderly or aide in a hospital can lead her to medicine, nursing, or social work. Camp counseling could interest her in teaching, recreation work, or camp management. Bagging groceries at the supermarket can lead her to explore entrepreneurship or business management. Helping with a political campaign may tempt her toward a career in government. Your daughter is likely to see the immediate connection in what she is doing, but you'll need to help give her an expanded view to see the broader opportunities that may be available to her if she pursues further education.

First Job Early job experiences are not always successful for adolescents. More than one young person is fired rather quickly because she doesn't seem to know what is expected of her. (F. W. Woolworth was fired from his first job and was told he wouldn't amount to anything.) It's important that parents help their daughters process such an experience. This is another opportunity for you to be a wise coach rather than judge your daughter as a failure. She may indeed judge herself that way. The result will be lost confidence and a potential anti-work attitude.

Before having a discussion with her, consider some of the reasons girls lose their first job. Sometimes adolescents socialize too much with other peers on the job or with friends who pay them a visit. They may also talk too much to clients or customers in person or on the phone. Although being friendly with customers is essential, talking too much is time-consuming and expensive to their employers, who see their payrolls disappearing. Teens don't often consider the cost of their excessive talking. Some supervisors will advise girls about this problem; others will simply fire them.

Some girls may lack assertiveness and initiative. That may manifest itself as not doing enough work because they're not sure what to do and are afraid to ask, or, in contrast, they ask too many questions because they fear making mistakes. Here the problem-solving approaches you've taught them at home will pay off. If they've learned to take initiative at home, they're more likely to take the initiative at work. Encouraging your daughter to observe others in their workplaces will speed their skills acquisition. Some coaching about how to learn a new job may even prevent her from being fired from her first work experience.

Another reason girls may have difficulty adapting to the work environment is that the typical minimum-wage jobs available to teenagers do not allow the freedom and choices they're accustomed to in their world of home and school. Conflicts may arise between job scheduling and other extracurricular activities, and employers may not always be flexible. Although many teens make appropriate adjustments immediately, some coaching tips before the experience and some problem solving afterward will help heal wounds and prepare teens for future success.

Modeling Positive Work Attitudes Your daughters will hear your descriptions of your own work. They will also hear their fathers' and grandparents' comments about their mothers' careers. If complaints about your career's taking time away from family predominate, they will soon chime in and make you feel guilty. They may also promise themselves to give their own children more time and not pursue a career that takes time from family life. On the other hand, if others describe your work as worthwhile, they are more likely to respect you and value a career for themselves.

If you have a good career, let your daughters know you enjoy your work and that it benefits the family for you to have a career. You can even add that you're probably a better mom because of the confidence you derive from your career. Although the salary may also be important, your daughters will be more impressed by your developed self-confidence. When you take your daughters to work, your colleagues on the job can build your status by telling your daughters how important you are. Don't hesitate to prompt them; you can return the favor.

HOW "GOOD LITTLE GIRLS" SHATTER GLASS CEILINGS

Susan Widham*

President, Beech-Nut Nutritional Corporation

Susan Widham's earliest memories go back to her family's first home, surrounded by a white picket fence. She was probably about five years old, and she can recall eating big sweet peaches from the tree in their backyard and being a "good little girl." She knew she had permission to walk around the block as long as she didn't step off the sidewalk. Within those clear limits she could keep herself busy catching little horned toads in the alley and playing with her younger brother and sister. She would even help her mother take care of her siblings, but what she remembers most about those early years is that it was very important to be good. She remembers herself as compliant, and she knew she was to do exactly what she was told.

Another pleasant family memory for Susan was her family's three-week summer trips traveling around the country. They camped out together in national parks, hiked up mountains, and absorbed the magnificent California coastline. Of course, she also recalls the continuous sibling squabbles, mainly about who would sit in front of the air-conditioning vent in the car. Her travels didn't really provide any special family warmth for her, but the spirit and excitement of adventure and exploration are what pervade her recollection of the trips.

The summer trip after seventh grade was especially vivid to Susan, not because of the trip itself but instead because of how it ended. Her parents left her to remain with their friends' family so they could return home and deal with their house, which had been vandalized and burned down by the substitute newspaper boy. He knew they were on vacation, and he and his friends broke in and got drunk on Susan's dad's wine. When they realized their out-of-control vandalism would get them into trouble, they started the fire to destroy their fingerprints and the evidence. Susan returned only later to see their destroyed home and remembers the drama of seeing their refrigerator melted into the wall and her model horse collection totally destroyed. Scribbled across her wall was "Horses suck." She remembers a deep sense of terror and violation.

As a result of the fire, the family had to live in an apartment for a while; Susan had to live with a cousin for a year so she could attend classes in the school district where her parents were building a new home. Living with her cousin was especially difficult because her cousin was an only child and, Susan recalls, was probably spoiled. The cousin was not happy about sharing the limelight with Susan, even more so in light of her parents' constant and invidious reminders that their daughter, who barely earned C's in school, did not achieve as well as Susan, who got all A's. Perhaps it was no wonder that Susan's cousin was not particularly fond of her.

From Susan's perspective, she was always shy, quiet, compliant, withdrawn, and especially "good" throughout her school years. She was also always an excellent student in all subjects, but she remembers liking math, science, and spelling best of all. From first grade on she read constantly, but her reading was concentrated on horses, the great infatuation of her childhood. First she read book after book about horses, then she collected models of horses, and finally, in third grade, she actually received her first horse.

Her passion for horses became Susan's focus and provides an excellent example of a young woman executive in the making. Susan's parents told her that they simply couldn't afford to continue to keep horses for her. Very quickly she learned to set her own goals and earn the necessary funds. In middle school she baby-sat regularly and devoted all her savings to maintaining her horses. When she thinks about her preadolescence, it seems her life was consumed by baby-sitting and horses; that only expanded in her high-school years. She never hesitated to take an extra job, working a little harder or rising earlier in the morning, if it meant she had the opportunity to earn some additional money toward her horse interest. She couldn't afford a trainer, so instead she bought a book that taught her how to train her horse for riding. She recalls wishing for an Arabian horse, but of course baby-sitting money wasn't sufficient for that, so she settled for a half-Arabian dapple gray colt. Although she couldn't really identify when she became competitive about her horses, she did remember racing with her friends frequently. She also recalls that she had one of the fastest horses and took great pride in the fact that she could beat just about all her other friends on their horses. However, even then she seemed to know how to meld competition with cooperation.

Camp Fire Girls provided more activities for Susan's early training for business leadership and an experience in which she combined both friendship and competition. During her elementary-school days, her closest friends were members of the Camp Fire Girls, yet Susan competed with them extensively through her activities. She recalls that she could earn beads for completing special projects, and she sewed them onto her jacket. She was determined to have more beads than anyone else. She recalls building a birdhouse, camping out overnight, and making a dinner for her family to earn those beads. The more she earned, the more she sewed on her jacket, and she recalls managing to stay ahead of all the other girls in her group.

Candy sales were the real test of Susan's entrepreneurial and competitive skills, and she wanted to be sure she could sell more candy than anyone else. She developed a plan to go into a neighborhood that had a high concentration of apartments and duplexes. The more doors there were in an area, the more doors she could knock on, and she was never hesitant, despite her shyness, about knocking on all those doors or about working longer hours. Even then, she was totally focused on her goal of selling the most candy, and she succeeded every single year.

Schoolwork was not an area that Susan recalls much about. Perhaps she felt that way only because she earned good grades easily. She remembers doing an hour or two of homework a day, but she spent most of her time on her horses. She was never best in any particular subject, but she graduated with honors and an almost perfect mathematics SAT score. Her verbal SAT score was not nearly as high but was well above average.

Susan had a very difficult time in high school. Her family had made a dramatic move to a very wealthy suburb. After the move, Susan went to a school that was different from any other school she had ever attended. She recalls that other students would receive sports cars when they turned sixteen, and the girls had worn makeup since they were twelve. Unlike Susan's own family, their families seemed to have limitless financial resources, and she never felt she fit in with these wealthy high-school students.

Susan was not isolated from friends; however, friendships were always interest-centered for her. In elementary school it had been

Camp Fire Girls and horses, and in high school it was horses and religion that provided her with a group of close and happy friendships. Her interest in horses led her to participate in rodeo planning, an important Texas high-school activity. Her religious interest kept her very busy in a Christian youth group called Young Life that provided Susan with both a sense of security and an opportunity for leadership. It was so meaningful to her that she continued leading such groups while she was attending college.

Although Susan was always youngest in her class, the only time her young age bothered her was when she had to wait so long to get her driver's license. Susan had only two boyfriends in high school, one in her junior year and one in her senior year. Before that she just wasn't much interested in boys, nor was she very involved in fashion or makeup. Horse activities and the friends who liked horses were much more fun for her.

Susan says that breaking through glass ceilings as an executive in business involved taking risks. She also explains that risks don't bother her now, as she has considerable confidence. During her interview we pressed her for recollections of risk taking, but Susan was fairly positive they didn't exist in her childhood. She emphasized again that she had been very shy and fearful of anything that posed a risk. She does remember specifically a close friend in elementary school who was very courageous. Her friend might jump to a tree branch and challenge Susan to try it, but no such challenge would tempt Susan. She even recalls the friend teaching her to smoke cigarettes in sixth grade. Susan did try it, but that was as far as her smoking went, and she and her friend soon parted company.

Susan reflected that she may have been inspired to take risks by observing her dad. He had given up his successful career as an architect to launch his own business. Her mother was angry and upset by his decision, but Susan was awed that he had the courage to start all over again on his own. Susan tended to side with her dad when she was younger, and she strongly identified with him. On the other hand, her brother, just a year younger than she, tended to side with her mom. Susan often felt angry that her mother would let her brother get away with almost anything. Furthermore, her dad would also go on special hunting and Scouting trips with her brother, and she wasn't allowed to join them. Although Susan gets along with all her siblings now, she does recall some resentment toward the brother closest in age to her while they were growing up, as he seemed to have the best of all worlds.

Susan's parents had met at Rice University. Her dad had graduated with a degree in architecture, but her mother, who was also an architecture major, had dropped out after the first two years of college. There was a fair amount of conflict between Susan's parents, increasing as she matured. It seemed to her that her father wanted her mother to be there for the children and for him in the traditional way that women were in those days. Her mother simply didn't seem to enjoy parenting or being a homemaker. She wanted more independence and was frustrated with the busyness and boredom of parenting four small children. She would escape her boredom via some very entrepreneurial volunteerism. Although she would have preferred a career, Susan's mother filled her life instead with presidencies of the Junior League, PTA, and other community organizations. She seemed to require continuous activity for fulfillment, and as far as Susan could see from her little-girl perspective, her mother was never there to listen to Susan but only to criticize her.

Susan recalls feeling that nothing she ever did was perfect enough. Her dad would listen to Susan's complaints and fears, and that helped her to feel less afraid and much closer to her dad. She always thought her dad was perfect when she was a child, although, of course, she realizes now that he had a few shortcomings. Although he never actually blamed Susan's mother, he would point out other female role models to Susan who were strong, good, gentle, loving, and emotionally available to their husbands and children—for example, his own mother, Susan's grandmother. It was almost as if he was trying to give her confidence in her ability to be different from her mother, with whom she was continuously at odds.

By the time Susan was in high school, the conflict between her parents was much worse, and her parents were separated several times and finally divorced. During those high-school years, Susan's mother often blamed her for the arguments, saying that she was the reason her parents fought, but her dad always reassured Susan that their problems weren't her fault. Although Susan never accepted the blame personally, she hated the conflict. Susan's mother did return to college and earned both bachelor's and master's degrees, and her father was supportive of her mother's education despite their divorce.

Attending college herself provided Susan some relief from the conflict between her parents, and she was very motivated to leave home rather than feel caught between her parents. Susan's parents wanted her to go to Rice University, their alma mater. Her dad was so interested in her going there that he even completed the application for her. Susan's preference was to go to Colorado State University, major in forestry, and, of course, ride horses. Susan was accepted at both, but when she chose Colorado State, her dad explained that he wasn't willing to pay out-of-state tuition at a state university, and if she didn't want to go to Rice, she really ought to attend a state university in Texas, where the tuition was more reasonable. Faced with the financial realities and that reasonable request by her dad, and pressured to make a rather rapid decision, she decided to go to Texas Tech University because her boyfriend was going there and it fit in with her dad's requirements. She broke up with her boyfriend soon after starting college, and after her sophomore year, Susan transferred to the University of Texas at Austin.

College was the one time in her life when the always-focused Susan lost direction. Her horses were left behind as she explored a variety of majors and new interests. At one point she tried majoring in microbiology. Then she enrolled in accounting, but she deplored it. Since she loved science and hated accounting, she thought she might like to be a scientist or doctor. She discovered that she would need to earn a doctoral degree, which might take an additional eight years. She was not willing to invest that much more time in school, despite the fact that she was an excellent student.

In her junior year Susan took an engineering course and enjoyed it immensely. She remembers building cars and learning about torque and thinking that she had finally found a passion and the right career direction. She then discovered that she would have to spend another three years in college if she wanted to major in engineering. She finally decided on a communications major primarily because it was the only major that would allow her to graduate on time and get out into the world of work, where she was convinced she would find appropriate direction.

The working world was a comfortable place for Susan. She had always had a job, from her baby-sitting in sixth grade to a variety of other jobs including salesperson in a women's clothing store, waitress, and laboratory assistant for a pathologist. She always felt she was a successful worker. Perhaps, she thought, a reasonable work experience rather than more schooling would help set her direction. She did return to school enthusiastically several years later, when her experiences in the work world made her realize that a master's degree in business (MBA) would be relevant to her career.

Susan was correct in her assumption about the world of work. Every job she took after college moved her up the career ladder. Even when she left jobs because of her husband's moves, first to Chicago and then to St. Louis, she seemed to be able to advance another step. Interestingly, when the interviewer commented on Susan's continued successes, she responded, as so many other women have, that she attributed her success to her good fortune. However, Susan admits that she has learned to be aggressive and outspoken when the goal is one that she believes in. There were always risks, but she developed the confidence that she could accomplish her goals once she put her mind to it. Work has always afforded her confidence.

It was after Susan's first child was born and Ralston Purina, her employer, had purchased the Beech-Nut Nutritional Corporation that she approached her boss, whom she met accidentally in the grocery store, and told him she'd like to be product manager for the baby food company he had just purchased. Beech-Nut had lost money for twenty years, but she was confident that she could turn it around. She left a comparatively stable job to try to reverse Beech-Nut's situation. As a mother herself, Susan was committed to letting other mothers know about Beech-Nut Naturals, the new name she had developed for the product. Susan Widham moved rapidly through the positions of product manager to director of sales to vice president to president. The quiet, confident, hardworking style she developed through her Camp Fire Girls and horse activities seems to be paying off well for Susan, who in her thirties is a mother of two sons and an executive who has shattered the infamous glass ceiling.

SHE BROKE WITH TRADITION

Nancy Collier
Part-Time Teacher and Homemaker

Although education and homemaking are traditional roles for women, Nancy Collier broke from tradition by becoming the only member of her family to earn a college degree. She trained and worked as an elementary-school teacher, and now, as a forty-three-year-old mother of three children and a physician's wife, Nancy works part time in the local public schools.

When asked about the influences that shaped her life and career decisions, Nancy described her rural upbringing, her hard work on the family farm, the fact that she was the oldest in her family and thus given more responsibility, and most important, Mary, her childhood baby-sitter.

Nancy was raised on the same dairy farm on which her mother was raised. Her grandparents acquired the farm in the second decade of the century and faced the challenges of farming. Hard work was accepted as part of life. With neither electricity nor modern conveniences, Nancy's grandparents raised dairy cows, cultivated crops, grew and preserved food, made clothing and rugs, cleaned clothes by hand, and lived off the rich land. When Nancy's grandparents approached old age, they retired to a small ranch-style house about a quarter of a mile away from the farm, and Nancy's parents took over the family farm. Nancy recalls her grandparents' strong work ethic but also remembers many winter evenings of playing Scrabble together in front of their fireplace.

Nancy's father was a farmer; her mother, a homemaker. Both of her parents earned high-school diplomas at the same high school Nancy attended. Actually, their earning diplomas was quite remarkable considering their adverse circumstances. Her mother was the only member of her family to complete high school. Her father was the oldest of three, and he drove other high-school children to school during the war for a small fee so he could continue in school.

Nancy is the oldest of four children. Her siblings still live and work in the community where their grandparents grew up.

Much of Nancy's childhood was spent doing chores on the farm. She milked cows, collected eggs, and helped harvest the crops. Because she was the oldest, she worked alongside her dad. If she had had an older brother, it would have been he rather than she who shouldered the farm responsibilities. She felt especially close to her father, but he gave her few compliments on her hard work for fear of her getting a "big head." She occasionally overheard her dad talking to their neighbors about his "hardworking daughter" and sensed her parents were proud of her.

Nancy's dad was very clear about his expectations. When the choice was between schoolwork and chores, chores came first. Once Nancy began to work on her physics homework in the barn while she waited for the milking to be complete. Her father scolded her for not attending to her chores. The expectation was that she would work hard on the farm and at school, marry a farmer, and have a family.

Nancy's mother's highest priority was that Nancy "be a good girl." That included good behavior, not getting pregnant in high school, not using drugs or alcohol, and being nice to people. Her mother also taught her not to act "too good." She was not to think she was special or any better than anyone else. From a young age Nancy learned to "rein in" for her mother. Even now, when she visits her hometown, she is very cautious about what she says, does, and wears. She remembers to be humble.

While Nancy was always expected to do more work, she also received special privileges because she was the oldest. When she was ten, her brother was born, and she was delighted to have a baby brother to care for. By the time Nancy was in high school, she used to help her little brother with his schoolwork, play with him, and occasionally baby-sit for him. She credits her interest in teaching to her experiences teaching her brother.

Nancy attended the same two-room parochial school from kindergarten through eighth grade. It was there she observed her occasional baby-sitter and role model, Mary, who was a number of years older. Nancy watched Mary being gentle, kind, and pleasant to people. Mary wasn't bossy, and she spoke to the younger children in the school, even though she was in eighth grade. Mary graduated from high school, moved away, went to college, and developed a career. When Nancy realized in seventh grade that she wanted to go to college someday, it was because she wanted to emulate Mary. Seeing Mary enabled Nancy to imagine what it would be like to leave her safe small town to further her education.

Nancy recalls being very happy in elementary school. She did well in all of her school subjects and played piano, read, spent a lot of time alone, ice-skated, and played softball. Her family didn't have a TV at home. Her work on the farm increased her confidence, and she participated in 4-H, exhibiting her dairy cows and entering sewing projects in local competitions. Frequently winning blue ribbons confirmed her skills to her.

Home life was somewhat less smooth while Nancy was in middle school. She remembers trying very hard to please her mother, yet always feeling that her mother was too critical of her. Also at that time, Nancy realized that her mother was not completely happy with her own life as a homemaker. Her mother's signs of discontent encouraged Nancy to contemplate other options that might be open to her. She believed there were few options available for women other than becoming a nurse, teacher, or social worker. Although Nancy was not sure what career she wanted to pursue, she was certain she wanted a career in which she could work with children.

Nancy blossomed in high school. She became more involved in activities, continued to help on the farm, and maintained her good grades in school. She was on the school yearbook staff, became student council class president, worked as a Sunday school teacher, and was successful in many more contests and competitions. (She was even selected as the town's "Dairy Queen," which gave her the honor and fun of waving from a convertible at all the local parades.)

Nancy had a very active social life and a very serious boyfriend. Her relationship with this boyfriend caused some tension at home. Nancy felt considerable pressure, was uncomfortable, and thought about how she might escape the scrutinizing eyes of her mother and the community. College would give her freedom and adventure.

When Nancy's parents realized she wanted to go to college, they weren't particularly supportive. They were worried about her being far away from home and were fearful that college would be an unhealthy influence on Nancy.

Among the forty-six seniors in Nancy's graduating class, only two students, she and the principal's daughter, went to college. She attended a small college about an hour from home, and it put an entirely different perspective on her upbringing. She had not even traveled beyond her small town, and her handmade clothes, for which she had earned 4-H blue ribbons, were an oddity. Compared to the other students, she felt uncomfortable, unusual, unsophisticated, and poorly prepared. Many of the students had parents who paid their way through school, but Nancy's parents paid only part of her college tuition. Nancy raised the rest of the money with dining hall jobs, baby-sitting, and work-study positions.

It took Nancy several years to adjust to her new surroundings. By her junior year of college, she finally invited some of her college friends home to meet her family. These college friends viewed Nancy's childhood experience completely differently. Instead of perceiving the farm as backward and slow-paced, as Nancy feared they would, they considered Nancy's experiences exotic and fascinating. Her friends helped Nancy reframe her childhood experiences much more positively. She became better at understanding the source of her values and determining how they fit in with her day-to-day adult life. She was very appreciative of the work ethic and perseverance her parents had taught her.

Even though she had internalized her mother's message that she shouldn't believe she was special, she began to see her "farmer's daughter" childhood as unique and empowering. It gave her the courage to break with tradition and achieve a college degree and a successful teaching career.

CHAPTER 4

SEE JANE LEARN

That Invaluable Education

Part 1: Findings

Most of the women in our study were successful in school and enjoyed it. They mainly perceived themselves as excellent or at least good students, although that varied somewhat from elementary to middle to high school.

The majority of the women, 80 percent, attended public schools. Sixteen percent attended parochial schools, and 5 percent attended independent schools. The national attendance proportions were 91, 9, and 3 percent, respectively. Figure 4.1 compares their school enrollment to the proportion of attendance nationally at each type of school.

It's very clear from our data that most of the women received their foundational education in our nation's public schools. However, compared to the national population, almost twice as many of these women attended parochial schools and more than twice as many attended independent schools. The percentage that attended parochial schools actually decreased from elementary to high school, while the percentage that attended independent schools increased between elementary and high school. The numbers in each career group did not vary much relative to type of school attended except for orchestral musicians. Compared to all other career groups, more orchestral musicians, 93

FIGURE 4.1

Comparison of School Attendance of
Successful Women to Prevalence in Society

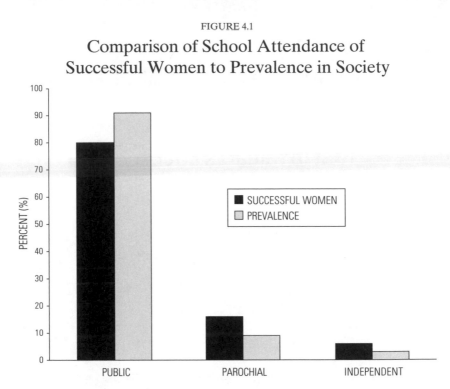

percent, received their entire education in public schools. That may be because so few parochial and independent schools offer the extensive music programs that public schools frequently do, or it may also be that parents' financial resources were directed toward music lessons rather than school tuition.

More women in this study attended all-girls schools than is the case in the general population, but specific figures for attendance at girls' schools at the time these women were there couldn't be found. Presently only 5 percent of this country's girls attend single-sex schools. Ten percent of the women in our study attended all-girls high schools, although only 4 percent had attended all-girls middle schools. The career groups that had the highest percentages of attendance in all-girls high schools were administrators of nonprofit business organizations, attorneys, scientists, and allied health professionals.

Martha James, a patent attorney from Ohio, remembers her all-girls high school as being critical to her realization that it was important to study. She also believed that it allowed girls who might otherwise not feel successful to find an area in which they could excel. Deborah Green, a research scientist, remembers her attendance at an all-girls high school eliminated much of the pressure she felt regarding boys. Science teacher Mary Sadowski enjoyed attending an all-girls high school and now teaches at one. She remembers having the sense that girls could do anything and is delighted that so many girls who attend the school where she is a teacher study advanced math and sciences. Pauline Black, now a college professor and researcher in biology, attended both high school and college in all-female institutions and indicated she was not even sensitive to issues of gender discrimination until graduate school and her career.

A much higher percentage of successful women, 13 percent, attended women's colleges compared to the total population. In 1976 it was estimated that only 1.5 percent of women who attended college were enrolled in women's colleges. The career groups that had the highest percentages of attendance at women's colleges included the power-broker professions (nonprofit and for-profit business, government, and law), and the traditional professions (allied health, education, and mental health). The groups having the least attendance at women's colleges were musicians, artists, media women, scientists, and physicians.

Many of the women in the study were very vocal about the importance of their single-gender college education. One woman artist proclaimed that attending a women's college changed her life. Business executive Amy Fox, who was very involved in politics at her women's college during the sixties, believes she developed the confidence that permitted her to become an executive in the public transportation industry. Some of the women, particularly those who moved into executive positions in business, mentioned that their businesses were eager to attract graduates of women's colleges. Perhaps the women's colleges were more effective in giving women opportunities to develop leadership skills. One physician recalled that her women's college made the transition to coeducation while she was in her third year. Almost immediately, most elected offices that had been held by women were taken over by the new male students.

BEST SUBJECTS

The women's best subjects, as early as elementary school, often predicted their eventual career choices. Regardless of career, however, most of these highly intelligent women were early and excellent talkers. The theory that girls develop their verbal skills earlier than boys seems to be upheld by this study. Many of the women were also early readers. The profession that had the greatest number of women who spoke and read very early were attorneys; perhaps this was a factor in their selection of the highly verbal law profession. For all professions except medicine, science, and media, reading was most frequently these women's best subject in elementary school. More media women considered English as best, with reading not far behind. Writing was selected by many women in the media as well; it was also a frequent choice for the educators. The physicians and scientists chose science and math most often, with reading and English not far behind. The allied health professionals frequently found science to be their best subject, although math wasn't chosen as often as it was for the physicians and scientists. Thus math may be an important separator between nurses, on one hand, and physicians and scientists, on the other. The women in law, government, and mental health selected social studies most frequently after reading and English.

As the women moved from elementary to middle and high school, their special subject strengths became even more pronounced. In high school mathematics continued to be a strong subject for scientists, physicians, and businesswomen. Physicians, scientists, and allied health professionals maintained their strengths in science. Social studies and history were indicated even more frequently by attorneys, politicians, and mental health professionals. Women in media, education, business, mental health, and those who became full-time homemakers indicated strength in English and writing. The artists and musicians were strong in English as well, but the second most frequently mentioned strength for the artists was social studies, and foreign languages were often cited by the musicians. For the total group, English was most frequently indicated as their best subject. This would be an unlikely best subject for a male population and should surely please English teachers.

Reading Dr. Mary Ainsworth,* a pioneer research psychologist, recalls, "My mother taught me to read when I was very young, and I can visually recall when I was two or three years old sitting in my crib surrounded by books and magazines. They also gave me the *Books of Knowledge* children's encyclopedia, and I loved it and read it constantly."

There were several other successful women who could visually recall their early enjoyment of reading in their cribs as well.

Science A medical scientist from Boston recalls: "My dad was a family practitioner who had his office on the first floor of our three-story house during my formative years. I wandered in and out of the office a lot and watched procedures like suturing. Dad often took my sister and me on hospital rounds. Although I recall thinking it was all pretty boring and ho-hum, I must have been intrigued. I do remember one day looking at a gram stain with Dad in his little office laboratory and being very excited when he told me, 'One day you might look in a microscope like this and find something no one else has ever seen before.' I was hooked."

Dr. Susan Lemagie,* an obstetrician and gynecologist, asked her parents for a chemistry set for Christmas when she was in the ninth grade. They obliged, and thereafter she would work on her chemistry experiments in the attic. When other girls were spending their allowances on clothes and makeup, Susan saved up her money for chemicals, flasks, and beakers. She was supremely happy in her own little world of science in the attic.

Sandra Calvin, an environmental engineer, described herself as "the kind of nerdy little kid who finished the math book early." Her teachers granted her independence, and she found working at her own pace to be "cool." Her mind naturally accommodated complexity. Even at an early age, Sandra combined and created complex systems. It was almost as if her work as a systems engineer was presaged by her taking out five board games at once and creating ways to connect them all.

Inspired by her biology teacher, medical researcher Dr. Linda Brooks, at age twelve, constructed a skeleton out of the bones of a cat. She and her friend worked for days, bleaching and preserving the bones, and finally gluing the skeleton back together for permanent display in the science laboratory at her junior high school.

Many of the women were inspired to enjoy science by their family's outdoor and nature activities. Research psychologist Dr. Mary Schneider* recalls being totally absorbed by nature. She set up aquariums with different ecological systems and one that simulated the natural environment for a salamander she caught.

Writing The women in our study who had memories of early writing experiences often directed their lives toward careers that involved writing. Sally Sahn, a media publicist for international athletes, remembers her first controversial newspaper editorship in sixth grade. She was willing even then to write about unpopular views. Dr. Sara Barts, a psychologist and writer, recalls writing her first stories and plays in fourth grade. She also remembers writing an imaginative story about being a slave coming from Africa. When she read it to her eighth-grade class, her peers listened with rapt attention. That was the first time she realized she could someday be a writer.

TEACHERS AS ROLE MODELS

Perhaps it will surprise no one that teachers at every level were found to be important and inspiring to most of the successful women in the study. MIT engineer Dr. Catherine Burns recalls wanting to be a first-grade teacher in first grade (like her teacher), a second-grade teacher in second grade, and so on, until she finally decided she might like to be a college teacher. Educator Roberta Wendt wanted so much to be like her teachers that she would emulate their handwriting. Her handwriting would change with each of her teachers.

More than one woman talked about falling in love or idolizing a third- or fifth- or tenth-grade teacher. The teachers might be either male or female, but the women's admiration always inspired their love of learning. Sometimes the admiration was extended to a school principal or guidance counselor. Business executive Margaret Karnes discussed her eighth-grade teacher-principal in the Lutheran school she attended. He taught her religion and also taught her values she still depends on in her daily business decisions. She even recalled very clearly some of his special lessons about honesty. Nurse Angela Sands recalls a sixth-grade teacher who reinforced not only her intelligence but also her kindness by giving rewards for good grades, effort, and kindness to others. Teacher Mary Sadowski was encouraged repeatedly by the nuns who taught at her all-girls Catholic school and remembers just hanging around after school to talk to her favorite nun. She and her friends sometimes missed the school bus because they didn't want to leave school. Mary was energized by seeing her teachers returning to school for master's and doctoral degrees, and the mother superior of the order, although she walked with a cane, would throw her cane into her fancy sports car and go "tooling around." Not only that, the nuns actually physically helped build their home. Mary remembers seeing the "sweet old ladies" put in sidewalks and lay bricks.

Teachers only supplemented the positive influences some of the women found at home. However, for some, like Dr. Ana Casa and artist Sandra Sheets, schools were shelters. It was Ana's French teacher who inspired her to go to college, and the inspiration of many caring teachers helped Sandra to survive her childhood. Librarians also helped them feel at home. My own guidance counselor, Henrietta Herbert,* was pivotal in my decision to attend college.

Specific positive influences can be found for almost all the women in our study, but it's also fair to mention teachers or counselors who, undoubtedly unintentionally but nevertheless unfortunately, turned girls off to school. Attorney Diana Doyle recalls a sixth-grade teacher who turned her off to math, some very uninspiring high-school teachers, and only one English teacher whom she truly enjoyed. There were quite a few women who complained that math teachers were the cause of their reduced interest in that subject. It is hard to know if the teachers were the problem or if the women blamed the teachers for their own math inadequacies.

Fortunately, and perhaps to no one's surprise, the examples of positive experiences with teachers and schools far outnumber the negative ones, but it should give teachers reason to pause when they realize the powerful impact they have on their students.

SPECIAL SCHOOL PROGRAMMING

Although schoolwork was usually easy for these women, less than 20 percent indicated that their elementary schools had programs for gifted and talented students. Some mentioned the important impact these programs had for them. A freelance writer from Little Rock, Arkansas, explains: "In junior high at a governor's program for gifted children, we produced a literary journal. I attended this program for six weeks every summer from the time I was eleven until I was fourteen. I got favorable attention for my writing. I published in *Scholastic* magazine and won a national Scholastic Writing Awards contest. The program made a lasting impression on me."

Research chemist Dr. Lisa Smith* recalls, "When I was in middle school, they selected students who took tests and got placed into gifted and talented programs. No program actually developed, but they gave us the option of leaving a subject and jumping ahead a year in that subject. That gave us automatic peers who were advanced. Being advanced was hard socially but not academically. They shuffled us into advanced classes, but there was a core of us who became advanced in every subject together. There was a real unification between us. Most of us were in the top ten of our graduating class. One woman is a biomedical engineer, one man has a doctorate in metallurgy from Johns Hopkins, one has a degree in toxic management and also worked on a Patriot missile. One is involved with arts and juried arts shows."

By middle and high school, more of the schools had specialized programs; therefore, the number of women in special programs increased.

Nevertheless, fewer than one-third of the women in the study took advanced courses in math and science in middle school, and fewer than one-half did in high school. The three most frequently given reasons for taking advanced courses were encouragement by a teacher, an interest in the subject, and a desire for challenge. The three most frequently given reasons for not taking advanced science and math were that they weren't offered, they were too hard, or other subjects were more interesting. Fewer than 1 percent of the women acknowledged that they didn't take the courses because they perceived them as boys' subjects, and fewer than 1 percent indicated that their worries about what boys might think of them prevented their taking science or math. However, other subtle forces were clearly operating. One nurse remembered it this way: "I think it was the norm in the mid-sixties for math and science grades to decline. My chemistry teacher told me to copy the work of the boy who sat next to me, as he understood the material. I hated to be dumb, so I quit asking, and just didn't learn anything, and then I kind of developed an anxiety toward the courses and just decided I couldn't learn them."

Most of the advanced programming was in the form of honors or advanced placement (AP) classes. AP classes were available only to the younger women in the study. Seven percent of the women took college courses while still in high school, although that practice was less common in earlier days.

SUBJECT AND GRADE SKIPPING

A whopping 25 percent of the women skipped subjects, and 15 percent actually skipped grades during elementary and secondary school, providing strong evidence that there is no relationship between skipping subjects or grades and major academic or social harm. Although some of the women referred to minor temporary social adjustments, most did not comment on the skips as causing problems. As a matter of fact, several who were not allowed to skip commented on the boredom that resulted. The school Dr. Susan Lemagie* attended wanted her to skip a grade twice. Her parents refused because they were concerned about her social adjustment. She remembers being bored despite her teachers' doing their best to provide enrichment and extra work. It wasn't until she entered a wonderful middle school with challenging classes that she loved school. She had good friends in the accelerated class, felt "smarter than the boys," won essay contests, and was finally happy.

When her parents moved and she had to change schools again, she was unchallenged and unhappy once more.

You'll recall that medical researcher Dr. Janice Douglas* skipped a grade in elementary school and indicated that this was the approach used by teachers in the segregated South, where there were no special programs to challenge students. When she moved to a highly competitive college-oriented school district in Ohio, the principal wanted Janice to repeat a grade. Her parents wouldn't permit that, however, and she quickly proved herself by doing well academically and earning the highest score in the entire ninth-grade class on her math achievement test.

Because research psychologist Dr. Mavis Hetherington* had skipped three grades by junior high school, most of her friends were older and dating, and she remembers thinking they were pretty weird to be interested in boys. By high school, however, she had caught up and remained friends with the same group of girls. By that time she understood their interest in dating.

The career groups that had the most grade skippers (approximately a quarter) were orchestral music, mental health, and medicine; however, there were some women in every career group who skipped grades. Very few of the women skipped more than one grade.

MIDDLE- AND HIGH-SCHOOL GRADE DECLINE

Because research suggests that grades decline for girls in middle and high school, particularly in math and science, the women in the study were asked about their academic performance in elementary, middle, and high school. Only 10 percent of the women indicated general grade decline in middle school, while twice as many indicated improvement. In high school, one-quarter indicated grade and achievement decline, and approximately the same number improved their achievement. More than a quarter lost confidence in math and science, and, again, another quarter actually continued to increase their confidence in both math and science. Confidence in math and science was separating out the women and determining the direction of their professional choices as early as middle school; this process continued in high school.

When the same question was asked in a way that was related to their self-perceptions of their school performance, it was clear that even more of the women viewed themselves as declining in academic confidence in middle school. Figure 4.2 shows the percentage of women who

FIGURE 4.2

Percentage of Successful Women Who Had Excellent
Academic Performance in Elementary, Middle, and High School

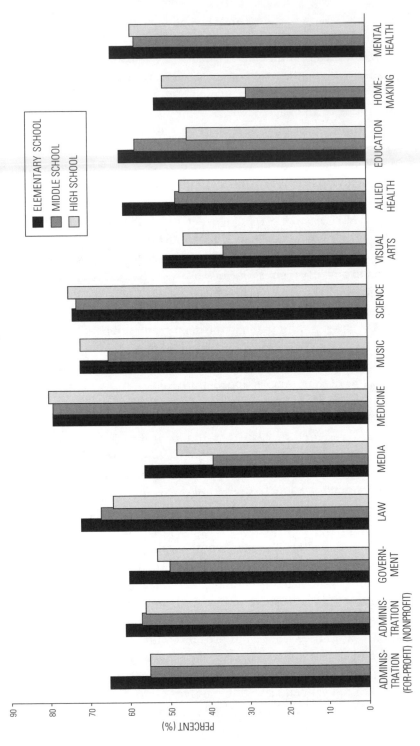

considered their academic performance to be excellent in elementary, middle, and high school. There was considerable variability by career group. What is evident is that only the physicians and scientists perceived themselves as consistently excellent throughout school. In other career groups, many perceived themselves as only good students in middle school.

The effect of middle school as an important threshold for intellectual confidence is corroborated by our data. The figure also shows that many women in some career groups did not perceive themselves as excellent students in middle school, and that perception did not change for high school. However, more women in media, music, art, and homemaking recovered their academic confidence and again perceived themselves as excellent students in high school. The probable reason for improved self-perceptions of the women in these careers was that fewer of these women took advanced courses in math and science in high school. Thus, by avoiding the more difficult classes, many women may have perceived they were better students in high school than they had been in middle school.

Both math and science confidence increased for approximately a quarter of the women during their middle school years. On the other hand, approximately the same percentage acknowledged having declined in confidence during that time. Dr. Melissa Sparks,* an assistant chief nursing director, had this perspective on the subject: "Not being great in math and sort of seeing math as something girls are not particularly good at—that would be something I would have wished had been different. I think that I was probably good in all sciences. Anything that had to do with math quantification, I just didn't understand the constant, let alone know how to plug in formulas and all the rest of it. I had to compensate for that all along because by the time I got into MPH [master's of public health] and doctoral programs, we had to come to grips with those courses, and I did, but it was never easy. I always felt like I was really disadvantaged by my mathematics experiences."

Attorney Michelle McGuire* truly dreaded mathematics: "When I was in high school, math continued to be my albatross, avoided like the plague, and I did horribly in it, made no effort in it because it was so bad for me. I was not impressed with the teacher at that time and didn't take any great interest in really making an effort as far as math was concerned. That became a problem also in my relationship with my mom because I was just doing so poorly in math and not making the effort and this was not making my parents happy. That haunted me through-out high school. Fortunately, there were classes like 'You and the Law' and things like that when I was taking more of an interest in law."

Some of the women lost their confidence in math only temporarily. Dr. Lisa Smith,* a research chemist, remembers: "I had chronic bron-chitis that would come back again and again, so I missed a lot of school and began to slip because school wasn't as easy to make up as it used to be. In some ways it was easier to get behind. I think my key problem was that I didn't do my homework. Math is not a spectator sport. You can't miss. I missed some critical stuff, and I began to do very poorly. I was getting a D in algebra.

"When my oldest brother, who is a mathematician by trade, found out I was getting a D in algebra, he had a fit. He made me get out of bed every morning at 6 A.M. and sit at the dining room table. He said, 'You're not doing your homework. Nobody gets a D in algebra unless they don't do their homework.' He made me sit there and do my home-work. I would cry. I wouldn't understand it, and he would help me get through it. That completely turned my grade around."

Jody Hill, a vice president of economic development, reported: "When I was in eighth grade I was placed in the Algebra 1 class. Through the first three or four weeks I struggled. I was failing all the quizzes, and nobody could figure out why I was having such a hard time because I had always been a math person. I had always been in honors classes. My mother took me to see Gordon, who was very mathemati-cal, a geophysicist or something like that. I spent an hour and a half with Gordon, and all of a sudden I understood everything. After my time with Gordon, I'd gone from making a 55 on a test to getting an A on the retake test. My parents and I all knew that I could do the work. My teacher at the time was probably marginal, and I didn't get the math, but Gordon was able to explain it. I understood it immediately, and I took advanced math all through high school and college."

While some women were losing confidence in math, others actually gained it. Dr. Catherine Burns, now a professor of engineering at MIT, recalls doing math independently in middle school, surpassing all stu-dents in her class and perhaps even her teacher. Medical researcher Dr. Janice Douglas* recalls competing with her cousin about who would do the best in math. Sometimes he would do better than she, and some-times she would do better. The competition helped Janice's confidence.

When the women were asked if their interest in boys and social life caused them to be less serious about their schoolwork during this time, 16 percent acknowledged that they had.

GRADUATION RANK AND AWARDS

This highly intelligent and hardworking sample of women had average graduation ranks in the top 12 percent of their high-school classes and average SAT (Scholastic Aptitude Test) verbal and math scores of 620 and 610, respectively. Unfortunately, those SAT scores were based only on the half of the women who reported them. Many did not know their SAT scores or had not taken the tests.

More than half of the group of women reported receiving awards at graduation, and a third of them received more than one award. The awards were varied and included art, academic, athletic, and even typing awards. Approximately a quarter qualified as National Merit or Commended Scholars, although the National Merit Scholars program was not yet in place at the time when many of the women who participated in the study were going to school. For most of the study participants, success and achievement were fundamental throughout their school years.

Part 2: Advice

Successful women in both traditional and nontraditional careers were educated in every type of school imaginable, from large urban schools to one-room country schoolhouses, and from coeducational public schools to all-girls independent schools. A significant number of our women were also educated in parochial schools, both coed and single-gender. That doesn't mean your selection of schools is not important. It is important that schools provide environments that encourage and value learning and provide challenge for your daughter. It is also helpful if your daughter is able to find at least some peer support for learning in her school.

CHOOSING THE RIGHT SCHOOL

As you evaluate your daughter's present school placement, the most important questions you should ask yourself are, "Does my daughter say she feels reasonably smart in this environment, and is she working hard?" In elementary school, if she's a "bookworm," a "tomboy," or a "good little girl," these are indications that she's in the right school. In middle school, if she feels different and self-critical, but nevertheless smart and hardworking, the school is still all right. If she's no longer working hard and believes that her social life, boys, and avoidance of learning are high priorities, you may wish to explore both your parenting priorities and other school options, especially if peer pressure to underachieve is affecting your daughter's learning.

If your daughter is on the right path, she's writing for school newspapers, exploring science materials and ideas, participating in student government, performing in drama or debate, or being excited by music, art, or sports involvement. By high school, she should be taking advanced subjects in her areas of strength and interest and be very busy with other interesting extracurricular activities. If she's being labeled by others as a "brain," that's in her favor, although she may have mixed feelings about it. If she's engaged in learning and activities and enjoying herself socially as well, so much the better, but a busy, happy social life is not mandatory for a good school environment and may, in some cases, be counterproductive.

If you think the school environment is interfering with your efforts to help your daughter feel smart, then consider changing schools if that is possible. You should explore school possibilities carefully so that your daughter doesn't think you are blaming her teachers or being disrespectful to her school. After searching for other alternatives, you may decide that your daughter is already in the appropriate school. Furthermore, if she is already in a school that fits with your values, economics, or plain convenience, it may be much better to communicate your concerns to her teacher or make some compromises rather than actually change schools.

At the elementary level, your main concerns should be whether your daughter has a challenging curriculum and whether teachers are sensitive to the importance of calling on girls as frequently as boys. Many teachers announce early to the class that they will alternate genders when calling on children. Although such an announcement is not absolutely necessary, a visit to the classroom will help you to determine if girls are being encouraged to speak up in class. If your daughter is fearful and doesn't volunteer, it might be a good idea to arrange some behavior-modification techniques for encouraging her to express herself early. Figure 4.3 includes a plan that almost always works with quiet and fearful girls.

If your daughter is outgoing and communicates well but you believe that other girls do not get the opportunity to speak out, it's worth sug-

FIGURE 4.3

Encouraging Your Daughter to Speak Up in Class

Tell your daughter privately that you would like her to speak up or answer a question at least once a day in class. Explain that each day when you talk with her about school, you'll ask her if she has spoken up. If she has, you'll put a star on the calendar. If she's very young (kindergarten or first grade), the star may be enough to get her started. If she's older, she may wish to save the stars or points for a gift. She does not need to receive the stars on consecutive days to receive credit. After she's received her first gift or is speaking up once a day, you may wish to credit her with a star only on days when she speaks up twice. Once she is in the habit of expressing herself, she won't require the stars, and you will gradually be able to forget about the speaking-up game.

Explain your plan to your daughter's teacher and ask her to at least notice if your daughter does take the courage to raise her hand. It's important for the teacher to recognize her, but not to fuss, overpraise, or share with the class that anything special has happened. Overpraise or too much excitement about her finally speaking up is enough to pressure her back into her shell. This approach almost always is successful with very quiet and fearful children.

gesting to the school principal that the teachers have a staff development session on how to encourage girls' participation. Many excellent teachers report that they simply weren't aware that they called on boys more than girls; indeed, it's often a technique they use unconsciously to prevent the boys from getting into trouble.

A Challenging Curriculum A challenging curriculum may be difficult to provide. Most teachers either believe they are already challenging all their students or, if they realize they aren't, will simply admit that given their overwhelming responsibilities of coping with other students (25 or 30 in elementary school, and up to 150 in middle or high school) who also have special needs, they simply can't meet the needs of all of them. Teachers and parents may not view lack of challenge as a problem because that lack of challenge will build your daughter's sense of intellectual confidence in elementary school. However, lack of challenge is likely to have the opposite effect when she enters higher-level schools if she isn't accustomed to working reasonably hard. It's important for her to learn to make a commitment to effort early in order to develop future confidence.

If you're worried about a lack of challenge, you have at least five choices to consider. First, communicate your concern to the teacher. Be optimistic and respectful. She may be able to change your daughter's assignments or give her enrichment work.

Second, you may want to design home enrichment to fit with your daughter's curriculum. This can be done in cooperation with a teacher. For example, if the class is studying volcanoes, your daughter, with your assistance, could research a particular volcanic disaster and make a model of the volcano and city, before and after; find out about a place where there is worry about volcanic activity, and try to communicate via the Internet with people experiencing an active volcano; write an imaginary story about living in a volcanic area; produce a play with others about a volcanic eruption; and so on. Your daughter's imagination, the teacher's ideas, and your creativity can make the study of volcanoes important in her learning memory.

Third, you can go to the school psychologist or to an out-of-school professional psychologist to ask for an evaluation and a professional intervention to help plan a more challenging program for your daughter.

Fourth, you can join a local or national parent support group that positively advocates for a challenging educational program, and receive encouragement and information from other parents.

Finally, you can visit other schools in the area to determine if they can provide some challenging curriculum for your child. You will have to project ahead to your daughter's attendance at middle and high school when considering tuition at either a parochial or independent school. If you have limited means, it may be more important to postpone private resources until later, when your daughter may become developmentally more vulnerable.

Although you have similar choices available to you for middle and high school, the structure of upper-level schools may cause communication to be more difficult. It may also be more difficult to implement change because usually more teachers are involved. Also, peer pressures affect both your daughter and the school decision-making process. Keep in mind that many of the successful women felt different, and those feelings may, in fact, have been important to their learning to be resilient. It is unlikely that your daughter will be harmed in the long run if she feels somewhat different. It is important, however, that she continue to feel smart and challenged. Be sure that her middle-school years offer her challenging courses in every subject area. Many middle schools do not offer high-level math and science courses. Also, your daughters need challenging writing and literary experiences.

Middle school is the first time some girls are almost totally distracted by boys, and some girls think that being an "airhead" is somehow a new definition of being a girl. Although interest in boys is healthy and normal during preadolescence and the teen years, if interest in the opposite gender distracts your daughter from the learning process, this is the time to consider whether she would benefit from a single-gender school or a different school that gives children the opportunity to take advanced courses.

Your daughters require challenge even during middle school. Their brains don't stop growing during early adolescence. If they lose momentum during those years, they may also lose the belief that they are smart, hardworking, and independent.

It's important not to overreact to minor school problems. The successful women in the study did not attend perfect schools. Many of these women found school to be too easy, and some remember at least temporary periods of boredom. Changing schools makes sense only if it's likely to provide a more supportive and/or challenging environment for your daughter. It's important to remember that your daughter does not need to be at the top of her class to feel smart. If she is in a challenging school environment, she can say to herself, as did Judge Edna Conway, "All the kids in this school are smart, so even if I'm in the middle, I'm doing fine." That may foster a better life adjustment than being at the top of the class. A school in which girls believe it's cool to be smart encourages all the students to want to learn more.

By middle and high school, if your daughter is performing poorly because she is being influenced by a very negative peer group, sometimes a change in school can be helpful. At our clinic, we have had good results in distracting some girls from negative peer groups by moving them from public to parochial school and vice versa. However, before you assume that school change will make a magical difference, consider that every school has some negative kids, and your daughter may indeed find them again.

A Too-Challenging Curriculum It is also possible for your daughter to have a school curriculum that is too challenging. If your daughter has uneven abilities or learning disabilities that are not recognized or considered, she could be feeling helpless and frustrated. Even if your daughter has above-average abilities, she could be feeling frustrated (and unintelligent) in a school that does not provide appropriate curriculum adjustments for her.

Schools are required to provide evaluations, and teachers are often helpful in adjusting the curriculum for students with learning problems or disabilities, so the first step is to express your concern to your daughter's teacher. You're likely to have an easier time persuading a teacher to help with a disability than to help you provide more challenges. However, if you've already made appropriate efforts, and if you have the option, you may wish to consider schools that have smaller, more personalized classes. Smaller is not always better, but if your daughter is working hard and not feeling smart, it certainly makes sense to consider other options.

ENCOURAGING INTELLECTUAL CONFIDENCE— THE IMPORTANCE OF TEACHERS

Academic strengths seem to direct children from elementary school onward. There are obviously differences in aptitudes; however, research has given us evidence that teachers' and parents' expectations affect children's achievement considerably. It can therefore be assumed that teachers' and parents' gender-related expectations about girls' achievement may encourage their reading, English, and writing skills and discourage their math and science competence. If you further consider that mothers and predominantly female teachers are conveying early messages to girls about expectations, it becomes even more important to focus attention on expecting girls to do well in all subjects.

Math and Science Competence To the extent that the future can be projected, it looks as though the best-paying jobs will involve at least some math and science competence. Technical careers as well as the world of business expect mathematics competence. If women are to achieve gender equity in income, more women will need to move into these higher-paying fields. To give your daughters the greatest number of choices, encourage their love of and comfort with math and science early on. If parents and teachers expect girls to be good at math from the beginning, more of them are likely to select careers that are and will be open to them.

As early as the preschool years, encourage little girls to like math and science. Only if they feel smart at these subjects and can observe adult women in science will they pursue developing these strengths.

From early childhood on it's important to talk science, read science books to girls, buy science-related toys and games, and even create scientist dolls. It's also important to count and measure and describe a world full of number problems. There are number toys, sports scores to count, recipes to measure, catalog prices to add up, money games, math tricks, and board and card games that involve counting and comparing numbers.

The goal is for your daughters to feel comfortable in the real world of science and math. They need to think of themselves as inventors, explorers, scientists, and computer experts. You can enhance that image by noticing and labeling those skills early. Incidentally, you don't have to label your daughters as best in the family in math and science. Despite respect for individual differences, all the kids in the family can be good at math and science. Just assume it runs in the family, even if it hasn't before. Talk is powerful.

Teachers can foster math and science interest in girls by encouraging classroom competitions and naming girls to be captains of math teams as frequently as boys. When they create cooperative science groups, they need to be certain to name as many girl team leaders as boys. Girls can be encouraged to enter projects in science fairs. Women scientists can be invited to visit classrooms to talk about their research.

Many of the women believed that their math decline was related to a specific math teacher. That may or may not be true, of course, but some people who are very good at mathematics have difficulty making it easy enough for others to understand. Because math concepts are built one upon another, if your daughters don't understand a concept, they could lose confidence easily. It is an excellent idea to provide tutoring help to girls who find math difficult. Sometimes that little bit of extra help can build skills as well as confidence and permanently improve their math achievement.

All women do not have to be involved in math and science to achieve success. There are many women in careers where verbal and social competence and understanding are primary. However, many of these careers are more competitive and more difficult to enter. Furthermore, women in the verbal professions tend to earn less. It is important that women choose careers in which they can love their work and are good at it. Math is not for every woman, or man, but your earliest expectations can provide your daughters with more options.

Reading and English The most effective way for children to learn to love to read is to be read to. Parents can begin reading to children, holding books with them, showing them pictures, and talking about them during their first year of life. By eight months, research tells us that babies can distinguish familiar words. That ability may begin even earlier. Parents who read to children in those early months of life find that children are less likely to rip up books at the usual paper-tearing stage because they have learned that books are somehow special. Even if babies don't understand the words, the beginnings of verbal learning and concentration are taking place. Family reading can continue until children are teenagers. Even a once-a-week family reading time will encourage the love of reading. Varying the readings from biography to fiction to science to poetry to exploration will encourage your daughters to broaden their curiosity and tastes in reading. Stories of successful women seemed to have been especially important to the women in our study and have the potential to inspire your daughters as well.

Children who learn to rhyme also learn to read more easily. Nursery rhymes and rhyming everyday words will encourage their abilities to distinguish sounds. (The Rimm children remember that things were as "cold as a bold" and "warm as a form"—only nonsense rhymes, but perhaps they were helpful.)

Children learn to speak by imitation. Use correct English early, and hire child-care providers who speak well and appropriately. Children can also learn more than one language early, either by you carrying on your own language tradition or by learning the language of a child-care provider. It's also important that children are exposed to English early even if it isn't your native language. Children who enter a school where all children speak English are at a great disadvantage if they don't know English. Dr. Sara Barts recalls worrying about speaking up because she wasn't certain which language she should use to answer the teacher correctly. Considering that girls tend to speak up less than boys, discomfort with language could further lessen girls' verbal assertiveness.

Listening to stories on tape will encourage children's listening skills and vocabulary building. Also, the public-radio program *Rabbit Ears Radio* provides stories for children to listen to, which will improve both concentration and a love of literature. Books on tape that the whole family can listen to while traveling together encourage listening skills, verbal abilities, family bonding, and improved travel behavior.

Writing Writing can also begin early for children. Start by giving them the opportunity to tell stories, alter stories, or finish your stories. When they can write a few sentences, letters to Grandma or to friends who have moved away can help them learn to put on paper what they'd like to say. Creating books, even ones with few words and many pictures, gives them an experience of authorship. As soon as they are able, teach them keyboarding on the computer. You may soon have a family newspaper, and this may eventually encourage your daughter to be editor of a class newspaper. The Internet, when carefully monitored for appropriateness, can provide motivation for girls to communicate in writing, and e-mail is surely a fun type of communication for your daughters. Writing to pen pals has always been an excellent way to encourage writing, and it's as effective now as ever. Sometimes teachers will help your children find pen pals.

Participating in writing workshops and writing contests and attempting to get written work published in children's magazines and newspapers can be very effective motivators for your daughter's writing. Don't be surprised if your daughter faces writer's block for the first time after winning a writing contest. Winning a contest can put pressure on children, particularly on perfectionistic children. Remind your daughter that she is unlikely to win every contest she enters or have everything she submits accepted for publication. Give her examples of famous authors who submitted their books and stories hundreds of times before finally becoming successful. Encourage your daughter to play around with ideas with the realization that authors aren't usually satisfied with everything they write, but sometimes the very work they are unhappy with ignites a spark for their readers. Writing a lot is the secret to becoming comfortable with the written word. If your daughter knows she is expected to write multiple drafts of everything, she will be encouraged to continue without feeling like a failure each time she's criticized by a parent, teacher, or friend.

If your daughter has trouble accepting your criticism, agree to write your comments on her paper lightly with pencil. Ask her to read over and consider the suggested changes, choose only those she'd like to use, and then erase your comments afterward, to emphasize the message that you're not imposing your criticism on her. If you do any writing for your own work, you can be a role model for learning to take suggestions by asking your daughter to proofread your work. She can use the same approach that you use. That will prevent you from needing to make changes you'd rather not make. Girls are often unable to take criticism well, and that ability is absolutely necessary for building resilience as well as skills in writing or almost any other field. It may as well start at home, where your daughter knows she's loved.

AVOIDING MIDDLE- AND HIGH-SCHOOL GRADE DECLINE

Perhaps the best way for your daughter not to see her grades and confidence decline as she moves into larger schools and more complex learning is for her to understand that school will take more effort and that you will expect her to work harder. But what do you do if your smart daughter suddenly starts acting like an airhead or becomes determined to please only the boys? It is time for you to talk about smart girls and dumb girls and what their futures look like. It's also time to remind her, and your sons as well, that smart boys like smart girls. It may even be important to remind her that she needs to be honest with her teachers, her family, and especially herself.

If your daughter does run into academic problems in middle school, brief tutoring could build her confidence. However, if you think peer pressure is the issue, it's time to push for some involvement in activities that will bring her together with more achievement-oriented kids. Chapter 5 will include more about extracurricular involvement, but you should think about your daughter's strengths and interests, because she won't want to leave nonproductive friends unless she can tie herself to another group of peers who share her interests. Sports, drama, or music involvement may help your daughter change her peer group. Although there's no guarantee that the kids on the sports team, in the play, or in the band are all achieving, the requirement that they invest time in productive activities can teach them some discipline that is likely to generalize to academics. Religious programs often provide good opportunities for philosophical discussion, intellectual challenge, and socializing with thoughtful peers.

It seems that only positive involvement and busyness in excellent activities can prevent your daughter from spending all her time and energy looking through fashion magazines and spending hundreds of hours shopping in an attempt to be beautiful. Of course, some of that is perfectly normal adolescent development, but if it can be balanced with a bevy of strong interests, you will have much less to worry about. Your daughter can best find herself through her strengths. Help her to discover and value them.

BUILDING CONFIDENCE WITH ADVANCED COURSES

Encourage your daughter to stretch herself. Teach her to love challenge. Believe in her ability to take on hard tasks, though if she seems to be feeling too much pressure, back off—but only a little. The fact is that girls can't build confidence by avoiding all the hard classes.

Girls, particularly those who are excellent students, are often afraid to take a course in which they won't achieve an A, but real confidence comes from earning a B in a difficult course that everyone thought they couldn't handle.

Encourage your daughters to take the risk of enrolling in advanced courses if there is any indication they can handle them. Many girls have felt much more comfortable in single-gender math and science classes because they at least get a chance to speak up or ask questions. If your schools don't provide opportunities for advanced classes in science and math in middle and high school, advocate for them for your daughters as well as for the other students.

Grades are important to all students, but girls tend to be more conscious of and worried about grades. They tend to avoid classes if they fear the grade will bring their averages down. Many schools weight honors and advanced classes, which encourages more students to enroll in them, and the students will therefore discover they can succeed in these challenging classes. Weighting systems differ by schools. Most simply use a system in which a B in an advanced course receives the same weight as an A in an easier course. It sounds like a simple plan; however, it's quite controversial in many schools, where teachers debate which courses are complex enough for weighting. For students, however, weighting is a very effective way to encourage risk taking because it minimizes the risk slightly. Your daughters may be motivated to take advanced physics if a B is weighted the same way an A is in an easier course, and they may realize that taking an easier class may actually be a disadvantage for their grade-point average.

ACCELERATING TO PROVIDE CHALLENGE

Research continues to support subject and grade skipping as effective approaches to challenging children who are able to learn at an accelerated pace. There is no research that suggests it does social harm, but there is considerable research indicating that the process is academically helpful. Occasionally students who have skipped subjects and are enrolled in two different grades find it confusing to explain their status to peers; some in this group have indicated it might be easier to be all in one grade.[1] Once in a while there are some peer problems immediately after skipping a grade, but they soon disappear. Sometimes girls who already had peer relationship problems continue to have them. For the most part, however, skipping can cause less confusion than many other approaches to providing challenge within the classroom.

Only a very small percentage of children should skip a grade, and it should be done only after a very thorough psychoeducational evaluation. If you believe your daughter is unchallenged, even if she seems contented, it's a good idea to have a professional evaluation done by an expert in the area of gifted education.

Girls seem to be less willing to take the risk of skipping a subject or grade than boys. They tend to be hesitant about leaving their friends. If you accept their wish to stay with friends as a rationale for not moving to more appropriate academic work, you are giving them the message that their social life has a higher priority than their learning. If they believe their social life is the highest priority, they may use that as an excuse for avoiding many challenging experiences. Furthermore, they may fear they will be unable to make new friends or that they can't be friends with children who are in different grades. If they are candidates for grade skipping, be supportive and give them the confidence they'll need for taking risks in the future.

Many will tell you that grade skipping will be detrimental to your daughter's social life. However, that detriment may be an advantage to your daughter in other ways. Teachers who have considered allowing their own children to skip a grade but decided not to for social reasons are particularly vociferous about telling other parents not to let their children skip. As you will see in a later chapter, many successful women did not have very extensive social lives anyway, whether or not they skipped a grade. There seems to be no reason to blame the issue on grade skipping.

Subject and grade skipping build confidence in students. Children will permit themselves to work hard to catch up on what they've missed, discover that their efforts are effective, and feel smart even if they are not at the top of the next class because of the grade skip. Skipping builds confidence in the same way that retention in a grade steals confidence from children. Children are always comparing themselves to others. If they believe they can learn faster and better, they feel good.

There is an important fringe benefit to skipping a grade or two during elementary or middle school. Many of the successful women in this study pursued many years of education, and most of them also had families. The ticking of the biological clock has been a major issue for the women of this generation. Finding time for babies amid professional degrees and residencies is extremely difficult. Saving a year early on, when your daughter may be bored, can result in gaining an extra year on what nature considers to be an appropriate time for childbearing. It is a reasonable consideration when deciding about skipping a grade, providing your daughter's evaluation suggests she might benefit by advancing in this way.

One final note: If the school is adamant about not allowing grade skipping, it's not a good idea to become embattled over the problem. The continuous struggle may cause your daughter more harm than a little bit of school boredom. Find opportunities for enrichment instead.

TEACHING YOUR DAUGHTERS
TO VALUE THE SIGNPOSTS OF SUCCESS

Of course, it's most important to motivate your daughters toward the love of learning, but if you scoff about the importance of grades, your daughters have much to lose. Students who have good grades almost always enjoy learning. On the other hand, there are many children who think they should have the right to pick and choose to learn only what they'd like to learn. They will provide you with many an intelligent argument about how "grades don't count as long as we're learning." The underlying problem is that they may be worried that they wouldn't get the good grades even if they tried. Children who are uneven in their abilities, have learning disabilities, or who haven't developed a work ethic are infamous for excuses about grades.

Getting good grades is a good habit that will open doors for children from kindergarten through college and for the rest of their lives. Although it is important not to pressure your daughters to become obsessed about grades, they need to place value on those important evaluations of their performance.

Children are not very good at projecting the future. A good education is not just doing what you want to do and learning what you want to learn, although ideally much of every child's education will involve that. Your daughters need to be prepared for experiences of failure. Recovering from those experiences through resilience is an important part of success. That does indeed mean that they may have to accomplish tasks and study subjects and even take tests that are unpleasant for the sake of jumping the hurdles that will lead them to successful careers. Don't buy into your daughters' excuses. Encourage the good grades as well as the learning.

You may wonder if you should monetarily reward your kids for grades. Very few of the successful women in the study were paid for grades. More often they considered the praise reward enough. If your kids are doing well and they ask for money for each A, I suggest you give it to them, although you should certainly emphasize that you know it's not the only reason they work hard. If they're doing poorly, money for grades hardly ever pays off. Underachievers don't usually have the confidence to deliver the grades, and they soon give up. If you're going to reward your underachievers for anything, it's better to attach the rewards to effort in short-term goals, such as getting all the assignments done on time, doing extra work, and so on. It will likely result in better grades, and they can feel they earned the grades by working harder. The concept that working harder produces better results is an important one to learn.

Prizes and awards look good on your children's records. The excitement of awards, seeing their names in the newspapers, and the articles that you cut out and hang up on your kitchen bulletin board are their signposts of success. Even if they get only a few, they'll feel good, so you may wish to encourage them to try for those awards. Sometimes entering less popular contests can give them a better chance at winning an award and help build their confidence.

THE ALMIGHTY A

Although many parents struggle with trying to encourage their daughters to study, do their homework, and do a little more than is expected, there are some parents, and many girls, who struggle with the opposite issue. There are many adolescents, and even young adults, who have overlearned the lesson of achievement. Instead of being encouraged to work a little harder, to do a little more than is expected (or at least all that is expected), these girls need to be told to do less than they are doing. They find they can't have fun or do anything with their friends or family unless they have overstudied. They say they won't enjoy going to the mall with friends if they aren't absolutely certain they've studied sufficiently for a test.

The pressure these girls have internalized and the drive they feel does not come as a direct message from their parents, although teachers often assume the problem is caused by parental pressure. Usually their parents are also urging them to back off, because by the time these young women come to see me, they have bitten their nails to the quick or are experiencing headaches and stomachaches.

It is difficult to help an internally pressured girl to back off from her overstudy. Her overstudy and perfectionism have made her so successful that she continuously receives positive reinforcement for working too hard. Thus when she overstudies for the chemistry test, she finds that not only does she get the A+ she was hoping for, but the teacher announces in amazement that she has earned the highest grade on this difficult test that anyone has ever earned in the last ten years. Furthermore, she is competing to graduate first in her class. There are other students who have all A's, so to keep herself in first place, she needs to take the greatest number of advanced placement classes possible and receive A's in these. If she's first, she will get an automatic scholarship based on merit. She also realizes the advantage first place carries for getting into her choice of colleges.

If you have such a daughter, you know how many times other parents have commented on how fortunate you are. On the other hand, your daughter's peers may well have said that she's not much fun and too brainy. Many of these girls do have good friends, but their friends have largely given up on encouraging them to come along to activities. The reality is that for some girls this behavior works perfectly: They receive their scholarships, they get into good colleges, and then they struggle with even more pressure in college, and in medical, law, or graduate school. Eventually, however, they need to cope with the indefiniteness of the real world, where they cannot overstudy for the test. While hard work can pay off, A's will not necessarily be forthcoming.

It is that big picture that I try to give the young women I see in the clinic. If you have a daughter who is experiencing that kind of driven pressure, she will need help backing off a little at a time. If the girl is planning to put two hours into study, could she take the risk of studying only an hour and a half? This is a very foreign concept to her. She usually feels that cutting down will increase her anxiety about the test. "Getting by" has never been her strong suit. Yet knowing that she can actually make herself so physically sick that she would have no choice but miss school, miss the play, miss chorus and band, and miss being valedictorian is enough to help her realize that she must slow her pace.

If you have such a daughter, don't waste your time feeling guilty. You've probably done a great job of parenting. It's your daughter's own success as much as the praise that coincides with that success that has caused her to internalize pressures. Notice whether you are a role model for overwork, and if so, find time to relax and have fun with your family. Help your daughter to balance work with fun. Try to do that before she gets into the overwork pattern, but if you do see her working too much, tell her that overwork, too, can cause serious, immediate, and lifelong problems.

WHEN A WOMAN IS AN "UNCOMMON MAN"

Dr. Diane Butler*
Private-Practice Pediatrician

Dr. Diane Butler's high-school valedictory address summarized well her direction, although at the time she couldn't have predicted where her path would lead. She urged her fellow graduates of the Class of 1964 to "take the initiative . . . for themselves and their country . . . to strive to become the uncommon man." She advocated that they develop perseverance, moral integrity, and sincerity of purpose. Diane's high-school address eloquently reflected who she was and the principles that would guide her through adulthood.

Diane's family and academic environments set the stage for her later education and career. Diane consistently excelled in school and always seemed intrinsically motivated to study and learn. She would complete her homework on Friday nights before she would let herself enjoy the weekend. She was a hard worker and considered herself smart but not brilliant. She loved science and math and excelled in both, which she believes was natural because her mom loved science and her dad taught math, so Diane expected to be "best at both." She received science and math awards upon graduating from high school. Achievement was part of a continuing family tradition.

Diane was actively involved in dance, music, Scouts, and reading; she watched very little television. She was a Scout leader for younger girls and baby-sat in middle and high school. Later she realized that her experiences with younger children influenced her in her eventual career choice.

Both her parents had high expectations of her, were firm and supportive, and were intelligent. During her middle- and high-school years, Diane's parents urged her to be strong and independent and not to bow to peer pressure.

Diane was true to her studies and her love of learning, but perceived herself as not being popular and a loner. She thought others may have considered her to be "prudish and stuffy." She was told she was not a social person, and she believed it. She did not consider herself "socially adept." Although Diane dated in high school, it was sporadic and not based on popularity. She "just didn't go along with the crowd" and always felt somewhat different and alone.

Although Diane's parents made it clear that Diane needn't be held back by her gender, they did provide some very ambiguous messages that perhaps reflected the times in which she grew up. Diane never felt restricted from activities merely because she was a girl. She described herself in childhood as a tomboy. She "climbed trees, ran races, and was involved in sports to the extent that they were available at the time." On the other hand, her brothers, one older and one younger, were expected to go to college because they were boys. Diane was expected to go to college only if she was smart enough, and perhaps that was another component of her drive for achievement. Although she acknowledges feeling pressure from her parents to achieve, she had interpreted that as pressure to achieve in school, not in a career, and she indicates that the pressure never bothered her.

Diane's excellence in math and science, paired with her lack of social confidence, led her initially to a career as a medical technologist, where she believed she would not need to interact much with other people. She had earned excellent grades in college but believed that other careers in the medical field would require her to be socially skilled as well as "naturally brilliant." She didn't believe she was either. Diane worked hard in her position as a medical technologist and quickly moved into research with several physicians. She learned all she could from the laboratory but came to feel she didn't fit in because she saw herself as more goal-oriented than her peers.

As Diane began to feel somewhat unfulfilled with her work as a medical technologist, she also discovered the personal satisfaction of helping patients. She gained confidence in her ability to relate to people, and was encouraged to consider becoming a doctor by the physicians with whom she worked. Through her six years as a medical technologist, she gained the confidence she needed to be an "uncommon man," and she entered medical school at the then-atypical age of twenty-eight.

Although Diane's parents always expected her to have both marriage and career, Diane was still unmarried when she decided to go to medical school. Her mother expressed fear that she would "educate herself out of a husband" and discouraged her from enrolling. Nevertheless, Diane felt medical school was the perfect direction for her and decided she would rather be single and happy than married and unhappy. However, she never actually had to make that choice. Diane met a man just prior to entering medical school who shared her values.

They commuted several hours weekly to maintain their relationship until Diane completed medical school and they married. Diane's mother was pleased and proud of both her daughter's medical career and her marriage.

Although Diane was initially uncertain about which specialty she would select, she found herself drawn to pediatrics. From her past experiences in Scouting and baby-sitting, she had developed a special love for and ability to communicate with children. Diane viewed pediatrics as the ideal specialty for her because it was both a caring profession and an art.

Diane completed medical school in three years in a special accelerated program. She had already received a master's degree in science before entering medical school. She doesn't feel that she was treated differently in medical school just because she was a woman, although she indicates that perhaps there existed an "old boys' club" among the surgeons. During her surgery rotation when an older surgeon defended the rigorous schedule as necessary "to build character," she remembers responding assertively that she would prefer *not* to develop character like his. Diane Butler has continued to assert herself in uncommon ways, recently separating from her group pediatric practice of thirteen years to start her own successful practice.

When asked about her most important role models, Diane named three. First and foremost, Diane identified with her mother and believes she was an important and fantastic role model. Although her mother had interrupted her own education to support her husband's college work, she returned to college to get her degree in her mid-fifties and entered a career in teaching in her late fifties. Diane admired her mother's commitment to education and career, and was influenced by her mother's continuous interest in science as well.

The role model for her philosophy of life came from Diane's reading. Ayn Rand, through her books *The Fountainhead* and *Atlas Shrugged*, helped Diane to create a philosophical foundation by which to guide herself.

Medical school provided a third important role model. Diane was inspired and influenced by a pediatrician she acknowledged as the first woman doctor she had really known. Diane realized that "this is the kind of person I would want to be," although she explained, "In terms of actual people, I really carved out my own person. I picked and chose from a lot of pieces of different people . . . to end up with my own ways of doing things."

Diane gave birth to her first child, a son, immediately after her residency; she was then thirty-four, which at the time was considered old for a first-time mother. A daughter, born a "blue baby" who required open heart surgery at eight months of age, followed three years later. Diane credits her husband for his continued support and inspiration, his entrepreneurial encouragement, and his strong commitment to fatherhood and sharing of home responsibilities. To Diane, he is the most important influence in her adult life. She feels that other men might have been intimidated by her high-powered career and would not have tolerated so successful a wife. Diane's education and income, she says, "don't faze" her husband or her in-laws, who provide another generation of support for the family. She believes she and her husband have an ideal relationship. She hopes their marriage can provide a good model for their own two children.

It appears that Diane, now in her late forties, is living out her valedictory address by perseverance, moral integrity, and sincerity in an effort to be the "uncommon man" she spoke of, and a happy one at that. It is difficult to imagine that this charismatic, successful, and socially confident physician, wife, and mother was the lonely, isolated, and prudish adolescent she remembers.

FINDING A CAREER THAT COMBINES PEOPLE AND SCIENCE

——

Angela Sands
Registered Nurse

Angela Sands was enrolled for six years at a large midwestern university because she just couldn't decide on a career that was right for her. She was diligent in her studies, but to her disappointment, her grades in college were not what they were in high school. She does admit that there were times in college she lost confidence in her intelligence and was even depressed. Socially, she often felt shy and inadequate, but her very close group of friends helped her through those hard times. She knew she was doing something different because there were few other women in the science courses she loved. As the first in her family to complete college, she was taking some risks and felt a little like a pioneer.

As a child, Angela wanted to be president of the United States when she grew up. In adolescence, she thought veterinary medicine was the perfect way to combine her teenage absorptions, science and animals. While in college, she seriously considered engineering because many of her closest friends were engineering majors. She knew she could manage the initial math classes but feared she wasn't analytical enough for the advanced math. Furthermore, she preferred working with people. So she switched to physical therapy, quite certain it would work for her. But then a counselor warned her that very few students were being accepted into that major and suggested she try nursing in the meantime. It was a good recommendation, because Angela's B average was not sufficient for acceptance into physical therapy. Nursing minimized the math requirements she disliked but combined her love of people and her love of science. Undoubtedly part of Angela's career decision was related to her strong identification with her nurturing mother, to whom she could always go with her problems. She wished to play a similar mothering role herself and wanted a career that would provide flexibility so she could balance it with being a good mother.

Angela admitted she also identified with her dad's practical hands-on activities, which also enhanced her interest in nursing. Because her dad had no sons, he did things with his daughters he probably would not have done otherwise. He would often have Angela help him fix an engine or repack wheel bearings as he provided a constant narrative. He would also let her help with house repairs. He motivated her to take shop and electrical classes in high school, often questioning her about what she was learning. When friends teased her dad about having five daughters, he would refer to them as his "harem." Angela usually rebuffed such comments with "Dad, we are *definitely* not your harem!"

The relationship Angela's dad had with his family was somewhat unpredictable. During Angela's elementary-school years he traveled frequently, and her mom took charge of the family. The girls became quite accustomed to this pattern of care, and Angela remembers resenting when her dad increased his time at home during her high-school years. Her mother was easier; her dad was firmer. He dictated too many rules, which Angela sometimes renegotiated with her mother. Despite the difference in their parenting styles, she realized even then that her parents were reasonably firm without being too rigid.

Angela was somewhat rebellious with her dad, but she was basically a "good kid" during high school. She hung around with a small group of good students during her teens, although she considered the boys to be "friends that were boys" rather than actual boyfriends. She spent a lot of time with Bill, who lived out in the country among the cornfields. His family had a pond for swimming, and the kids could blast their radio as loud as they wished without disturbing the adults. Angela did the driving, and her friends would pile into her parents' car and go places, mainly to Bill's farm. Angela thinks of her high-school days as wonderful, although her social life never distracted her from her high achievement.

Angela received plenty of take-charge experiences as the oldest of five sisters. Of the five, only two completed college, and Angela believes that's directly related to mixed messages about college received from their parents, neither of whom had earned college degrees. Her dad had dropped out of Notre Dame, and Angela sensed college had been a negative experience for him. Angela's parents expected them to be good students in high school, but beyond that they were ambiguous.

Angela was always an excellent student; she graduated twelfth in her class, and was considered to be brainy and a bookworm. Even early on, her science and math skills were as strong as her verbal skills. Angela and her sisters all have special memories of their sixth-grade teacher, Mr. Bains. He had an incentive program in which his students could earn "Mr. Bains money" to save up for special activities or treats. Students could earn the play money for good grades or for being kind to others or volunteering in the community. Angela earned a fortune in "Mr. Bains money," which confirmed to her that she was a really smart, nice person. Angela loved the plan; it was a winning-in-competition experience for her.

In the middle grades, Angela's academic self-confidence was further confirmed by her automatic placement into honors classes, where she continued to earn mostly A's. She never doubted her intellectual ability, nor did she perceive that her new interest in boys had any negative impact on her grades.

There was one significant negative experience for Angela in middle and high school related to band. She played clarinet, and the teacher arranged a competition for chair placement. The band students would anonymously judge who was best by listening to the two players. When students came out of the contest room they would be either cheered or humiliated, depending on whether they had won or lost the contest. The clarinetist in the first chair was in the position of warding off those who wished to move up. Although throughout school Angela always sat in either first or second chair, she abhorred having to "always be better than everyone." Finally in senior high school, although she enjoyed playing her clarinet, she quit band because she detested the competitive atmosphere. She couldn't recall if she was in first or second chair when she finally left the program, but she does remember the competitive discomfort.

Synchronized swimming, a totally cooperative venture, was more to Angela's liking. She also loved being in the school play and playing on a noncompetitive intramural volleyball team. Although Angela usually avoided competitions, she does recall her excitement when she won an award for being the best typist in her class.

Angela's dad's messages about girls being able to do anything paid off for her in high school, when she assertively volunteered to be statistician for the hockey team. A girl had never held that position before, and she carried out her responsibilities while she and her friends also admired and jested with the boys on the team. They all had crushes on the boys, and watching the team members was much more fun for her than the statistics.

Angela continued as an excellent student in high school. She was involved in plenty of school and social activities, but she resisted negative peer pressure. She was independent enough to combine a fun social life with high academic standards (she spent three hours a night doing homework). She was never considered one of the popular kids in school, but neither was she unpopular. She was considered one of the smart kids, but not a "genius"; one of the athletes, but not really a "jock." Angela was comfortable with not being at the top and actually preferred it that way.

One of Angela's favorite high-school teachers taught business education. The teacher was young and unmarried, and Angela and her friends thought she was "so cool" that they visited her at her home. That friendship with a teacher gave them good feelings about learning.

Travel proved to be a tremendous step for Angela in building her sense of independence. Her ninth-grade social studies class took a trip to Washington, D.C., and earned part of the funds for it through school projects. Her parents were hesitant about giving Angela permission to go, because not only was it expensive, but she had never been away from home without them. Angela had saved up money from her baby-sitting jobs and convinced her parents that she could handle the trip responsibly. She remembers clearly the fun bus rides and the visits to the monuments and buildings, but most important to her was the satisfaction that she had earned most of the money for the trip. She never forgot that first travel experience and used its success to expand her traveling experiences while she was in college. The travel, for which she always earned the money, opened up a whole new world for her, encouraged her to take risks, and built her personal self-confidence.

As Angela reflects upon her present lifestyle and career, she believes she made good choices. Her engineer friends have difficulty balancing their family responsibilities and their careers. At age thirty-five, Angela believes that nursing offers her versatility, flexibility, and the opportunity to fulfill her most important loves—working with both science and people as well as finding time to be a great mother to her two young children.

CHAPTER 5

ACTIVE GIRLS, ACTIVE WOMEN

Part 1: Findings

It's not surprising that the busy, interesting, successful women in our study were also busy and interested little girls. Perhaps they received their preparation for managing the complexity of their lives as successful women from learning the organizational skills that were needed to manage their complicated schedules in childhood.

MUSIC

Highest on the women's activity list was involvement in music in many forms, including piano and other musical instruments, band, orchestra, and chorus. Some of the women found their identities in their music, while others found their social lives there. Some found self-discipline through practice that generalized to other skills. Still others found a related nonmusical career. A violinist from California explained how she and her music became interconnected: "When I was eight years old and about to start violin lessons, I told my mother, 'I'm not a violiner yet, but I will be someday.' For me, being a violinist is not a career choice but rather an essential part of who I am, similar to being a wife and mother. In many ways, you become a violinist before you choose what career to pursue, and therefore the choice has already been made emotionally before you have a chance to make it intellectually. I believe that the conviction that 'this is what I am, not just what I do' is essential to being a really good violinist."

Here's how Norah Baines, a New York City flutist, became engaged in her music: "At ten I started playing the flute. I loved the physical feeling of using my breath to create such a beautiful sound. It was the most beautiful sound I ever heard. In middle school, music became my escape from social and academic competition. I could practice in my room and escape from the competition I felt with my sister. I entered music competitions and won almost all of them. I had carved out a niche for myself."

It wasn't only musicians who became absorbed in music. Medical researcher Dr. Janice Douglas* played piano from kindergarten through high school and practiced independently simply because she enjoyed it.

It was very common for women in our study to view their musical group (orchestra, band, or music camp) as a social facilitator. "Participation in musical activities, which were fun, provided a creative outlet as well as social opportunities, taught me the value of discipline and hard work, and taught me how to perform under pressure," said a physician. "My interest in music led me to work on the concert committee, which opened doors to many different situations and developed problem-solving, financial, communication, and socialization skills," an entertainment executive commented.

A musician described her summer music camp as a great place to meet kids (not just girls) who were as passionate about what she loved. "So, instead of being the 'different,' special kid, I felt one of a large group. When I became a leader there, popular with many kids and respected by faculty and kids, my confidence soared. The coed nature of these orchestras also created a nice social network where 'dating' seemed less important." A computer scientist from California explained that her study of music in elementary school brought her to electronic music in high school, which then led to electrical engineering as a career.

Dr. Sandra Calvin, an environmental engineer, never had to work hard at math and science. Instead, she learned the value of hard work from her music instruction. She knew she was not naturally talented in music, but it was an area in which she wanted to achieve. In high school, Sandra remembers practicing her oboe for hours to master a difficult part. Later this rigor translated into an academic context. When her college work became difficult, she knew that she could master it with the same careful concentration.

Editor Liz Ludlow's* piano experience taught her to appreciate music in her life. "I think that early musical training had a big impact on me. I've always been very interested in the arts. I've been an avid dance fan; I go to the ballet and modern dance. It helped me in my first job, which was as an arts and entertainment writer. I lost all interest in piano in high school, but I'll never regret the experience."

The findings of this research suggest that music is definitely *not* a luxury in our schools, but an important tool for learning many skills that generalize to other kinds of learning as well as to successful careers.

RECREATIONAL READING

Next highest on the activity list for these women was reading, with more than half of the women indicating that they did a great deal of reading outside of school. Their reading provided them engagement, escape, knowledge, and mentors. The verbal professions—media, law, education, and mental health—were home to the women who did the most reading as children. However, reading was selected frequently by women in all professions. Many of them remembered being called "bookworms." A journalist from Little Rock, Arkansas, explained, "Books were my salvation. As a child, I felt isolated, different, and hungry for a richer life. Books provided that. I felt authors of children's books were kind and wonderful adults who had cleverly reached out to me across time, understanding me, and addressing things I cared about."

GIRL SCOUTS

Girl Scouts was extremely popular for women in this study. About half of them belonged to Scouts in elementary school. The professions that had the most Scouting involvement were science, law, government, and mental health. Least involved were the artists, allied health professionals, and homemakers. Although most of the involvement took place at the elementary-school level, some girls went on to take leadership positions in Scouting through high school, and for others, Scouting became an important social outlet during a period when many felt isolated from the dating scene. Scouting became their community and an avenue for leadership, accomplishment, confidence building, and creative exploration. Furthermore, Scouting automatically provided girls with the opportunity to see women in leadership roles. Psychologist Dr. Anne Caroles remembered her volunteer Girl Scout leader as being ahead of her times. Because of her, Anne realized that women could do things beyond what she had previously thought. Perhaps it is the absence of male leadership at Girl Scout camps and activities that helps girls realize that women are capable of so much more than what some girls' experiences suggest. Margaret Karnes as well as many others remembered selling the most cookies in their troop.

SPORTS

The younger women in the study were more involved in sports than the older women because there were very few athletic opportunities for the older women, although even some of the older women considered themselves tomboys and athletes as children. About a quarter of the women in the study were involved in sports by high school, about three times as many as were involved in cheerleading. The professions that had the most involvement in sports were science, medicine, business, media, and education, in that order. Many of the women, particularly those in the first three professions, mentioned that sports taught them how to cope with the competition they met in their professions.

Least involved in sports were the orchestral women and artists. Undoubtedly their intensive participation in their art left them little time for sports, or perhaps artists simply tend not to be interested in athletics.

One physician recalled her sports experiences this way: "My participation in sports gave me an appreciation of how hard I could push myself. It taught me to achieve with hard work and how to deal with failure, even when you work hard." Another physician said, "Participation in organized sports has played a critical role in my development and my success in a traditionally male world. Exposure to sports as a teenager and college student taught me to win, to lose, and to strive to achieve my personal best. In college and after college I competed on an elite level as a rower, winning the national championship and medaling at the world championship. I was one of two women training with a group of men. Success in this group set the stage to train and compete with male surgeons without carrying any major chips on my shoulder."

There is research that suggests that gifted boys who participate in sports are more accepted by their peers. Perhaps, considering the value placed on athletics in our society, it is not surprising that these highly

intelligent women also found that sports facilitated their social acceptance. Another physician gave us an example: "Sports was really important for me because I was a spindly kid and if you were real scholastic,
you got picked on a lot. Sports gave me an identity other than that of
'school worm' and a place to belong. I swam, and I had a very demanding coach. She really worked us hard, and that critical ninth- and tenth-
grade year, I spent my summer working out because I wanted to make
the team very badly. I became very strong. In the early part of my
sophomore year, people began either to lose their interest in school or
to be very motivated to achieve. There was this girl who was a tomboy,
and during high school she got away from scholastics. She always
wanted to pick on me and have a fight with me. I finally said, 'Maggie, if
you really want to fight, we can fight, but I swim six miles a day, and I
can beat the shit out of you.' That was it. She never harassed me again.
With the exception of scholar-athletes, kids who are really scholastic
get picked on."

Dr. Leigh Carter, an educational researcher, recalled how sports led
her to admire her mother. Leigh had always admired her dad and
thought of her mother as uninteresting by comparison. Leigh was training to shoot targets with a rifle and was becoming quite good at the
sport. She aspired to be on a college rifle team someday. One day she
decided to try her hand at bow and arrow shooting. She set up a target,
took aim, and missed repeatedly. Her mom, who was watching her from
the kitchen, came out and said, "Leigh, it looks like you're having a
hard time there." Leigh's mom took the bow and arrow and pointed to
the garden hose on the other side of the yard. "See that hose?" she
asked. "Watch this." Then her mother shot four arrows into the hose.
Leigh recalled being very impressed and having a new respect for her
mother's competencies from that moment on—and off they went to
Sears to buy a new garden hose.

Despite the lesser involvement in cheerleading compared to other
sports, many of the women who were cheerleaders commented on how
it provided them with confidence and how much they enjoyed it.
Although having girls cheer for boys is a sexist tradition, there seems to
have been no harm done for the attorneys, politicians, scientists, writers,
and teachers who enjoyed it. Liz Ludlow,* an editor, was quick to point
out that cheerleading equipped her to be her city's cheerleader as editor of an important magazine: "One of the experiences that shaped me
was my experience on the cheerleading squad in high school. We were

in the state championships. The whole thing, from the minute I decided I wanted to be a cheerleader, taught me so much. The skills needed to make the squad, the discipline, the networking—the 'schmoozing'—might be a little part of why you make the squad. Then there is the goal setting and being part of a tight-knit group once you're on the squad. We spent more time practicing than the football team; two hours after school, home for dinner, then two hours at night. Working together to be the best taught me a lot about teamwork and sticking with the project, skills I use in my job as editor. I feel I'm in a cheerleader role, and this magazine is a cheerleader for my city."

It is a measure of freedom for girls to be able to extend their athletic competence beyond cheerleading, however. Many of the older women in the study who described themselves as "tomboys" commented on the unavailability of sports in their time and their belief that they probably would have enjoyed them. With more girls' sports available and more women role models for sports participation, girls will undoubtedly expand their participation and increase their learning opportunities from that participation.

STUDENT GOVERNMENT

By high school, about a third of the successful women were involved in student government. Perhaps not surprisingly, the power brokers in our study were also frequently power brokers in high school. More of the women in government today (fully half) were in student government in high school compared to the women in the other professions. Nonprofit organizational leadership had the second most involvement, followed by attorneys and businesswomen. Least involved in student government were the musicians, artists, and mental health professionals, in that order. Quite a few women also ran for school office, although they didn't always win—perhaps a good experience for building the kind of resilience necessary for running for office in the real world.

Deborah Goldman, a director of government affairs, ran for president of the student council and came in a very close second. She developed a campaign theme and a support group. "I think my parents helped me to see that being number two wasn't a defeat because I continued to be competitive with the person who ran against me. We went back and forth on a lot of things. Sometimes she won; sometimes I did."

State senator Elizabeth Quinlan was one of the few women in government who lost her social confidence during middle school. Despite the fact that she didn't think of herself as a leader, she was elected president of the freshman class. She agreed that her friends must have seen her leadership qualities despite her wilting self-confidence.

Dr. Laurie Stuart* learned resilience that would help her with the pressures of her eventual profession. Every year she ran for student council in her very large high school and every year she lost. Finally as a senior, she was elected and can still recall the jubilation. Her perseverance was finally rewarded.

DEBATE AND DRAMA

The women in the government and law career groups were most frequently involved in debate in high school. Many of those in the same two career groups, as well as those in business and organizational leadership and in education were also involved in drama. Not at all surprisingly, the women in media had the most involvement in drama, with more than half being active in high-school drama. Those who actually became media performers often began their rehearsals as early as elementary school. Donna Draves, who is now a television news anchor, recalls receiving lots of encouragement from her mother for her creative activities. Even in elementary school, she performed for audiences in drama, debate, and speech. She remembered winning speech contests and believed they were very important for her academic and social confidence.

OTHER INTERESTS

Other frequently cited activities included dance, art, hobbies, outdoor activities, writing, and science activities. The women often described how specific experiences gave them confidence and discipline in other areas of their lives. Here's an example of an artist-sculptor, Jean Cobb, who found herself involved in a multitude of atypical girl activities: "I was never taken with girl stuff. I was never really taken with boy stuff, either. I don't think I identified myself as a feminine person, and I was very involved already in activities that most people didn't think girls did, like sports, journalism, photography, and those types of things. I was good at and a leader in sports, and I had incredibly high energy. I was the photographer for the yearbook in high school, and I learned how to develop and enlarge and print photographs. I covered wrestling matches, football games, debates, and dances. These were all really important to my high-school life and my self-confidence."

TELEVISION

Most of the women had television sets in their homes while they were growing up, although 40 percent had no television while they were in elementary school. By their high-school years, only 10 percent didn't have television. Almost a third of the women watched television approximately an hour a day, and a little more than a quarter watched it approximately two hours a day. Only 10 percent of the women indicated they watched it for three to four hours a day. Although there were slight variations among careers relative to the amount of time spent watching television, only the full-time homemakers watched significantly more television than other career groups. On the other hand, there were individual women within almost every career group who watched many hours of television. Television news anchor Donna Draves watched television at least four hours a day, and by age twelve had decided to become a famous television news anchor.

TIME ALONE

With all this involvement in extracurricular activity, one might suspect that these girls were overprogrammed, except that almost half indicated they played and spent considerable time alone during elementary school. That percentage decreased to 25 percent by their busy high-school years. Sally Sahn, who was brought up in rural Indiana, loved art and dance and spent many hours practicing dance. She participated in Scouts, took piano lessons, had many hobbies, enjoyed reading and writing, and was often outdoors but nevertheless spent considerable amounts of time alone, as there were no neighborhood children nearby to play with. Catherine Burns, an engineer, was actively involved in music and Girl Scouts, but despite plenty of social activities, she always valued her time alone. She remembers her older sister trying to hug her and Catherine saying to her mother, "Just get her away from me. I want to play by myself."

Part 2: Advice

Based on the busy and interesting lives of the women in the study, it seems good for your daughters to be absorbed in activities and interests from the preschool years onward. Parents who are already taxiing their daughters to lessons should feel encouraged in their efforts. However, you also need to be selective and set limits. Because many of the women remembered valuing time alone in their childhoods, it is important not to overprogram your daughters. It also seems sensible to prevent neighborhood socializing from invading your home, thus leaving children no time to themselves. Teaching your children to tell their friends that they need some time to themselves provides good practice in assertiveness and will prevent them from being dependent on continuous socializing.

Your daughters' temperament will also guide their involvement. Very social children may push you toward permitting overinvolvement, and you may wish to limit their selection of activities. Fearful or shy children may avoid involvement, and you may thus need to make some decisions to enroll them in classes rather than give them choices. Shy children, when asked if they'd like to participate, will often respond negatively because of their fears. That often precipitates a power struggle of persuasion: Their fears and anxiety increase as you argue, and so do yours. Especially when they're young, consider instead telling them you've enrolled them in an activity you're sure they'll enjoy. They'll have time enough for making choices after they develop the confidence that comes with successful engagement.

Shy children especially often enjoy mother-daughter or father-daughter activities. Group activities such as Brownies, where Mom is a leader, or parent-child swim classes are good starter activities.

THE MAGIC OF MUSIC

If possible, we suggest you begin music lessons during your daughters' preschool years. Consider the findings of this study of such high participation in music and also of other research findings that exposure to classical music, learning the keyboard, and choral music at the preschool level may actually enhance spatial skills. Early music lessons of some kind may be especially important for girls who score low on tests of spatial skills. Suzuki music instruction, which teaches preschoolers to repeat the sounds and rhythms they hear, seems to be especially appropriate for very young children. However, more traditional approaches to music lessons are also suitable provided the music teacher feels comfortable teaching preschool children. Brief practice sessions fit a preschooler's attention span better, and practice during the preschool years will undoubtedly require considerable parental support.

Sometimes preschool children don't seem ready to take lessons and will resist any practice. We would suggest discontinuing lessons for a little while with the idea that they can be resumed later for another trial.

Even if children resist taking formal lessons or parents have difficulty finding suitable teachers, children can listen to music, play toy musical instruments, and sing or dance to music to learn about rhythm. Preschool dance lessons not only help children to feel comfortable with music but teach physical coordination, concentration skills, and gracefulness as well. When you select a preschool or day-care center for your children, be sure the school provides adequate opportunities for musical participation. Singing, playing rhythmic games, and playing simple musical instruments should be included on their activity list.

THE LOVE OF THE PRINTED WORD

Encouraging a love of reading and writing combines your daughter's need to learn a skill with an emotional closeness to the printed word. It's important to realize that although an important source for pleasure reading is books, computers and the Internet have also opened up a huge source of additional reading. When reading is extended to computer resources, the sense of competence in reading also extends to confidence with computers. Because computers are now an important component of all professional careers, facility and comfort with them are as important today as was the love of books that was typical of the women in our study. Furthermore, boys in the classroom tend to be more interested in computers, which are often connected to math and science competence. Connecting computers to reading and writing will assist girls in enjoying them. Three- and four-year-olds are ready to begin computer use.

You may wonder about the concept of home and school rewards for reading. For those who already love to read, the reading material itself is intrinsically rewarding, and of course no rewards are necessary. However, rewards can encourage the many girls who resist reading. School and library contests and even family rewards for the number of books or pages read can entice the reluctant reader to push her concentration a little more. Large rewards will probably not accomplish more than stickers, stars, honors lists, or pizza points.

Also consider tempting your daughters who are not readers by giving them fast-moving adventure books as gifts. Nancy Drew books have invited girls into reading for several generations. The quality of the literature may be less important than the fun the reading presents, especially initially. Many of the women in the study were inspired by biographies of successful women and read those biographics numerous times. There are more biographies of women available for children than ever before. Check with your librarian to locate appropriate biographies of women that match your daughter's interests and developmental readiness.

Recreational writing can be fun for your daughters. Writing and acting out plays in elementary school, corresponding with pen pals, creative writing, and expressing feelings in journals and diaries are typical interesting outlets for your daughters. Don't be critical of your daughter's early writing. Too much criticism can stifle her creativity before she builds self-confidence. Encourage your daughter to start a class newspaper when she's in elementary school or to join the school newspaper staff in middle or high school. Family newspapers are fun for kids and can easily be integrated into e-mail. Computers make journalism seem very professional to kids. Photographs and interviews can be part of the process. Grandparents and other relatives love them, and they can ease your daughters into the writing habit, which in turn may lead to many successful careers as well as provide important emotional expression for them during childhood and adolescence.

SCOUTING OPPORTUNITIES FOR INDEPENDENCE

Girl Scouts or Scout-like organizations are a good choice for developing skills, confidence, and independence in girls. Although the quality of the Scouting experience may depend a great deal on the leadership of a particular troop, consider that Scouts are an early single-gender activity that may open up leadership and assertiveness opportunities. Girl Scouts gather their own wood and make their own campfires; they hike challenging trails and learn to use tools; they lead sing-alongs and march in parades. They accomplish and achieve without boys making fun of their skills or doing the adventurous jobs for them. Furthermore, Scout leaders are often women of action and good role models of accomplishment.

Earning Girl Scout badges is also an excellent way for girls to learn goal direction and motivation. They can plan tasks, select from a choice of activities, and receive appropriate token rewards (colorful woven badges or, in other groups, beads) for their accomplishments. Furthermore, they are encouraged to develop a wide variety of interests.

On the other hand, with so many women in careers, good leadership is in scarce supply. It isn't as common for mothers to volunteer in community activities as it used to be. Successful mothers who are already overwhelmed may find it easier to send girls to lessons where a paid teacher takes the responsibility for leadership. We would suggest some creative approaches to sharing leadership responsibilities so that you, as a parent, have some specific mother-daughter time reserved to help all girls. If you can co-lead a Scout troop as a team, your share will be appreciated, and each leader will feel less burdened. Your volunteering provides multiple benefits. Not only do you make an important contribution to girls, you will have special bonding opportunities with your daughter, gain status in your daughter's eyes, and can observe your daughter's interactions with peers.

Scouting is pioneering work. It can provide the kind of healthy risk taking within a social setting that your daughters will require in their careers. Girl Scout camps can permit your daughters some independence in environments that emphasize activity rather than parading themselves as fashion icons for the approval of boys. Girl Scouts cross international boundaries and can also afford your daughters the kind of learning and understanding that will help them in careers that require cooperation with people of many different backgrounds. Judging by the omnipresent Girl Scout cookie sales, there are still many active Scouts around, although, sadly, Scouting has all but disappeared in some communities.

In addition to Scouting, religious groups, summer camps, and other all-girls organizations provide environments that encourage independence. You won't know whether your daughter will benefit from such an activity until she's tried.

In short, an all-girls organization seems an ideal practice place for learning many of the skills that pioneering careers require. It will take the mothers and professionals of today to keep Scouting and other all-girls activities growing and changing to meet the expanding needs of our daughters.

SPORTS AND PHYSICAL FITNESS

Although your daughters may not elect to be involved in team sports, it seems important to encourage participation in some sports experiences. Individual sports and physical fitness activities kept up over a lifetime are critical to both physical and mental health. Sometimes girls think they need to choose between being smart, artistic, creative, or athletic. Help them to understand that physical activities should be part of everyone's lifestyle. Of course, it's important that parents model this principle by being involved in physical fitness activities themselves.

Involvement in physical activities should begin during the preschool years. By the time your daughter is three or four, you can practice catching and throwing balls with her, or give her the opportunity to swing a plastic bat or hit a golf ball with a club. Your daughter can shoot baskets into low basketball hoops. Gymnastics, dance, ice skating, in-line skating, bicycling, and swimming are a few of the activities that can begin by age four or five. All these activities give girls the message that sports are fun and are equally available to girls and boys. If your daughter has brothers, they can join in, but don't allow them to let her win just because she is a girl. Giving her and her brothers a balance of winning and losing experiences is important even during their early years. Also, as parents, you can participate in those activities with your children.

When girls are given opportunities to learn physical skills early, they are less likely to be inhibited during adolescence and less likely to worry so much about what others think about their appearance. They are simply too busy playing a game or practicing their skills to think constantly about their appearance. Physical fitness becomes a natural, healthy way of life. Even girls who may be poorly coordinated can improve their coordination, and thus participate in social activities that involve physical fitness.

By adolescence, sports and fitness participation should feel as natural, necessary, and comfortable for girls as it does for most boys. In addition to the health benefits of physical exercise, girls will learn to cope with cooperation and competition. They'll also learn the resilience and self-discipline that so many women in our study referred to. Furthermore, they'll more easily find a social neighborhood. If they don't fit in with the popular kids, they'll fit in with the kids who like to go biking or are on the track or swim team. Two very important fringe benefits are that exercise helps to fight depression, and that if sports are a natural part of growing up, girls are likely to feel more comfortable with their bodies.

Despite all the benefits of exercise, you may find your teenage daughters prefer being couch potatoes. You may indeed find them watching soap operas for hours and worrying about their weight and appearance for the remaining hours. Their peer group may discourage exercise or sports; societal pressure during those years can be both extensive and intense.

Family hiking, biking, canoeing, skiing, or camping trips may help if you can convince your teens to join you. If not, search for summer programs for teens that are physical-fitness-oriented. If your daughters find a group of friends who enjoy outdoor physical activities, they'll soon enjoy them as well and may be willing to join you in the future.

One caution relative to unwilling teens and sports is that if you over-praise your daughter about her abilities in order to encourage her to join a sports team, your encouragement may backfire. If you tell your daughter she'd probably be a star of the volleyball team if she'd just give it a try, she is unlikely to take the risk of trying. Furthermore, if she does join, she may experience your overpraise as pressure, and it may cause her to be more fearful. It's probably better to encourage her to join a sport for the fun of it, perhaps pointing out that the team travels to other schools or even has social gatherings and thus may give her opportunities to meet other fun kids. Although it's good for girls to join new activities even if their friends don't, if your daughter is especially hesitant, you might mention another girl she knows and likes who does belong to the team. If you suggest she ask one of her present "couch potato" friends to join her on the team, that could work, but it's more likely not to. Her friend may convince her not to join, or if they both join with a negative attitude, you may find they both soon drop out.

If you're a friend of your daughter's friend's parents, you may wish to join together to encourage your daughters. Once you succeed in getting your daughters to join, remind them they need to be committed to the team for the season because a team depends on all its members.

School teams may be quite competitive; therefore, not all girls will make the teams. Consider intramural teams, recreation centers, Girls and Boys Clubs, and Y or church teams as other alternatives. They can be just as much fun, and usually everyone is allowed to play. Again, the fun of meeting teens from other schools and communities may be an important enticement to your daughters.

If your daughter is especially asocial or intellectual, playing on sports teams can really help her overcome her isolation. Whether girls are too social or not social enough, sports facilitates much more than physical fitness.

PRACTICING POLITICS

Don't dissuade your daughters from running for president of the student council because you remember it as a popularity contest, or because she claims it is just that. Even if she loses, and some kids must lose, there is much to be learned from the experience. Even when Suzanne Daniels lost repeatedly, her parents encouraged her to try again—and now she's a state senator. Giving talks, rallying friends to support her, and even nominating herself if she believes she'd like to try the job are all healthy for her assertiveness. The applause when she wins or her acceptance of losing after making an effort are healthy experiences in building confidence and resilience. If she's afraid to risk running for president at first, even being secretary, despite the gender stereotyping, will provide her with a good initial experience.

Also help your daughter to think seriously about what the role of representing others means within the school environment. Instead of the overused parents' and kids' message that student councils don't accomplish much, help her to understand that creative leadership within the school setting can make the school a better place. Assist her in developing campaign strategies as well as realistic goals for her participation in student government. Even planning dances and homecoming parades are full of confidence-building and organizational opportunities.

Let your daughter know that most administrators are open to suggestions that fall within the power of student populations. Creative student leaders can often get their voices heard in local newspapers, can ameliorate the drinking and drug problems in many schools, can support school building projects, and can even expand extracurricular activities or student lounges. Remember how television producer Denise Dennison led her class in a campaign to permit girls to take shop class. Explain to your daughter that political change is always slow and that it involves debating differences of opinion. Revising rules and regulations is cumbersome at every level of government. Schools are a good beginning for understanding the democratic process and teaching girls purposefulness and independence. Empower your daughter early to make small improvements in her world.

School can be a training ground for your daughter's future decisions about political participation. Women have made huge inroads into government compared to a generation ago. Nevertheless, this country and the world need your daughter's leadership. Even if she doesn't become the first woman president of the United States, it won't hurt her to start thinking that it's possible. We do have a female secretary of state and very powerful women in many state and national government positions.

OPPORTUNITIES FOR SHOWMANSHIP

Even many "good little girls" often crave attention. Certainly many rebellious adolescents seem to have a voracious need to be noticed. It seems fairly normal for adolescents to feel as if their every word or action is being observed by others. Drama, debate, and forensics are ideal experiences for appropriate attention getting. All three of these activities combine helping girls to feel smart while teaching them the important skills of presenting themselves to a public for both entertainment and judgment. There is risk taking involved. On the other hand, all of these activities require effort, self-discipline, and learning new skills. These activities are especially good for girls who may have "lost their voices" during the preadolescent, middle-school period.

With school drama, however, there is often a problem. Many girls try out for the school play, but very few get parts. Those who don't are often quickly discouraged. Consider encouraging your local recreation department to initiate a drama group for teens. It can include visiting the theater as well as acting and designing sets and lighting. It's a wonderful way to keep teens interested and busy. If there's an adult drama group in the community, its members may be willing to coach the teens and even include some of them in selected plays. Sometimes there are drama groups for young children, and your teenage daughters may be able to assist and help teach the younger children. Local repertory theater companies may also offer drama opportunities for children and teens.

If your daughters enjoy drama, encourage it as a skill that will be helpful for all careers. It would be better not to encourage every girl who thinks she's a budding actress to aspire to Broadway theater. Actresses, even very talented ones, often spend years waiting on tables while waiting for their lucky break. Only a tiny percentage make it into this glamorous and hardworking lifestyle. Your daughters are likely to admire the glamour without realizing the hard work and lack of opportunity. You may feel some conflict between stealing your daughter's dreams and being realistic, but despite all the precautions, participation in elementary-, middle-, or high-school drama is mainly an excellent experience to encourage. If girls can gain skills and confidence from participation and use those skills in the many other careers that will be open for them, they will undoubtedly be better off.

Debate, forensics, or speech clubs are typically open to all students in middle and high school. Although they provide excellent learning experiences, debate is selected more frequently by boys. Girls may fear the judging or losing involved in competition. They may not like the "brain" label that is often attached to such intellectual contests. Debate coaches might attract more girls if practice debates were held in social studies or science classes to provide a trial experience for girls who might not come to an after-school activity. All-girls debate teams might also spark some interest. Debate team travel to other schools could be punctuated with some socializing to entice girls to join. Forensics and debate classes for credit could provide some school time for the extensive preparation required for good debating. Women in politics and law could be invited to visit the school to talk about the importance of high-school debate, forensics, and speech for their particular professions.

Most important, parents should encourage their daughters to become involved by showing their own interest in debate topics and activities. It's crucial to question yourself about subtle personal worries that your daughter may be less popular or be labeled as too "brainy" if she joins intellectual clubs and activities. If you have those feelings, your daughter may be sensing that you're holding on to an old-fashioned definition of a girl.

Debate provides an excellent opportunity for your daughter to learn assertiveness. Don't help her to back away from this risk-taking opportunity. The assertiveness she gains will help her achieve in whatever career she chooses, especially law, government, or business.

ACTIVE GIRLS ARE MORE INTERESTING

Girls who are engaged in interesting activities have more to talk about, more to share, and develop more confidence. Whether it's art, dance, diving, in-line skating, 4-H, or religious activities, they're receiving the kind of stimulation that activates them and gives them sensible control over their lives. They have a variety of healthy ways to spend their time. They learn to plan and balance their lives and learn important skills for balancing family and careers in the future. And they have fun in the process. They find people or groups of adults and youth who naturally share their interests. This, too, prepares them for the normal socialization of adulthood. They will be less pressured by teen norms based on girl-boy relations, alcohol, or drugs.

Girls who have few interests are in temporary trouble. Soap opera fantasy, sex-oriented fashion magazines, and films will move in to fill the vacuum. Pleasing boys and staying thin may monopolize their thoughts. They'll shower for hours and endlessly do and redo their makeup. They'll lie on their beds and listen to music for days. If the current fad represents devil worship or violence or a mind-controlling cult, take the behavior seriously and get help. If their music is only romantic, you can breathe more easily and consider their enjoyment of it normal. However, if it preoccupies them entirely, it is a problem. Some is normal; too much may be symptomatic of depression, loneliness, or a lack of confidence.

Most adolescent girls go through some strange transitional development. You won't need to toss out every CD, poster, or magazine to get them back. However, if the material your daughter is listening to or reading is too extreme, we do suggest you take a stand. Let her know you've listened to the lyrics or read the material and that you don't approve. If it's really inappropriate, you do have the right to toss it, even if she's purchased it with her own money. She'll call it censorship; you can call it parenting. However, you, too, will need balance. If you become too restrictive, she'll fight you in the name of independence and rebellion, and you may lose more than you gain.

Many adolescents spend a considerable amount of time talking about fashion. After all, there is a legitimate reason to be interested in the fashion world. It offers many careers. Consider that two women in our study, Helen Gurley Brown* (former editor of *Cosmopolitan*) and Kathleen Olds* (former editor of *Glamour*), were encouraged in their interests in fashion by their mothers. If your daughters are interested in dress design, the clothing business, marketing, or media, fashion can be very important. If you find them spending too much time looking at themselves in the mirror or scanning fashion magazines, however, try to redirect their interest toward real-world applications. Perhaps they can find a mentor in fashion design or visit a college that has such programs. Needlecraft, sewing, or designing clothes can be creative outlets for your daughters. Programs through 4-H encourage skilled creation of clothing. There are so many ways they can channel that interest and receive appropriate encouragement. Although making appearance central to your daughter's thinking can be unhealthy, help her to see real-world applications of her fascination with clothing rather than negating her interest. There are many potential careers open to talented businesswomen in the fashion industry. And if your daughter develops good writing skills, there may be opportunities to write for fashion magazines.

Because positive activities are so important to your daughter's development, it isn't a good idea to withdraw them as punishments. You'll do your daughter a great disservice by taking gymnastics away because she hasn't completed her homework. Parents often come for counseling with depressed and rebellious daughters who've had all their interests and activities barred because of rule infractions. What these parents don't realize is that in taking these positive activities away, they've also removed all opportunities to build a positive self-concept. Only social privileges should be forfeited for this kind of disobedience, and it's not even a good idea to take too many of those away. In Chapter 2 we emphasized the importance of staying in the coach position instead of becoming the judge. Although sometimes that becomes difficult and rebellious adolescents can get out of control, make every effort not to remove the very activities that keep your daughter positively engaged.

If your children have few interests, there are many ways to expand them. If they are preschool- or school-age, sharing your interests often encourages their involvement. Engaged and interested adults are role models and partners for the development of interests. Involving them will require your own engagement in activities. You may wish to retrieve some of your childhood interests to share with your daughters; for example, your children may be fascinated by your childhood stamp or coin collection or even your old doll collection if you had the foresight to keep it.

At any age, but especially during adolescence, children's interests expand if they have a peer group with similar interests. Classes and interest-centered camps can be very effective for starting your daughter networking with kids who are active and interesting.

When girls are hesitant about challenging themselves or becoming involved in activities because they may be perfectionistic and fear making mistakes, a good approach to teaching them motivation, perseverance, and self-discipline is to suggest they begin an activity in which they're not particularly talented so they experience real challenge. The fringe benefit of such an activity is that they don't need to set high expectations for themselves. Even if they learn to skate or play the violin in an average way, it will be an accomplishment.

TELEVISION: TEACHING TOOL OR TREACHERY?

Television has the potential to introduce your daughters to a multitude of interests. If they are watching the many positive offerings that television can provide, and if their viewing is limited to reasonable amounts of time, television can make an important contribution to your daughters' lives. However, there is so much on television that is gender-stereotyped and so much to tempt your daughter into the world where girls and women are romantic fools, brainless, or only sexual objects that it seems television is in many ways sabotaging the feminist movement. Even on family shows, mothers are typically portrayed as aggressive ogres married to playful and fun fathers who sabotage mother's power in an alliance with the children. They are not good role models for your daughters.

On the other hand, television now has many excellent and knowledgeable news anchors and program hosts who serve as role models for intelligent involvement. They ask probing questions of prestigious people and powerful world leaders. Furthermore, their combination of intelligence and charm will correct some girls' mistaken notion that pretty women are not smart and vice versa. My own television experiences with Katie Couric, Jane Pauley, and Anne Curry have been most inspiring, and surely Oprah Winfrey, Rosie O'Donnell, and many others are superb television role models for your daughters.

Very few of the successful women in our study watched more than two hours of television a night—data supporting the conclusion that it's not healthy for your daughters to become couch potatoes. To prevent your daughters from falling into the all-night television routine, keep the television in the living or family room for family viewing. At least you'll know where she is, and she'll be less likely to use television as an escape from homework or sleep. The same advice holds for computers. The Internet can be fascinating and fun, but when your daughter is in her room "surfing the Net," you won't know what she's doing or with whom she's communicating. If she's in the family room, your curiosity about her interests will seem much less like snooping to you and your daughter.

We need intelligent women to produce and take leading roles in television. The media has a powerful impact on our society, and girls who are interested in television and the Internet in challenging and exciting ways are learning the skills that will provide opportunities for future leadership. However, hours of watching the shopping channels, the soap operas, or cartoons are unlikely to foster the leadership we'd like to encourage.

VALUING ALONENESS AND INDEPENDENCE

Relationships have traditionally been of great importance to girls and women. The importance of other people to girls' self-concept is both a strength and a weakness. For all careers, strength in working with others fosters collaboration and sensitivity to the needs of co-workers and the organization. The flip side of the importance of social relationships is that girls and women are more likely to depend on other people and may be afraid to step out of a group to accomplish something unique. Both men and women seem to be less accepting of independent women than they are of independent men. Independent women are often described as competitive, lonely, or aggressive, all with a negative connotation.

It isn't necessary to force your daughter to be antisocial to give her the confidence to be independent. However, it is important not to become worried and anxious if your daughter enjoys spending time alone engrossed in her own interests. It's very important not to describe this being alone as negative or strange, as many parents and teachers do. The teachers in our study were a particularly social group as children. As a result, they may worry more about a girl in school who is a loner and more independent than most. Their worries may be conveyed to parents, and eventually such combined adult anxiety about such very healthy independent behavior will convey the message that being alone is abnormal. This would be much less likely to happen for a boy who loves to make model rockets or practice throwing a ball into a hoop by himself. Similar behavior on the part of a girl is often labeled shy, strange, and lonely.

Preserve some time alone for you and your children separately, beginning in the preschool years. Also allow for informal play. Time to cultivate one's imagination or do one's own work can become a comfortable tradition. When too many friends call and visit, encourage your daughter to explain to them that she's working on a project or doing something with the family. Girls who are constantly involved in social activities are often at a loss for something to do because they are unaccustomed to being with themselves. By adolescence they may find themselves bored or depressed if they're not socially occupied. By adulthood, they will certainly fear taking on the challenge of pioneering professions that may place them with few friends. Executives can feel very lonely at the top, and dependent women may fear the loneliness if they've not learned independence.

On the other hand, our study includes some very social girls who grew up to be very successful and independent women. Cultivate independence in your daughters, but be sensitive to the individual differences among children.

A FAMILY SURROUNDED BY MUSIC

Louise Andrews
Orchestral Musician

It is not a surprise to find a grand piano at the focal point of the Andrews family's living room. Music, family, and church have all coexisted as far back as Louise can recall. She can visualize her whole family singing enthusiastically as her dad played one of his many instruments. He never read music, and the whole family were only amateurs, but mother, father, aunts, and uncles all played, and everyone sang. By age four Louise's dad had taught her to play the ukulele. She played a whole repertoire of Disney and popular songs using the chords she learned from her dad, although she certainly could not read a note.

Louise desperately wanted music lessons. Her brother, five years older, played the violin, and by age six Louise wanted to play one, too. Small violins weren't available at the time, and Louise's parents didn't have the money to buy a small instrument even if they had been. Furthermore, teachers refused to take such young children for lessons. Louise's parents thought that tap dancing might be a good temporary substitute to assuage Louise's thirst for music lessons, and Louise loved the tap lessons, but they were not enough.

When she turned eight Louise began taking piano lessons for fifty cents an hour from a wonderful woman who came to their home to teach her and her brother. When this teacher discovered Louise's unusual talent, Louise became the center of her teaching. For example, Louise started with a book called *Teaching Little Fingers to Play,* which was supposed to be a book for early beginners and should have lasted for several months. After the first week, both Louise and her brother played the whole book. In astonishment, the teacher turned to her mother and said, "I'm sorry, Mrs. Andrews. I know these books are expensive, but we already must get your children the next book." Soon Louise was learning chords and theory and progressing rapidly through one book after the other. Each time she'd say to her adoring teacher, "Gee, I don't think I can do this," and each time her teacher would respond, "Why don't you go ahead and try?" At the end of Louise's lesson the teacher would take extra time to play duets with Louise, and soon she was playing complex piano pieces. Louise found she was accompanying sing-alongs with friends and at church, and she could play most anything.

Simultaneously Louise had also begun taking fifteen-minute violin lessons at school every week. After a short time, the string students could play in a small orchestra. However, by high school Louise expected to discontinue her music lessons, which were already such a large part of her life, and prepare to become a secretary, because she was an expert typist (she had begun typing lessons at age seven and had won multiple typing contests). Although Louise recalls that early testing in elementary school showed she was highly intelligent, her parents didn't share that information with her at the time, and it never occurred to her that she might go on to college. Although she and her brother had been expert spellers, and indeed she was even a city champion speller once, learning and education were for the love of learning rather than building blocks toward a higher education or a career.

Louise's dad had only an eighth-grade education and was a welder. Louise's mother had graduated from high school and attended a year of normal school so she could teach, but she devoted her life to enriching her children's lives with learning and music. Louise's parents had made the deliberate decision that her dad would supply the bread for the family table and her mother would economize in many ways at home so she could be there for the children and teach them. Her dad often worked overtime, and the children hardly saw him during the week. However, when he was at home, whether it was late at night or on the weekend, he was very available and loved playing with the children. Louise remembers her family as a close-knit one, involved in gardening, checkers, and card playing, including pinochle. The backyard was filled with other kids, and when it was too hot to stay outside, they'd go in the house and play chess or Monopoly. All the neighborhood families knew each other, and it felt safe because the parents always looked out for each other's kids.

In high school Louise's life changed. She had expected to stop all lessons, as her older brother had, but somehow she was signed up for violin in school anyway. She didn't much like the high-school string teacher, Ms. Sawyer, who was very hard on her and tried to correct all her bad musical habits. Louise recalls that this teacher would "jump on her" for every little mistake, and she felt endlessly "picked on" and humiliated. She was definitely thinking she should quit, but her brother urged her to continue a little longer. By this time the teacher was providing challenging music unlike anything Louise had learned before, including Bach's Brandenburg concertos. The complex music enticed her. Also, she joined a larger and better string ensemble, and suddenly the teacher became more supportive (or perhaps Louise was just getting better at playing and perceived it that way). Ironically, that high-school string teacher, whom at first Louise despised, became a very important and influential mentor for her.

Louise would often assist Ms. Sawyer in teaching other children. Once while she was helping other students, Ms. Sawyer suggested that Louise expand her variety of instruments and introduced Louise to the viola.

She never had her own viola, but she enjoyed playing the viola that belonged to the school, and later, when she auditioned for the Eastman School of Music, she chose the viola as her preferred instrument.

By the time Louise had graduated from high school, she thought she might like to be a music teacher like Ms. Sawyer. She wasn't absolutely certain, however, because the school administration didn't seem to appreciate Ms. Sawyer. Although Louise didn't understand the political dynamics that were taking place, it seemed to her that Ms. Sawyer wanted to facilitate inspiring experiences for her students but was being frustrated in her attempts to do so. While Louise could see the appeal of teaching as a career, she was also fearful of the limitations.

Louise never took private music lessons in high school until Ms. Sawyer announced to a group of her more talented musicians that the Detroit Conservatory of Music was going to offer a free class for talented musicians, and at the conclusion some of them would be awarded a scholarship to attend the conservatory during their senior year. Louise was one of three students who won. Thus she received her first high-level private lessons from the conductor of the Windsor Symphony Orchestra. He also let her borrow a variety of music she couldn't have afforded to purchase, and she was introduced for the first time to a great repertoire of serious music.

Louise got almost all A's throughout school. There was never any grade or confidence decline during her middle-school years. She was younger than most kids in her class because she had entered school at age four, but that never seemed to bother her. She recalls some very special teachers during her middle-school years and especially adored her seventh-grade teacher, who somehow managed a class of forty-five students in two grades and also introduced Louise to her love of poetry and literature. In eighth grade, Mr. Paul prodded her to enter and win the citywide spelling bee even though she was nervous about participating. He also introduced the class to algebra, which Louise loved, just because he thought the class should have more challenging work. Louise recalls that she was hesitant about taking on challenges, but her teachers would encourage her, and her successes gradually helped her feel more intellectually confident.

In high school Louise found that her older brother's clear expectation that she must prepare for college conflicted with her own expectation that she would prepare to become a secretary in the business world. Her brother, whom she so admired, was absolutely appalled that she thought she would be happy sitting at a secretary's desk for a few years and then being a housewife. He insisted she schedule a program that would include college preparation, along with the program that would prepare her for the secretarial career that she believed was expected of all girls, and a third program that would allow her to take both the string and choral music she so loved. As a result, her high-school schedule included typing, stenography, music theory, violin performance, music arrangement, four years of Latin, honors English, honors history, chemistry, biology, algebra, geometry, and advanced math. She simply enrolled in almost everything, although she recalls being disappointed because she had no room in her schedule for physics. Despite her schedule, her grades remained high, and except for geometry and gym, she managed all A's and graduated third in her class. Louise does recall, and wants other teen girls to know, that on some days she cried because chemistry was so hard. Although she never quit, she admits that there were days in which she wanted to give up in desperation. She also felt socially isolated from many of her class-mates and thought that some resented her success.

From childhood on, church choir and religious activities had domi-nated her outside time. Her musical ability in church encouraged church teachers to involve her in almost every activity, including sum-mer Bible school, Sunday school, and, of course, every choir group they had in the church. Louise had perfect pitch, and the choir groups appre-ciated her help. She reported that in high school she spent twenty-seven hours per week involved in music, including practice, lessons, and musi-cal groups.

Louise attended the Eastman School of Music on a partial scholar-ship to become a music teacher. She was not yet that advanced on the viola, but she played piano, organ, violin, and sang as well. Her dad was unemployed because Detroit was having many economic problems, but despite that, her parents saved so she could continue on to her second year at Eastman. She remembers hearing her parents' friend say to her dad, "Why are you killing yourself and working so hard and saving for your daughter when you know she'll just get married and have chil-dren?" Her dad's reply was, "What happens if her husband dies and she has to support her children?"

When Louise decided not to return to Eastman, her parents were astonished. However, Louise found her private viola teacher at East-man disappointing. She wanted more help than he was accustomed to giving, because he usually worked with more advanced students. Louise found her academic program difficult as well and lost confidence in herself. Much to her family's initial disappointment, Louise returned home to Michigan to continue her study. When she transferred to the state college, she lost a scholarship she had originally received, but the school assured her that if she could prove herself academically and also play in the orchestra, she might be able to earn another. Louise double-majored in German (she loved foreign languages) and music, proved she could maintain an A average in her academic area, and earned a full scholarship for her remaining time in college. She lived at home and needed only transportation and money for books. Louise played every job she could get, from nightclubs to light opera to substituting in orchestras to earn money for her expenses. She had an inspiring viola teacher (only about six years older than she), who also played for a symphony orchestra. He remained her coach even after she graduated from college.

Louise played and substituted in small orchestras at first and then had her first audition for an orchestra in Canada. In those times, tryouts were on a stage in full view of the judges. She was later told that there was a very anti-American attitude in Canada at that time, which perhaps explained why they hired a Canadian instead. Her next audition was in Baltimore, and her parents drove her there to provide support. She thought she had performed quite well, but at the end of the day she was informed that they believed she lacked experience. Discouraged again, she wondered where she would get the experience if no one would hire her. Although it could have been a bleak trip home, her parents turned it into a family vacation and tried to be encouraging. Their attitude was, "If you don't get in one place, you'll get in another," but at that time Louise seriously doubted their wisdom and, even more seriously, doubted her ability.

Two of her friends contacted her about an audition for a violist in their orchestra. Furthermore, the orchestra was having some financial problems, and some of its members were leaving. This looked like an opportunity for her. Her friend Fred provided her with a list of pieces they were likely to use. Louise had played all but one, a Bartók concerto, which he said they would surely ask her to perform. She borrowed the score from the library and mentally studied it repeatedly. When she got to her audition and faced the conductor, she actually played the piece for the first time. According to Fred, she played it superbly. When the conductor asked if she had done the piece with an orchestra before, she had to admit she hadn't. She finally was offered her first contract for $6,500 a year, a salary that even then was extremely low. Louise met her husband, Robert, in the orchestra, and they wished to be married, but suddenly found themselves in the throes of a very bitter strike. There was no contract and a hostile stand-off. They postponed their wedding, and she and Robert walked the picket line together.

When Louise was asked whether she found many women in her orchestra when she first joined it, her answer was surprising. Apparently the orchestra realized that they could keep costs down by hiring married couples who together could make a living, but whose separate salaries were quite low. Thus it was known as a couples orchestra—one of several orchestras that used this approach to both accommodate couples and cut costs. Most other major orchestras at the time had very few women, and at some orchestras there were even rumors that the conductors propositioned women who were auditioning. It was even implied that the only way a woman was going to get a job in an orchestra was to sleep with the man on the podium. Today auditions are blind and held behind a screen to prevent racial, age, or gender discrimination, but Louise acknowledges that to some extent the judges often know whom they're listening to anyway, and some discrimination probably continues. Louise doubts, however, that sexual harassment is still an issue in orchestral selection.

Louise and Robert, now in their early fifties, continued to play in the same orchestra for many years. Because her husband plays a less-common instrument, he doesn't work full time, and Louise has played full time for many years. She'd like her husband to have the opportunity she's had and has indicated that she would be willing to leave her orchestra job, which she loves, in order to follow him if he were able to find a better opportunity.

When Louise was asked about what made the greatest contribution to her career, she shared the following: "At the risk of sounding like a paid commercial, I was fortunate to have a strong, supportive family. Originally farmers, my parents believed in hard work, honesty, and integrity. My grandparents provided similar models for me. I was continually praised for my talent and discipline in academics and music. Each of my parents spent time with me every day—reading or cooking with my mom, gardening with my dad, or making music together. My older brother was close and advised me. Family dinners with other relatives usually resulted in musical jam sessions and hours of card games and chats. That strong family ethic sustains me still."

CAPTURING THE "PULSE OF YOUNG WOMEN"

Helen Gurley Brown*

Former Editor in Chief of Cosmopolitan *Magazine,*
Currently Editor in Chief of Cosmopolitan *International Editions*

With one year of post-high-school training as a stenographer and typist, Helen Gurley Brown emerged from anonymity to author her best-selling book *Sex and the Single Girl* and become editor in chief of Hearst's *Cosmopolitan,* turning it into a best-selling magazine, which would subsequently have thirty-two international editions. Her creation, "That Cosmopolitan Girl," was a beautiful, sexy, yet independent woman who was very successful in attracting and pleasing men. Ironically, Helen's philosophy of life was both feminist and antifeminist in the same breath.

Helen believes her writing reflected that which was "true and made sense to her." Mainly she views herself as realistic and honest, and she considers her solid common sense the result of needing to cope with a difficult childhood realistically. She states, "There was no time in my life to do drugs or to be spoiled." As to the central role that sex played in Helen's writing, she describes that, too, as true and honest and a reflection of what women really feel. She wrote about sex because she believed "it was delicious, pleasant, important, and always felt good" to her, and her writing reflected those authentic feelings.

One wonders how such success can come to a young woman who was born in the 1920s to traditional parents who themselves were in a marital relationship that was cordial but not loving. Helen was a second daughter and a second very difficult birth for her mother. Helen's mother was trained and worked as a teacher; she would have liked to have continued to teach school, but her husband, as was typical of professional men of the time, would not permit her to have a career. Helen identified with her mother, whom she remembers as having a "splendid brain" and a great interest in fashion. She was very feminine and sewed elegant clothes for her daughters. She hand-smocked Helen's dresses, "a painstaking process you don't see anymore that involved embroidery needles, silk threads, and lots of fussing." She was professional enough to have hung out a shingle had the times allowed it. Helen's dad bought her mother a sewing machine to sew for her daughters, but it was not to be used for a career.

A characteristic of Helen's that she does not attribute to her mother is charm. Helen's charm and personality came, she believes, either from her father or as a way of compensating for her perception that she was not particularly pretty during her high-school years. She describes herself as having had "terminal acne," which was treated by a doctor twice weekly. Although Helen was popular with girlfriends, she didn't attract much attention from boys, and knew she'd have to make up for her "mousy" appearance by using her intelligence and personality.

Helen was an excellent student throughout school and a good writer. Dance was important in her life, and she practiced consistently, taking dance lessons from her elementary-school years through high school; her mother sewed beautiful costumes for her dance recitals. Perhaps the years of dancing also helped foster in her mind the importance of fashion, beauty, attention, and applause. As an adolescent, Helen was religious and actively involved in choral music through her church choir. In middle school she considered herself both shy and a show-off; she wore long evening dresses at parties but remembers herself as too shy to have fun. She received considerable and welcome attention by writing and performing in school plays, but in high school, to her disappointment, she couldn't get parts in the plays. An important source of audience attention disappeared. However, she was president of the Scholarship Society and World Friendship Club, active in debate, successful in writing competitions, and valedictorian of her graduating class. It was in high school that she "became a personality" and further developed her intelligence to compensate for self-consciousness about the acne. In her senior year the student council president asked her to the prom "at the last minute" because he thought, "Gurley can dance, and she can take care of herself." A successful, happy prom resulted in a nice romance that lasted a year.

Helen's remembrances of her relationship with her dad are positive, although she believes he would have preferred having a son. "He was a good sport about it and never made me feel bad about being another daughter," Helen reports. Ira Gurley was a wonderfully accessible playmate to his daughters, taking them many places, going on rides with them at the state fair, reading to them, and telling marvelously funny stories, including one about removing the sand from the Sahara Desert one grain at a time. She also recalls her dad helping her and her sister enter contests, several of which Helen won. Helen recollects her dad's warmth, her sitting affectionately on his lap, and a relationship full of love.

Helen's brief, loving relationship with her father ended tragically when Helen was ten. His life was cut short when the door of an elevator slammed shut on him as he jumped into it, killing him and leaving Helen with only the memories of a charming, smart, and fun-loving father who was a success story in the making. Her dad had attended law school and then entered the state legislature. He was assistant game and fish commissioner and earned a high salary for those days ($25 per week). Her father was also popular, and Helen thinks he would have become secretary of state if not for his tragic accident.

Although Helen's memories of her dad were positive, she recalls her parents' marriage as being far from warm. Helen's mother had married Helen's dad at the request or insistence of her own parents. Her mother actually broke off a relationship with another man she would have preferred marrying because her parents viewed Helen's lawyer father as a more suitable mate for her. Helen didn't think her mother ever really loved her father. She didn't consider her parents very compatible, nor did she believe that they had a very satisfying sex life. She believes that her highly intelligent mother must have felt resentful when her father voted against women's suffrage. She remembers her mother's complaints about not being allowed to work. Helen even recalls a comment her mother made about her dad's accidental death suggesting that his rush to jump into the elevator while the door was closing was probably only to "show off to two women." Helen doesn't know if that's what really happened, but the comment surely suggests some problems and resentment in her parents' relationship.

Family disaster struck again when Helen was fifteen. Her sister contracted polio and was to be an invalid in a wheelchair for the rest of her life. Despite a situational depression, her mother carried out her parenting responsibilities with dedication and commitment, continuing to drive Helen to dancing classes, sew for her, and make every effort to permit her to have normal high-school years. She never expected Helen to take on adult responsibilities before she was ready; however, after graduation from high school, Helen felt obligated to earn money to help both her sister and mother. They could ill afford college, and a year of secretarial school to learn typing and shorthand seemed the most expedient way for Helen to make the necessary financial contribution to her family. Helen dedicated herself to taking care of her sister and her mother.

Helen appreciates and admires her mother. She gave Helen a love of beauty and a good eye for fashion (she would have liked Helen to become a fashion designer), encouraged her daughter's intelligence, and permitted her independence, despite personal sacrifice. Although her mother gave her the message that most mothers gave during her generation, that is, to save sex for marriage, Helen appreciates also that her mother "didn't mess up sex" for her with a lot of negative sanctions and prohibitions. Helen recalls that when she was nine and visiting her grandmother, her uncle, only twelve, was sexually interested in her. He pursued her all summer and finally persuaded her to pull down her pants and show him her "cock." She obliged and remembers his unsuccessful attempt to have sex with her, which she recalls as "not a bad experience" and not at all repulsive or scary, as many children might. After several years of feeling fearful and guilty for not saying anything about the incident, she finally recounted it to her mother. Helen was pretty sure her mother did not like sex, but she accepted the story and didn't criticize Helen or Helen's young uncle (her own brother). Today such action would likely be reported as sexual abuse, with all the resulting social service repercussions and investigations. From Helen's point of view, she is only thankful that her mother "didn't tamper with my sexual experiences in any bad way" and never "screwed up my sex life."

Helen's adult success stories are well known. Her first secretarial position paid her $6 a week. She moved from secretarial work to copywriting after winning a writing contest, although she didn't at that time have any idea about what a copywriter did. She authored her best-selling book mainly out of fear that she would lose her copywriting job. She tried unsuccessfully to start a magazine, then accepted when Hearst offered her a year's salary to revitalize a flailing *Cosmopolitan*. Her appreciation for the support and encouragement provided by her husband, David, "a prince of a man," was conveyed strongly in her interview.

Certainly Helen Gurley Brown's life provides a model of how to triumph over difficulty with hard work, dedication, perseverance, and integrity. The difficult question for parents may be in accepting Helen's message. They may debate whether in capturing the "pulse of young women," Helen fostered positive self-fulfillment for young women or created more problems for many young female adults who already put too much value on appearance and the importance of men's attentions. Helen contends that her critics never actually read *Cosmopolitan*. While her books and *Cosmopolitan* always stressed the importance of looking as good as you can (and doing whatever you needed to do to get there) as well as the importance of having a man in your life to love and have sex with, Helen claims her main thrust was not toward being "dependent on men's approval and admiration" but to be enticing enough to attract a man in a skewed population (more eligible women than men) while at the same time developing your full potential in a career that could give you a good life with a man—or without a permanent man if necessary. Helen says her credo is Freudian: Work and love are equally important for a woman as well as for a man.

CHAPTER 6

See Jane Win, and Other Formative Experiences

Part 1: Findings

POSITIVE EXPERIENCES

Competition, Awards, Exhibitions, Elections, Publications The women in the study were asked to indicate the most positive and negative experiences they remembered from their childhoods. Figure 6.1 shows the experiences remembered as most positive. Competition was chosen by more than a third of the women as an important positive experience. It was selected most by the total group as well as by every career group. Furthermore, four of the other frequently mentioned positive experiences—awards in a talent field, exhibitions of work at school, elective office, and publication of written work—are often based on competition or comparisons. Thus, of the categories of positive experiences selected by these successful women, five involved competition. Obviously many of these women were highly competitive. This is a striking reminder of how important competition is in the educational process.

Some of the women declared their feelings about competition with pride, while others barely whispered them, as if they were ashamed of expressing their feelings. Amy Fox, a business executive, remembered: "I thrived on competition. I was valedictorian of my class. In elementary

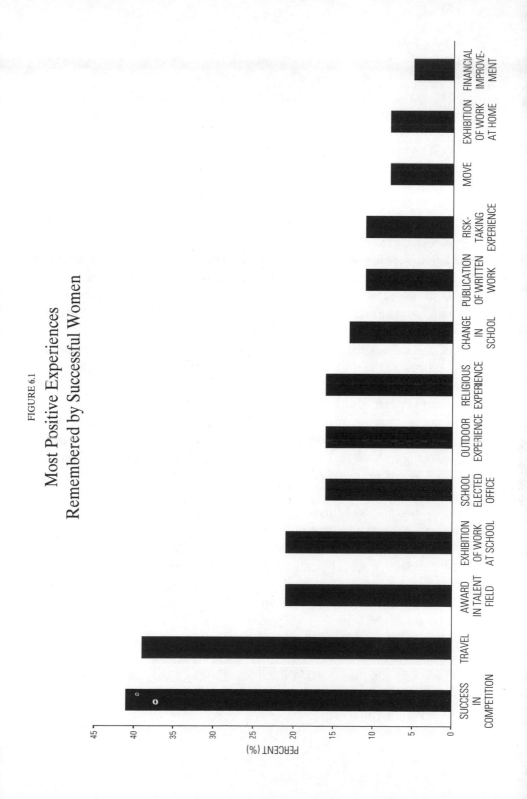

FIGURE 6.1

Most Positive Experiences
Remembered by Successful Women

school I won an essay contest and read my essay on the radio. In high school I won a writing contest and, as a result, I was given an opportunity to be a regular reporter for the local newspaper."

Dr. Sandra Calvin, an environmental engineer, recalls: "I was motivated by competition. I competed in sports and music. I couldn't even imagine playing volleyball without keeping score. The competition of vocal and instrumental placements spurred me on. I wanted to see who was best, and it never bothered me to lose as long as I could improve."

Janet Winters, an assistant superintendent of instruction at a large school district, described her family's very competitive environment. Both of her parents were athletes when they were growing up, and she recalls they used to play cutthroat chess. The public relations director of a health care agency recalled winning several acting and speech tournament trophies and speed-skating competitions. The defeats were exciting, too. She actually raced against Bonnie Blair, an Olympic gold medalist. Although she lost, her comment was, "That was okay by me. She was *fast!*"

Dr. Patricia Robertson always loved science, but when she was a semifinalist in the Westinghouse science program and saw that 80 percent of the winners at the famous awards dinner were boys, she knew she was different and that she would be a scientist. Harpist Sheri Rand would get "competition nerves" and watch her hands tremble on the harp. One day she decided that nobody really cared if she looked nervous or not, so she had better stop being nervous. Somehow that insight cured her of her trembling, and she relaxed and decided the competition was fun.

Scientist Jessica Moreno had this to say: "People have said I'm competitive. I am always surprised because I don't see myself as competitive, but you don't get to this point if you're not competitive. I do know I intimidate people. I don't try to. Usually I'm so overwhelmed with self-doubt that when people think I'm intimidating, it astounds me. I'm competitive with myself. I want to meet or exceed my own goals. I don't judge myself by how I stack up to other people except for a marker as to maybe where I should be. If someone has done something, and they are at a similar place in their career as I am, I think, 'Gee, maybe that's where I should be as well.' I don't want to say I have to beat that person. I want to live up to my potential. I always realize that there are a lot of people who are smarter and more ambitious than I am."

Of course, not everyone felt as positive about competition.

Madeleine Lane, a violist, remembered preferring not to compete. She recalled that her mom, who was also a piano teacher, pushed her to enter competitions. She never wanted to, because she thought she could play just for her own satisfaction. Her mom continued to push, and she was afraid of losing, so she just kept winning.

Laura Geuther,* a full-time homemaker with a college degree in business, explained that she was simply not competitive. She tried out for cheerleading and did very well, but dropped out before the finals because she thought other girls wanted it more than she, even after she was told she would make it. Laura never tried to get elected for office, either, but was anyway. She seemed to be motivated by reason and fairness rather than winning or being best. Despite her lack of competitive motivation, she was very successful in almost everything she attempted.

Winning in competition was punctuated with exhilaration and emotion for Sherry Stevens, an author and psychologist, but losing was frightening. Having the highest grades in her first-grade class, being selected for a leadership award at age eight and not even understanding what the word "leadership" meant, earning the highest score on a math achievement test in her entire eighth-grade class, and earning the highest grade-point average for one grading period in high school were all extraordinarily motivating. They made her want to be best, to be a winner, to be conscientious, to feel special, to feel smart. For her, however, there was also the flip side of winning. Although she felt confident she could be smart, she didn't take advanced math in high school for fear of getting a B, which would ruin her A average. In college she received a B+ in math and decided that math was not for her and that she would therefore never take another math course. The passion for winning was not yet matched by resilience. That came later in her life.

Dr. Penny Sarans, a reading educator, considers competition to have a very negative effect on her: "Competition really punches you down. You know you are worthless if you lose. . . . If it's win-lose, I don't want the situation. I want to enjoy the experiences, but I don't want to be devastated because I didn't get whatever I wanted." Although Dr. Sarans was referring to her perspective on competition now, her own childhood was not one in which she remembered winning. She had not been a very good student, she had a very difficult childhood (her parents were divorced), and it wasn't until after she was married and had children that she was inspired to attend college and graduate school. Perhaps it was her childhood memories of feeling like a loser that alienated her from any competition.

Travel The second most frequently cited positive experience for the women during their elementary-, middle-, and high-school years was travel. The women referred to positive experiences with their families, with other children at camps, and independent travel to visit relatives or to other countries. Some mentioned annual trips with their grandparents that left them with unforgettable memories.

The women's families made some remarkable efforts to broaden their children's worlds and in many cases made major financial sacrifices so their children could learn from their environments. As any parents who travel with children know, not all such trips are pleasant and easy. Yet these women remembered their childhood travel experiences in most positive and impressive ways. Travel was equally important to women in all career fields. These stories come from educators, scientists, psychologists, artists, nurses, and business executives.

Educator Laurie Mitchell recalls, "My parents took us traveling every summer. My dad planned for us to visit every national park in the country, and we actually visited all but Acadia National Park in Maine. We would stop and read every single monument sign. If I fell asleep in the car, my mom would awaken me abruptly and demand that I look at the view or a sign because I might never ever be in this special place again. To this day I cannot pass a monument or sign without stopping and reading every detail."

Environmental engineer Dr. Sandra Calvin remembers, "I was the fifth of six children, and my parents didn't have much one-to-one time with me. My dad would save up his vacation time so we could pile into the family station wagon and drive to the national parks to camp and hike for five weeks. I grew up loving nature because they were vacations that were enriched with learning about the biology and geology of the areas we visited. My parents encouraged all kinds of scientific interests."

And Sally Sahn, a media publicist for international athletes, remarked, "My high-school graduation present was a trip to Finland and Germany to visit my 'brothers' and their families. They had been AFS (American Field Service) students and had each lived with us for a year. I traveled within Europe by myself at age seventeen—a great learning experience! It gave me the confidence to go on to a large university. I knew then that I could really stand on my own."

Outdoor and Religious Experiences Many of the women in our study referred to outdoor and religious experiences, which were often intertwined. Several of the women recalled religious-camp experiences that bonded them with the outdoors, religious commitment, friendships, and leadership experiences, all at the same time. Sometimes the outdoor experiences were tied to the roots of these women's love of science; other times they were related to risk-taking experiences and independence or the love of travel. Guidance counselor Dr. Karly Rheam recalled, "There were camps I attended, both with my family and as a preteen and teenager. They were affiliated with our church denomination, and there were different age groups and different camps, and we usually went twice in the summer. There was comparatively a lot of freedom, lots of people to interact with. I lived out in the country in a fairly isolated area, so socializing with people was sometimes difficult. But the people who came to camps were right there. We were close in physical proximity, and we were out in the woods, on a lake, which I loved. That was one whole experience that just kind of stretched from when I was six until . . . well, I still go back to it."

Physician Dr. Alice Petrulis* attended Catholic Youth Organization camp for only two weeks each summer; however, it was the best social experience she ever had, and she remembers those summer camps better than any other experiences during her middle-school years.

Not all religious experiences involved the outdoors. State senator Elizabeth Quinlan recalled the impact of her Catholic religion: "My parents knew that the way out of poverty for us was education, education, and education. They, as a couple, taught us all the values touted today as necessary to raise happy, productive, and good citizens. Our Catholic faith was at the center of our lives, and I feel that the social teaching of Jesus Christ was a precursor to my service as an elected official. My family, church, school, and community provided the backdrop for my life today. The call from President John Kennedy to 'Ask not what your country can do for you, but rather ask what you can do for your country' struck a responsive chord in me. The institutions I belonged to had done their job of preparing me for my life of service, and life of service it is." Jody Hill, a vice president of economic development, remembered her very positive experiences with religion and church: "It was a big part of my life. My mother was always at the church. She worked at the church running a nursery school. She was on the vestry, and she was a lay reader. It wasn't until I was a junior or senior in high school that I realized she was the first female lay reader. People ask me about my mother being a priest and how I feel about it. They think that's weird or something. The whole time she was doing this, it seemed very normal."

Church and synagogue groups also provided a socially comfortable community for quite a few women and provided them with opportunities for leadership. Some women who hadn't felt particularly popular in school often mentioned a religious group in which they were elected to office or felt included. Some were active in their religious affiliation at the state or national level, and they served as officers and organizers at those levels. Martha Howard, a director of human resources for a Jewish community federation, remembered that her commitment to a religious/cultural youth group gave her leadership opportunities, public speaking experience, and responsibility. And scientist Dr. Carolyn Borth recalled, "I did get involved in a synagogue youth organization while in high school that I think gave me a boost in confidence because I held some leadership positions in that organization. It was the first time I was in a situation where I could be smart and not be considered some sort of nerd. It was an important experience, and I stayed involved in that organization throughout high school."

Risk-Taking Experiences Only 11 percent of the women in the study indicated that risk-taking experiences were influential positive experiences for them, and most of those experiences occurred during their high-school years. Traveling independently was one to which many women referred. For example, when Sarah Wells,* artist-photographer, was eleven, she traveled to Paris with her mother. Her mother left her there for a month with an aunt and some friends. She remembers that her exotic aunt had many artist friends and was very inspiring. Even during the college years, most of the women referred to their risk-taking experiences as related to unusual trips or outdoor experiences that provided them with the opportunity to get a different perspective.

NEGATIVE EXPERIENCES

Figure 6.2 shows the most negative experiences remembered by the women when they were growing up. Isolation from peers, the illness or death of a family member, moves, and changes in schools were

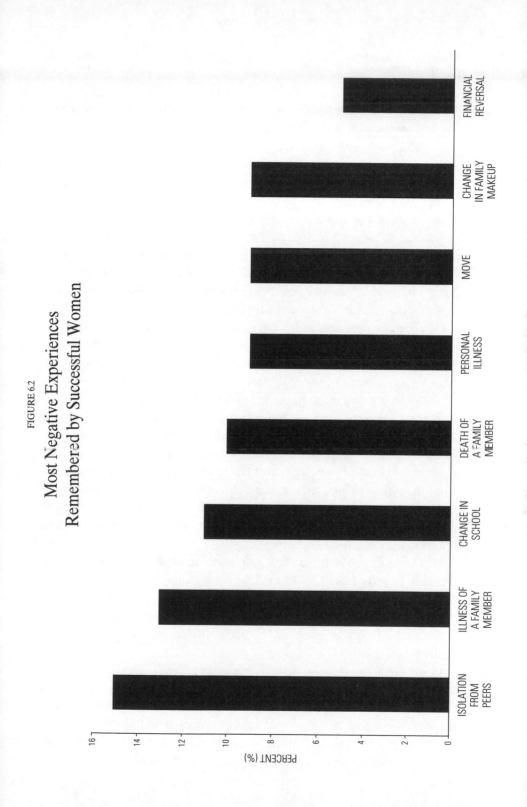

FIGURE 6.2

Most Negative Experiences
Remembered by Successful Women

ISOLATION FROM PEERS
ILLNESS OF A FAMILY MEMBER
CHANGE IN SCHOOL
DEATH OF A FAMILY MEMBER
PERSONAL ILLNESS
MOVE
CHANGE IN FAMILY MAKEUP
FINANCIAL REVERSAL

PERCENT (%)

mentioned most frequently. Financial reversals were mentioned least frequently.

Isolation from Peers Although isolation from peers was the most frequently mentioned negative experience, only 15 percent of the women indicated it as a problem. Yet, in the interviews with the women, many more of them talked about times when they felt isolated. Surprisingly, the percentage of women who felt isolated was higher in elementary school than in middle and high school. In contrast, during the interviews most of the women referred to middle and high school as the times they felt most isolated. Perhaps that's because most adolescents occasionally feel isolated but don't necessarily view their isolation as negative. Feelings of isolation may have been a negative experience for some but were a positive, maturing process for others. Some of the women found ways to cope with their isolation. Dr. Carolyn Borth remembers, "I was always a smart kid and always somewhat socially isolated—like a nerd, sort of. That was always the price to pay." Her feelings of being labeled as "nerd" or "brain" and paying a price were echoed repeatedly by many of the women. Some women saw themselves paying a price for being good students; others used their academics or interests as an escape and didn't mind the isolation. Donna Jacobsen,* an artist and illustrator, escaped through her art: "I was less social than most and sometimes felt isolated. My art was my outlet. My work was exhibited in school, and I won art contests. Surprisingly, my English teacher influenced me as much as my art teachers. I would illustrate authors, poets, literature, and received much encouragement for my artwork as I applied it to English. Art was all-important and helped me cope with my isolation."

Dr. Anne Caroles, a psychologist, used academics for escape. She recalled, "I didn't ever feel like I fit in in elementary school. I went to Catholic school with a very rigid order of nuns. There was a lot of really harsh discipline, physical kinds of harshness and abuse. Academics was the place where I could really, really succeed, and so, I really, really succeeded."

Figure 6.3 shows that the percentages of women who indicated that isolation was a negative experience varied among the career groups. Three times as many artists remembered feeling isolated as did women in government, among whom only 7 percent remembered feeling isolated.

Other careers with high percentages of women who indicated feelings of isolation were attorneys, media women, musicians, scientists,

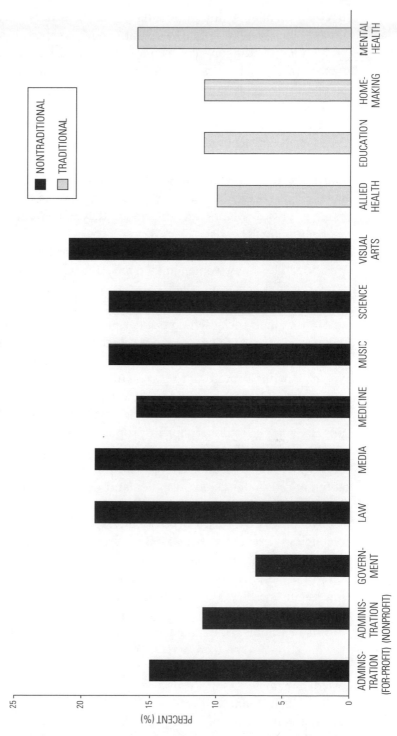

FIGURE 6.3

Most Negative Experiences:
Percent of Successful Women Who Remembered
Isolation from Peers

doctors, mental health professionals, and business executives. The greater social isolation felt by the attorneys compared to that of the women in government is particularly surprising because many of the women in government were actually trained as attorneys. Despite their similar training, it is perhaps the greater social experience of the women in government that attracted them to those positions.

Fewer women in the traditional career groups, that is, educators, allied health professionals, and homemakers, recalled experiencing isolation. There were also fewer leaders in nonprofit organizations that experienced isolation. Perhaps feelings of isolation and difference during their early years helped to prepare the women in the nontraditional careers for the isolation and difference they would encounter in their pioneering fields.

Appearance, concern about weight, and worries about acne were mentioned by many women in the study. It's unlikely the women were truly rejected because of their appearance, but surely they often felt ugly, too fat, or unvalued, particularly by boys. Some women acknowledged that their social self-concepts were tied to the approval of boys. Their academic confidence was not, which for some provided an important escape. In all cases, these women relied on their brains, their perseverance, or their interests to cope with their disappointment in their appearance. Orchestral musician Amelia Tyson perceived her problem as academically motivating: "The fact that I was never glamorous or popular may have done a lot to propel me into greater success at a career. Unfortunately, female beauty is a two-edged sword that can actually limit a girl's real achievement. If the fact that a girl is beautiful automatically opens doors for her and gets her extra approval and attention, why should she work really hard at anything?"

Psychologist Dr. Karen Brooks's interest in boys was related only to belonging: "I've always been kind of envious of people who had more of a sense of entitlement, a sense of belonging, legitimacy or something. I never experienced that. I wasn't in the 'in crowd,' and the boys had no interest in me. I was overweight, and I felt just completely helpless about doing anything about that. I guess that made me double my efforts at school, making the grades because the other stuff was out of the question. I wanted boys to like me because that would affirm that I was okay and valuable, but in my heart of hearts I really wasn't interested in them."

Although Donna Draves was thin, she admits she never felt thin enough and was actually very competitive about being thinnest. She recalled that there were two girls in her class who were skinnier than she, and she remembered saying, "My gosh, that scares me."

Dr. Dana Larsen, a scientist, never worried about her weight because she was so thin, but she admits she used not eating as a control issue with her parents, who would try to force her to eat and told her she should "take eating lessons." She also admits that her mother and grandmother put much emphasis on appearance and clothes, which perhaps was related to her need to be thin.

Some of the women experienced racial or religious difference as isolation, but others, although they felt different because of their religion, did not seem to feel isolated. Business executive Amy Fox recalled, "I felt somewhat different because I was Jewish and none of my friends were. I believe that experience gave me an appreciation of many cultures. By junior high school, I felt isolated, socially awkward, ugly, and introverted. I was even less social in high school and felt very isolated. I went to a women's college where I was accepted, found a social group, and was very assertive in antigovernment politics during the sixties, and I finally felt like I belonged."

There were very few African-American students in Judge Edna Conway's classes, and as a result, she often felt isolated and different. She attended an all-girls Catholic high school and didn't date at all because there were no African-American boys in the partner boys' school. At that time it was definitely not acceptable for African-American teens to date Caucasians. Even being friends with Caucasian girls was difficult.

Nevertheless, Edna was motivated to prove herself. That motivation was reinforced by her feelings of difference from her cousins. She felt caught between her older and younger cousins. Her older cousins didn't want her around, leaving her to play with the younger ones. In Edna's words, she felt as though she had "an emotional scar or something." Edna decided she would show them by achieving and doing better than they did. Her cousins attended college but eventually dropped out. Edna not only completed college but graduated from law school. Yet she felt different and isolated in each new school.

Illness and Death The women in the study were queried about family health problems in several ways. First, they were asked about unusual illnesses or allergies they may have had during their preschool years, and one-fifth responded that they experienced those. When asked to indicate negative experiences during their elementary-, middle-, and high-school years, 13 percent of the women recalled illnesses or accidents during the elementary years, but only half as many indicated these problems during middle and high school. Either these women became healthier as they matured, or they became accustomed to health problems and didn't consider them to be negative experiences. The women who experienced accidents and illnesses sometimes viewed them as growth experiences. Dr. Alice Kranz, a psychologist, said, "I had very serious knee surgery when I was in high school. I was about fourteen years old. It was all from gymnastics, and I was on crutches for long periods of time. I had always been very social, and then all of a sudden I went into the hospital. I was supposed to be hospitalized for a day, and I was in for a week and was out of school for three weeks. I did all my work at home, but my friends were off doing their social things that high-school students do. I was stuck on my crutches. They all came (twelve of them) to visit me one day. They had all been yakking, and I went downstairs on crutches and they all left. Nobody even asked me a question. That was a big change in my life. It was as if they didn't really care about me, but I learned I could be on my own. From then on, I actually began to enjoy being on my own."

Orthopedic surgeon Dr. Ruth O'Keefe* explained how an accident shaped the direction of her career: "I was a musician when I went to high school; I wasn't a scientist. I went to a very academically oriented high school, and in order to take band my freshman year, I had to take an academic course the summer before. So I took biology. Just before high school started, I had a bad accident and smacked my mouth, injuring my teeth, so I couldn't really play my horn. I was falling in love with my biology teacher, and I started hanging around the chemistry lab. One of my best friends was a great lover of science, lover of chemistry, lover of learning, so I really kind of lost interest in music and gained interest in science. Thank God I had the accident."

Dr. Lisa Smith,* a research chemist, recalled how her illness managed to almost get her lost academically: "I had chronic bronchitis that would come back again and again. I remember going to the children's hospital, and I remember having a lot of problems with my health in terms of not being able to breathe. I missed a lot of school and began to slip because school wasn't as easy to make up as it used to be. It some ways it was easier to get behind. I found myself getting D's in math. If it hadn't been for my brother's help, I probably would never have caught up."

Illness and death of family members during childhood obviously affected some women. Fourteen percent of these women's mothers and

13 percent of their fathers suffered a serious illness sometime during their childhood. Three percent of their mothers and 6 percent of their fathers died when they were growing up. For those who lost their parents, the impact was great. Some of the women talked of the continued inspiration of their deceased parent, and others shared stories of extreme resilience and suffering. Interestingly, some of the women also talked about their very different responses to illness and death compared to those of brothers or sisters. For one sibling it seemed empowering, while another often experienced depression. Our numbers are too small to hypothesize the cause of this differential response, but it does seem that the successful women who experienced a parent's death were given responsibilities and power beyond their years and had to draw upon their own resources because there was no one else to fall back on. Physicians Dr. Chantel Dothey* and Dr. Janet Smith, *Cosmopolitan* editor in chief Helen Gurley Brown,* and artist Sandra Sheets were all dramatically affected by the illness or death of a family member but assumed new responsibilities because of their problems. Dr. Dothey struggled with childhood bone cancer, and in addition her mother was very sick. She recalled: "My mother had multiple sclerosis when I was five. It made me aware at a young age of the reality of life. She would give me a list, and I would get groceries instead of visiting with friends. I had some adult responsibilities. I was missing something. We were taking care of her instead of the other way around."

For the most part, resilience, independence, and optimism were the typical responses to family illness and death for the women in this study, although that may not have been so for other family members. Our women seemed to learn their own strength through their experiences.

Moves and Changes in Schools Approximately the same percentage of women considered their moves and changes of schools to be positive as considered them to be negative, related to either better or worse social relations with peers or an increase or decrease in academic challenge.

Dr. Penny Sarans recalls being very socially uncomfortable and unhappy in middle school, but upon entering high school, she became very comfortable and socially accepted. Her high-school years were happy ones mainly because of the social acceptance. "In middle school I felt isolated and friendless. When my parents told me we were moving, I viewed it as an adventure. In senior high after the move, I met friends and became very social. My social life dictated the clubs I joined. I joined activities where my friends were, dated a lot, and had lots of friends. I didn't get into any trouble, had good but not excellent grades, didn't worry about my grades, and just followed my interests."

Executive Susan Widham* found her move in high school to be difficult because the social standards were so much more sophisticated and materialistic. She adjusted by finding friendship groups among those who enjoyed horses and in her religious group.

Academic changes made the difference for television producer Denise Dennison and obstetrician Dr. Susan Lemagie.* Denise had been an early reader, had skipped a grade, and was at the top of her elementary-school class in her urban school setting. When her family moved to a suburban setting where the academic program was ahead of that in her first school, her teachers and parents viewed Denise as making an excellent academic adjustment, though she remembers it as very difficult and further recalls that she no longer felt like the excellent student she had been, perhaps because she was no longer the best student in the class.

Dr. Susan Lemagie* had been bored and unchallenged in elementary school. She attended a very challenging middle school and loved the honors classes. Then her parents moved the family to a small town in another state, and Susan found herself in a small high school with little challenge. She was furious at her parents for forcing her to move. Although she participated in high-school activities and earned excellent grades, she felt frustrated, bored, and resentful. She knew what an intellectually challenging environment was like and was angry that she had to leave something so exciting.

It would seem, based on these women's experiences, that it was not the moves per se that were problematic but rather how the new school curriculum or social life compared to that in the girls' former schools. However, for some women the sheer number of moves made a huge difference; for example, Sandra Sheets, an artist, lived first in hotel suites and then single hotel rooms with her mother and sister after her father died. They went from being wealthy to being penniless. Sandra attended several different schools each year until she became terrified of any change in surroundings.

Financial Reversals Very few women, only 5 percent, recalled that financial changes had either a positive or negative impact on them. Rosemary Kovacs* recalls, "I was the last child. My sister is fifteen years older than I, and my brother is twelve years older, so I grew up like an only child on a farm. My parents were both second-generation American citizens. They didn't finish high school, but they were well read and were intelligent. We were really poor, but I didn't know that at the time, and it never bothered me."

Some of the negative experiences were more dramatic. It was hard for teachers to imagine Dr. Lisa Smith's* poverty: "When I was in sixth grade, there was a bad hurricane. My parents were in the paper business, and all the paper mills were shut down. We lost everything. We had to mortgage our home. In the seventh grade, I had a teacher who was very abrasive, and whom I did not like at all. I handed in the first homework assignment on a half sheet of paper, and he embarrassed me by saying in front of the class sarcastically that I was too poor to afford a whole sheet. I was very upset, and there was no way to make him understand that paper was actually really difficult for me to get. Because all the paper mills had shut down, we had to purchase it by the box from Canada. It was really expensive, and my family couldn't get it. I was too hurt to explain all this to my teacher."

Part 2: Advice

The role of competition in preparing children to be successful adults is the subject of controversy. However, it cannot be ignored in parenting and educating your daughters. Parents and educators alike will need to help girls to learn to cope healthfully with competition if they are to be expected to enter careers that have been dominated by competitive men. Ideally women will be assertive enough not only to survive in what were formerly male-dominated fields but also to modify those fields to make them psychologically more comfortable for both men and women.

As you teach healthy competition to your daughters, it's important to emphasize that most of our successful women remembered winning as motivating and exhilarating, but they also coped with failures and losses. Some of the women, mainly those in traditional women's careers, avoided competitive activities or disliked them intensely. More of the women in all career groups were involved in competitive activities as they matured into the teen years. My research on underachievement shows that underachieving children are often highly competitive individuals who do not cope well with losing. As you teach your daughters to compete, all elements of these findings need to be incorporated so your daughters will be motivated to succeed and will not be easily discouraged. They will need to cope with competition whether or not they enjoy it. Your daughters will need to be resilient, because all children and adults must deal with losing experiences.

Children's preschool years seem to include four elements that are foundational to coping with competition. Adjusting to sibling competition, which will be discussed in Chapter 8, is very important to developing children's confidence. Praise, as discussed in Chapter 2, can provide either motivation to win or fear of failure. Early school experiences and game playing are two other important ingredients that serve as a foundation for both motivation and resilience in competition.

Your daughter's preschool experiences, whether they occur in an actual preschool, a day-care setting, or in-home care, will establish a label or reputation for her because this is the first time she will be compared to her peers. She'll feel more or less attention and praise addressed to her by her teachers. Although teachers attempt to make the preschool environment appropriately noncompetitive, even very young children unconsciously compare themselves to others. Your daughter's early environment should not give her the feeling she can't keep up with others, or else she will feel like a loser from the start. On the other hand, if it gives her the feeling that she is way ahead of everyone else, it can also be harmful because it could cause her to feel too competitive and as if she must always be ahead of other children. Of course, if there are children of different ages in the preschool environment, your daughter can attribute her failures and successes to her age. Appropriate attitudes toward challenge are learned early; even during the preschool years, learning patience, perseverance, and confidence is part of coping with competition, and these skills will stand her in good stead as she matures.

Game playing is the most overt manifestation of competitive learning during the preschool years. Don't be worried if your daughter cries or has a temper tantrum when she loses a game during those early years, and definitely don't feel sorry for or get angry at her for her behavior. It's natural for children to hate to lose; some even cheat in order to win. If they cheat to win, you can take the opportunity to teach them about honesty and good sportsmanship. Don't overreact, but use losses in games or sports as opportunities to help your daughters learn about healthy competition. One mother, frustrated at her young daughter's poor sportsmanship, asked her why she had such difficulty losing. Her daughter's bright response perhaps said it all: "I don't know; ask

God. God made me this way." Indeed, God may have made all children and adults wish to win until they either learn to cope or give up on the fun of winning.

Your daughters should experience the fun and exhilaration of winning. You can cheer for them and get excited with them as long as they have opportunities both to win and to lose and you don't prevent them from losing or feel sorry for them. The little girl who is permitted to win all the time may be in deep trouble in the competitive world she must enter; the going will be difficult for her when she doesn't win everything, and she may become so fearful of losing that she avoids challenges and risks. Losing may feel intolerable; perfectionism may be overwhelming. My clinical observations do show that parents, and perhaps especially dads, tend to be more supportive and feel more sorry for girls in competition than they do boys. Dads will often challenge or tease their sons, and fathers and sons even banter back and forth about losing, but that's not so with daughters. It is not unusual for parents to suggest that brothers let their little sisters win, which builds confidence for brothers because often they know they could win, but for sisters it builds dependence on winning. They soon sense that people are supposed to let them win, and confidence does not emerge if girls know the boys are only letting them win because they'd probably cry or feel bad.

Elementary-school-age children can become involved in school and interest competitions in their areas of strength. Sending in stories and poems for publication and participating in spelling bees, sports, 4-H events, and music and art contests are all appropriate during these years. Children love to see their art or stories exhibited at home, in their classroom, or at the grocery store, and even exhibition at grandparents' homes seems exciting and like winning to them. If they're photographed for the local newspaper as winners, be sure to clip the article, make copies, and exhibit it on the kitchen bulletin board or mount it in a scrapbook. Your excitement about their winning is motivating; there's no need to downplay it.

Of course, your daughters won't always win. They may only place second or third, or receive honorable mention. They may receive absolutely no recognition at all. These, too, are learning opportunities. They can learn to be excited and happy for a friend or sibling. They can learn to congratulate the winner, although they may find that difficult at first. They can hear you say you loved their story or picture but that we can't all expect to win. Experiencing a loss is a time when you can encourage your daughters to try again, improve with practice, or develop a new competitive strategy. You can be disappointed with them, but do try not to feel too sorry for them. They will have other opportunities, and remember, they're learning resilience.

There's no reason to encourage your daughter to enter every contest. Indeed, it would be healthier for her to enjoy participation in some noncompetitive activities. She can simultaneously learn to enjoy both noncompetitive and competitive activities. However, if she's never interested in competing, you could tempt her into competition by getting her involved initially in areas where she would have the opportunity to at least place second or third. Music contests at early levels and 4-H and Girl Scouts are excellent for providing many opportunities for winning and less likelihood of losing entirely. At the elementary-school level, competition should not be so fierce or so frequent as to discourage your daughter. A gradual introduction to competition is beneficial.

One kind of competition that I don't recommend for children is beauty contests. Beauty contests and child modeling teach children to center their attention on appearance, charm, and fashion. Adolescence and young adulthood are likely to be very difficult for these girls if the natural beauty of their early childhood is difficult to maintain during puberty. Many teens in our society still struggle with issues such as acne, awkwardness, and weight. An early childhood in which beauty and fashion have been emphasized will make the occasional skin eruption during adolescence seem like a curse; it can mean that a few more pounds make a girl feel obese, ugly, and depressed. Being more moderate and less centered on appearance in the early years will help your daughter to resist the societal emphasis on appearance that will be there regardless of her family influence. Then, if she turns out to be a beautiful teen, the attention she receives will be a pleasant surprise but is less likely to be central to her life. In the meantime, she will have developed the value system of a smart, hardworking, and independent woman.

By middle and high school, there are many opportunities for competition. Math teams, creative problem-solving teams, academic decathlons, ensemble contests, dance teams, and sports teams help children to enter competition in the company of others before going it alone. There are local school and community contests as well as state and national competitions. Winning at the local level gives girls opportunities to try their skills at higher levels. It also gives them interesting opportunities to meet motivated young people who are also both competitive and social. Sometimes contests give teens opportunities to travel as well, and this, too, is beneficial. An excellent resource book for finding competitions is *Competitions: Maximizing Your Abilities* (F. A. Karnes and T. Riley, Prufrock Press, 1996).

All this can sound very tempting to your daughters. However, if they're fearful of taking the risk of losing, they may defer to less productive activities, such as idle chitchat and endless shopping. Your reassurance that they'll surely win may only cause them to feel more pressure and avoid participation. It's better to let them know they'll learn and have fun from the participation, win or lose, in order to encourage them to take the chance of entering contests.

Let their interests guide you in your encouragement. Your daughter can pick and choose the kinds of competitions that develop her interests and skills. If she loves music and prefers not to compete, that option should be available to her unless it's your interpretation that irrational fear of losing is preventing her from attempting the opportunity. Then a little push from parents may be just what she requires to take her first risks. Even the parents and teachers of some of the orchestral musicians seemed to need to insist occasionally that their daughters and students compete. Once your daughter is victorious a few times, you're unlikely to need to continue pushing. Furthermore, if she seems to have unusual talent in music, it is important that she learn to cope with competition in her area of excellence.

It is not always easy for parents to interpret their children's attitudes about competition. "Good little girls" learn that they should be good sports and may act as if they're good sports even when they feel anxious about the risk of losing in competition. They may avoid competitive activities and enter only contests in which they are fairly certain of victory. They may not reveal their feelings to their parents and may not even be honest about their feelings to themselves. A guidance counselor told this story about a middle-school student who had completed an achievement inventory, the Group Achievement Identification Measure (GAIM), and had scored low in the part of the test that measures competition.[1] When the counselor shared the girl's score with her mother, the mother questioned the reliability of the test because she was so certain that her daughter handled competition well. The counselor recommended the mother talk to her daughter about the issue. Much to the mother's surprise, her daughter broke down in tears, explaining to her mother for the first time that she hated competition. Many girls deny their feelings about competition and will acknowledge them only if they feel they are in a safe environment. Teaching girls to be resilient must truly begin with their honest acknowledgment of their feelings about competing and their fears of losing. Mothers may wish to share their own feelings about competition with their daughters or at least may wish to describe the feelings they remember from their teen years.

Winning in competition is so exhilarating and so motivating that every girl should have opportunities for winning. However, you will have to be an advocate and perhaps even a volunteer to keep competitive activities thriving in your schools in an educational era when many educators believe that competition is harmful to children. Furthermore, you will need to be sensitive in order to recognize whether your children are overinvolved in competition and too stressed by it. It's when they view it as a game and losses can roll off their backs that they can gain skills useful in playing the career games of life. They will definitely need support during the learning process. Every girl needs to recognize the temporary nature of winning and losing experiences so that winning is always viewed as a possibility and losing is never viewed as a permanent state.

TRAVEL IS WORTH THE TROUBLE

As you pack your children and what may seem like all your worldly possessions into your minivan or camper, you may indeed be wondering if travel is worth all the effort. Americans seem to have a love affair with travel, and it has a great impact on their children. Certainly the successful women in our study reminded us of how important travel was to them. Travel with their families was viewed as both an adventure and an educational experience, and travel alone or to a camp was considered an important step toward maturity, independence, and social fun. Visiting with grandparents, aunts, uncles, and cousins not only was valued but helped girls to develop a variety of family mentor relationships. Apparently it's all worth the effort.

Although up to about age three travel in itself is usually significant only for the parents, by ages four and five you're probably already building a few unique memories. By school age not only are you building memories and enriching learning experiences, you're also building independence and probably enhancing creativity as well. By age five children can travel independently on the airlines.

As you travel with your children, you become role models for learning and interests. If you stop to read the monument signs and study the history, geography, and sociology of the communities you visit, you make travel a valuable learning experience for your children. Even stops at the souvenir shops can provide learning, despite the fact that you may be thinking they're mainly full of junk (many are). On the other hand, that is where you'll find the books and pictures that will permanently engrave any particular trip on your children's memory. Those are the educational souvenirs that they will bring into school as they talk about their experiences or write about in a research paper. Travel tied to curricula that children have studied or will study in school is always particularly meaningful.

Travel also provides an opportunity to create your own traditions and your own travel humor. Special games that are played on the train or plane or in the car, special closeness that may at the time seem too close, and special sayings like "Are we there yet?" and "This is my side of the seat" or "Whose turn is it to sit next to the air conditioner?" are all created in the crowded but intimate space you share in the vehicles that convey you to your destinations. How can we forget a child's asking us to "turn the hall light on, please, Mommy" from his sleeping bag in the tent? Although you all may become weary of the crowding together and the living with just the basics, memories and closeness are created and are worth the sacrifice if you can expend the extra energy required.

When the whole family gets together at the grandparents' farm, apartment, condominium, or house, and aunts, uncles, and cousins are involved, there are new possibilities for building relationships, and new stresses as well. (Consider that new stresses encourage and help children learn to adjust.) Sibling rivalry may expand to cousin rivalry, and parents have a superb opportunity to be role models for family cooperation or competition. It may take some prior planning to provide an opportunity for your children to see a loving family working and playing together rather than the chaos that sometimes results from crowded quarters. Don't hesitate to simplify meals and chores. Disposable plates may not be as elegant as china, but they mean more time for fun. Sharing in the laundry and cleanup and expecting your child to participate can make a large family holiday a treasure despite the turmoil. Overlooking small disasters can permit the family to focus on the positive experiences. You may have to redefine this time as family time rather than an adult vacation, but wholesome family bonding can result.

Consider also that if both parents have careers, travel needs to provide not just education and fun but also time for true vacation or rest.

Many resorts accommodate two-career parents by providing camps and child care for part of the time so that adults can enjoy each other without the children for a few hours a day and know that their children are being cared for and having an adventure as well. Indeed, for parents who are accustomed to having their children in day care, a vacation with even their own children on a full-time basis may feel overwhelming and not like a vacation at all. Consider the several purposes of your trips and plan ahead so that you can include activities for all members of the family.

Of course, you can travel too much. When tempers and tears mar trip after trip, you may want to take a break from traveling. If every trip becomes a disaster and your kids are jaded with museums, monuments, and even our country's magnificent national parks, it may be better to spend more time at home. By the teen years, a camp counselorship, an opportunity to be a lifeguard, or a job delivering pizza may help your teens appreciate your earlier family travel. It may be time for them to travel with a youth group or independently in a foreign exchange program.

Parents can encourage schools to provide group travel to foreign countries. Such travel is usually an extension of a foreign-language program and provides both language and cultural immersion. Trips to Washington, D.C., New York City, or Chicago may be related to social studies or literature or drama courses. Many schools already have such trips. If not, your suggestions may begin a school tradition that can have an impact on your children and many other children in the future. Usually students organize opportunities to earn at least part of the travel expenses, and that, too, adds to the value of the experience. Such trips typically require parental support, so you may need to volunteer to contribute your vacation time to supervise a group of teens in Mexico, but you could have a learning experience in the process, and your teens may actually appreciate your coming along provided you offer them some privacy.

TEACHING ABOUT GOD AND MOTHER NATURE

Learning about one's religion and experiencing the outdoors don't always go hand in hand, but summer experiences out-of-doors and even winter camping experiences often seem to provide special opportunities for children. By the preschool years, YMCAs, churches, and Jewish community centers frequently provide day camp experiences that are more likely to be unique compared to the normal day-care experience. Children can simultaneously learn about religious traditions and good values while they learn water safety and to appreciate the beauty of a lake (or indoor pool). By age seven or eight, your daughters can go to camp for a week or two, and many Y's, churches, and synagogues do provide such opportunities.

Sometimes parents brag about "not sending their children away" because they care too much about them, but quite frankly, that's old-fashioned and represents a time when women built their self-esteem based on only their parenting and homemaking responsibilities. Your daughters can take their first steps in building independence away from home. They may not be willing to go the first time, but chances are you won't be able to keep them away in the future, and like many women in the study, they'll have wonderful opportunities to learn more about their religion, nature, or both, while discovering they can make it on their own. Furthermore, they'll build some wonderful friendships and increase their writing skills (and, with some luck, not your telephone bills) by keeping in touch with newfound friends through letters or e-mail.

Attending religious education programs that combine social and religious life during the teen years can be very important. For teens who may not be absorbed in the school social culture, churches and synagogues provide opportunities for leadership, organizational skills, and developing friendships. As adolescents search to understand their personal definitions of religion and God, religious discussion groups often help them sort out their ideas and their sense of identity by highlighting goals beyond their immediate needs and wishes. Furthermore, group leaders can often be supportive to them and to you, even when teenage rebellion makes parent communication difficult. Religious camps usually include physical activities and exercise as part of their daily routine, and that, too, is healthy for teens. Because religious groups also provide community service opportunities for youth, your daughters can become meaningfully committed to helping others instead of being totally self-absorbed. For a girl who is overly worried about diet and weight, volunteering to help in an impoverished community where lack of food is a genuine issue may provide insight. In a few cases girls may be sufficiently inspired to select pioneering careers in professional church leadership, an area that is still predominantly filled by men and would certainly benefit from the presence of women.

Unrelated to religion, outdoor experiences also provide your daughters with opportunities to pursue physical fitness, a sense of independence, and an introduction to and exploration of the natural sciences. Indeed, many women scientists received their inspiration from their families' love of nature and the outdoor experiences that were a part of family life. If as a family you're lacking knowledge on how to manage in the great outdoors, join a family-oriented group for biking, hiking, birdwatching, or wildflower collecting. Check the Internet or yellow pages for a list of groups in your area of interest. Once you've learned the skills as part of a specialty group, you may wish to apply them independently with your family.

If your daughter's afraid of an ant and considers exercise to be a walk through the mall, there's even more reason to expose her to outdoor experiences. As mentioned previously, Scouting and camping groups often provide such opportunities, but perhaps she'll fight that because it's so direct. Think about her strengths and her interests and find an outdoor opportunity that fits. Camps that specialize in creative writing, drama, sports, foreign language, music, and art often have summer opportunities outdoors, and she may find herself hiking if only to paint a picture or write a story. A little bit of "roughing it" can only be healthy for her and may even get her beyond squawking and squealing when she sees a bee. She may even forget to put her makeup on!

PROVIDING AN INCREASINGLY LARGER BOX

"Thinking outside of the box" has become a common term for creative thinking. It emphasizes viewing events or people or ideas from perspectives different from what is typical for one's self, family, or group. The concept fosters the importance of risk taking compared to thinking only in traditional ways. Although many girls are not known for their willingness to take risks, it is that inability to take a chance that has prevented some women from entering careers where risk taking is required. Because parents have the responsibility to protect their children and, particularly in the case of their daughters, have often overprotected them, perhaps the analogy of letting them out of the box would be better stated as providing an ever-enlarging box for them to explore.

The analogy of providing a larger box fits very well for the preschool years. Beginning with the crib, moving to the playpen, and then to the childproofed home, backyard, and school, it's important for children to be in safe spaces that permit them to explore their world in a manner appropriate to their developmental needs. Issues of safety dictate how large their box can be and when you can let them out of one box into a larger environment. If they are permitted too much freedom, they may play with electrical wires, run into the road in front of a car, or get hurt in some other way.

Teaching a child to swim is another example of how parents gradually permit their children to take risks. Many of you reading this book will have at some point taught your children to swim. You didn't just throw your children off the diving board into the deep end of the pool. Instead, you introduced them to the water gradually, holding them closely at first, then gradually helping them move through the water with water wings or the equivalent. Next came lessons and swimming without support. As your children's skills improved, you gave them more freedom and independence, and finally they were on their own swimming and doing water sports freely because you could trust their skills and judgment.

Permitting your children to visit friends' homes and knowing the families of those friends keeps the safety lid on while permitting more freedom. Providing supervised camp or travel experiences permits freedom within limits. Encouraging your daughters to be friends with children of different races and religions further extends your children's box.

Once children have been given freedom, it is psychologically difficult to have it withdrawn. Your children will feel controlled when you remove freedoms they've already become accustomed to having. However, they will also feel controlled, stifled, and eventually angry if you do not increase their freedom as they mature. Too much freedom too early and too little freedom later on produce similar symptoms of rebellion.

For the most part, you can measure the freedom you give your daughter by comparing it to what you would give your son. Many of the women in the study complained that they were not given the same freedom their brothers received. Nevertheless, the facts are that girls may be more vulnerable unless you equip them with the tools to protect themselves. Sports may make them stronger, and the martial arts may provide some self-protection techniques. They may learn to use Mace where it is legal, but despite all the safety gadgets with which you can equip them, they are more likely than your sons to be raped in a dark parking lot. They simply will have to use the university escort service or walk with a buddy, and when you finally let them out of their boxes, you will need to warn them of the real risks. Even if they label their parents as overprotective or naive, when they travel to high school or college you will have to make contact with school authorities ahead of time to determine the risks and prepare your daughters for them. That is common sense, not overprotection.

You are also a model for risk taking. If you always insist on doing things the same way, and if you fear trying a new route, a new restaurant, a new city, or a new movie, you can expect your daughters to follow your pattern. If you're afraid of spiders or the dark or a storm, expect your children to be fearful also. Furthermore, if fathers take risks and mothers don't, it teaches daughters those gender-stereotyped roles. Sometimes with the busy schedules families have today, it's difficult to make spontaneous changes. However, it's important for your daughters to see your flexibility. Furthermore, you may even want to label flexible behavior overtly to heighten your daughters' awareness of the ease with which you can make changes. She will be growing up in a world of continuous fluidity and change, which will prepare her best for change in the workplace and the continuous societal changes she's likely to face in the future.

EVEN DIFFICULT ISOLATION CAN TEACH RESILIENCE

Social isolation was experienced as sadness and self-doubt by many of the women in the study. However, in some cases it felt to them as though they were simply different and did not fit in with the majority of their peers. For the most part, isolation gave the women in our study more time alone to dedicate themselves to a specific interest or to learning activities. They may even have developed the confidence that they could succeed as loners. In some cases they found other social groups in which they were not isolated. Those two adjustments seem to be good approaches to use when helping your daughters cope with feelings of difference and isolation.

During the middle-school years especially, but even in high school, girls' social interactions and cliques seem to depend heavily on scape-goating other girls. Thus "We're together, but we won't let others in our group" seems a common way for preadolescent and adolescent girls to connect and feel close. Those cliques can be somewhat fluid, so some girls who were "out" may soon be "in" and vice versa. In other cases the groups seem to be quite rigid, with some girls permanently excluded. Whether the exclusion is temporary or permanent, many girls seem to suffer from it.

Parents who come into my clinic usually report that their daughters are especially sensitive, bright, creative, and insightful but aren't accepted by the other girls. Sometimes there is a socioeconomic, race, or religious issue separating the girl from the others, but more typically the separated girl has different interests and is less steeped in the mainstream culture of fashion, makeup, boys, and so on. Sometimes another girl may be competing with their daughter for leadership and may fear losing to her if she's included in activities. The parents are usually feeling sorry for their daughter, and the girl is also feeling sorry for herself. They often blame the school for not handling the problem or blame other girls' parents for the problem. Of course, schools and families do need to take the responsibility of teaching children to respect individual differences, to be kind and sensitive to others, to be better friends, and not to form exclusive cliques; yet the pattern continues.

There seem to be at least four important lessons your daughter can learn from being left out by the other girls. First, she needs to understand that she is not the only girl who is sometimes left out, although it may feel that way to her. As research psychologist Dr. Mary Schneider* pointed out, it's helpful not to compare "your insides to someone else's outsides." This is an important lesson that will prevent girls from feeling isolated. They may not look isolated to others although they feel alone. Furthermore, others may feel just as isolated but may not appear that way from the outside.

The second lesson will be important to resilience. Your daughter needs your support to know that it's all right to walk a school hallway alone and that being different and alone some of the time doesn't make her a bad person. Indeed, successful women need to be independent and will feel alone many times. Teach courage instead of teaching a girl to feel sorry for herself in the name of sensitivity. She can be both sensitive and strong.

The third possibility is how competition affects your daughter's friendships. A well-adjusted and successful high-school student, Maggie, explained that she was disappointed and didn't exactly understand why her former best friend, Brianna, no longer wanted to be friends with her. Both Maggie and Brianna were excellent students and were involved in many similar activities. Brianna was seeing a psychologist for depression and explained to Maggie that she felt she never could do anything as well as Maggie, but when she lost a boyfriend whom she really liked because he became friends with Maggie, that was the last straw. Brianna just felt bad when she was around Maggie. Maggie repeatedly argued with Brianna that she did many things well, but Brianna was not listening. Instead she was continuously comparing herself to Maggie and just felt inadequate. Maggie accepted the loss with regret, but mostly couldn't quite understand why Brianna had to be friends only with kids who didn't do as well as she.

The story is an excellent example of how competition can interfere with friendships during adolescence and leave many successful girls feeling isolated. Maggie had no alternative for maintaining Brianna's friendship except maybe purposely not doing her best in her school-work, extracurricular activities, and social life. She realized she would have to befriend others who didn't feel as threatened by her success.

The fourth part of teaching a girl to cope with isolation involves teaching social skills. A teacher or outside observer can typically help with these problems. Sometimes children have mannerisms or habits that are truly offensive to others and isolate them unnecessarily. We all remember the girl with the oily hair, or the girl who smelled really bad, or the one who bragged all the time, or the one who talked too much, or the one who was so quiet that no one was patient enough to listen to her. Those skills can be taught after the problems are identified.

Parents may miss the social problems entirely. Ask teachers to help you observe the problems, and remind them you won't be offended by their advice. You can always decide whether or not the missing social skills are fine according to your values or whether your daughter really needs to wash her hair more often or stop talking so much. You may be able to help your daughter with these skills, or you may wish to send her to a counselor. Group counseling can be especially effective for teaching your daughter social skills, and school counselors often under-take such social-skills groups.

Although girls do need to learn the resilience of moving forward independently, social skills will be important for your daughter's sur-vival in a successful career and in the relationships of adulthood. Ado-lescence requires plenty of social skill learning.

WHEN YOUR DAUGHTER IS FEELING DIFFERENT

Because so many of the successful women described themselves as feeling different, it tempts one to believe that feeling different is a building block for individuality and resilience. Those feelings of being different may be only part of the developmental stage of finding one's identity, but they do seem to be common to kids who are motivated by creativity. Many teens who come into my Family Achievement Clinic struggle with the issue of their difference. Sometimes they report that it causes them to feel lonely and isolated. Other times they corroborate their difference by pointing out their unusual clothes or nose rings or by telling me about the psychedelic lights in their rooms at home. Sometimes they discuss their unusual thinking. I usually describe these young people as marching to the beat of a different drummer, because their parents almost always say they have always done just that.

If young people feel different, sometimes they seem not to want to be reassured that other young people also feel this way. It's almost as if it is their wish to be so unique that keeps them isolated, and their unique-ness depends on your not knowing others like them. However, they're very vulnerable to feeling madly and intensely in love with another young person who perceives himself as isolated and different. Some-times the breaking up of a relationship of that intensity is extraordi-narily painful for the pair. Other times a girl tires of competing with someone who perceives himself as more different than she.

If the feelings of difference are tied to clothes or room decor or strumming the guitar, try to help them to differentiate layers of creativ-ity. The surface layer is the one that makes a girl feel unique and excited temporarily; for example, setting the styles for other kids, or being the first to discover a new music group. It is exhilarating and not bad in itself; however, it is only a token of what a person's potential for cre-ativity can be. That surface layer will never put food on the table or lead to a successful career or be recognized as a major contribution to soci-ety. However, in my clinic, I point out the valuable symbolic meaning to young people who are struggling with this issue. It helps them to inter-pret their personality as one that thrives on discovery, invention, and unusual thinking. It emphasizes and helps them understand that they will be happiest and most fulfilled in a creative profession. The creative teen feels as if she's found an ally who understands her need for cre-ativity because of my understanding her value of creative expression.

The next step is more precarious. I will point out to these vulnerable young people, who aspire to be different but also fear their difference, that creative people who make a societal contribution, and incidentally perhaps even a living, base their creativity on in-depth study, practice, and knowledge, and that education and self-discipline are the keys to providing them with a career in a field where they can express them-selves creatively. Sometimes they've heard that story already from their parents, but usually they seem to listen. Perhaps they feel understood because their difference is valued by someone other than their parents. If the creative young person is already into heavy drug use, it may be difficult to turn her around, but more often the advice encourages her to try a little homework or to engage in some creative writing or art or actually practice her music. Consider that such girls may be fearful of putting forth too much effort lest the new effort not produce the admiration they desire, thus threatening their fragile adolescent self-concepts. They worry that they are not as "creatively talented" as they thought.

If the young person is already self-disciplined and that is part of her definition of her difference, the task is much easier. She may then need only to find a peer group that shares her creative interest. Even if her acne or weight is causing her a serious problem, finding friends who share her interest frees her from the "weird" label she's been identified with in school. If she has met some friends who share her creative interest in a summer or special program, she will be able to cope better with the isolation or loneliness when she's back at her own school, where her diligence has been valued only by the adults in her life.

WHAT YOUR DAUGHTERS CAN LEARN
FROM ILLNESS AND DEATH

Research on eminent men found a higher proportion than expected who had experienced the loss of a parent by serious illness or death. Clearly this doesn't mean that the men haven't suffered serious emotional losses; rather, it means only that their career achievement may not be adversely affected. Many of the successful women in our study experienced the death or illness of a parent as well. The significance of this finding is that although illness or death in the family is likely to make it more difficult for the surviving family members, parents who lose a spouse to death can be resilient enough to encourage their daughters' success. The women in the study who did best seemed to be those whose surviving parent permitted them to continue school involvement and were role models for positive coping with difficult losses. These mothers or fathers often successfully balanced home, parenting, and job. The girls were frequently given more responsibilities in terms of assisting an ill parent or earning some additional money to help out, but the message from the single parent, or from an ill or dying parent, was always that learning and education were still the highest priority. What that means to the parents who unfortunately find themselves in such a difficult circumstance is that although their daughters may be psychologically disadvantaged by a parent's illness or death, they can develop sufficient resilience to adjust and live a good life. It is important that their education be emphasized and that they not be forced into adulthood before they're ready, although they can often handle greater responsibilities than the typical teen without harm.

Even if you personally struggle with depression because of your loss, it is likely your daughter will overcome her traumatic loss and adjust successfully provided you can keep going and give her the opportunity to see you responding with strength. Ironically, death or illness in a family can actually provide a confidence-building experience for your daughter and inoculate her against the more negative activities that distract other teens.

MOVING CAN BE A POSITIVE EXPERIENCE

Moving is actually a risk-taking experience for children as well as for their parents. As a result, being a role model for a positive and adventurous approach to moving is your highest priority for helping your children adjust better to moving. Research indicates that the lives of highly creative people frequently involved considerable moving. Moving actually helps children see the world from alternative perspectives. This does not mean that we recommend that parents move their children for the sake of creativity; rather, it says only that in our mobile society, it is likely that parents will have to move their children, and that there is no reason to feel guilty about it or to give up important career opportunities because you fear your daughter will feel lost without her best friend.

Research shows that moves become more difficult as children reach adolescence, and moving during the middle- or high-school years is most difficult of all. If your daughter is resistant to the idea of moving, talking about it is important. Let her know you'd be happy to both listen and help her make the adjustment. Make yourself available when she wants to talk about issues related to the move. To make the idea of moving more acceptable, you can hold a special sleepover party for her and her closest friends before she leaves. Some interesting note cards might be nice party favors to help her and her friends stay in touch. Promised telephone and/or e-mail time will help your daughter know you're being supportive. A cassette tape exchange works well for special messages, and photograph exchanges help to keep long-distance friendships close. Plans for a yearly visit can be considered, although sometimes such plans disappear as new friendships develop.

Be sure to visit your daughter's new school with her before she begins classes. If the school can arrange a partnership with a student in her class so that she can become familiar with at least one person from the start, it will help her meet other friends, and she'll gradually become more comfortable. To smooth the transition, help your daughter identify activities in the new school that are comparable to activities in which she was involved in her old school. Reassure her that it usually takes a little time to make new friends, but she'll surely find some eventually.

Try not to ask your daughter repeatedly if she's made friends yet. That will only put pressure on her. Instead, encourage confidence and caution. Particularly in middle and high school, suggest she first assess the different crowds or cliques to determine which ones share her values and interests. Perhaps she'd like to invite a new friend to your home for a visit (even if some of the boxes are still not unpacked).

Talk to your daughter's new teachers to determine if the school's curriculum is about the same as her former school's. If it seems more challenging, arrange for a temporary tutor until your daughter catches up on her work. If the curriculum isn't challenging enough, determine if there are other resources in the community to enrich your daughter's learning. It won't hurt her to be bored in school for a few weeks, but you may want to communicate with the school principal if she's repeating too much. Consider, too, that your daughter will be comparing herself to the students in her new classes. She may not be willing to share with you that she doesn't feel as smart as she used to in her old school. You may need to help her make this adjustment. Try not to get into the position of negating or opposing the new school, or your daughter will surely turn off to her new environment.

Social standards may also be different. You will need to decide whether purchasing a few new fashionable outfits is worthwhile to help your daughter fit in or whether you simply need to help her decide that her own values are different and important enough to stay with and just feel a little different. At least be sure you're available for discussion of these difficult issues with your daughter.

You will be adapting, too, and of course that will put stress on you as well. Let your daughter know that you, too, are adjusting, but try hard to model enthusiasm and an adventurous spirit. Explore your new neighborhood as a family. Check out the museums, concerts, and theaters in the area. You may even wish to check the malls and flea markets. If your daughter succeeds in making you feel guilty, you may find yourself regretting the move, which will only make relocation more difficult for the whole family. Guilt has never been helpful to parents, but empathy and creative problem solving can help your daughter adjust.

MONEY IS SMALL STUFF

Despite the fact that most couples work at developing their resources and worry significantly if they don't have the financial resources they perceive their daughters need, very few women talked about positive or negative memories related to increase or decrease in wealth. Although more than half of the group of women came from lower-socioeconomic-status homes, their memories seemed to be much less about financial deprivation or material possessions than about role models who were hard workers. Mary Train is a successful business executive in the computer technology industry, where she recalls pioneering as the only woman in all-male industry for many years. Mary reminded us that her Ukrainian immigrant mother was a cleaning lady who struggled to put aside money for her college education, and she continues to view her mother as her most important hero. Her mother's commitment to earning, saving, sacrificing, and encouraging her daughter's education had more positive impact on Mary than the negative effect of their limited resources.

Perhaps knowing this can take some of the pressure off families who struggle financially and worry about the adverse effect on their children. Building your relationship with your daughter far exceeds in importance the material possessions you can provide for her.

AN INDEPENDENT "FIRE-EATER"

Catherine Burns, Ph.D.
Professor of Civil Engineering

Catherine Burns doesn't look like a fire-eater. The petite woman in a bright yellow suit would remind one of an elegantly dressed lady about to attend a women's social luncheon were she not surrounded by blackboards covered with complex mathematical formulas. At age thirty-six, Catherine, a professor at MIT, loves her work even though she works more than fifty hours a week. For her it's almost self-indulgent. Ten hours a day she gets to go off to her office and work on neat problems, leaving her family behind at home, which suits her well. She said, "Some people exercise, some people read, some people shop. Work for me is my time, and I feel as if I am doing something for myself. On the other hand, when I'm at home, I'm focused completely on my husband and my children."

Catherine manages to maintain a happy marriage and raise her two daughters. Despite her incredible confidence when discussing her work, she was much more hesitant when she talked about raising her children. She believes she lacks the intuition necessary for making the right decisions about her children. In fact, she talked about the natural talent her nanny and her children's preschool teachers have with kids. Her confidence diminished when the subject changed from career to kids.

Catherine always had a very good relationship with her parents while growing up. Although neither of her parents has a college education, Catherine believes that both of them had high expectations for her. She isn't really certain, however, that they actually expected her to go to college. Catherine remembers only that they wanted her to be a hard worker. Her father would repeatedly say, "You can do anything you want if you work hard," and "Nothing comes for free." She remembers identifying with her father because of his positive attitude toward hard work. Catherine believes her mother lacked confidence and independence, and as a result made it a high priority to instill independence in her children. She succeeded; Catherine was always independent.

Catherine was the middle child of three, between her older sister and younger brother; ironically, this is not a birth order that usually predicts great independence and success. She attended public schools and was always an excellent student. In elementary school Catherine was actively involved in music, playing piano, saxophone, and drums. She also belonged to Girl Scouts, but spending time alone was always an important priority to her.

Prior to Catherine's interview, she asked her mother what she remembered about Catherine's childhood. Her mother's response was, "Tell them you were just competitive and wanted to do your best from the time you were born." For example, the competition that sometimes adversely affects girls' confidence in middle school only encouraged Catherine to race ahead. She was placed in an open classroom where she could work at her own pace. She remembers not only being ahead of all the other students in math but also being far ahead of her teacher. Catherine had incredible intellectual confidence, for good reason. She always felt that if she couldn't get it, "who could?" She was clearly always the best student, and she consistently received A's. She was always drawn to math. She never required any prodding or monitoring from her parents. She thrived on classroom competition. She loved to win and rarely experienced losing in any intellectual competition during those early years.

Catherine continued her excellent performance in high school, and she added several competitive sports, including tennis, skiing, and running, to her many musical activities. She loved to win but took her sports losses in stride; indeed, most of the losses she experienced were in sports. She described herself as being about average in sociability and found little time for partying in her very active life.

Catherine was a National Merit Scholar in high school but had no real idea of what she wanted to do after graduation. She had always wanted to be a teacher, but her guidance counselor suggested that because of her high grades and excellent ability in math, she might like to become an engineer, and "at least there were jobs in engineering." Based on her counselor's advice, she decided she'd start by majoring in engineering, although she hadn't the vaguest notion what engineering was all about.

Neither did Catherine have any idea about where she wanted to attend college, and her parents knew absolutely nothing about the various colleges, so they didn't even try to advise her. Most students from her high school applied to the state university. Catherine sent for a Dartmouth application only because she knew some friends who had gone there. Because the Dartmouth application was thick and would take a long time to complete, and also because she realized that Dartmouth was expensive, this extremely gifted young woman decided not even to apply there and chose to attend the state university instead.

Catherine adjusted easily both academically and socially to college. She completed math, computer science, and engineering classes but was still uncertain about engineering. She called her mom to get guidance. Her mother responded, "No way am I going to give you advice on that, because I will be blamed for the rest of my life," and she added, "I learned my lessons from those haircuts." Catherine's mother recalls that Catherine would ask, "Should I have long hair or short?" Her mom would answer, "Short." Then after it was cut, Catherine would say, "See, Mom? You made me get my hair cut."

Catherine married her present husband two years after college, and prior to entering graduate school. Part of her graduate work involved four years of study at Georgia Tech. She had to live apart from her husband to complete her studies for that entire period of time. They visited back and forth for weekends and vacations, and somehow managed to keep the marriage alive and well. Although living apart was a major sacrifice, she acknowledged that her habit of being independent sustained her.

At MIT, where she earned her master's degree and doctorate, Catherine faced her first real academic challenge. For the first time she found herself thinking, "If I can't do it, I may be the only one who can't." She began telling herself, "Well, that's okay. There certainly are smarter people, but I have other strengths. I suppose they'll come in handy." Catherine would never let herself quit until she made a real effort at something. Then, and only then, would she let herself decide if she liked it or not.

Catherine has won some impressive awards. When people congratulated her, she would say, "Well, I was lucky." Finally one of her male colleagues pulled her aside and told her that she deserved it and it wasn't just luck. He suggested that she just say thank you instead of making excuses, and he pointed out to her that women always say, "Well, it was luck" or "Well, it was timing, because they want to fund women and minorities these days," and so on. Catherine considered this an important lesson, but ironically she still considers herself to be mainly lucky.

As Catherine reflects on her success, she indicates she was most motivated when she was faced with a challenge. Interestingly enough, although competition was so important in Catherine's childhood, she describes her present approach to research as collaborative. Mostly Catherine collaborates with men. There are very few women in her field, and those she knows have not shown an interest in collaboration. In her field the norm seems to be not to collaborate but to build empires instead. Nevertheless, she prefers collaboration. She's concerned she may not get tenure because she's in such a competitive environment and because of some of her priorities. She always wants to be home with her kids by six o'clock, and most of her male colleagues work much later. Her goal isn't to be a tenured full professor. Rather, she phrases it this way: "Let's see if I can do something. Can I have fun along the way, enjoy myself, and also be successful?"

Catherine perceives that being a woman in her profession is much easier now than it was ten or fifteen years ago. She feels well supported, and in some ways she believes her life has been easier because she's a woman. The men are pretty serious about encouraging diversity in the workplace, and they tend to accommodate her lifestyle. Occasionally she makes her concerns explicit: "Yes, I take my career seriously, but no, I don't want to meet at five-thirty at night because I want to go home to be with my kids."

A colleague of Catherine's described a problem that he saw in many female engineers: "We had 'fire-eaters,' some great women in this place. Now it's as though a lot of them are into the age when they're having babies, and there is this huge transformation. These fire-eating, hard-working women are now completely disinterested in what they're doing. They just don't have their heart in it." This same man observed that "Catherine must be a genetic mutation, because she's not like that. She has retained that 'fire-eating' quality." Also, people have talked to her about tenure, saying, "Won't things calm down when you have tenure?" Her response is that if she gets tenure, she'll ask herself, "What's next?" She may start her own business at that point. She may engage in some completely new type of collaboration. She certainly doesn't expect to slow down.

Catherine frequently reminded her interviewer of how much her mother wanted to instill independence in her children and how her father emphasized that positive, hard work would lead her wherever she wanted to go. It seems they were certainly successful in their parenting goals. Independence and hard work seem to be the threads that wove through Catherine's childhood and continued into her adulthood. Those goals were the first priority for her parents. Both she and they succeeded in their goals. She is indeed an independent "fire-eater."

SPIRITUAL PASSION PERMEATED
HER CHILDHOOD

Miriam Kane
Rabbi

Rabbi Miriam Kane remembers always having had an intense yearning for religious involvement. She also identified with her dad's spirituality. Although he didn't consider himself very religious, Miriam thought he had a religious soul. She recalled their family visit to Mount Rushmore and how awed her father was at the sight of it. Somehow his comments about the monument made her feel he had a deep spiritual belief in God. Her own spiritual passion was also nurtured by an Orthodox rabbi's wife, a Hebrew-school teacher, a very religious

Catholic friend of her mother's who lived with the family for a year and went to mass every day, a religious Lutheran male friend in high school with whom she has remained friends, and a religious great-grandmother who died before she was born but about whom she heard much from her grandmother (and for whom she is named). These role models were all passionate about their religion and had a dramatic impact on Miriam's wish to lead an intensely spiritual lifestyle.

Considering Miriam's spiritual zeal, a religious career would have seemed a natural mission. However, her religious career began only after she earned a master's degree in business and worked as a credit analyst in a bank for five years. The business career simply didn't fill the spiritual bill for Miriam, so at age twenty-six she completely reversed her career direction and decided to attend rabbinical school, where she was the only woman in the class.

Miriam's parents did not raise Miriam to be an observant Jew since they were not very observant themselves. Despite that, Miriam became extremely interested in her religion when she was about eight years old. Her Orthodox Hebrew-school teacher invited her to her home for a Sabbath dinner, and Miriam was inspired by this beautiful, humble, and pious nineteen-year-old teacher and her husband, who studied Torah all day long.

As Miriam became more active in religious services, a rabbi's wife began inviting her to be with them frequently. The family was Ortho-dox, and Miriam was enticed by the wonderful lifestyle, the close fam-ily, the regular celebration of the Sabbath with music and love, and the spirituality that seemed to surround their family. Miriam remembers the music with some humor because the rabbi's wife was tone-deaf, but her off-key singing never deterred her. She would bang out the music on the piano and sing with an enthusiasm that enthralled Miriam. She was dynamic and passionate about religion, and Miriam bonded with her in a special closeness.

Miriam attended religious services frequently, usually alone, but sometimes with her brothers. Her parents attended only infrequently, and Miriam recalls that when in her teens she coaxed them to become more observant, her dad took her aside and made it clear that he and her mother had their own beliefs and that she should respect them and stop pressuring them about their religious participation. Her father's criticism made Miriam very cautious and caused some temporary feel-ings of isolation and aloneness. Although that isolation related only to her religious concerns, it made her teen years with her family a little more tense, since she was so immersed in her religious thinking.

In other ways Miriam was always very close to her family. Miriam was the only girl, the oldest of four children. Her dad had been a high-school math teacher and was promoted to become a high-school principal and then a school superintendent while Miriam was growing up. Miriam's mother had been trained as an English teacher but was a full-time homemaker during Miriam's childhood. Both parents loved learning, and they inspired Miriam to set learning as her highest priority.

Miriam was always an excellent student in every area but was especially strong in mathematics, much to her mother's surprise, because her mother had never been very strong at math herself and thought mathematics was typically a boy's subject. Miriam was so good at math that she and her dad would have math conversations at dinner while the rest of the family just listened. French was also a strength for Miriam, but their whole family shared and loved French; eventually everyone in the family spoke French, and they would have conversations in French over dinner.

Miriam took her schoolwork seriously. Her homework and study definitely came first. Miriam remembers idolizing her fifth-grade teacher. She recalled, "When you're in love with a teacher, it's easy to be in love with learning as well." Miriam took all the advanced courses she could and always earned the highest grades. If there wasn't an honors course in a subject, she was totally bored. Of course, she'd do her work anyway, but it felt deadly to her. Everyone referred to her as "smart," and she had no doubt at all about her intellectual ability. Indeed, she graduated first in her class and was a frequent winner of academic awards and competitions.

Despite the admiration she received for her academic accomplishments, she realized that her academic ardor prevented her from being "popular," and in many ways she wished she could be popular "like the cheerleaders." She never even considered underachieving, but she knew she was paying a social price, and although that never detoured her from her love of learning, she often wished for more social acceptance and would have loved to have had a boyfriend in high school. She decided she was just too smart for the boys to take a chance on her.

She was always active in extracurricular activities and was president of her school's National Honor Society chapter. She was in drama, choir, and marching band, and worked on the literary magazine and yearbook, but it was the religious groups she belonged to that gave her friends and a social life. She belonged to Orthodox groups in which the boys took all the prestigious religious responsibilities and there was no socializing with them. She also belonged to a Zionist youth group that wasn't as religious, where she could socialize, sing, and dance with both boys and girls and still be fervent in her Judaism. She was frustrated by the conflict that in the Orthodox world she couldn't do what the boys did—have a bar mitzvah or lead a service. Instead, her uncle arranged for her to read the Torah in Hebrew at his Conservative synagogue in Philadelphia. She learned her part entirely on her own from a cassette tape, and she so impressed the congregation that she heard them say she was the best bar mitzvah boy they had ever had. At age thirteen, it was an exhilarating experience for Miriam.

Despite all the other role models Miriam had, she was very close to her family. As a young child she identified with her mother, and she remembers that her mother was her best friend during almost all her life. However, in adolescence Miriam identified more with her dad because of his religiosity and his intelligence. Her mother would always tell her that she was like her dad because he was so smart. In fact, during her mother's interview, her mother posed a significant question. She wondered why so many mothers who have highly intelligent daughters constantly tell them they are like their fathers. That is what Miriam's mother did, acting as if she were not as intelligent as her husband. As Miriam and her mother think back, they realize that her mother's lack of intellectual confidence helped to sabotage their relationship during Miriam's teen years, when Miriam felt a lot smarter than her mother and looked up mostly to her intelligent father, whom her mother had taught her to respect.

Both Miriam's parents were strict with her, but she thought they were not as strict with her brothers. For example, when Miriam wanted to get a job, they explained to her that her job needed to be school, but her brothers were allowed to work for pay as well. It may have been because she was first in the family, but she really thought it was because she was the only girl.

Miriam felt close to her three younger brothers, and they always respected her and considered her an authority figure. She had plenty of nurturing leadership experience right in her own family, and she admits that some of this has helped her in her position as rabbi, where she finds herself often mediating relationships just as she did with her brothers.

Miriam's childhood was truly enriched. As a family they went to museums, theaters, and concerts and filled their lives with learning. They traveled throughout the country every summer, and Miriam even put a spiritual spin on their travels. She observed her father's awe in his admiration of nature, and she, too, felt awed by this beautiful country. She remembers her dad's amazement while watching shooting stars, though he was fascinated not only by Mother Nature but also by the creations of artists and musicians. Mount Rushmore and classical music enthralled him, and somehow that also tied Miriam to a sense of his spiritual nature.

In high school Miriam traveled to Israel. The trip provided a spiritual tie to that country and an even deeper link to Judaism. After high school, Miriam went off to McGill University in Montreal to major in French. At college she found a close group of Orthodox Jewish peers, and she also mixed with students who were not Jewish and were involved in French culture, which she loved. For the first time she dated Jewish men. In her high school she had done very little dating. Also, Miriam loved being in an environment where her friends also valued learning. She was no longer alienated from others, because they shared similar values. When she graduated she wanted a career, but she ruled out becoming a rabbi, although a close friend encouraged her to try that direction. Perhaps the fact that, as a child, she had seen only men leading religious services was a factor in her decision. Miriam chose instead to get a master's degree in finance, and she enrolled at New York University. By the time she finished her finance internship, she knew she was moving in the wrong direction. Nevertheless, she worked in the world of finance for five years before she decided there was no place for her but the rabbinate. Orthodoxy was not open to her and never will be, but the Conservative Jewish seminary was permitting women to enter. Although Miriam was the only woman in her class, she loved it, and she knew she had finally found her calling.

At age thirty-seven Miriam has been a rabbi for five years, and in many ways it's everything she wanted. However, she has encountered a few troublesome matters. She was always successful at pleasing every-one in her family and school, but now she finds it quite impossible to please everyone in her congregation. Also, Miriam and her husband, a computer analyst, would like to have children in the future, and although it wasn't clear from Miriam's interview that there were fertil-ity problems, she does not yet have a family. Perhaps with time Miriam will be able to have it all, but for a young woman who was always able to be successful in every endeavor, not being able to plan her family may be especially difficult.

As Miriam looks back on how she was parented, she is appreciative that her parents never set limits on their expectations for her. Both parents encouraged her to break with tradition; her mother would say, "Why shouldn't a smart girl become anything she wants to be?" In a sense it is ironic that although normally Miriam fervently leads her congregation in carrying on the Jewish tradition, it was possible for her to take this leadership position, typically held by men, only by being courageous enough to break with tradition.

CHAPTER 7

SOCIABILITY, SHYNESS, AND INSECURITY

Peer Relationships

Part 1: Findings

In comparison to their less-accomplished peers, many of the successful women in the study did not view themselves as very successful socially. That was especially so during middle and high school. During the elementary-school years, almost half of the women indicated they were about average in sociability, but by middle and high school that number decreased to about a third. Furthermore, almost 40 percent considered themselves less social than typical in middle and high school (see Figure 7.1).

Perhaps the busy academic and extracurricular lives of these women precluded extreme social involvement. They were immersed in activities and interests, but not nearly so involved in partying. As noted previously, many indicated they felt lonely, and many more considered themselves different during their middle- and high-school years. Quite a few recalled being shy. Journalist Janet French* provides an example: "I was truly shy when I was in high school, although I was only shy in certain ways. My friends thought I was funny and they enjoyed my friendship and I enjoyed theirs, but there was a high-school hangout that I was afraid to go to because I thought if I walked in there, everybody would be looking at me. I felt like I wasn't pretty, and I had terrible acne for

FIGURE 7.1

Self-Perceptions of the Sociability of
Successful Women Compared to Their Peers*

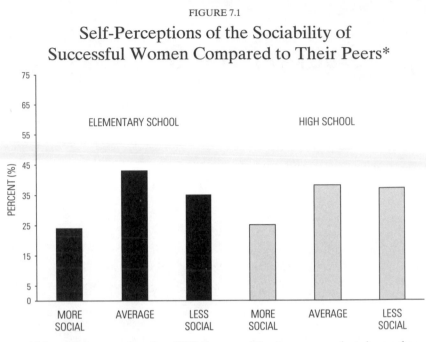

* May equal more or less than 100% if women did not answer or selected more than
  one category.

years, which is the bane of any young woman. My mother also gave us
home permanents, and she didn't believe in fads, so we were never
allowed to buy into the current fads. We always had good sensible
clothes. I remember in the early years, we had to have a navy blue suit or
a bottle green suit, or a black suit, and that was our basic clothing."

Veterinarian Rochelle Breen found that shyness prevented her from
socializing but also encouraged her in the academic arena, where she
knew she could "shine." That feeling was echoed by quite a few of the
women. They could escape their fears through their studies and receive
recognition for scholastic success.

Sociability varied among the career groups, sometimes in the direction one might intuitively expect and other times not. If we use the term
"popular," which is what teens use to describe being more social than
typical, only a quarter of the total group considered themselves to be
popular. Figure 7.2 compares the career groups by the percentage that
perceived themselves as less social and probably not particularly popular in high school. Popularity in high school did not divide neatly by traditional and nontraditional careers. However, for the most part, the
women in the more social professions were also more social in high

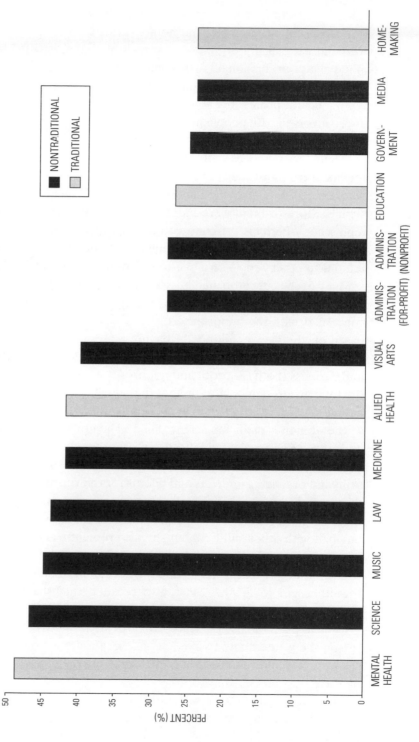

FIGURE 7.2

Percentage of Women Who Considered
Themselves Less Social Than Typical in High School

school. It certainly is not surprising to find the women in media, education, government, business, and homemaking to be among those who were more social; nor does it seem surprising that scientists, physicians, allied health professionals, artists, and musicians were less involved in social life. It was, however, surprising to find that the attorneys and mental health professionals were less social, particularly because they are so involved with people in their careers.

The women in the science, music, and art professions were less social in elementary school as well, and those in the people professions, except for law, were more social even in elementary school. The only women who seemed to reverse their sociability were the mental health professionals. More of them were more social in elementary school than in high school. Perhaps the contrast in their involvement with peers was related to the beginnings of their analytical and introspective talent in relating to other people on a one-to-one basis rather than in groups.

Many of the educators had busy social lives during their entire childhoods. Perhaps that is why so many teachers today are often especially concerned with the importance of socialization in schools. For them, based on their own childhoods, having many friends seems a critical measure of healthy emotional adjustment. The women in government and business (both for-profit and nonprofit) were also more social than the total group, demonstrating that they displayed early the important people skills necessary for their careers.

The women in medicine, science, mental health, law, orchestral music, and art were less social than those in most other careers, particularly by high school. Their high-school years were an important time for honing skills and practicing interests and talents for their career goals. Many of the women were simply not in the mainstream of teenage social life.

Research psychologist Dr. Mary Ainsworth* recalls playing some baseball with other children, but she also remembers feeling different because she always liked to read. She used to walk home from school with another girl, telling her all about what she was reading and "boring the other girl to death." Mary also recalled that she was different because she "wasn't as pretty as other girls."

Clinical psychologist Dr. Karen Brooks acknowledged that the only reason she wanted boys to like her was because that would affirm that she was okay and valuable, but in her heart she really wasn't interested in them.

Another scientist, Dr. Lisa Smith,* explained that she wasn't what her mother anticipated socially. She wasn't really "feminine" and was voted by her class as most likely to succeed. There was no way she would have been voted funniest or easiest to get along with. Instead, she had a small core of friends that she was very close to, but she made it clear to others that she had no interest in being involved with them. Her mother would say, "Have more tact; it wouldn't kill you to be nicer to them." Her mother was disappointed that she really didn't care about clothing. Lisa recalls three girls in her high school who never wore the same outfit twice. These girls wore fur coats and dragged them around from class to class because they didn't want to put them in their lockers. Lisa considered them "fluff chicks" and just didn't have the time or energy to be involved in that nonsense.

Several women described their high grades as a "social cost" they had to pay. Internist Dr. Susan Rehm* recalls that she stopped raising her hand to make contributions in high-school classes when she found out her peers disapproved of her excellence.

Attorney Michelle McGuire* also remembers prioritizing her homecoming dance as most important. The dance was on the same day as the SATs, and she was homecoming queen. She was much more concerned about her hair and shoes than about the SATs. She can remember distinctly just picking test answers randomly because she wanted to leave early. Even if someone had told her at the time that the test was going to have a substantial effect on her life, she wouldn't have cared. The homecoming dance was the only event on her mind.

HOMOGENEITY OF FRIENDSHIPS

Figure 7.3 shows that more than half of the women had friends who mainly valued learning and good grades. About 40 percent had friends who had various attitudes about learning and grades, and only 4 percent indicated that their friends did not value learning and grades. This pattern held true throughout the women's elementary- and secondary-school years and supports what parents have known for years—that peer influence is important. Furthermore, the pattern of having achieving friends held constant for all careers. Journalist Rosemary Kovacs* said, "I was on the school paper, in the National Honor Society, and in band. I had a group. We were 'The Clique.' We were the smart group." Dr. Alice Kranz, a psychologist, was typical, too: "In junior high school we went skating every Friday night, and then on Saturday night somebody had a party. We spent a lot of time together hanging out at people's houses. I had a very active social life in eighth and ninth grade. Pretty much all weekend was spent with my friends, but they were all good students."

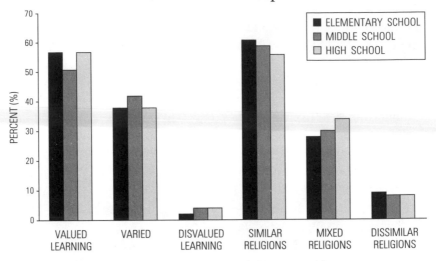

FIGURE 7.3

Peer Relationships

And violist Marilyn Bergman recalled, "I had a group of friends; in fact, we all lived close together, but were not great lovers of going to dances and things like that. We walked to school, we had our entertainment activities together after school, and our parents were always interested in what we were doing. We liked to roller-skate and play baseball. We did things in each other's homes and had Halloween and Christmas parties. We were always interested in actively participating in positive activities, and I guess that's why we called ourselves the Agenda Club."

Not all the women had such positive peer involvement. Guidance counselor Karly Rheam recalled some negative peer influences: "In middle and high school most of my friends didn't value learning, and I didn't fit in. I thought differently than they. I studied very little (half an hour a day). My grades were good, and math and science were easy. I took honors classes and graduated in the top ten percent of my class."

For someone like Dr. Janet Winters, an assistant superintendent of schools, middle school brought about some dramatic changes that were pretty much enforced by her parents: "I was a little bit of a tomboy. I was a catcher on the boys' team, so I had my mitt. When I went to junior high school, we had a noon break when we could go outside and play ball or whatever. Then my mother made me wear a dress, and I had to have my hair long and curled, the whole bit. Suddenly, even though I had my mitt, the boys wouldn't allow me to play anymore. It was extremely traumatic for me. I came home in tears, crying, 'What am I going to do during recess?' My mother said, 'Oh, you can't play with them anymore.' I had played with these boys since I was young. And then my mother said, 'There'll be dances; you'll be very popular.' She was right; I became popular. In fact, the boys all took me along to dances with them, and suddenly I had a very different relationship with the same boys, and I liked it."

Most of the women (about 60 percent) indicated a fairly homogeneous peer group in terms of religious and cultural values as well as achievement. About 10 percent indicated their friends had different religious values all through school, and only about a third had a mixture of friends relative to both cultural and religious values.

Some of the women remembered specific incidents of prejudice in their childhood. Orchestral musician Claire Hunter recalls experiencing integration in the South and racism from the perspective of her Caucasian family and friends. She remembers playing the organ for an African-American friend's wedding and being told that she was "crossing the line." She felt so bad for her African-American friends, and she didn't feel she fit in with her white friends because they were so racist. Medical researcher Dr. Alyssa Gaines recalls being one of very few Jewish students at an exclusive independent school and remembers the cutting remarks, specifically references to her "Jewish nose."

TOBACCO, ALCOHOL, AND DRUGS

Very few of the women in the study were regular smokers during their childhood and adolescence. At the middle-school level, only 2 percent smoked every day, and 82 percent had never used tobacco. By high school, only 6 percent smoked regularly, and 66 percent had never smoked. During the college years, however, the number of regular smokers increased to 18 percent and only half had never smoked. Tobacco use was also analyzed by the age of the women because of the assumption that the research on the negative effects of tobacco use may well have had a differential impact on their smoking habits. A full quarter of the older women in our study had been regular smokers in college. However, 12 percent, only half as many, of the younger women smoked regularly while in college. Paulette Lisy,* a successful entrepreneur, recalls how her smoking began: "My parents were very trusting, very unsuspecting. I never did anything really bad, but I was terribly bored in school. I would smoke a cigarette every single period in the bathroom to see if I could get away with it. I did. I would smoke in the bathroom just for excitement, just for something to do, and thus began a long-term smoking habit that I eventually managed to quit." This kind of incident was a playful reminder of their teen years for some of the women. For others, it was the beginning of a serious habit. Most of the women in our study, however, never started smoking at all.

The percentage of women who had never used alcohol declined dramatically from middle school to college, as would be expected, from approximately 80 percent in middle school to less than half in high school and to only 15 percent in college. The percentage that used alcohol every day, however, was only 1 percent from middle school through college. This was not a group of addicts; however, many of the women were involved in social drinking. In middle and high school, most used alcohol "a few times a year." By college, a quarter of the women used alcohol once or twice a month, and a fifth used it once a week. When analyzed by age group, the differences went in the same direction as tobacco use, although the differences weren't as great. By college there was less alcohol use by the younger group than by the older group.

Artist Brenda Tate recalled her attempts at sampling alcohol and drugs. Her first taste of beer was "gross," but she and her friends got very drunk. On the way home they almost drove into a pole, and that close call frightened her away from alcohol for a long time. She tried "speed" the first time right before a volleyball game and couldn't pay attention to the game. She tried it again at a school retreat. She hated the feeling it gave her of being out of control; thus she ended her drug experimentation.

Drug use was of particular interest to our research since many of the women were in college or graduate school during the late sixties and early seventies, a period of significant drug use by young adults in our society. Although 90 percent of our women never used drugs in high school, that number declined to two-thirds by college. Less than 1 percent of the women cited regular drug use. Drug use once a week was indicated by less than 1 percent at the middle- and high-school levels, and by only 4 percent during college. Most of the women indicated they used drugs "a few times a year." The only drug used by more than 1 percent of the women was marijuana, and that was used by approximately 12 percent of the women in high school and a quarter of the women during their college years.

Drug use differed significantly between the older and younger women, with older women using drugs less at all levels despite the fact that many of the older women were in college during the 1960s and 1970s. In high school, 94 percent of the older women hadn't used drugs, compared to two-thirds of the younger women, and by college three-quarters of the older women hadn't used drugs, compared to slightly more than half of the younger women. In summary, there were very few women in the study who used drugs regularly, many who did not use drugs at all, and a fair proportion who experimented with marijuana, mainly while they were in college. Although percentages of drug use are not high, they are higher for the younger women than for the older women, reflecting the increasing direction of drug use in our society. Figures 7.4 and 7.5 show the data on tobacco, alcohol, and drug use by the women in our study.

FIGURE 7.4

Percentage of Successful Women Who Never Used Tobacco, Alcohol, and Drugs in High School and College

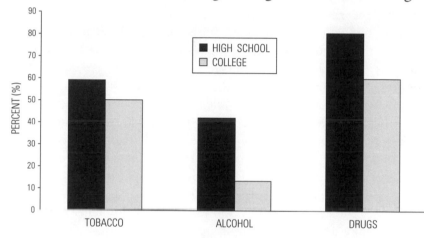

FIGURE 7.5

Percentage of Successful Women Who Used Tobacco, Alcohol, and Drugs in High School and College Once a Week or More

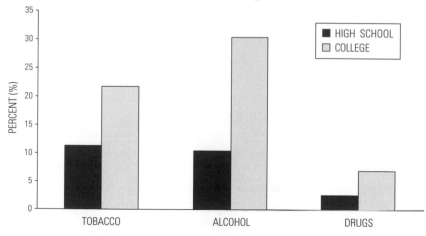

Part 2: Advice

Parents are often in a quandary about their children's social issues. Mothers may wonder if their own experiences are appropriate for guiding their daughters toward healthy social adjustment in a very different society. Fathers may question how they should respond to their daughters' social and dating dilemmas when these are so very different from their own experiences.

From early on, fairy tales guide children toward gender-stereotyped role expectations. How can parents change the delightful fairy tales of princesses and helpless maidens to encourage a prototype of a smart, independent, adventurous, risk-taking girl who accepts challenge and competition? Parents may wonder if girls' exposure to those stories will cause their daughters to continue fantasizing about being the Sleeping Beauties and Cinderellas of yesteryear.

Certainly there is no evidence that the spunky women in our study were deprived of the typical fairy-tale literature of our culture. Most of them were such voracious readers that it's hard to believe any literature escaped their reach. Perhaps it is enough to explain to your children that fairy tales are just that, and that real women are different. Stories of adventurous girls and biographies of great women seemed to have inspired our women even in juxtaposition to the fairy tales.

Television tales, however, cause more serious problems for young people. Many adolescents of both genders are seriously hooked on soap operas and often use them to interpret how to act socially and get on with their peers. Many girls spend countless hours watching the "beautiful people" of these programs play musical beds.

It may be better to watch a few soap opera sessions with your teens as a basis for good discussions about reality. Even when they say they know the difference between fiction and the real world, it's worth emphasizing some key points about weight, fashion, beauty, love, sexual relations, assertiveness, and reality. Figure 7.6 includes excerpts from an essay written as a school assignment to provide a teenage perspective.

As noted earlier, many of the teachers in our study tended to be quite social when they were growing up and are more likely to compare and interpret your daughters' social behavior based on their memories of their own social lives. Thus the girl who is a bookworm, who prefers to play sports with boys, who is physically less mature, or who doesn't dress like the other girls could be seen by her teacher as lonely, sad, different, or—hardest of all for a parent to handle—poorly adjusted. You

FIGURE 7.6
"Watching" for Role Models

Movies and television shows are often the primary forms of entertainment for young girls. However, the women portrayed in movies and on television are often false role models for teenage girls. Oftentimes, movies and television shows portray women who value physical appearance, have promiscuous lifestyles, and have defective personalities.

From movie stars to the sitcom mom, most women in these shows are thin and beautiful. The producers tend to show women valuing physical beauty above inner beauty. Not only is there an emphasis on the women establishing their self-worth based on appearance, but the respect of others around them is also based on appearance. Some teenagers see this example and force themselves to fit between the narrow margins these movie stars have portrayed. Many teenage girls are misled by the false picture portrayed by the movies and television into thinking less of themselves.

There are two basic types of personalities found in the average soap opera. The first type of woman is a pretty, jealous type that uses her intelligence to deceive others around her. The second type is usually a naive, male-dependent type who has no grasp on what it takes to be successful.

Teenage girls often idealize the women in the media and follow these examples. Movies and television shows send false or mixed messages to teens in terms of what is morally and ethically correct. They create a lot of unnecessary pressure on girls at a very important time in our lives.

Virginia Miraldi
Age 15

will need to determine if this difference is something you want to change or support. If she does not seem lonely and sad, it is important to explain your daughter's independent personality rather than try to change it. If the teacher's interpretation as well as your daughter's suggest your daughter requires some social-skill changes or simply a change in the way she dresses, these changes could make her happier without taking away her independence.

There is a delicate balance between helping your daughter establish her individual identity and encouraging conformity to peer norms.

IDENTIFYING YOUR DAUGHTER'S SOCIAL COMFORT

The three main conflicts suffered by adolescent girls who are searching for their identity are related to school achievement, girl-boy relationships, and beauty. These are, of course, intertwined, but we will simplify them into three distinct categories in order to offer advice for parents.

Most girls are unlikely to underachieve in elementary school. The combination of having mostly female teachers as role models, the emphasis on being good little girls, and the small-muscle coordination that seems to help little girls develop nice penmanship easily combine to prevent the underachievement problems that so many boys develop during the early grades. On the other hand, by about fifth grade, when the curriculum gets more complex and peer pressure encourages less effort in school, many girls find themselves in a dilemma. In some ways they say they'd like to continue to be great students if they could. On the other hand, straight-A students aren't really popular, so they think maybe it would be better to study less, to forget to hand in a paper, or even to intentionally mess up on a test. Some girls will only think about this conflict, while others may actually act on it. Some of this latter group may try these behaviors only once or twice. Others may get into the habit of not studying. For such girls, underachievement becomes their new pattern, and they may lose confidence in their ability to do anything about the problem, particularly in math and science.

Many women in the study alluded to the social sacrifices they made to maintain their intellectual integrity. It will help your daughter know that she's not alone, and it will help you to have the courage to let her know she mustn't sacrifice her integrity, much as school administrator Dr. Janet Winters's parents did: "I picked up very quickly that roles are different in terms of academics. I basically caught on that boys didn't like you to be too smart. I was very good in math, and I had told my mother that I deliberately missed a problem on a test so that I didn't have a perfect score. My parents went into a big lecture: 'You will not do that; that is ridiculous. If you are capable of getting the top grade in math, go for it.' I took their advice and decided not to worry about what the boys thought. I won the state math contest in algebra as a freshman and beat all the boys in the school. That ended the conflict for me." Janet stopped making deliberate mistakes, but if it had continued, as it does with many girls, her entire achievement pattern might have changed.

There are many middle and high schools in which the peer norm is to achieve. If your daughter is underachieving in that type of environment, perfectionism, learning problems, or too-high expectations may be at the root of the problems rather than negative peer pressure. Sibling rivalry pressures—that is, when a brother or sister is an excellent student—may also be causing your daughter to give up on achievement in some areas.

WHEN YOUR DAUGHTERS CENTER
ON THIN AND BEAUTIFUL

When girls develop an interest in boys, some very confusing behaviors begin to take place, and the girls themselves become very confused. They see their friends change the way they walk or talk when boys are around, and they watch some friends who weren't popular suddenly become popular. They see friends change their values entirely. They see changes in the way peers dress and wear makeup, and they try to determine what will work for them, and indeed, what they want to work for them. For many, having the tools to attract boys feels like an urgent and earth-shattering need: "If Mom and Dad won't let me dye my hair, I think I'll just have to cut my wrists to show them how serious I am" or "If I can't have my own telephone to talk to Justin, I'll just run away from home." When girls make these threats, it is usually to manipulate their parents into getting what they want; however, their feelings seem real to them, and their needs feel immediate and powerful. These threats are frightening to parents, but the girls are often so angry and desperate that your explanations of why you can't let them do as they want seem to fall on deaf ears. On the other hand, if you make the mistake of giving in to your daughters' desperate pleas and anger, you set the stage for continued and more intense manipulation.

Your immediate responses to your daughter when she makes those outrageous requests need to be wise and thoughtful: "Abby, I'll need a few hours to think about your concern" or "You know that Dad and I always talk about these issues." Your daughter may recognize this as a delaying tactic, and indeed it is, but because you've not said absolutely no, she'll wait patiently in hopes that she'll get what she wants. This may also give her some time to cool down enough so she can explain why she's so concerned, and you can respond more sensibly and give her a slightly more long-range perspective. The slowing down of the decision-making process for impulsive and spontaneous adolescents seems frustrating, but it is very effective for teaching your daughters to postpone their own gratifications and become more thoughtful young women.

Suppose you tried to do the right kind of parenting, or perhaps you admit you messed up on a few things, and you find your teenager obsessed with her appearance and weight. If she has lots of boyfriends, she may believe her appearance is what's keeping them. Sometimes she thinks about her weight all the time and doesn't even relate it to her relationships. Furthermore, her weight often becomes a competitive issue with her friends or with popular kids, so she doesn't feel thin unless she's the thinnest.

When your daughter's thoughts are centered on her weight, the first behavior you have to examine is your own. Many mothers in our society talk constantly about dieting and do their own fasting and bingeing. Many fathers in our society make continuous comments about their wife's weight gains or losses. Indeed, it sometimes seems as if society is obsessed with weight, glamour, and appearance. We *are* an overweight society, and of course medical research shows that too much weight is not healthy, so we have the dilemma of encouraging good health while minimizing the impact of glamour and body self-consciousness on our daughters. That is further confused by our own wishes to be both healthy and sexually attractive to our spouse, or to other men or women if we're not married.

Our daughters are surrounded by both junk food and obsessions with thinness. Teenagers don't typically worry as much about health and assume they will live forever. Given all those paradoxical pressures, it is no wonder that so many young women struggle with marginal eating disorders, while some slide into the extreme eating disorders of bulimia and anorexia nervosa.

Your observations of your daughter's eating habits are crucial. If you notice only the typical teen behavior of occasionally skipping a meal or overindulging in snacks from time to time, there's no reason to panic. Do become sensitive to what you and your daughter's father may be saying about her weight and weight in general. Minimize weight talk except as it relates to health. Be sure to avoid sarcastic comments about your daughter being too fat (or, if you're the dad, your wife being too fat). You may even have to take her brother or sister aside to explain the importance of not making such ugly comments. More than one patient's bulimic pattern began after a sibling or peer in school teased her about being fat. You can't do much about comments by other teenagers, but you can restrain your own negative comments about other people's weight. Your daughters and sons are listening.

If you, either mother or father, have reasonable communication with your daughter, this is a good time to talk with her privately about any worries she has about her weight. She may share what she's feeling, or she may deny she's concerned. If you're the mother, tell her that women have come a long way and that she should value herself for much more than her attractiveness to boys. Of course, you can rein-force your belief that health is important and tell her that you under-stand she may feel self-conscious about her weight. Rather than provide her with a list of appropriate foods, ask her if she'd like an appointment with a nutritionist to plan a healthy diet. If you believe her weight worries are causing her serious problems, this is a good time to persuade her to visit a psychologist who specializes in eating disorders. It is also a critical time for fathers to reinforce to their daughters the important values of developing themselves into intelligent, active, and independent women and to let them know that boys who are interested only in appearance won't be very good long-term friends.

Although it may be obvious to you and to those who know your daughter that she is starving herself (anorexia nervosa), bulimia is often hidden even by otherwise open adolescents and young adults. A bulimic adult who came to my clinic put it this way: "At age fifteen, I learned what I thought was this neat trick. I could eat all I wanted and still stay thin. This neat trick still haunts me at age forty. I was divorced once and am now dating a wonderful man. I fear that if I tell him about my problem, he'll break up with me. My teeth are rotted from the vomit, and I live in embarrassment and fear that my recurring problem will never go away."

Bulimia is a perilous disorder, and any symptoms need to be taken very seriously. Subtle signs are one worn-down fingernail (the one on the finger used to induce vomiting) or a dental examination that shows fillings that are shinier than typical. The food bingeing is often paired with compulsive exercise and amazing secrecy. Although outpatient psychological care may be effective, it's not unusual for young women with serious eating disorders to require hospitalization so that calorie intake can be carefully monitored.

It's important to realize that even the most honest young women may play elaborate games to hide their food intake. Night raiding of refrigerators or cupboards, taking jobs in bakeries where they can eat undetected, swallowing hundreds of laxatives, or adjusting a scale so their parents think they weigh more than they do are only a few of the tricks these disturbed young women play in an attempt to stay perilously thin.

It seems to require a dramatic experience or fear to break through these young women's defenses and convince them that their thinness may be bringing them near death. Indeed, some do die. However, if anorexic and bulimic women are confronted by parents or siblings, or if they find the courage to share their problem with someone, they feel tremendous temporary relief, and often this is the beginning of the solution to the problem. Unfortunately, the struggle that lies ahead is difficult. The fear that they will gain weight is irrational yet so obsessive that it takes priority in their lives. Part of coping with an eating disorder involves developing interests, coping with competition, and valuing oneself apart from one's appearance. Self-acceptance without expecting perfection of oneself is close to these issues as well. There may also be important family issues.

Because eating disorders are so complex and parents need to be involved in the therapy, parents also may deny the seriousness of the problem. It is almost as if there is a family conspiracy of silence, with daughters hoping they will not be found out and parents wishing that they are only imagining the symptoms.

WHEN YOUR DAUGHTER IS IN THE WRONG GROUP

There seems to be nothing more difficult for achievement-oriented parents to tolerate than seeing their daughters unite with a negative group of peers. Students who don't value school are often also anti-parents and pro-alcohol, tobacco, drugs, and promiscuous sex. They thrive on irreverent and often obnoxious music, and your daughters will probably proclaim that they are good and loyal friends and are indeed much kinder to her and less shallow than the "preppies" and "jocks." They will be secretive, call you controlling, and protest that you have no right to control the friends they choose. Very few women in our study were immersed in this kind of negative friendship group, although a fair number mentioned brief brushes with such friends during adolescence. If your daughter is deeply involved, she should get psychological help, but you will almost certainly have difficulty convincing her to get that help. Even if you can manage to tempt her into seeing a psychologist once, she will probably consider it a waste of time and assume that you and the counselor are wrong and want only to change her.

There are some preventative strategies that work well, and there are some solutions that work some of the time if your daughter is not too involved with a negative group. We hope you're reading this early enough for prevention.

Preventative Strategy #1: Avoiding Pressures for Friendships Many of the anti-school girls I have worked with were lonely, attention-seeking, and sometimes aggressive as elementary-school-age children. Parents and teachers have been anxious about their lack of friends even when they've had a few. Parents and teachers often put pressure on the girls to make friends, and the girls connect having a large group of close friends with healthy adjustment. They learn that adults are disappointed in them because they don't have friends, and they become so anxious about friendships that they're willing to do almost anything to be included in any group that will validate them. They develop a deep resentment toward the bright, achieving kids who have not accepted them and share that resentment in order to build solidarity with another group. In some ways they believe that "goodies" are bad, which makes "baddies" good because they are good to each other, although they may appear tough or mean to outsiders.

When your daughter is a little lonely, it's important to label it as independence even though you realize it isn't easy for her. In that way you avoid putting too much pressure on her about making friends and becoming popular. Use this lonely time to help her to learn skills and develop interests that will enable her to share activities with others. For example, learning to play chess will encourage her to play with other girls, or developing an excitement about music or art will give her a passion to share with other positive young people who also enjoy her interests.

Preventative Strategy #2: Avoiding Conspiratorial Relationships Rebellious adolescents have often been overempowered by parents who are divided. A mother who allies with her daughter against her dad, or a father who allies with a daughter against her mother, teaches a child that relationships become closer and more intimate when two people share a common enemy. Learning to feel close to a person only when there is a common enemy can become a very negative but intense habit, which transfers naturally to finding a peer group or even a boyfriend who is against school or against parents.

This alliance-against-an-enemy relationship with a parent becomes an even greater risk during or after a divorce. Mothers who have been rejected by their husbands are especially vulnerable to engaging their daughters in intimate details about the unethical or insensitive behavior of their husbands. Although it seems at first that daughters are understanding and value the intimate sharing, that too-intimate practice almost always backfires. Teens are torn by the conflict and attracted to the power of the father, who often seems willing to become much more permissive than the rejected mother (perhaps to attract the daughter to his side). Dads tend to prefer that their daughters become less inhibited and more open, in order to justify the new lifestyle that the fathers may have adopted. Girls may be attracted to the new freedom they are offered. This usually initiates rebellion in the daughter against the mother, who has already been hurt and is trying to teach the daughter to be ethical. It doesn't seem fair to the mother, and it often isn't. Divorce is no time to assume that your daughter is mature enough to be your counselor or confidante. Not only are you placing your daughter in an impossible dilemma, but you're also teaching her disrespect and rebellion toward her dad, which will in turn cause him to teach your daughter disrespect for you. Furthermore, you're giving up your adult responsibility when your daughter may require it most.

Preventative Strategy #3: Helping Girls Adjust to a Move Another important prevention takes place after a move to another community. In Chapter 6 we recommended having your daughter paired with someone initially when moving to a new school. The person with whom she is paired can often make her feel more comfortable as well as include her in a positive friendship group. Thus the selection of that person should be made carefully. You can probably do that most diplomatically if you share with the teacher or counselor your daughter's most positive interests. If you do this, it is more likely that she and the girl with whom she is paired will have activities or interests in common.

Sometimes negative or needy kids are selected by teachers to pair with new students in the hopes of helping them. Of course, the neediness may work, but the negativity is unlikely to help your daughter find nice friends. Caution your daughter that finding good friends takes time, and there isn't really a hurry about it because you're certain that eventually she will find a few good friends. A wish for quantity encourages the quest for popularity, which may or may not turn out to be a good thing, depending on the values of the popular peer group in the particular school.

Solution #1: Changing Schools There are several possibilities for solving the negative peer group issue. In Chapter 4 we recommended changing schools under certain circumstances. That works most effectively at the beginning of a negative peer group relationship, before your daughter is overly engaged with the group. It also works best if the negative group does not live in the surrounding neighborhood and if your daughter and her friends don't drive yet. It's more effective at the middle-school level than at the high-school level. However, it was effective for some women in the study and has been extremely powerful for some girls who have been clients at the Family Achievement Clinic.

Solution #2: Prohibiting a Friendship Also somewhat effective in middle school and possibly early in high school, but not likely beyond that, is a clear message to your daughter that you wish her not to befriend a particular individual or group. You'll need to justify the prohibition by explaining that you find their behavior unacceptable and you'll only permit them to be friends outside of school if you see a change in the other girl or girls. If both parents agree on that philosophy, your daughter is likely to accept it. If you as parents don't agree, don't waste your time prohibiting the friendship. Your daughter will ignore the message she doesn't like if she receives an equally powerful message that she prefers from her other parent. If either of you believes that your daughter should have the right to choose any friends she wishes, she will, regardless of one parent insisting she be more selective. This is an important communication that the two parents should talk through carefully. Again, if you have had a difficult divorce, your daughters are more vulnerable, and the prohibition is unlikely to be effective.

Solution #3: Substituting a Positive Relationship The most positive technique for removing a girl from a negative peer group is somehow getting her involved in a positive peer experience, such as a fun enrichment program, a special-interest group, drama, a summer program or camp, or a youth travel program. If your daughter isn't too negatively involved but just a little rebellious, participation in a school program in another country will often elevate her to an entirely different self-perception. Living with another family in a foreign country may put her in a position where she not only must respect limits but will appreciate her parents much more. Participating in an opportunity abroad provides her with a pro-school status that will undoubtedly alienate her anti-school peers. Furthermore, such an opportunity can provide her with significant positive attention in her own school as well as in her host school. For families that don't have the financial means for such opportunities, there are exchange programs that offer grants/scholarships or suggestions for student fund-raising. Even participation in the student fund-raising activities will give your daughter a positive direction and a positive peer group.

Solution #4: Entering Contests Encourage your daughter to enter a contest or activity in which she has a chance of winning or getting an important part. Don't hesitate to talk to a coach or teacher privately about your efforts to reverse her negativism. Winning kids are often excluded from peer groups that are negative about school. Winning a speech or art contest often provides status to students and causes them to appear more interesting to positive students. Sometimes a victory is enough to separate a teen from a negative peer group.

Solution #5: An Exciting Family Trip An exciting family trip is also an option for distracting your wayward daughter from negativity. Time away from peers in an entirely new environment can channel your daughter's independence. One-to-one trips, although they may not be entirely effective, may be important in reducing tension temporarily and enhancing family closeness. One parent and one teen may be better than the entire family because the teen is more likely to relax if sibling rivalry issues are not present.

If you introduce any of these potential separators to your daughter, don't expect her to like them. She'll fight you if she is pressured to participate. They shouldn't even be suggested as choices, or she surely will not make them. You can, however, permit or even encourage her to make choices among them. For example, which country she would prefer or which summer creative writing program seems most interesting are the types of choices that she can make effectively and that will encourage her independence and lessen her resistance.

HOW MUCH HOMOGENEITY IS GOOD?

The argument related to cultural homogeneity or heterogeneity goes back a long way. It was at my high-school graduation in Perth Amboy, New Jersey, that the speaker addressed the audience about whether our country should be viewed as a melting pot or a symphony orchestra. Even then I preferred the symphony orchestra approach of main-taining many cultural traditions, languages, and cultural richness and valuing the blending of differences. At the Family Achievement Clinic, whether parents of children come from Iran, Mexico, India, or the Ukraine, they are encouraged to continue their language and to pro-vide cultural instruction whenever possible. The political correctness of homogeneous cultural groupings seems to vary with the times, but our research substantiates that children brought up on islands of their own cultural values can become comfortable in college and adulthood in the mixed cultural milieu that this country offers.

PREVENTING SMOKING AND DRUG USE; DELAYING ALCOHOL CONSUMPTION

You are unlikely to be able to prevent your daughters from smoking if you or your spouse smokes. With the barrage of evidence about the harm tobacco causes, it is difficult to explain how conscientious parents who love their children can continue to smoke. Of course, the only answer is that it is a difficult addiction to break, and if you are continu-ing to smoke, at least you need to explain to your children that you wish you had never picked up your first cigarette. Although that's most likely to work only if you quit, don't leave the message unsaid.

If your daughter experiments with a cigarette or two, that's not a rea-son to overreact, but it is a reason to be very clear about your strong opposition to her even experimenting with them. You may want to sound stronger than you feel. Addiction takes hold quite easily with young people. Furthermore, young people who get involved in smoking in middle school are often opening the gates to other addictions.

If your daughter is smoking with friends regularly, there's a very good chance she is not in the kind of crowd that will foster her achieve-ment. Like most other issues, cigarette smoking is easier to prohibit early and indeed is difficult, and sometimes impossible, to prevent by high school. If you don't smoke, at least you can prohibit smoking within your home. You don't have to be subjected to your children's passive smoke, and while that may push your daughter to smoke at the home of a friend whose parents are more permissive, she will at least learn to respect your limits.

There are several schools of thought on alcohol use. One group believes that if families drink in moderation and use alcohol as part of their holiday celebrations, introducing their children to a few sips of alcohol during an appropriate holiday takes away the "forbidden fruit" temptation and thus prevents teens from viewing alcohol as a vehicle of rebellion against parents. Other families believe that their children should not be allowed to have any alcohol at all. No research supports either approach, although as with tobacco, alcohol abuse by parents surely encourages alcohol abuse by children.

Many parents look the other way when they know their teens are drinking. Some confiscate car keys so that their teens won't drive, but permit them to party with alcohol in their homes. Such parents are being role models for breaking the law, and they should not be surprised if their children follow in their footsteps and find themselves involved in legal problems even beyond drinking. They've given their kids permission to be selective in regard to which laws they will obey.

I believe parents should give their teens the message that alcohol consumption at parties is definitely illegal, and they probably had better not have even a single sip, or else they're as vulnerable to being caught as others who are drunk. They might be better off accepting the role of designated driver, a graceful approach to avoiding drinking. On the other hand, if they require a ride home under any circumstances that make them feel uncomfortable, they should not hesitate to call you. You should promise to be there and that they won't have to face an inquisition—at least not at the time, although it's fair to have a reasonable discussion afterward. There's not much sense in threatening punishment; if you do, they won't call when they need you, and you will not be able to prevent either the abuse or the potential accident when they drive under the influence of alcohol or drive with others who have had too much to drink. Encourage your daughters to join SADD (Students Against Drunk Driving). The organization will drive the message home better than you can. SADD has saved many teen lives and has also made it socially easier for teens to decline alcohol.

Parents who experimented with drugs in their teens or twenties struggle with an honest approach to preventing their children from experimenting with drugs. Furthermore, parents often believe they need to reveal to their children that they were not so innocent as their children believe. We encourage you not to rush into confessions to your children. Your daughters don't need to know about every experiment of your youth. Your telling them will grant automatic permission to do as you did and go at least one step beyond. After all, most kids like to outdistance their parents.

If you're concerned that not telling them will encourage them to hide things from you, be assured they'll hide some things from you anyway, and indeed they should. While good communication is important, expecting your daughters to tell you everything is enmeshment, and permits them no privacy or independence. On the other hand, if your daughters specifically ask you if you experimented with drugs as a teen, it's important to be honest. One can't build trust on lies. You can, however, explain that you wouldn't do it today because, first of all, the drugs of today tend to be much more potent, and second of all, there was a lot that was unknown in your day about the harm of drugs. We recommend that you then give an example, the worst one you can remember, of a friend or an acquaintance who was permanently harmed by drugs. Perhaps this will at least encourage your daughter to be cautious. Do remember that if you actually give her permission to experiment, she will undoubtedly see it as permission for much more than an experiment. Zero tolerance for drugs is reasonable. We now know that marijuana adversely affects motivation and short-term memory, and that it is an entry-level addiction that predicts use of other drugs.

There are obviously many issues involved if your daughters are already using and abusing tobacco, alcohol, or drugs, but dealing with those issues is beyond the mission of this book.

MAKING HER MARK

Donna Draves
Television News Anchor

By around age twelve, Donna Draves had decided she wanted to be a famous news anchor, like those she watched on television. At age thirty-five, she has made a name for herself as a local news anchor in a large northeastern city, and while her childhood dreams were of national rather than local television, right now she is comfortable because her family is a high priority for her.

Donna's ecstatically happy with her career, her family life, and her national network of friendships. She loves the popularity, prestige, and excitement her television career delivers. She finds her work challenging, interesting, fulfilling, and financially rewarding. She also acknowledges the downside, which includes very long and late hours, extreme pressure, and considerable worry about her appearance. Her day often begins at 6:30 A.M. and ends as late as 11 P.M. Balancing her family responsibilities and her career sometimes does feel overwhelming.

Donna's earliest memories of her childhood involve reading and art. Her mother was a high-school English teacher and an artist and encouraged Donna's love of books and artwork. Donna recalls that very early she had special artistic talent; however, it seemed to disappear with maturity. On the other hand, her love of books has had a long-term impact. Dolley Madison, Amelia Earhart, and Eleanor Roosevelt were heroes who inspired her wish to someday make her own mark in society.

Reading wasn't considered "fashionable" among Donna's peers, and her love of reading actually became a problem for her. Even early on she felt pressured to do more of the activities approved of by popular girls. Donna's activities included playing the piano, writing creative stories, and involvement in speech, drama, and Girl Scouts. In elementary school, she especially enjoyed performing in front of audiences. She also took various lessons, such as dance and drama, but tended to quit the lessons soon after she began because she often felt awkward, even clumsy, compared to the other students. Learning the steps was hard for her, and she felt that everyone in the class was better than she. Instead of explaining to her mom how bad she felt about her inadequacy, she would just tell her she didn't like the lessons. Her mother never forced her to complete the lessons or any course she enrolled in. She continued her speech lessons because she had a great memory, and she knew she could excel at and even "be best" at speech. She won many speech contests and continued with speech throughout high school.

Donna attended a small Catholic elementary school through eighth grade despite the fact that she was Episcopalian. Her beautiful, artistic, and talented mother was actively involved as a volunteer in the school. She was proud of her mother and thought she was the most beautiful mother in the school.

In third and fourth grades, Donna didn't like math because it was difficult for her. She blamed the teachers and told her mother she was bored. She recalls that her mother was very understanding about it, always taking Donna's side and feeling sorry for her. She even thinks her mom might have gone to the teachers to complain for her. In retrospect, Donna feels her mother was a little too understanding. Donna acknowledged that right from the start she was figuring out how to get out of things she didn't like or do well.

When Donna was in fifth grade her mother developed health problems and discontinued her teaching career temporarily. Her mother was in and out of the hospital frequently and had surgery several times.

Donna remembers that she herself often pretended to be sick during the years that followed. She simply preferred staying at home, day-dreaming and watching television, fantasizing about being grown up and on television, and always wishing she were older.

Despite her frequent absenteeism, Donna was an excellent student and was identified as gifted. She loved the creative writing that was part of the program, but hated the math and considered it useless. When she was assigned individualized math work in the gifted program, she didn't do the work because it didn't interest her. Donna recalls very clearly her exasperated teacher in the gifted class asking to see her work, discovering she had done none, and scolding in outrage, with her finger in Donna's face, "Get back to your desk and do your work!" Immediately afterward Donna pretended to be sick again and stayed home for about six weeks. She danced around much of the day, watched TV, and did little else. Even the maid who was caring for her while her mother was at work announced, "You ain't sick." The maid was right, yet to this day Donna believes her parents thought she was. They took her to a specialist who couldn't identify the problem, so the feigned illness continued on and off with no recognition that Donna was only "sick" of school.

Both of Donna's parents had high educational expectations for her, but she perceived her mother as having higher expectations and as being more firm with her than her father. Her dad was devoted but traveled a great deal as a business executive. He tried to cope with both her mother's and her own frequent complaints of illness and loved and adored them both. She and her mother would spend hours talking together, but they rarely did anything and were never involved in any physical activities together. The creative enterprises and the book discussions of her earlier childhood disappeared, and in place of activity there was only idle chitchat.

When asked whom she was most similar to, Donna denied identifying with her mother, mainly because she had never viewed herself as being as pretty, thin, or smart as her mother. Donna's mother had won beauty contests in high school and college and had also been a scholar. Donna never considered herself as being like her dad, either, although she had a very special relationship with him and thinks of him as the most giving and generous person in the world. Instead, she identified with her grandmother, whom she remembers as being cute and fun and always very happy. "She was just good and kind," Donna recalls, "and although she is sick with Alzheimer's now, whatever it is behind her eyes, when she looks at you, you know that deep inside that kindness is still there."

Donna still finds her grandmother remarkable and considers her to be "a superior being." She explained further, "It's not because she's the most brilliant person in the world, although she's very smart, but there is something about her that you know is so wonderful." Donna says her grandmother really appreciated the things that are supposed to be appreciated, and society never got into her head and corrupted her; she just worked and was a happy person. When she was in college she worked as a dental assistant, and she traveled out into the countryside and took care of poor people's teeth.

Donna thinks she looks like her grandmother but wishes she could have her "profound face." Her grandmother maintained her beauty in a way that Donna believes she never will. She sees herself as more stocky in build, not as slender as her grandmother, but thinks that's because her grandmother took better care of herself and exercised regularly.

Donna also sees herself as most like her grandmother in the sense that she's willing to be friendly with anybody and everybody. She explained: "I model myself after my grandmother. I know everybody's name in my grocery store, including the guy who sweeps the floor. I think my grandmother taught me the joy of valuing all people. She taught me not to write others off just because they're uneducated. My grandmother is always kind, open, and happy, and I'm really like that, too."

Although Donna feels very close to her younger brother, she remembers having felt jealous of and pressured by him. She also felt less intelligent and less athletic than he. Donna described the competition she felt with him by explaining that he was a "mathematical genius" and was selected for a special higher-math program for which she was not. In some ways she wondered if her brother's mathematical talent contributed to her hatred of mathematics. He was a great basketball player, and she described herself as a "klutz." It seemed to her that her parents were all wrapped up in his accomplishments. She felt fortunate when she began to win more speech contests. It gave her a special niche and helped her to deal with the feelings of inadequacy she experienced when she compared herself to him. She also felt more socially successful than he, and she valued that. It seemed to her that she had to avoid participation in activities or areas in which her brother excelled because they automatically made her feel inadequate.

Donna remembers her middle-school years as very precarious for her, and had it not been for her competitive victories in speech and the motivation they provided, she believes she might have headed off on the wrong path. She and two other girls in her class were very interested in boys. She was very pretty (although she didn't think so at the time), and popularity was her highest priority. She recalls being considered cool, popular, maybe even a show-off, and she was quite difficult during those years. She would go with her anti-school friends to a theme park and smoke and look for boys. They were her best friends, and she was going nowhere with them. As Donna reflects on it, she thinks of that time as one that could have changed the direction of her life entirely. She realizes that her temporary anti-learning, anti-parent peer group almost brought her down, and had it done so, she would have missed out on so many other opportunities. Those friends never went on to college, as far as she knows, and Donna shudders as she thinks of what she might have missed. Somehow the attention she received for her speeches separated her from them. So, in a sense, she was rescued from a downhill trajectory of underachievement by her winning speeches. She thanks her inspiring speech teacher for redirecting her to the excitement of speech contests. Gradually she was accepted by a different set of girls who were good students and who were all college-bound.

When asked about the importance of appearance in her life, Donna admitted probably putting more emphasis on it than she would ever want her own children to do. She recalls from pictures of herself that she had been a beautiful little girl, admired by all for her looks. However, during adolescence, she went through a very unattractive stage. She recalls that she had a terrible complexion, and her skin is still pitted as a result. She recalls having had terrible eating habits, alternately starving herself and eating junk food. She believes that may have contributed to her terrible skin condition, which she then covered with heavy makeup.

Donna remembers looking in the mirror and thinking how unattractive she was. Not only did she think she was not very pretty, but in her words, she wasn't "even plain-looking." Her skin was bad, she had a round face, and she was just "not very cute." Before she went on to high school, she remembers thinking, "Well, I won't be popular because I'm so unattractive, so what in the world can I do to make my mark?" She decided she was a pretty good writer. Her mother had taught her to write, and she loved writing in elementary school, so she thought maybe she could be a literary journal editor or write for the high-school newspaper.

High school represented a dramatic change for Donna. Her parents chose to send her to an independent high school, and she had some difficulty adjusting to a student population that was very different from what she was used to. Some of the students were very accelerated, highly intelligent, and excellent athletes. All of the students came from a very different socioeconomic class than Donna was accustomed to, and most of them were extremely wealthy.

While in high school, "miraculously," Donna recalls, "I actually got a lot cuter. I ended up sort of leaning on my looks as a crutch because I was so insecure. It never occurred to me to actually try to learn a sport or get involved in school activities. I don't think I even tried to do anything in high school."

Donna remembers worrying constantly about her weight, even though she was very thin. She discovered she could just pass up food. Although she never became anorexic, she played little tricks where she wouldn't eat all day and would then go home and eat a light dinner and her parents would think she was okay. Then on the weekends she would sleep until 3 P.M. so she wouldn't have to eat. By not eating, she would remain the size three she wanted to be when she went out with her boyfriend at night.

Donna realizes now that this ploy was ridiculous, stemming as it did from a lack of confidence in herself, and she believes it had a long-term effect on her adult muscle tone and endurance. She doesn't feel physically fit and bemoans her early poor eating and personal health habits. She recalls two girls in her class who were "skinnier" than she, and she found that scary. She felt unattractive unless she could be thinnest. Even in this area, she constantly compared herself and felt competitive.

In high school Donna's grades and achievement improved, but she wasn't in any highly accelerated classes, and there were so many smart students in her school that she just felt "dumb." Donna studied and did much more homework in high school. Despite her good school performance, Donna believed she couldn't achieve much of anything, as she wasn't good in sports, was poorly coordinated, and was terrible at math. Furthermore, her brother was a superachiever. She recalls, "I wanted to be a superachiever at something, so I concentrated on nothing else but popularity, looks, and boys, and just loafed all the time."

When asked why she thought she was so boy-crazy, Donna said she attributed this to both her insecurity and competitiveness. She thought if she could have become renowned for being smart or athletic, it would have helped to direct her energy, and she might have been more confident and easygoing. Furthermore, she thought her family encouraged her early dating. She read lots of teen magazines, and focused on hair, makeup, and appearance constantly. At age fourteen she wished she were twenty-two and tried to look that way. She doesn't remember any objection from her parents, so television stars and teen magazine models became her most important role models. Perhaps hearing about her mother's successes in beauty contests also encouraged her in that direction.

Being popular and pretty remained Donna's first priority. She felt pressured to have preppie clothes and was intimidated by her classmates' wealth and beautiful homes. She was on the planning committee for the prom and was selected for the homecoming court. She remembers her life centering around her handsome, popular, and smart boyfriend.

As Donna reflects on her relationship with her parents while she was in high school, she remembers that there was considerable conflict between them and her and that they were pretty hard on her. Her relationship with her dad was better than that with her mom. She thought that they prevented her from having as much fun as her friends, yet she always felt loved by her parents and recalls that at least they were "neither dumb nor drunk," and that they always wanted the best for her. Furthermore, they rarely punished her, though they did follow through on the rules they set. In many ways, she realizes now, the pressure they put on her and the limits they set were really good for her, but at the time she was mainly annoyed and angered by their rules.

Donna decided she would graduate from high school a year early and accept a scholarship to a small women's college. She never shared with anyone that her real motivation for leaving high school was that she had broken up with her boyfriend and, perhaps more important, realized that someone else would be elected homecoming queen. Donna simply could not face the failure. She describes herself as a "cover-your-butt" kind of person who basically hides her failures because she finds them so difficult to cope with. She adds that there are some things that it's charming to be not so great at, and those she's happy to reveal. However, not being most popular was not something she was willing to cope with in high school, so going to college early on a scholarship seemed like a wonderful and honorable alternative. Consider that other young people faced with these feelings of failure might have made much worse choices, such as quitting school or sleeping with many young men.

Donna's time at this small women's college at age seventeen was a smashing success. She was a star at the college, took leadership roles, was popular, and became campus queen as well as a very good student. Her major was journalism and TV. After a year and a half, however, she transferred to the large state university and was suddenly very lost. She continued to excel in her journalism and TV classes, however, and thanks to them, she graduated, though just barely. She had an internship with a major television station, and a television anchorwoman to whom she feels very indebted was an important mentor during those difficult college days.

Donna remembers "getting it in her head" that other kids were somehow better than she. She wanted to find something that made her stand out from them, and she thinks that's really one of the reasons she chose a television career that put her so much in the limelight—to try to be something other people would find remarkable. She thought, "They'll say, 'Oh, God, look what Donna did!'" She also acknowledges that because she felt dumb and shallow at some points in her life, it never occurred to her "to do anything that would require me to be highly intelligent, like medicine or science." Furthermore, she had confidence in her verbal skills because of her speech training and confidence in her social skills because of her popularity. Thus she chose her career because it was one of the few things she actually believed she could do.

After a terrible and brief first marriage, Donna is in a happy second marriage and has two children. It's only recently that she's really come to terms with her driving competitiveness and finally feels a sense of contentment with her place in life.

When Donna reflects on her career, she realizes that she has "made her mark." She has a great five-year contract that will provide her family with financial security even if it is not renewed. She has managed to "show up" her former classmates who were so wealthy and successful. Finally, she doesn't feel so pressured to win, mainly because she finally views herself as a winner. When she thinks about her serious pitfalls, which fortunately were only near misses, she's very thankful she had the drive, the perseverance, and the resilience to survive times that could have stolen from her the success and happiness she has today. Donna Draves knows that being as competitive as she is is a two-edged sword.

CHAPTER 8

Parents Do Make
a Difference

Family Relationships

Part 1: Findings

Most of the successful women in our study not only perceived themselves as smart girls but also viewed their parents as intelligent people.
Three-quarters of the women considered both their parents intelligent;
13 percent thought their fathers were more intelligent than their mothers; and 8 percent thought their mothers were more intelligent than
their fathers. Only 3 percent of the women believed that neither parent
was very intelligent. You may recall from the first chapter that fewer
than half of the women's dads and only a quarter of their mothers had
completed a college education; thus, despite their lack of higher education, their daughters appreciated their parents' intelligence. It may well
be that fathers' additional education gave them some advantage in
their daughters' perceptions of their intelligence, but many of these
women's parents had not even completed high school. Our data make a
strong case for children learning to value and respect their parents'
commonsense intelligence. For example, executive Margaret Karnes's
father had no more than five years of education in his native Hungary,
but Margaret observed his great ability to learn from his environment,
his great foresight and ability to predict the future, and his excellent

and logical decision making. She also respected her mother's level-headed ability to balance her father's too-creative decisions with realistic common sense, even though her mother had little formal education. Margaret often felt embarrassed by her parents' accents, but she had no doubts about their intelligence.

Sixty-eight percent of the women found both their parents to be supportive. However, when there were differences in the support parents provided, twice as many of the women (16 percent) found their mothers to be more supportive than their fathers (8 percent). A full 7 percent of these women found neither parent to be supportive. This data seems to imply that while support from both parents is ideal and certainly best for children's developing achievement, nevertheless a considerable percentage of these women, almost a third, found success despite the lack of support of one or both parents. As you can see by a few of the following comments, even when there was a perceived lack of support, there was clearly a strong influence. Gretchen Instrom, director of an adolescent health center, credits her incredibly supportive family. "They never let me down. The excitement of my own children over my attending graduate school was of great value to me. Also, my husband attended graduate school and changed careers at age forty. We all cheered for one another, even though our changes meant less income for the family." And Judge Beverly Abrams believed her mother had the most influence on her. "She encouraged me to choose a nontraditional career and go to law school. She knew I needed the challenge and status of an unusual, different career that wasn't pigeonholed only for women."

Novelist Samantha Hollingsworth was, surprisingly, motivated by her mother's lack of support: "My mother's consistent skepticism was a goad. All my life I've tried to impress her. I finally made it last year when Random House bought my first novel." Lorraine Wolfe, a business consultant, rose above her family's dysfunction, but never stopped wanting to impress them. "My parents were in constant conflict and disorganization. They provided little support for any of us in our nine-children family. Oddly enough, I continue to want their approval. When I was asked about my delight at becoming a partner in the prestigious consulting firm I'm now with, I recall thinking that I really wanted to please my parents. I also remember how in eighth grade I made a purposeful decision to psychologically leave my confused family and take charge of my own life. That was when my D's and F's became A's, and when I decided I wanted to be like June Cleaver on *Leave It to Beaver*."

When the women were asked about the five most supportive relationships during their lives, mothers came out highest, with fathers a close second, and grandparents and other relatives somewhat further behind. The percentage indicating parents as most supportive declined only slightly from elementary to middle to high school, and it wasn't until the college years that parents took a backseat to professors and peers.

Grandparental influence was selected as very important by almost a third of the women during their elementary-school years, but that figure diminished to approximately 20 percent by middle school, high school, and college—still a considerable number, because the assumption must be made that many of the women's grandparents died while the women were growing up.

Other family support, including that of aunts, uncles, and cousins, was considered very important by an impressive 20 percent. Below are some women's statements about the importance of other family members. Notice that the comments about grandparents are sometimes in contradiction to each other. Some grandparents emphasized grades, while others placed no emphasis on school achievement; nevertheless, despite their differences in emphasis, the grandparents seemed equally effective in their inspiration to their granddaughters. Two attorneys gave differing perspectives on how their grandmothers influenced them. Lynette Hathaway recalled, "My grandmother was my rudder and compass during a very rocky childhood. Even though she is a very religious and conservative woman, she has never made me feel ashamed or 'bad' about my nontraditional choices. When I was in grade school, she would make a big deal of my report cards and give me a quarter for every A. I believe that her early support and encouragement helped to make me an academic achiever."

In contrast, Colleen Noon remembered best the unconditional love. "My grandmother gave me the greatest gift one could ever give a child: She loved me unconditionally and had no expectations of me other than to be a good, kind person. While she had no education, she was wiser than any person I've ever known because she understood human nature and only expected me to be true to myself. Her arms were a refuge; her house was my home."

Jacqueline Owen, who works in corporate law, recalled her grandmother's influence this way: "She was a black woman in Georgia born in 1885. She had a master's degree, and all five of her sisters attended college. She was amazing." And Carol Chandler, a television news producer, remembered being inspired by two aunts who were both nuns.

"They sent me their textbooks before I even started school. From those phonics books, I taught myself how to read and write by age four. My aunts were the most educated people in my family. They were both school principals. They saw my potential and told me to never stop trying."

IDENTIFICATION WITH PARENTS
(AND OTHER ROLE MODELS)

The women in our study indicated high identification with their parents, although the percentage that identified with their mothers decreased somewhat as the women matured. When asked whom they thought they were most similar to when they were in elementary school, twice as many (50 percent) chose their mothers, compared to those who chose their fathers. Approximately 20 percent chose someone else, often a teacher or other relative, and sometimes a television hero or a neighbor. By high school only a third chose their mothers, but a quarter continued to identify with their dads.

Charlotte Peters, the general manager of a weekly newspaper, recalls going to work with her father a lot during her younger years. "He taught me a solid work ethic at a young age. I spent more time with my father than my mother, and therefore identified with him more. He taught me work values and supported my dream to become a newspaper publisher."

Pastor Faye Schultz was influenced by her strong family background of clergy. "My grandfather has great gifts as a pastor. My uncles, aunts, and cousins are also involved in a wide variety of ministry. My eldest uncle encouraged me to attend seminary, although very few women did. He was a bold supporter of women in the ministry. I had many good role models in the ministry."

The director of an independent school saw her mother as her main role model: "My mother's example as a successful journalist and loving mother was the most powerful influence in my life. I had no career aspirations, yet my mother's example left me no other model. Although she always said, 'Mothers should be at home, not at work,' I did what she did, not what she said."

Business executive Holly Barringer was greatly influenced by and identified with her father. "During my high-school and college years, my father received several promotions and became a very important man at one of the most prestigious corporations. I was proud of him and yearned to emulate him. In the meantime, my mother, who was seven and a half years older, began to achieve high status and eventually became the head of the computer division of a well-known computer company. I wanted to achieve at their levels. I felt I had all the drive, ambition, and talent of my father in me."

Some women did not respond to the identification question at all, and the percentage that did not choose mother or father varied by career. Many women were very clear about the family member with whom they identified; others barely mentioned similarities between themselves and their parents, and still others absolutely rejected any identification with either parent.

Figure 8.1 compares identification figures for the women in the study by career. Although more women in every career identified with their mothers, the careers in which the most women identified with their mothers were homemakers and allied health. The careers in which the most women selected their fathers for identification figures were mental health, science, and medicine. The career groups that selected "others" most often for identification were music, art, and education, and the "others" they selected most frequently, to no surprise, were their teachers. The data for the most part corroborate what one would intuitively assume, and in the case of science and medicine, what has been previously found: Nurturing directions are encouraged by mothers; interest in the male-dominated fields of medicine and science is supported by fathers; and in the specialized arts, teachers are a strong source of encouragement. A surprising finding was the number of mental health professionals who identified with their fathers. As we'll discover further, the mental health professionals were different from almost all other career groups in many ways. Also not surprising was the finding that many teachers identified with their own teachers; many recalled playing teacher by kindergarten age, even lining up blackboards, chalk, and school desks for their younger siblings and friends.

Because the majority of the women in our study identified with their mothers, it became even more important to determine whether their mothers were full-time homemakers or whether they provided role models for careers. Although more than 80 percent of the mothers of these women were full-time homemakers when the women were preschoolers, a proportion that was constant across all careers, many went into the workforce or continued their education as their daughters matured (see Figure 8.2). By these women's high-school years, only 39 percent of their mothers continued full-time homemaking. More of the mothers of women in traditional careers continued to stay home

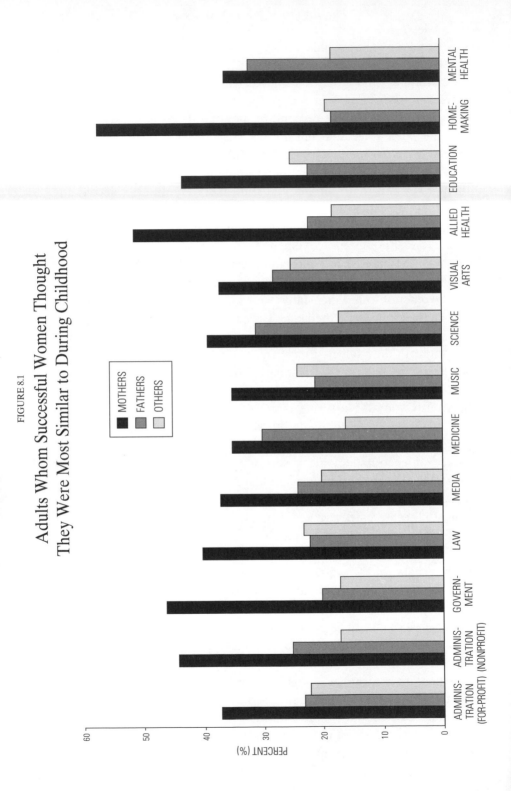

FIGURE 8.1

Adults Whom Successful Women Thought They Were Most Similar to During Childhood

FIGURE 8.2
Percentage of Women Who Had Mothers Who Were Full Time Homemakers During Their Childhood

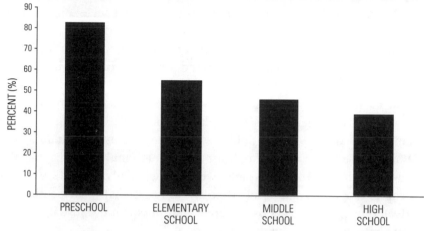

during their daughters' childhoods. Both scientist Dr. Carolyn Borth and psychologist Dr. Sara Barts recalled that their mothers were committed to their homes, but they also always worked side by side with their dads in their stores.

Most of the homemakers had a strong identification with their mothers and valued their role in the family. Laura Guether,* a full-time homemaker, had a college degree and a career in business. Both her sisters had earned college degrees and chose careers; however, she viewed homemaking and parenting as her highest priority. "Our parents worked very hard to make sure that their daughters could be what they wanted when they grew up. They gave us confidence and helped us to realize by example the importance of having a parent at home for your children. Children need someone at home who cares about them personally."

Figure 8.3 emphasizes how important mothers' modeling was for their daughters. A much smaller percentage of the mothers of women in traditional careers returned to school for further education while their daughters were growing up. Almost half of the physicians may have been particularly inspired to pursue an extensive education because they observed their mothers continuing their education. Nearly a quarter of the mothers and 15 percent of the fathers of the women in the study achieved higher degrees during their daughters' childhoods.

Medical researcher Dr. Janice Douglas* recalls that her parents were going to medical school and dental school during the first four years of her life. When she and her husband married in their first year of medical school, they, too, assumed they would continue their education even if they had a family. They knew it could be done because it had been done by her parents.

Dr. Patricia Williams, an assistant professor of science, explained how her mother was an example of the importance of education and independence: "My parents acrimoniously divorced after a seventeen-year marriage. My father remarried immediately. All of us kids and my mother moved to Los Angeles and were on food stamps while Mom went to school. I was in high school at the time. When my parents divorced, my mother chose to go to law school so she could support her family. She also said she would never be dependent on a man again. While those days were difficult for the whole family, I think that she served as an example of a woman who took control of her life, pursued a career she liked, and excelled at it. I am sure that those sentiments affected my ability to choose a career and pursue it because it was fun and because I would remain independent."

FIGURE 8.3

Percentage of Successful Women Who Indicated Their Mothers Continued Their Own Education While the Women Were Growing Up

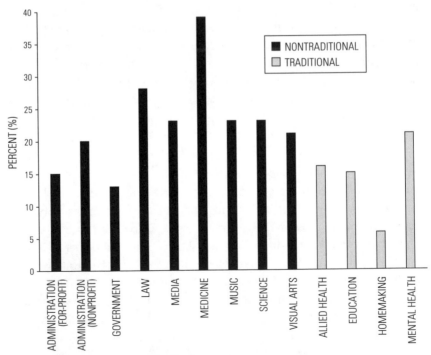

Judge Edna Conway had many positive role models, but Edna recalls vividly a negative role model that influenced her. It was a woman who used to ride the bus regularly on Edna's route to school. The woman had four or five children who were always screaming or crying on the bus, and from Edna's perspective, she looked "so poor." Edna remembers thinking, "I don't want to be that way," and she concluded that only a college education would deliver what she wanted.

FAMILY SIZE AND BIRTH ORDER

More than half of the women came from medium-sized families of two or three children. Nine percent were brought up as only children, a quarter came from large families of four or five children, and 8 percent came from very large families of six or more children. Birth order varied considerably by career groups, but almost half of the entire group were firstborns, which is considerably more than would be expected (see Figure 8.4). Thirty percent of the women were middle children, considerably fewer than would be expected. Twenty-eight percent were youngest in the family. Only children were not calculated in the birth order results.

The traditional concept that firstborns are more successful and middle children are somehow disadvantaged in terms of achievement and success was upheld by our data. Oldest children are often given more power and attention in the family and thus tend to seek more power

FIGURE 8.4

Birth Order of Successful Women: Total Group

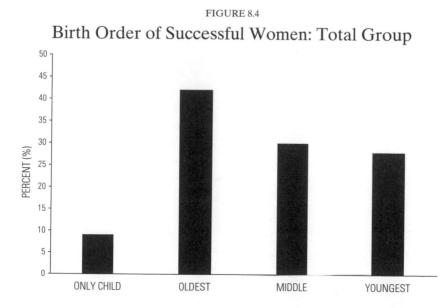

and leadership in their careers. Oldest children also tend to be tradition bearers, less creative, and less rebellious. The largest percentage of oldest children was in government and education, with almost half of the women in each category being firstborns. As children, they typically ended up taking care of their siblings, were put in charge, and baby-sat a fair amount.

Homemakers included the most middle children (almost half), followed by allied health professionals (40 percent). Being middle children did perhaps decrease their motivation for high achievement, as well as encourage their desire to be nurturing. Perhaps they wished for more attention and thus wanted to compensate by giving more attention to others; equally likely is that they learned to be comfortable sharing attention and thus chose careers in which they'd receive less individual attention and status.

In science, law, and music there were more women who were youngest, and not as high a proportion of oldest children as in some of the other careers. Perhaps these careers attract more youngest children because they are more creative.

Finally, and again surprisingly, the mental health professionals included more women who were youngest in the family—perhaps a tribute to their rebelliousness or to their childhood efforts to understand the relationships that surrounded them. One psychologist recalled that her older siblings were always in charge at home, but she also remembered trying to figure out what got them into trouble so she would know what to do or what not to do to stay out of the same kind of trouble. She also recalled spending a lot of time trying to understand how all the people in her world interacted. Perhaps she was not the only psychologist who was introduced to understanding relationships by insightful observation from the position of the baby of the family.

Although it is interesting to recognize the importance that birth order has for the selection of careers, it would be wrong to overrate its importance when guiding your daughter's career direction. In every career group, there were women of every birth order category. While birth order may encourage a woman to move in certain directions, it alone is not a determinant of success in any specific career.

SIBLING RIVALRY AND RELATIONSHIPS

The women in the study described their relationships with their siblings more in terms of the roles they played compared to their siblings rather than in terms of overt competition. For example, musicians, dancers, or artists often described their art as providing their special space in the family and how a sister or brother recognized the special talent as their sibling's and thus stepped out of that arena to create their own academic, social, or athletic space. The more extreme the rivalry, the more territorial siblings were. In some families the siblings were labeled as "the smart one," "the social one," "the athlete," "the musician," "the artist," and so on.

Even more dramatic was the way siblings took on contrasting roles—dominance or dependence, for example, "brilliant" compared to "smart and hardworking." In sister pairs, the more dominant female sibling was typically the successful woman in the study, and it was also her perspective of her sister's dependence that was described. In brother-sister pairs, "brilliant" was a descriptor almost always attributed to a brother, while "hardworking" tended to be assigned to the sister. For example, educator Roberta Wendt described her brother as brilliant. He could just show up and get good grades, while she had to work really hard to do that. She was also very social and wanted to be part of almost every organization. Her friendships were important, too, so she was busy every minute, but she never considered herself brilliant. That paradigm also fits with the sibling relationships of the clients who often attend Family Achievement Clinic for treatment of underachievement. It is the brother who is typically described as gifted and underachieving, and the sister who is viewed as hardworking but not especially gifted. When the women described treatment of their brothers and themselves by their parents, many commented on the slightly different treatment they received. Even when their parents had high expectations for their daughters, there remained significant gender-stereotyped roles, and some of the women even talked about how their brothers were revered and put on a pedestal.

Educator Roberta Wendt recalls, "I remember when I was in junior high school occasionally thinking that my brother was allowed to do so much more than I, and my mother's reply was, 'He's a boy and he's four years older.' I fought that so much. I would say, 'What does being a boy have to do with it?' She would say, 'Well, we just want you to be safe.' I'm sure she was worried about me getting into a situation that I couldn't handle with a boy who was stronger than me or something, but I remember resenting that because I thought I could handle anything. I knew how to take care of myself, I made good decisions, so why would they not think I would be fine? Except for that, my childhood was idyllic."

Dr. Sandra Calvin, an environmental engineer, admired her older sister because she was a good athlete and musician and had a great sense of humor. She was particularly close and somewhat maternal with her younger brother. Another brother was two grades ahead of her and had a learning disability. She used to help him with his homework, and he introduced Sandra to his friends as "the smart one."

Rhonda Baker, a graphic artist, commented that she was always different from her sister. Her sister was domestic, and her room was always neat and clean. Rhonda raised fish and gerbils, and aquariums filled her room, which she described as a "pit." Rhonda was like her dad, and her sister was like her mom. Her sister is a full-time homemaker; Rhonda has always worked outside the home in an art-related career.

Sally Sahn, a media publicist, explained the differences between her and her sister this way: "My sister was quite the opposite of me. She was very feminine in her dress and interests and was definitely not a tomboy. We grew up in contrast to each other. I did most of the talking for both of us. My sister was very quiet. My strength was in the verbal area, and my weakness was in math and, later, science. My sister didn't like to play outside with me but instead preferred dressing up. In a picture of us as children, I'm in shorts with my hair all messed up, and I'm hanging from the swing set, and she's got gloves on and a little sailor dress and anklets and Mary Janes for playing outside. My sister received her college degree in business and is presently a bank teller."

Amy Fox, a business executive, talked about how she bossed members of her family: "I was the oldest sister and pretty much ordered my sister around. She was very reserved. I eventually ordered everyone around, first my father, and during my teen years I had lots of battles with my mother as well, as I tried to run the family. I liked running everyone and was pretty feisty, as was my mother. Mom was a full-time homemaker and part-time teacher. My sister is a full-time homemaker. I manage five hundred employees in an extremely complex transportation system, and I continue to enjoy running things."

Judge Edna Conway remembers her sister as being very negative and complaining, moody, and pessimistic. Although the older of two sisters is often the more successful, in this case Edna, the younger sister, was the one to step out on her own. Edna's sister went to four or five colleges before she finally graduated. As Edna observed her sister's failures and bad choices, she said to herself, "I won't make the same mistakes. I can be successful."

Several women alluded to special privileges or talents that were developed because they had no brothers, and they were convinced that they benefited by being in an all-girls family. Civil engineer Dr. Catherine Burns recalled, "Probably the most important factor in my achievement was that I was the oldest daughter in a family where there were no brothers." And nurse Angela Sands explained, "In our family, because there were no boys, my dad just figured from the beginning that he was always going to do things with his girls that he probably would have done with boys if he had them. He would always have one or the other of us girls helping him fix the car and would explain what he was doing."

It was tempting to believe from the interviews that a no-boy family would make a difference in directing girls toward nontraditional careers. Although we analyzed the data to determine whether an all-girls or only-girl-among-boys family made a difference, there were no statistically significant findings that suggested that the makeup of these families made the difference despite the unique individual stories. In some families the absence of boys made a difference, and in others it made no difference at all.

RELATIONSHIP WITH PARENTS

This group of successful women mainly viewed their relationships with their parents favorably while growing up, although more women indicated a good relationship with their mothers than with their fathers. True to the developmental expectations of adolescence, relationships weren't quite as smooth during the teen years as they were during earlier childhood. Eighty-one percent of the women considered their relationship with their mothers to be excellent or good during elementary school, and 64 percent described their relationship with their father in those favorable terms. By the teen years, a little more than half of the women described their relationships as favorable with their mothers; half said the same of their fathers. Most of these women were not very rebellious as teens, but neither were their relationships perfectly smooth.

Physician Dr. Alice Petrulis* simply never had any huge gripes or adversarial relationships with her parents in middle or high school. "However," she went on, "that doesn't mean we didn't go through a stage when we thought we knew more than our parents. There simply was no major rebellion. We were all very goal-directed and independent."

Only 13 percent of the women described their relationships with their mother or father as poor, even during their high-school years. On the other hand, that percentage makes one realize that despite severe difficulties with family relationships, girls can mature to be successful women.

When relationships between parents and daughters were analyzed by age groups, there were no significant differences in the quality of relationships with parents between the younger and older women of the group. We speculated that family relationships might have degenerated among the younger women; however, that was not the case with our group.

Most parents of these women were considered firm in their disciplinary approach. Both parents were firm for slightly less than half of the group. Neither parent was firm for only 10 percent of the group, although that increased to 15 percent by adolescence. Although the changes in firmness were not great, the percentages indicating firmness moved in the expected developmental direction, with at least some parents easing up as their children matured. It's interesting to note that many more mothers were firm than fathers. Attorney Michelle McGuire* recalled, "My parents were strict from the standpoint that they enforced the rules. They were always very willing to look at every situation and make a judgment on it. For example: 'Where do you want to go? Okay, it's a basketball game, and then are you getting something to eat after, and where will you be eating? If it's at Denny's, you'll be home by eleven.' They wanted to know at all times where I was and what I was doing. If I had a reasonable explanation to their questions, I was permitted to go. They were fair in that regard. If I was going to the mall to hang out, it was permitted for an hour, not four. They enforced the right elements but still let me do everything I pretty much wanted to do."

A public relations director described her parents as giving her plenty of freedom and independence. "But they were strict. I always had a curfew, and I had to keep it. I blew it sometimes, and I got grounded for it, so there were definite rules, no doubt. I saw my parents as very overprotective. They didn't even want me to go to pajama parties at friends' houses. They just didn't believe in it. Eventually they came around, and I was never deprived ever in my life."

Although the parents of the women in most career groups were similar in their positive, firm approach to discipline as perceived by the women, there were a few interesting differences among the career groups. Among attorneys, there was less firmness by both parents, and more who had mothers who were firmer than fathers. Perhaps the attorneys' mothers were role models for the strength and assertiveness necessary in law, or perhaps the arguing with their mothers that the attorneys did during adolescence predisposed them to be attracted to a litigious profession. Attorney Diana Doyle became accustomed to argument and tension during adolescence, when her relationship with her single mother became much worse. Their conversations led to arguments, and they yelled, screamed, and even locked each other out of the house. Diana could hardly stand being around her mother, but her mother persisted in trying to improve communication.

The opposite was true for the allied health professionals. Fathers were firmer than mothers for many of them, perhaps giving them practice in being assistants to men (consider that until recent years, most doctors were men). Nurse Angela Sands recalled that during her elementary-school years, her dad traveled frequently, and her mother handled most of the discipline. In high school Angela's dad was suddenly back on the home scene. He was stricter and allowed less freedom than her mother. She was very angry and rebellious with her dad, although she saw her mother as understanding and protective.

The mental health professionals indicated the least firmness by both parents of all the career groups. It is interesting to note how these differences in firmness affected the relationships between the women and their parents. More of the attorneys had poor relationships with their mothers during adolescence. Mothers were perhaps placed in an "ogre" position relative to fathers, and these girls often identified with their fathers. More of the allied health professionals had poor relationships with their fathers during adolescence. For them, the firmer father may have been placed in the role of the "ogre." In both cases the negative relationship focused on the firmer parent. However, when neither parent was firm, the opposite response took place: The women were rebellious with both easy parents. Thus more of the mental health professionals, whose parents were less firm, seemed to have poor relationships with both parents.

It appears that children so desperately need limits that a lack of limits causes more anger and rebellion than clear limits do. Our findings support the conclusions from developmental research that the best family discipline is united and authoritative (rather than authoritarian). Neither authoritarian nor very liberal discipline seems to be as effective for family relationships, and certainly united discipline seems to be most effective for raising secure, confident, achieving children.

RELATIONSHIPS BETWEEN PARENTS

Few of the parents of the women in the study were divorced, although quite a few women recalled an increase in conflict between their parents during their childhood. Approximately three-quarters of the women believed their parents had a reasonably good relationship during the women's elementary-school years. By high school that percentage had decreased to 62 percent. This change may be related to an actual decline in the quality of their parents' marriage with time or to the increasing maturity and perceptions of the women by their teen years. Six percent had parents who were divorced while they were in elementary school, 4 percent more in middle school, and 4 percent more in high school, for a total divorce rate of 14 percent for the overall group. There was twice as much parental divorce for the parents of the younger women in our study than the older women (20 percent compared to 9 percent), undoubtedly a reflection of the times and the increasing number of divorces.

Divorce rates of parents were fairly consistent across career categories with only a few exceptions. They were especially high for the women in media and somewhat higher also for the women in medicine and science. The lowest divorce rates were found in the families of women in art, education, and homemaking. It is difficult to hypothesize why these careers differ, though one might suggest that women in the traditional occupations of homemaker and teacher came from families that provided role models who encouraged them not to break with tradition. One can hardly use this rationale for the artists, however, nor is there any way to explain why, for example, the scientists would have had more divorced parents than those in another nontraditional field such as law. All of these women's parents, however, tended to reflect less divorce than was prevalent in society as a whole while they were growing up.

Some of the women mentioned that their single mothers were role models for their own confidence and helped them to realize they would need to be, and could be, independent. Louise Behrens, an orchestral musician, recalled, "My mother was the best example I could have of a caring parent and a career woman. Although she never had the opportunity to play in a major orchestra, she was a fine violinist and still is a good teacher. Perhaps because she was single so much during my childhood, I saw early on that women need to be able to support themselves."

Mary Sadowski made a fine adjustment after her mother's divorce, but one thing she really hated at the Catholic school she attended was that the students were always being told that their parents would go to hell if they were divorced. In no way did she believe her smart, hard-working, divorced mother would ever deserve to go to hell. It also made her angry that in school they were always required to make Mother's Day and Father's Day cards. She would cross out "Father" and write in "Uncle." She recalls also hearing the priest say, "Kids who are trouble-makers come from broken homes." She knew the priest was wrong because her mother was so good, and she was trying to be just as good.

Joyce Colby, business manager of a school district, described the impact of her mother's achievements: "She was determined to be suc-cessful, and she opened an antique store to supplement her nursing income when I was thirteen. Her drive and determination rubbed off on me. I learned persistence and perseverance, and I knew women could make it on their own."

Earlier research on divorce confirms that single mothers who are themselves achievers and have adjusted to their single status do not have any negative effect on their daughters' achievement. Their daugh-ters' adjustment seems directly related to the mothers' positive adjust-ment. Unfortunately, most studies have shown that divorce has a much greater negative effect on boys' achievement, and for both boys and girls there may of course be other emotional side effects that weren't measured by this study. For example, attorney Risa Stone described her parents' divorce as having an effect not unlike an earthquake; there were aftershocks for a long time. She recalls questioning what was wrong with her and blaming herself for the divorce. She believes she repressed her feelings at the time but continues to have trouble trusting commitments and relationships. Although she was thirteen when her parents divorced and was always an achiever, as an adult she's not yet sure if she ever wants to get married and have children.

Part 2: Advice

The positive support and the coaching approach to parenting explained in Chapter 2 continue to be effective for building family relationships. As a parent of a very well put together family reminded me, it seemed to her that if she noticed and labeled her three children's positive behaviors, they simply became more positive because the children assumed those positive words characterized them. Such an approach certainly contributes to a mainly upbeat family atmosphere. For par-ents to lead in such a positive way, they need to feel confident about themselves and their parenting. Perhaps that was what Dr. Benjamin Spock had in mind when he suggested on the very first page of his first book that parents must trust themselves. At least from the perspective of the women in our study, their parents were intelligent despite the fact that the majority of them did not have advanced formal educations. This seems in sharp contrast to the feelings of some parents I see in my clinic, who sometimes believe their children are more intelligent and more sophisticated than they. Furthermore, the parents who come to my clinic often seem to feel an almost desperate need to please their children all of the time. They often have problems making decisions or recommendations for their children unless they are sure their children will find the decisions acceptable.

Giving children too many choices begins during the preschool years and becomes more and more problematic as they get older. It's as if parents believe they require permission from their children to say no to them. It is this enabling of overempowerment that seems to initiate the ensuing battles and resulting judgmentalism. Children who are in the habit of making all the choices often make quite a few inappropriate choices because they simply do not have the maturity to project the consequences. Because consequences are not always immediately obvious to the children, the parents must, of course, point them out. Children then get into the posture of defending their own choices. Parents rehash their reasons, and finally, when their children resist their parents' reasoning, the parents must resort to threats or punishments to enforce their requests. Of course, sometimes coaches resort to punishments as well, but only after more appropriate coaching efforts fail.

Figure 8.5, which provides several approaches to discussing report card grades, contrasts judging and coaching. Believe it or not, judging seems a lot more prevalent in real life. When you find yourself constantly judging, repeat to yourself, "Be a coach, not a judge."

WHEN YOU CAN'T BE A COACH

There are, of course, times in your daughter's life when you won't feel like being a coach. If your daughter has always been strong-willed, if you've already overempowered her, if your coaching hasn't been effective, or if she is so rebellious that you feel a punishment is absolutely required to set a clear limit, then it may be time to don your judge's robe and, we hope, also a demeanor of wisdom to determine appropriate consequences. Take your judge role seriously. Don't judge like the parent in Figure 8.5. Think of yourself as a thoughtful and sagacious

---

FIGURE 8.5

Judging Versus Coaching: Your Daughter's Report Card

Judging

Mother: What's wrong with you today? Bad report card again?

Daughter: Well, it's not so bad except for math. It's just that Ms. Alper's a bad grader. Everyone in the class has bad grades.

Mother: That's a familiar excuse. Why didn't you go to your teacher and get some help instead of waiting until you got a C? You just never plan ahead. I suppose your other grades aren't much better. It looks to me as if you need a consequence. I guess if you're not mature enough to get the help you need, you're not mature enough to drive. When you get all your grades above a B, you can have your license back. It doesn't seem as if you even care about your future.

Daughter: It's not that bad. There's not much sense in driving if I always lose my license! (Slams bedroom door)

Coaching

Mother: You seem disappointed. Is it your report card?

Daughter: Yeah, Mom. I thought I'd get a B in math, but I got a C.

Mother: It sounds like you need a little help to get where you belong. I was pretty good at math. Would you like me to take a look at it, or would you prefer setting up an appointment with Ms. Alper? I know you can turn the grade around next quarter and bring your semester grade up. You know I'd really like to help you catch up, and once you have it put together, I'll just stay out of it again. What's fun about math is it keeps you working.

---

adjudicator with the responsibility of responding to your daughter's misdemeanor in a manner from which she can learn for the future.

Consider that the punishment should match both the severity of the crime and her recidivism. That is, if this is a first-time offense, a warning and probation may be quite enough. If you've already tried probation and your daughter is a repeat offender, you will probably need to take away a privilege or special event. Although you may wish you could ground her for life to assuage your anger, life imprisonment, even when it is only in her room at home, will only inspire her to try to get even with you, and your home will become such an unpleasant and angry place that even you will undoubtedly wish to escape. You'll soon rescind your punishment in desperation, and your daughter will feel like she's successfully manipulated you again.

Consider carefully what you can take away. Taking something away that your daughter doesn't care that much about will not drive your point home. You will have to take something from her that she is really looking forward to or might be an especially fun experience. She will be angry at first, but she may either become explosive or tell you she doesn't care at all. You'll have to determine whether what she says accurately describes her feelings or if it is a manipulation she's using in the hope you'll change her punishment. If the punishment is a good one, your daughter will feel angry. However, if you haven't overpunished her, with time she'll realize you set a reasonable limit, and although she may not have liked it, in perspective she will believe it was fair.

Before you announce your decision, determine carefully if you have enough power to enforce your punishment. Consider whether your daughter could ignore your punishment and disobey you anyway. Following are some examples of reasonable judgments that might deter your daughter from further crimes without accelerating her anger and misbehavior.

Your daughter, a senior in high school, skips classes twice during a particular week. You receive a school report. In exasperation but with control, you remind her that her semester grades are far from exemplary, that these grades will count toward college, and the teacher was acting responsibly by assigning her an F for each math class she missed. You further question her reasons, which are something like "My friends and I overextended our lunch hour, and math is the most boring class in the world." You express to your daughter the seriousness of the problem and your disappointment at her irresponsible behavior, and she promises you it will not reoccur. This is a first offense. You explain you will not punish her as long as you can trust that it won't happen again.

Three weeks later you receive another letter from the school. Your daughter has been absent from math class for three consecutive days. You are about to explode. Don those elegant robes of justice. A consequence is probably going to be necessary. Hear your daughter out first, although it's unlikely she will have an acceptable, honest excuse. Consider her plans for the next few weeks. Missing the drama club play in which she has responsibilities or the volleyball game will punish her club and team more than her. On the other hand, she's been looking forward to that concert for a long time and even saved her own money for the ticket. She isn't going to love your news, but trust is trust. Perhaps she'll think about what she's doing before she casually extends her next lunch period.

If there are two judges in the house, you had better confer with the other one before you issue your judgment. There should not be the potential for appeal. Your daughter is not really in court as long as the two of you agree and the judgment can be final, reasonable, and binding.

BEING RESPONSIBLE ROLE MODELS

Adults don't really have the choice of being role models or not. Children and adolescents learn about the world by watching adult behaviors and the consequences they experience for those behaviors. They may copy behaviors unconsciously if they see that the behaviors are being rewarded, or they may avoid behaviors if they see them punished by society. Social learning theory tells us that three variables—nurturance by the adult, similarities between the child and adult, and perceptions of the adult's power—increase the likelihood that children will emulate the behaviors they observe. Presidents, senators, business leaders, teachers, athletes, doctors, media people, film stars, and Nobel Prize winners all have the potential for becoming powerful role models for children. For girls, however, there remains a paucity of female world leaders, prominent business executives, or Nobel Prize winners. Although there are an increasing number of prominent women in all fields, media and film provide the most powerful and obvious role models for girls. Perhaps that helps to explain the overwhelming number of girls who view their future as totally tied up with beautiful clothes, makeup, and romantic affairs with men.

Although many women in the study found role models in the biographies they read, and indeed many also found mentors in their work or other adults in their world, the most powerful sources of role models for girls are their families and schools. Thus parents, grandparents, and even older siblings become important role models for children. Adults are constantly being watched, emulated, and evaluated by the children in the family; therefore, adults not only live for themselves but are automatic teachers. Schoolteachers, too, are powerful role models for girls.

The fact that girls and their mothers share the experience of being female enhances mothers' responsibilities. When the women in our study often began by identifying with their mothers and then changed to identification with their fathers, it was often a matter of being attracted by their fathers' power and distracted by their perceptions of their mothers' powerlessness. When they commented that they knew they didn't want to be a "housewife," it was because they perceived the homemaker role as powerless, compared to what some of their professional fathers were accomplishing. It is also possible that their mothers' roles seemed powerless because their dads didn't overtly value what their mothers accomplished. With all apologies to those women who have chosen to be full-time homemakers in this generation, it seems that unless you are taking a strong leadership role as a volunteer, and unless that role is valued by your spouse and children, your daughters are unlikely to view you as powerful. On the other hand, our study provides evidence that if you continue with your education or return to the workforce as your daughters get older, even when they resent your taking time away from them and complain about your work, they will more likely respect you. Furthermore, by way of role model identification, they will develop more confidence in their ability to pursue higher education and be successful in a career. If they view you as a powerful and happy mother and homemaker, they are more likely to decide to be full-time homemakers.

Mothers who struggle and give up are role models for failure; mothers who persevere and succeed are models for resilience. Mothers who continue careers in which they are unhappy are role models for passivity; mothers who are excited about their careers and their contributions are role models for optimism and success. Mothers whose conversations center on appearance, fashion, and weight loss encourage daughters to make those attributes central to their self-definition. Mothers who discuss their accomplishments based on their intelligence and hard work encourage girls to take pride in their intelligence and achievements.

Fathers who complain about their wives' educational and career motivations diminish their wives' power to be role models to their daughters. Fathers who brag about their wives' accomplishments encourage their daughters to value education and success. Fathers who don't participate in homemaking tasks diminish the status of the homemaking responsibilities of their wives, and if the wives enjoy homemaking, their power is also diminished by their husbands' lack of participation. Fathers who participate in homemaking responsibilities and value their wives' homemaking contributions increase the status and power of their wives and encourage better relationships between their wives and daughters. Fathers who constantly remind their wives to go on a diet automatically remind girls that thinness is critical to the approval of men. Fathers who do not discuss weight and dieting and instead emphasize their wives' other qualities, such as kindness, independence, and assertiveness, communicate to their daughters that these qualities will be admired by young men and that appearance is less important.

This generation has made a complex transition. What instinctively feels right for men and women to say about the roles of both men and women in their families is based on how they were brought up. It is often counterintuitive to share power, to value both adults' careers equally, and to recognize dual responsibilities for raising children and completing homemaking tasks. Your daughters will grow in confidence when they see partnerships of power and respect in their parents. As the adults in the next generation, equality will be more comfortable.

Stop and think about what your children hear you say about your careers, your education, and your distribution of homemaking chores. Don't get in the rut of repeating the same complaints. Optimism and resilience are contagious. Successful women in the study were marked by both. Your daughters are more likely to learn these qualities if you press yourself to act those parts more forcefully. Furthermore, the more you act them, the more natural they will feel.

Parents in our society are often overwhelmed and overworked. To maintain your optimism, you will need to set priorities. Parents, together or singly, will simply not find enough time to accomplish the details that were accomplished when your father had a wife for the specific purpose of being a homemaker and mother. Your children will not miss those details because they have not experienced them. If you bake cookies with them every three months instead of every week, they will still experience the fun, warmth, and good taste of the traditional sampling of the cookie dough.

INVOLVING OTHER RELATIVES

Aunts, uncles, and grandparents may no longer live down the block. Fortunately, there are new ways of communicating, and automobile and air travel are so common that despite geographic distance you can be close. Telephones and e-mail can provide daily and weekly visits. Children's vacations that come during parents' working hours can sometimes be spent with a willing grandparent. The inspirational bonding with other relatives that many women in the study shared is still possible. The greater the number of powerful and inspiring family role models who surround your daughters, the more likely your daughters are to see their potential for making contributions to society. The messages of high expectations can be reinforced by family members.

There is also risk in setting family expectations. It is just as easy for other relatives to set negative expectations for your daughters. Grandparental favoritism can cause problems for the children who are not favored and can certainly be problematic if grandparents favor the boys or have old-fashioned ideas that girls exist only to be admired for their beauty. If grandparents have these gender-stereotypical expectations of your children, you will need to be assertive in correcting them and bringing them up to date about the new expectations that can be set for girls. If you explain to them how important their messages are to your children, you may be able to convince them to see the greater potential in your daughters. If you can't change their perspectives, at least you can interpret them respectfully to your daughters and help them to understand that their future will be better if they're stronger and more independent.

MAINTAINING A WHOLE SMART FAMILY

Children seem to be born with feelings of competition with their siblings. This rivalry always exists, even when parents proclaim that their children are not jealous of each other and are always kind and nice. Sibling rivalry does not only mean that children argue or fight with each other, although many siblings do some of that. Sibling rivalry is also expressed in the birth order differences described earlier in the chapter. It is expressed in the differing personalities (aggressive or submissive, talkative or quiet, disorganized or neat) and the different interests ("I was the dancer, she played the flute"; "I was the gymnast, she was the smart one"). There is often a territorial competitiveness that parents perpetuate in the name of individual differences and keeping peace. Unfortunately, it may put each of your children in a box that is too limiting.

It is hard to discover a way to encourage individual differences without heightening competition between your children. It is important for all your children to feel intelligent and creative, for all your children to have reasonable social adjustment, and for all your children to be physically fit. Helping them to feel competent in all those areas without their having to be best in the family is your task. You shouldn't tell your daughter who says she'll never be as smart as her brother that she's so much better at gymnastics. Instead, acknowledge that she may not be as intellectually gifted as her brother as measured by IQ or achievement tests, but that does not mean she is not highly intelligent. Intelligence is a complex construct, and there are multiple intelligences. She has a great deal of potential for using her good brain for accomplishment. You might also point out that if she lived in another family, she might be considered the smartest child, so feeling like the second, third, or fourth smartest child in this family gives her no disadvantage in school or in the world. I usually point out to children who are feeling at a competitive disadvantage in their family that admiring their sister's or brother's intelligence or skill often helps them to cope with their uncomfortable competitive feelings. If they celebrate their sibling's victories, they, too, will feel supported in their own victories and defeats. Furthermore, there's a great advantage in school if the whole family has a good reputation. Even when kids slip a little, teachers assume they're capable and they'll soon catch up.

It is important that parents recognize the pressure siblings feel by comparison to each other. The pressure is exacerbated when parents actually make comparisons, but the siblings compare themselves even if parents don't. The concept of "dethronement" is explained in Figure 8.6 and is useful for parents' understanding of dramatic changes in their children and the effects of sibling rivalry on their children.

Here is an example from my clinical work to emphasize the concept of dethronement for understanding your own family. Jonathan, a very bright ninth grader, had been underachieving in school for years. Despite an IQ score in the superior range, his grades were C's and D's. After meeting with his parents and setting up a study plan, Jonathan's sister, Alison, found it necessary to talk to me. Alison, an eleventh grader, had a history of excellent grades and wonderful social adjustment. Her parents had assured me that Alison was "practically perfect." Furthermore, she was confident and mature, and her sole perceived problem was that she struggled with math and could only manage to get a B (her only B) in that subject.

Alison initiated our conversation by explaining that she could help her brother get good grades by working with him every day. She was confident that her plan would be better than any plan to have him work independently. She seemed so earnest and determined to help her brother, and I was pleased and wanted to encourage her support for her brother. To provide Alison with insight about the issue, I posed the situation this way: "Suppose Jonathan turns his underachievement around and begins getting A's on his report card. How would you feel?" Alison

FIGURE 8.6

The Concept of Dethronement

When children are small, they require small amounts of power. As they get older and grow in maturity and responsibility, they should have expanded power. They shouldn't be treated as adults before they are ready. They can look forward to adult privileges and power, and they can gradually earn adult status.

Only children and oldest children are frequently treated like one of the adults in the family. It's reasonably easy for parents to accommodate one child, and they frequently do so, sometimes at the expense of the other parent. Thus, these children become accustomed to equal adult status, and sometimes more than equal power. They may sound exactly like little adults as they boss other children or insist on being treated as an equal to their parents.

Adultized children gain the social, intellectual, and apparent emotional sophistication that emerges from a close and enriched experience with their parent. They may have more mature insights into behaviors than their peers. They may, however, suffer from the feelings of insecurity and powerlessness that emerge with too much adult power. They may feel insecure because they simply don't know how to limit themselves. In classroom and peer relationships, where they aren't given adult status, they may feel "put down" or disrespected in comparison to the way in which they're regarded at home. They actually feel "disempowered" relative to the feelings of being overempowered at home.

The most difficult risk of adultizement is "dethronment." When another sibling is born or the parent remarries, the child may feel irrationally and extraordinarily jealous, although he knows he should be happy about the new member of the family. Dethroned children typically exhibit negativity, anger, or sadness. Their personalities may change so dramatically that parents, teachers, and even doctors may assume they're undergoing clinical depression.

Source: *Sylvia Rimm's How to Parent So Children Will Learn,* by S. B. Rimm (New York: Crown Publishing Group, 1996).

indicated that it would make her happy. Next I asked, "Suppose Jonathan, with his newfound confidence, becomes very good at math and thus is allowed to work at an accelerated pace in math. If he then does so well in math that he actually surpasses you, not only in his grades, but is also put in a more advanced math class than you, how would you feel?" Intuitively and without thinking, that sophisticated young lady exclaimed, "I'd die, I'd really die!" There was a brief silence, and then Alison said quietly, "I think I understand."

This case only reinforces the many others in which an underachieving brother's turnaround causes problems for a high-achieving, well-adjusted sister. More often than not, the comments by the sister to the parents are something like this: "Why are you making such a fuss about my brother's good grades? I get good grades all the time and no one gets so excited about those." Sometimes the responses are more subtle, like actually not handing in a few assignments to get some attention from parents. Almost always I'm able to forewarn the parents about the problem and prevent it. That perfect daughter is facing dethronement unless she receives some extra positive feedback and support during her brother's transition as well as some understanding about the pressures she's feeling.

Probably the way to most harm sibling relationships is not to acknowledge that it is normal to feel competitive. If parents add guilt to the already pressured feelings, children have nowhere to go to talk about their feelings. Certainly children view parents' treatment of their siblings differently than it is perceived by the parents. Just as certainly children will believe you treat their siblings better, even if you don't. It is important to stop and talk about there being more to relationships than competitive performance, reminding your children again that winning and losing are always temporary results; the race is not within the family but within the outside world, where the whole family can be successful.

FIRM AND POSITIVE PARENTING

Both parents were firm for most of our successful women, but only one parent was firm for quite a few. When one was firm and the other was less firm, anger seemed to be directed toward the firm one. I describe rituals in which one parent sabotages the other's power as "ogre or dummy games." Apparently these rituals did not prevent success for the women in this study. Nevertheless, they caused a more stormy adolescence. The stormiest teenage years came when neither parent was firm.

Interviews with the women gave further insight into their parents' approaches to discipline. Most of them seemed to have been coached rather than judged. The women talked about occasional punishments during the teen years, such as losing driving privileges for a weekend, but most of the women were given considerable trust by their parents. Some had specific curfews; others just took the responsibility of telling their parents where they were and the time they planned to come home. Firmness does not require continuous punishment. Positive expectations are more effective.

How do you raise your daughters to question and think, not be overly fearful, and yet not constantly push limits? Girls learn patterns all during childhood that they integrate into their personal courage. If preschoolers' explorations of their world are constantly greeted with a no, the world becomes a place to fear. They cannot find a place where they can be good. On the other hand, if they are given too much freedom, they get into danger or trouble frequently. When parents sometimes get angry and sometimes not for the same behaviors, the world becomes unpredictable, and they must push limits to determine what is allowable and what is not. A safe structure in which children can explore their world but can gradually learn there are some things they may not touch feels much more predictable and trustworthy.

As girls mature, exploration of their world should broaden. A family that says no too often continues to keep a girl fearful. A family that gives continuous mixed signals—a no that changes to a yes, a yes that changes to a no—teaches children to push limits continuously. It's this continuous pushing of limits that leads parents to overuse punishments. Parents should envision themselves as wise and thoughtful people and reserve judgment until they have heard their children's positions. Then they should respond wisely and confidently with a few good reasons so that they are role models for rational behavior. Once they have heard their children out, firmness is required. If they're wishy-washy at this point, children lose confidence in their parents' judgment. Furthermore, they will not accept their parents' first answer as permanent, and the irrational arguing ensues.

If you have guided your daughter with high expectations, by her high-school years you will be able to use guidelines instead of rules. If your daughter has pushed limits continuously, you will need to use a firmer set of rules with flexibility to permit her independence. Some guidelines for high-school girls follow.

- A general curfew seems appropriate as long as there is flexibility for particular activities.
- It's reasonable to encourage girls not to date, visit malls, go to movies, or have parties on school nights, when they should be either doing schoolwork or participating in extracurricular activities.
- Parents should know where their children are and have their teens call when they change locations. Girls should not be at a friend's home when parents are not around unless you are certain that there's no risk of invading partyers or male guests.
- Televisions and computers are better located in family rooms; that way, if the Internet or e-mail is being used, teens don't have excessive privacy.
- Bedroom doors should be open when boys are visiting; better yet, visits could take place in the family or living room. Teens should be given some privacy, but total privacy isn't necessarily good for them, even when they tell you that's what they want.

If you have a good sense of trust between you and your daughter, cellular phones and beepers can help keep you in touch and continue to give your daughter considerable freedom. She can feel free to take the initiative to call you from a friend's house if she feels she needs to be picked up, if she's delayed, or even if she simply requires a little support.

Your daughters will need reasons for your guidelines, and you will want your daughters' input. They'll be particularly concerned about the guidelines that affect their privacy with boyfriends. Be honest with your daughters. Tell them that sexual intimacy can be so intense that they can easily be drawn into relationships more intimate than what they may be ready to cope with. Knowing that a door is open is surely some deterrent for them and their male friends. Indicate that you don't plan to stop by without giving some warning, but they're not yet ready for complete privacy. Of course, these guidelines will vary with your own value system, but early and frequent sexual involvement prevents a young woman from concentrating on her interests, talent, career, and identity development. While relating to males is healthy and normal, intense and all-consuming relationships steal time and attention from other healthy endeavors, and thus become a serious problem.

Although guidelines vary with peer groups and value systems, and you surely want to take all that into consideration, you may find that you're an "ogre" compared to other parents; or perhaps you may be considered too liberal with your children. Search your soul, increase freedom as your daughter shows she can be trusted, and bite the bullet and remain firm when necessary, even if you feel unpopular.

LEADING A FAMILY ALONE

Divorce, death of a spouse, or a personal independent decision may make you the only parent for your daughters. Most single parenting is done by mothers.

As discussed previously, enjoying your work and talking about your contribution and satisfaction provide a positive model for all your children. Because you have no one to share family leadership, you're going to have to plan to find time for fun, travel, and humor as well. Sometimes those roles are stereotyped as belonging to fathers. The important point is that as a single parent, you have to plan for being both father and mother to your children, which isn't an easy assignment. The following recommendations won't make it any easier.

Because of the pressure on your time, you may easily find yourself inviting them along for typical adult-only occasions, such as out to dinner or to a movie with your adult friends. Certainly some of that will be fine, but if it becomes a regular habit, you will find that your children always want to go along. They may expect to be part of the normal adult conversation. Furthermore, they may talk to you as if they are adults and expect equal power with you. They may transfer the adult behavior they hear about into their child or adolescent world, where it's a poor fit. They may wish to emulate adult dress and want to wear clothes that you consider too "sexy" or mature. In your effort to include them, they may lose their sense of limits and consider themselves one of the adults. You will, in turn, lose the power to guide them.

Avoid intimate conversation with your children about their other parent or others you may be dating. Sometimes children don't even understand your descriptions, but they will feel the intimacy and learn your attitudes. If you feel angry at their other parent, even if it is justifiable, they may learn to be angry, not only at their parent but at all adults. If girls grow up distrusting men, they may have difficulty having trusting relationships with men in the future. If mothers constantly complain that their former husbands don't provide them with enough money, it will seem to children that men are all-powerful and women aren't, and they may wish to emulate their dads and turn their anger toward their mothers.

If your child's other parent has died, do share stories about that parent. Memories of the parent can help you to inspire your children toward achievement, responsibility, and kindness. Be cautious even in positive sharing, though. Don't destroy opportunities for your children to accept a new parent at some time in the future should you choose to remarry. Always remember that despite grief at your loss, you can continue to live a good life, and your children will adjust only as well as you do. You don't need to hide your grief from your children, because your grief permits them to grieve. However, it is important that your grief doesn't take complete, permanent control of your life.

As independent mothers, you are excellent role models for self-sufficiency. However, your children also need to see you in healthy social emotional relationships. Your daughters will be watching your relationships with men, but they can view only what is obvious. It's not a good idea to get your children involved with all the men you date. Go out with men without your children, and postpone their getting involved until you are more certain of your relationship. Furthermore, if your daughters observe you inviting a continuous stream of men to sleep at your home, it will be hard to explain to them that intimacy and responsibility go hand in hand.

When you "fall in love," regardless of your age, you are likely to feel quite adolescent. Ideally you'll have some supportive friends to help you through this. If your daughter is also adolescent, she will simply not understand or respect your strange behavior.

Occasionally fathers lead a family alone. For the benefit of those fathers who read this book, daughters can certainly learn achievement and responsibility from you as well as from their moms. However, there are girl topics they may not want to share with you. It would be good for your daughters to have the opportunity to bond with an aunt or female cousin so they can have an adult for "girl talk."

Your daughters will also be watching you to observe how you treat women and how the women around you act toward you. It's not a good idea for you to share your bed with your daughters. Also, the statement made above about a continuous flow of bed partners for mothers holds just as much for fathers.

If you are a single mother or father, have confidence in your parenting. Because you don't have a partner with whom you can talk things over, find support from other adults or from a counselor. Single parents have heavier responsibilities for role modeling because they are doubly powerful in the lives of their daughters.

SEARCHING FOR BALANCE AND
THE RIGHT PATH

Diana Doyle
Insurance Attorney

Diana is thirty-three years old, two years out of law school, and working as an insurance lawyer at a large firm in New Orleans. Even though she's been very successful in her profession, she is still paying off her student loans, has moved several times to follow her husband, and has a sense that being an attorney might be an intermediate step toward another career. Yet she enjoys her work and describes the process of becoming an attorney as a remarkable ego boost.

Diana follows in a line of successful career women. Her paternal grandmother was a successful businesswoman who earned a business degree when very few women even went to college. After losing her husband in World War II, her grandmother put her business degree to work running her husband's factory in Hungary. Despite the pressure from Communism, she led the company toward financial success. Diana's mother, too, has a successful career. She emigrated from Hungary to the United States, where she became a successful geologist at a large research institute.

In contrast, Diana's maternal grandmother always served as "the example of what happens if you don't have a career." She, too, lost her husband in World War II, but she had no schooling or training. After the war, she emigrated to Israel and worked long, hard hours as a cleaning lady. She just barely made enough to live on and struggled throughout her life. As a result of these role models, Diana never doubted that she would develop a career for herself. Throughout her childhood, her mother and paternal grandmother taught her the importance of financial independence and intellectual fulfillment and emphasized those values over getting married and having children.

Diana's mother and father were divorced when Diana was three years old, and she lived primarily with her mother. She had a very intense but mostly positive relationship with her mother. Because Diana was an only child, the two of them spent a lot of time together. Weekday evenings were quiet in their home. Her mother was tired from the workday, and typically they would sit together and read for hours. Occasionally they would watch TV together.

Her mother worked one day a weekend and took the other day off. On Saturdays Diana would go with her mother to her mother's lab and play there. She would play with different colors of tape, and put liquids in beakers and roll them around in a mixing machine. She took ballet lessons near her mother's office, and would wander into the anthropology museum across the street. Diana remembers spending hours looking at the Egyptian jewelry exhibit and making up stories to go with the artifacts in the museum. She became very good at entertaining herself. Sundays were reserved for her and her mother to do a shared activity. Once a month Diana chose the activity. Often they would go to the zoo, museums, the children's museum, or the beautiful formal gardens at the park. Occasionally they would stay home and read together.

Diana recalls the important role that her paternal grandmother played in her childhood as well. Though Diana's parents were divorced, her mother and paternal grandmother remained close friends. They lived in the same apartment complex, and each morning Diana's mother would drop her off at her grandmother's house for child care. Diana loved spending time with her grandmother, who was very smart, charismatic, and warm. She chatted with bus drivers, kissed saleswomen, and was always laughing—all this despite her inadequate English and heavy foreign accent. People were drawn to her and admired her, and Diana loved their time together. Her grandmother was upbeat, positive, and wise, and Diana admired her resiliency, especially considering the suffering and adversity she had experienced in World War II.

Diana's mother also had a great impact on Diana. Her mother had also gone through much adversity but was a model of independence, strength, optimism, and success. She always counseled Diana never to rely on a man but to be her own person. Her mother explained that a man could complement her, but she should never let herself become dependent. Both Diana's parents presented marriage as a choice, never a requirement. They said the same thing in regard to children.

When Diana's grandmother died, Diana was thereafter cared for by a woman from Okinawa. Diana savored the time spent at this woman's house. She enjoyed the attention she received, and played with the woman's daughter. Diana recalls being very active during her elementary-school years. She rode bikes, roller-skated, and played outside. She and the other children would also play with dolls, play house, and mash up berries and make little pies; she confessed that she and her Japanese friends would be quite mean to two little kids who were younger than they. During that time, ironically, she attended a private elementary school known as the "Peace-Love" school. She was an excellent student, easily performing well, but apparently the "peace-love" message failed in application to her play with those two little neighborhood friends.

As Diana became a teenager, her relationship with her mother became much more complex. More of their conversations led to arguments, and Diana decided to live with her dad for three months. She expected respite from the pressures of living with her mom. While she was there, however, her dad assigned her essays to improve her writing. At the time she was very resentful and thought, "Some respite. I'd rather be with Mom." In retrospect, however, she is grateful for this writing-intensive summer. It made her feel much more confident, refined her writing skills, and actually improved her relationship with her father despite the temporary friction.

Things become more tense upon her return to live with her mother. They raised their voices with each other constantly. They argued, yelled, screamed, and locked each other out of the house. Diana could hardly stand being around her mother. Her mother tried to communicate with her through newspaper clippings. She clipped articles Diana might find interesting and taped them to Diana's bedroom mirror. The articles always discussed topics such as women in professional careers, ways of financing an education, or ways to ensure entrance into a good college. Her mother was completely frustrated with Diana's lack of application to her schoolwork. Diana didn't care much about school; she got pretty good grades—about a B average, because the standards weren't very high—but was totally bored with academics. Her mother sent her to a psychiatrist because she was worried about Diana's disinterest in school. Diana went to a few sessions, but mainly considered the visits a joke, and they had no immediate effect on her attitude.

Diana turned to her peers. She belonged to many peer groups and enjoyed spending time with many different kinds of people. At times she'd hang out with the "preps," at other times, she'd be with the "druggies," and at yet others, the "artsy" types. Her high-school boyfriend was a "long-haired rock-and-roll type." She spent time socializing within each group and enjoyed the relative anonymity she experienced among them. She could act a certain way with one group and a different way with another, knowing that one group would never tell the other group who she "really was." Becoming popular was Diana's high-school priority.

During this rough time, Diana's mother tried to rehabilitate their relationship. She took Diana on annual summer trips to Israel to see Diana's maternal grandmother, visit the area where Diana was born, and travel around the Middle East. Diana and her mother called a truce during those trips. An important emotional bond was reestablished, but when they returned home, they reverted to fighting. The constant arguments continued almost through the end of high school. By Diana's senior year, their relationship began to improve gradually, and so did Diana's interest in school.

In college Diana became very interested in academics and suddenly loved school. She attended a large state university where she found the courses stimulating and the professors excellent. She began to date Jeff, a man who was eleven years older than she. He had worked his way through school and paid for his own education, and he believed in Diana's abilities to do well in school. The two of them spent hours studying together. He taught her how to study and tutored her in calculus. Suddenly she was on the dean's list and in honor societies. Even years after their breakup, Diana realizes how Jeff influenced her college experience. Because of him, she regained her interest in and excitement about school.

As Diana's academic interests deepened and her life improved, Diana became friends with her mother again. She began to call home more often and looked forward to spending time with her mom. They continued to take three- or four-week annual trips together, and even when they returned, Diana still felt at peace with her mother. Now they are close friends and spend many hours together talking about very personal things that go on in their lives, although Diana believes that her mother does hold back on some especially private issues, and so does she. Diana and her mother continue to use some of their old forms of communication: Her mother clips articles on professional women, women and the law, and finance and sends them to Diana, but now Diana truly values this helpful information. Diana has a great deal of respect for her mother. She realizes that her mother has lived through some difficult challenges, and she admires her mother's perseverance and strength.

What sparked Diana's decision to become a lawyer, although both of her parents were scientists and her grandmother was a businesswoman? Her ethnicity may have had something to do with her decision. She and her mother would be talking with each other—just chatting and having a conversation, only loudly and argumentatively, like most of her Hungarian family members did—and her childhood friends would ask, "Why do you and your mother always fight?" Diana never really understood this. As she saw it, they were not arguing, just talking. In retrospect, she realizes that she had automatically learned to speak very combatively. She was not afraid to confront people, and her speaking style was very argumentative. As she listened with her new sensitivity, she realized that other family members also had conversations that probably would be interpreted by outsiders as arguments. It was only their manner of speaking. Her comfort with confrontation was well suited to law.

Diana herself attributes her choice of the legal profession to a series of coincidences. While she was in college, she joined Toastmasters, the public-speaking group. She enjoyed the group and excelled at public speaking. A woman acquaintance once approached her and told her she was a very good speaker and that she should consider insurance law. She explained that women do well in insurance law and that there's a lot of room for women to be promoted in this area. Diana thought carefully about what she liked to do and decided that perhaps it would be a good path for her.

Diana explored the field by taking a job as an insurance adjuster after college. She had a lot of contact with attorneys on the job. At one time she was working with a problem client who had left her ring at a beauty parlor where she had her nails done, and was trying to get the insurance company to replace her ring. It just so happened that this woman worked as a secretary at a "fancy-shmancy" law firm in Philadelphia. When Diana denied her claim, the woman had her boss call Diana, thinking that he might be able to help her get her insurance money. Diana and the attorney went back and forth. She said to the attorney, "Let me ask you this. Is it your contention that we have to pay this claim because the ring was in secured custody and control of our insured?" He replied, "That's exactly what I'm saying." So Diana repeated her statement, and again he replied, "Yes." Then Diana said, "Let me read to you from our policy that specific exclusion." After their exchange, he said, "You know what? You'd make a great lawyer. You did a great job and you handled that well." His statement made Diana's day and clinched her decision. She was delighted to have an attorney from such a prestigious firm acknowledge her talent. She decided she would return to school to study law. She saved up her money, applied for student loans, and went to law school.

Diana has very mixed feelings about her career as an attorney. The public speaking, the bantering, and the decisiveness make her feel very competent and smart, but it's the day-to-day life of a lawyer about which she is not certain. She has no female mentors in her field. Although there are many women in insurance law, and quite a few in her own law firm, she feels they are unapproachable. Everyone bills their time on an hourly basis, so she does not feel comfortable just chatting with them. Diana also feels that the women maintain the aura of unapproachability to establish and reinforce their power. To add to the situation's complexity, Diana's husband has changed his job several times, and she has moved to five different states to accompany him. She has thus passed the bar exam four different times but has not been able to establish herself in a law firm. Finally, she believes the older men in insurance law have not yet accepted women as equals. She recalls one calling her "little flower." Women in law have to be tougher, and yet when they are aggressive, the men refer to them as "bitches." Diana finds this disappointing, but she has not yet figured out an alternative path. Obtaining her law degree taught her that she is smart and competent, and she is sure that in time she will find her way.

HARDWORKING AND CREATIVE, BUT HER FAMILY IS HER CENTER

Dr. Alyssa Gaines
Medical Researcher

If someone had told Dr. Alyssa Gaines when she was a first-year medical student that she was going to be a successful scientist, she simply wouldn't have believed them. She does believe that her success is only slightly related to her intelligence because, she says, "There are lots of people around here who are much smarter than me. I just learned how to work hard and became incredibly efficient."

Alyssa sat in her sunlit office at a prominent eastern medical school discussing her successful struggle to achieve tenure before the age of forty. Midway through the conversation, she turned and picked up the picture of her three children and said, "But of course, this is what it's all about. My family is really where the joy comes from!" Alyssa feels that her career is a great privilege and opportunity for her. She says she doesn't believe she'll ever accomplish anything great, but she loves her work and is incredibly successful. Despite her success, she referred continuously to her husband and children as being the major joy of her life.

Alyssa was the middle child of three sisters. Her mother was a full-time homemaker who was devoted to her family's needs. Her father was a hard-driving, brilliant, charismatic man at good times, but at difficult times was narcissistic and hot-tempered. Childhood with her father was like growing up in a whirlwind. Their house had no doors because her dad had broken them all down; nor could he find time in his busy career to give his children more attention. Yet, Alyssa recalled, they received plenty of valuable attention in the "spots that mattered," and much of the time her dad was tremendous fun to be around. Her father was a professor at the same university with which she is presently affiliated.

There was never any question in Alyssa's family of whether she and her sisters would have careers; it was simply assumed that they would. Both of her sisters are attorneys, and the three of them have always been very good friends. It's Alyssa's perception that they weren't very competitive with each other, although they were very different. Alyssa liked math and science from the start, and she was the one who would accompany her father to the hospital because she liked "the blood and guts." Her sisters didn't like going to the hospital because it made them queasy. Alyssa always wanted to have a chemistry set and did experiments on her own; her sisters were totally uninterested in chemistry. When Alyssa was six, she absolutely horrified her sisters by picking up frogs and doing experiments on ants.

Alyssa's parents were very supportive of her unusual interest in science, and when she was only in elementary school, they bought her a microscope. Alyssa also loved math and remembers needing math help from her dad only once, when she just didn't understand her teacher's explanation in calculus. Her dad sat down with her for three hours. He worked with her gently and neither yelled nor screamed. Thereafter she understood the beauty of calculus, and she always appreciated his very special explanation.

Alyssa's father had been trained as a surgeon, but his main interest was research rather than clinical work. He had published his most important research paper by the time he was thirty and had been appointed chief of surgery by the time he was thirty-nine. As a child, Alyssa thought he was smarter than anyone else in the world, and she admired him. She identified with him and wished she could be like him someday.

Alyssa attended a very exclusive private girls' high school beginning in eighth grade. Her school was certainly excellent academically, but she was one of only a few Jewish girls in the class. Furthermore, she was sure that many of the students were anti-Semitic. She clearly recalls the hurt when one of the popular girls told her, "You know, Alyssa, you'd really be quite attractive if you had a smaller nose." Alyssa was not happy at that school, although she appreciated its excellent program in literature and languages, and she admits she learned to write well. On the other hand, in her favorite areas of math and science, the school was somewhat inadequate. She recalls that in those days they were simply not "girl subjects."

Alyssa remembers herself as a smart, skinny girl who was bad at sports, was different from most of the other students, but who loved to act in the drama club's plays. She always questioned whether she was creative enough to be an actress, but ironically it was her acting that helped her socially. She was a good actress, and when she had the lead in the school play, some of the boyfriends of other girls in the school wanted to know "who the beauty was," and suddenly Alyssa held a reputation in the school for being "Miss Beauty." The younger girls gathered around her, and she realized for the first time that she might actually be quite pretty.

The school counselors told Alyssa she should go to Radcliffe because she was academically at the top of her class, but Radcliffe was not Alyssa's choice. She wanted to go far away to school, and she chose the University of Wisconsin. The school had an honors program that had stringent entrance requirements, including very high grades and SAT scores. That high standard caused her to decide the program was for her. However, after one year at the University of Wisconsin, she was unhappy and decided to leave. She blamed her wish to leave on her social discomfort. She lived in a huge dormitory, and it seemed to her that all the women were preoccupied with makeup and their appearance. She also acknowledged that the students in her classes were brilliant, but she never indicated that not being at the top of her class had anything to do with her discomfort.

Alyssa decided to transfer to the Harvard undergraduate program and found herself making a very difficult adjustment during her sophomore year. She had little interaction with any of the faculty except as romantic connections; they dated her, and she admits to a fair number of bed partners. She reports that if faculty behaved now the way they did then, they would surely be accused of sexual harassment, but when she was in college, her romantic relationships with some professors were not that unusual. She also dated some "strange" students, and she recalls making "one bad choice after another" in her relationships. She'd choose guys who were wild, crazy, and insecure. They would be mean and nasty to her, but she simply had no confidence in herself at that time.

Although Alyssa majored in biology at Harvard, paradoxically she avoided taking science courses. She decided that there were too many intense pre-med "nerds" in the science courses, and they always did better than she. They made her feel uncomfortable by comparison. Since she had taken so many science courses in her freshman year, she was able to take poetry and English literature courses instead. She did much better in those and didn't feel quite so intimidated by the English students. Although she worked very hard, her grade-point average was 3.4 at best, and that didn't help her intellectual self-confidence at all.

Excitement about research began for Alyssa with her undergraduate honors thesis, and when she reflects on those days, she still feels a fondness for them. She worked in her father's research laboratory, learning to do histology and using an electron microscope, and even writing a small research abstract with her dad. She found her first research experience thoroughly exciting and thinks that she might not have discovered how exciting research was had her dad not encouraged her in this way.

After college, Alyssa originally wanted to take a year off and teach English in Italy, but she had applied to medical school because she didn't have an alternative career plan. She didn't really think she'd be accepted into any medical school because her grades were only acceptable, not exceptional. On the other hand, her MCAT scores were very high, and her excellent interviews seemed to provide the entrée she needed; schools would frequently accept her immediately after her interview. When Harvard Medical School accepted her, her father dissuaded her from going to Italy to teach and reminded her she might not be accepted again if she reapplied.

After Alyssa's first few hours at Harvard Medical School, she was ready to quit. Her mom dropped her off on a Sunday evening at the dormitory, and she walked around trying to meet other students, whom she referred to as the "intense people." After a short while she called her mom on the phone, overwhelmed, and in desperation said, "Can you come get me? You have to take me home; I can't do this, I just can't do this!" She felt panic-stricken and totally claustrophobic. Her kind mom came and drove her home, fed her some chicken soup, and then promptly brought her back. After the first panic, she actually found she liked and was happier in medical school than she had ever been. She loved the science courses, as she always had, and she thoroughly enjoyed having pass/fail standards instead of grades.

Alyssa met her husband, Harry, at medical school. They started going out in the fall of her first year and were married six months later. Harry was the opposite of all the men she had ever dated: He was stable and self-confident, bolstered her self-esteem, and provided for her in so many ways.

In medical school Alyssa learned to love immunology, and for the first time she began thinking of herself as a creative person who was good at coming up with new ideas. In her last year of medical school, she found a mentor to work with on exciting immunology research. Her research was so outstanding that she received a prestigious award. Not only was this the same award her dad had won exactly twenty years earlier, but she was the very first female prizewinner. She has an extraordinarily vivid memory of the presentation of her award. The auditorium was crowded. Her father, her mentor, and her husband were all there. The awarding professor entered and announced, "Sometimes we award this prize to two people, but there really is no runner-up this time. This prize is awarded for *her*. . . ." Since there were four men and only one woman in the competition, most people knew Alyssa had won. Alyssa's dad leaped up and cried out jubilantly. It was a magnificent moment as Alyssa and her father enjoyed that victory in ecstatic synchrony.

Alyssa went on to do a residency in medicine but soon found herself bored with the clinical work. She went to a senior professor and said, "Is there a little research project I can do?" Thus began the next phase of her immunology research. Her project was successful, and she was again elated. She and her husband decided to do a research fellowship at the National Institutes of Health, and she wrote at least ten research papers during the three years she was there. She was incredibly productive because she accidentally learned that the secret to being successful was to be more efficient than everybody else. She learned she could do "at least nineteen things" at the same time, keep them organized, and get all of them completed successfully.

At the time Alyssa was doing all this productive research, she became pregnant, but only after being fearful that she might have fertility problems. Alyssa underwent a C-section for the birth of her first daughter. She tried to stay home and rest like she was supposed to, but because she had scheduled her medical board examinations and had already paid the high admission fee, she was determined not to waste her money, so she went ahead and took her medical boards. As soon as she was in contact with her colleagues again during the testing, she realized, "I have to go back to work or I'll be depressed." Alyssa returned to her laboratory and research, and her fears of depression disappeared.

Because her husband was a surgical resident and was working very long hours, their first baby was placed in day care soon after she was born. Alyssa and her husband tried to take turns picking the baby up at five o'clock, but because Harry moonlighted for extra income, Alyssa did 90 percent of the picking up, which meant she had to leave work by five o'clock.

Alyssa thrived on her work. After the birth of each child, she would bring her baby home and go back to work the very next day. That was the right approach for her, and she was convinced it was best for her children as well. Alyssa had an important advantage: By the time her second and third children were born, she lived in the same city as her parents. Although the children went to day care, her parents were always willing to help out.

Alyssa believes that she will never be a Nobel laureate, but she has fun and thoroughly enjoys her research. She particularly likes taking risks and doing new experiments. Alyssa insists that she is probably not as smart as many of the scientists with whom she works, but she does credit herself with a good imagination. She thinks of many new ideas, and she is no longer afraid to try them. She believes that if she doesn't take risks, she won't accomplish much. She attributes her ability to take risks to the balance her children and husband provide for her.

In her mid-forties, Alyssa thinks she is someone who started out with the usual difficulties and has just worked very hard. She's accomplished a great deal in a very short time, and she believes she is fortunate to be able to pursue scientific research. Although it may seem that science is at the center of Alyssa's life because she spends so much time at her work, she again affirmed as she pointed to her family picture, "They are truly the joy of my life."

CHAPTER 9

SEE JANE GO

Young Adult Resilience

Part 1: Findings

Almost all (more than 99 percent) of the women in the study attended college, although some did not complete their degrees. Most women in the study began college at the typical age of eighteen, but there was a wide range of ages at entrance, from fifteen through forty-eight. There were also some differences by career groups. Many of the scientists and mental health professionals entered earlier than the typical age; approximately a third of this group began by age seventeen, and 5 percent of the mental health professionals entered at sixteen. Some of the scientists and mental health professionals also began college later, in their twenties and thirties; some were as old as thirty-nine. There were even more early entrants to college among the musicians, physicians, and attorneys; between 5 and 10 percent began by fifteen and sixteen, respectively, and almost 40 percent by age seventeen. However, unlike the scientists and mental health professionals, none entered during later adulthood. No physicians or attorneys began college after age nineteen, and no musicians began college beyond age twenty. Surely the physicians and attorneys were sensitive to the length of the education that lay ahead, and apparently the musicians were so focused on their talents that none in our group postponed their advanced musical training.

Young age of attendance at college was never mentioned as a disadvantage or a problem by any of the women in the study. Psychological researcher Dr. Mavis Heatherington,* who had skipped three grades by college, indicated that when she started high school she couldn't imagine why the girls had been so interested in boys, but she did catch on eventually. Medical researcher Dr. Janice Douglas* remembered that she had been the youngest graduate of her high school, but that didn't prevent her from getting a perfect 4.0 average in college and graduating at the top of her medical school class. Neither did her young age cause her social adjustment problems in college or at any other point in her education.

Age of attendance at graduate and professional school varied dramatically by career group. Two-thirds of the physicians had begun medical school by the traditional age of twenty-two, and none began after age thirty. Pediatrician Dr. Diane Butler's* start at age twenty-eight was unique for the time. On the other hand, less than half of the attorneys entered law school at the traditional age of twenty-two, and a fifth began after thirty. Two women entered law school as late as forty-five. Only 11 percent of the women in business continued their education for advanced business degrees at the traditional age of twenty-two, but some of the women entered graduate school for advanced training at almost every age thereafter until age forty-four. Women in business are often encouraged to obtain a graduate degree for advancement on their job.

Approximately half of the women in our study attended public universities and half attended private colleges. About a third described their colleges as small; a fifth said their schools were medium-sized; and a quarter attended large universities. Thirteen percent received their education at women's colleges. As mentioned in Chapter 4, this was a much greater percentage than one would expect, compared to the overall population, but this may only reflect a bias in our study; more women who attended single-gender colleges may be sensitive to and interested in women's issues.

For the most part, our group of women liked college. Approximately 15 percent were either neutral or negative about their college years. Memories of college varied in a continuum between supreme happiness and serious disappointment. Dr. Lisa Smith,* a chemistry professor, recalled that as a freshman at Case Western Reserve University, she was so elated with her education that she felt like she had "died and gone to heaven." Dr. Sara Barts, a psychologist, recalls that the excitement of so many ideas and challenging professors made it feel as if her brain were "exploding with intellectual stimulation." On the other hand, artist Rhonda Baker wished her parents could have afforded an art institute rather than the university where she found her freshman art courses disappointingly repetitive of her high-school work, and Dr. Susan Rehm,* a physician, recalls that although her college was only a half hour from home, she was so homesick that if she heard the dog barking when she called home, she would cry. She adjusted by immersing herself in her studies and developing a relationship with the man she eventually married.

ACADEMIC ADJUSTMENT TO COLLEGE

An internalized expectation of completion of college was perceived as important by many of the women in their adjustment to college. Some considered completion of college to be an automatic expectation. Magazine editor Liz Ludlow* recalls that from the moment she could talk, she sensed she was going to go to college. Her parents began saving for college when she was a small child, and her mother began taking her for aptitude testing when she was very young. She took the PSATs nine times and the SATs three times. By ninth grade she was attending college at night. There was absolutely no "not going to college" in her family. Although she changed her major several times while in college, it never even occurred to her not to complete her degree.

The parents of many women in the study assumed their daughters would go to college, and so did the girls. For quite a few, marriage and a family were prioritized above college even though parents expected their daughters to be excellent students in high school. For those women, teachers and counselors were pivotal in their decisions to attend college. A guidance counselor, Henrietta Herbert,* was critical to my attending college. She encouraged me to apply for scholarships. Although I was always an excellent student and my parents valued education, it was assumed that I "should marry an educated man," and I had often heard that advanced education was the highest priority for males.

Dr. Penny Sarans recalls that college wasn't even a concept to her as a child. Her mother was a "secretary-clerk with no stenography." From her mother's perspective, upward mobility meant learning to be a secretary *with* stenography. She encouraged Penny to take that course plus typing in high school to be sure she could hold a secure job. Her mother's assumptions were based on her own difficulties finding a job. Penny decided to go to nursing school because at that time nursing school didn't take as long as secretarial school. Furthermore, she was able to receive a scholarship for nursing school. Despite her full scholarship, she failed the first semester. She found herself a secretarial job with stenography instead, and no one was too disappointed. Years later, after she married and had a family, her husband encouraged her to go back to school, and she finally completed her bachelor's degree one course at a time over a fourteen-year period. Once she discovered she was a scholar, she continued for her master's and finally her doctoral degree, and now the woman who never really thought much about the value of education for herself is teaching teachers how to teach reading.

Violist Kathy Drew attended the local campus of the state university and majored in mathematics. She was an excellent college student and adjusted well both socially and academically, but there were few music classes available to her. She transferred to a different campus, which allowed her to minor in music. She wished she'd had the opportunity to attend a conservatory, but Kathy's parents expected her to be married and have a family and have a teaching certificate as a backup.

The same percentage of women considered their academic adjustment to college about average as did easy (40 percent each); however, approximately 20 percent of the women found their academic adjustments to be quite difficult. Some almost didn't make it the first time, and others didn't make it at all. Sally Sahn, a sports publicist, talked about her difficult academic adjustment to college: "In high school, my close friends were all college-bound, so college and career were a natural selection for me. I attended a rural midwestern state university and enjoyed my college years despite a very difficult academic adjustment. I had very serious problems with my grades initially. I began with an underachieving attitude of 'Let's see what I can do without studying. I bet I can get a B in class without cracking a book or taking notes.' I got away with it in high school because I was able to learn by listening and was good at test taking. However, college was different, and I dropped courses and almost didn't make it until in my sophomore year I finally learned how to study effectively, change my attitude, and organize my time."

Musician Julia Christian recalls working hard in college and doing well but worrying a great deal about her grades. Julia's mother remembers that Julia would worry about failing a test at college. She would study hard and then be terribly disappointed if she earned a B+ instead of an A. It didn't seem like near failure to Julia's mother, and she would reassure her daughter. However, Julia's unnecessary anxiety persisted throughout college, although her grades continued to be excellent.

The grade-point average for the women in our study was 3.4 overall (where an A is 4.0) and 3.6 in their major areas. Despite their reasonable academic adjustment, many more of the women (34 percent) found college difficult than found it fairly easy (21 percent).

Internist Dr. Susan Rehm,* who specializes in infectious diseases, recalls her academic adjustment to college involved mainly determination and hard work. Brought up in a rural Nebraska community that had no special gifted classes in her schools, she conceptualized her task this way: "My basic notion of myself was that I am a person of average talent who overworks to the point where I can get somewhere with it. I always tried very hard and had the mind-set that if I did, I would probably do reasonably well. Calculus was my real weakness. I was both depressed and anxious and almost lost confidence in my ability to do math, so I went to the teaching assistants and even the professor for tutoring, and I made it through. It mainly took perseverance."

Decisions About Majors Only a third of the women in the study had selected their final major before they ever entered college. A fifth of the women selected it in their freshman year, and a quarter selected it during their sophomore year, the year by which decisions are typically expected. Twelve percent didn't select their major until their junior year, and 2 percent didn't select it until their senior year. About a third of the women changed their majors at least once; some changed majors two or three times before settling on their final choice. Some actually left college and returned after they realized what they'd like to study.

Obstetrician Dr. Susan Lemagie* began college as a pre-law major, then became ill with mononucleosis and dropped out to recover her health. Her parents were so upset that they insisted she be on her own financially from then on. During her illness, she read *Of Human Bondage,* a novel about a doctor, and she said to herself, "I could do that." She enthusiastically changed her major to pre-med and became much more goal-oriented. At age twenty-three, however, she was advised she was too old to apply for medical school despite her 3.9 average. She was also a member of Phi Beta Kappa and had scores in the ninety-ninth percentile on the medical school admission exams. She was annoyed and angry at a hostile interview for medical school in which she was asked why she got a B in folk dancing, why she took tennis pass-fail, and if she had friends. It seemed they were looking for a reason not to accept her. Finally the interviewer asked her how she felt about a court case in which three women were suing the medical school for not admitting them, claiming age and sex discrimination. Her response was, "That's a hard question. Those women are my friends. I just hope I don't have to do what they did." That ended the interview, and Susan received a letter of acceptance in the mail the very next day.

The record for changes in majors belonged to Karly Rheam, a guidance counselor. She changed majors seven times and admits that she changed whenever a course became too difficult. She would simply become anxious that she had chosen a too-difficult field. She was married in her senior year and then divorced thirteen years later. She had no clue until she graduated from college that she was considered academically talented. She read her excellent recommendations from school and began to think of herself as a scholar. She claimed that if she had realized how smart she was, she might have chosen to be a research scientist; however, she has no regrets at all about her present career.

Changes and Sequences The stairway to professional success for women was not always linear; indeed, it might best be described as "circuitous," going around and in and out, including a variety of sequences of education, marriage and family, and further education, sometimes in an entirely different field.

A full one-third of our group of women went on to graduate or professional school later than the traditional age for such attendance. Many of those women had changed their career direction entirely by that later date.

National television producer Denise Dennison left high school to begin her career in ballet. When that didn't work out for her because of injuries, she attended a "heavy-duty engineering school with lots of math and science," which she conquered despite her lack of math preparation or anticipation of any such career direction. During her internship in management science at a national television network, she discovered that the creativity of television production had much more appeal to her than the business management she was preparing for. She now finds herself far from either of her intended career directions, and although she sometimes feels disappointed about not having fulfilled her original dream of dancing, she knows that her present career is highly prized, and she values the creativity it provides.

Deborah Goldman, a director of government affairs in Washington, D.C., was a teacher first, but after her divorce she decided to attend law school. She recalls thinking, "Do I dare apply to law school? Do I dare?" Although she and her ex-husband had been divorced for a very long time, he was actually very supportive and instrumental in her decision. He said, "Why don't you just take the test?" So she did, and then she applied, thinking, "Okay, I'll send in the application, but I'm not serious." She was actually accepted to two out of the four law schools she applied to.

Former state senator Barbara Lorman* was initially invited to run for the assembly seat left vacant by her husband's untimely death. She rejected the opportunity, perhaps because it was so soon after his death. However, a year later, her state's Republican Party encouraged her to run for an unexpired term of a state senator. This time she consented, although with some hesitation because of her inexperience in government. She credits her years of volunteer leadership in the community while raising her family for providing important experiences that helped her in her role as senator. Although Barbara recalls her mother as being a strong, take-charge woman, and she remembers an abundance of political discussion with her father, she never projected that her homemaker status would lead her to the state senate. She served as a state senator for fourteen years and viewed her term as an opportunity to contribute to her government in grateful appreciation for what she as an American citizen has received. Barbara's parents were both immigrants.

Not only did many of the women change their career direction because of shifts in interest or even for chance reasons, but the feminist movement spurred women to new futures and provided these women many more choices than they had when they were younger. Some women followed a sequence of college, parenting, and then a return to school or the workforce in a very different career and with very different interests than they had pursued as undergraduates. For others, surprising career directions emerged when they were pursuing initial careers. Their career paths were indeed circuitous and often very different from the career paths of typical males of their cohort group.

SOCIAL ADJUSTMENT IN COLLEGE

Social adjustment in college was closely tied to academic adjustment, and approximately 80 percent of the women considered both to be either easy or average (Figure 9.1). However, a full 20 percent had difficulty with both, and some dropped out, either temporarily or permanently.

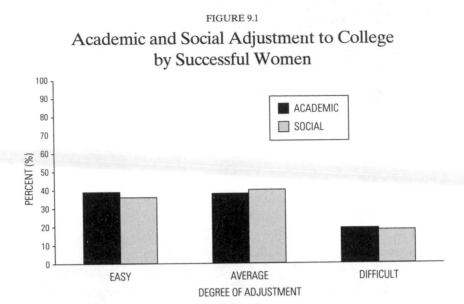

FIGURE 9.1

Academic and Social Adjustment to College by Successful Women

Margaret Karnes, a successful business executive, recalls that college just never seemed right for her. She couldn't find a fit at either the large university she first tried or the small college she attempted afterward. When asked whether the lack of fit was social or academic, she said she thought it was both. Although she acknowledged that she had indeed missed an important component of learning by not completing college, her ability to learn on the job sustained her in the years ahead. She was, however, very determined that all three of her children would complete college.

Dr. Sara Barts recalls that she never felt a social fit in either college or graduate school, although she loved the academic challenge of both. During her undergraduate education, she attributed the lack of fit to her culturally different immigrant background. She attended graduate school at a nontraditional age, while most of her classmates came directly from college. The age difference and her homemaker-mother role in life separated her from her unmarried young colleagues. Although she recalls feeling very different, it never prevented her from completing her degrees.

Dr. Ana Casa, a cardiothoracic surgeon and another first-generation American, also reported experiencing excellent academic adjustment but uncomfortable social adjustment. However, she always had a small circle of friends throughout college and medical school that provided her with the support she required. She did not attribute her social difficulty to her immigrant background and didn't understand exactly why she just didn't find a social fit. She thinks perhaps she was just not accustomed to fitting in. She had never considered herself socially comfortable during her earlier school years, either.

The women in both these cases, and in many other cases where social fit was a problem, were the first and only members of their families to attend college, so they really had no forewarning of what to expect. There were no family role models for college attendance or for professional careers.

Medical researcher Dr. Alyssa Gaines recalls her feelings of not fitting in at a large university. She acknowledged that the very bright students in her honors program were an impressive group, but she simply didn't fit in socially. She transferred to Harvard but wasn't all that happy there and felt she was surrounded by pre-med "nerds" who did better than she in all the science courses. Although Alyssa never mentioned competition affecting her self-confidence, her college experience was the first in which she was not academically at the top. It's significant also that she loved medical school, where there were *finally* no grades.

Compared to their high-school experiences, in college an even higher percentage of the women (80 percent) mainly belonged to friendship groups that valued achievement. Only 1 percent indicated their closest friends did not value school achievement. That's not surprising, because the peer norm at most colleges favors achievement. Veterinarian Rochelle Breen recalls that her high-school friends weren't that motivated and didn't accomplish much, but her college friends were motivated, ambitious, and hardworking, and they really had an impact on her.

The remaining women had mixed friendship groups. However, the homogeneity of friendships related to racial and religious beliefs diminished compared to earlier school years. Only a third of the women found their friends to have mainly similar religious and cultural values. On the contrary, some of the women who considered themselves different in elementary, middle, and high school found friends with similar values and religions when they attended college. Amy Fox, a business executive, felt lonely and isolated in middle and high school, but she found both social and intellectual acceptance for the first time at the women's college she attended. She became an immediate social leader in antigovernment politics during the Vietnam crisis, despite the fact that it separated her temporarily from her parents, who were first-generation Americans. They could hardly believe their daughter's anger at the country they felt so fortunate to be living in. Dr. Janice Douglas* attended college and medical school with a majority of

African-American students, and after her social isolation in her former Ohio high school, both she and her parents felt much more comfortable about her social fit.

The exploration of relationships with students who had somewhat different values expanded for most of the women in college. The importance of a close personal support group was described by many of the women. More than half considered their friends to be their most important models or mentors (see Figure 9.2). The director of a crime laboratory explained it this way: "I believe it's crucial for a girl to have a dependable support group of parents, siblings, family, and friends. Without a support group, I don't know where I would be today. I think few successful individuals can say they truly did it on their own. My parents have been a part of my support group all my life, for encouragement, as a sounding board, for advice, and so on. From grade school through college, the friends in my support group were positive influences. They never discouraged me from pursuing my goals. Although the members of my support group changed with time, I have always had a group I could count on."

The actual degree of sociability for these women while they were in college followed a very similar pattern to their earlier years in school, with a little less than a quarter considering themselves more social than typical, more than a third considering themselves less social than typical, and the remaining group considering themselves about average in social participation. More socially involved than earlier in school were the women in medicine, law, and art, perhaps because many of them found peers who shared their interests and were similarly focused. The teachers and businesswomen were more social than typical, but for the most part, they had also been more social in high school.

MENTORS AND ROLE MODELS

Figure 9.2 indicates our group of women's most important models during college. Professors ranked first as career mentors. Twice as many women were mentored by male professors compared to female professors (39 percent compared to 20 percent); however, considering that most colleges had many more male professors than females, the percentage of women selecting female professors was impressive, and greater than one would expect. Scientists, musicians, and mental health professionals selected professors as their most important role models more often than other groups, and homemakers chose professors somewhat less than other career groups. Homemakers also selected

FIGURE 9.2

Most Important Models or Mentors During College

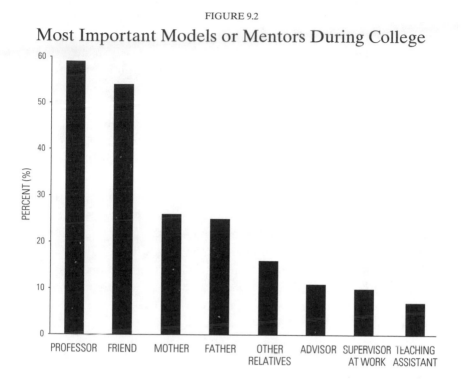

their parents somewhat more frequently than other peer groups, perhaps contributing to the high value they placed on homemaking.

Artist Rhonda Baker felt a special bond with one female professor and especially appreciated learning oil painting, composition, and watercolor from another professor with whom she often remembers butting heads. After reviewing one of her paintings, he would say something like, "This is just terrible." Then he would rip it up and throw it away and tell her to start over. Rhonda remembers being furious with him at those times but also realized even then that he was really helping her become a better artist by telling her to relax and "do what comes naturally." Rhonda believes he criticized her so harshly in part because he knew she was sensitive and he was trying to encourage her resilience, but also because he recognized her real talent. Rhonda's father's perfectionism and early direct style with her may have better prepared her for some of her more critical professors. She had already begun to develop resilience that prevented her from feeling discouraged by criticism. Instead, she learned to reframe her critics' powerful messages as proof that her talent was worth the criticism.

Liz Ludlow,* a magazine editor, was absolutely in love with her English composition professor. In fact, she went on to take every class that the professor ever taught at the University of Michigan. To this day, she stays in touch with him. He helped Liz in that important transition to her career as well. Prior to his influence, she had a notion that in order to be a success she had to be a doctor, a lawyer, or a businesswoman. She had never thought about being a writer or an editor. It was difficult for her to acknowledge that she could be successful working with the words she loved so much, but her English composition professor inspired and convinced her.

Environmental engineer Dr. Sandra Calvin was taking a graduate-level class as an undergraduate when a very aloof professor asked her about her future plans. When she told him that she was not planning to go to graduate school, he responded, "You've got to be kidding." This was what spurred her to consider going on in her education. When she was working on her final semester of her master's program, her major professor convinced Sandra to stay on for a Ph.D. and negotiated a deal for her so that it would take Sandra only three additional semesters. As a result of her professor's influence, and of course her own hard work, Sandra finished her doctorate.

A most important role model for Judge Edna Conway was John F. Kennedy. Paintings and photographs of him cover the walls and desk of her office. Edna was devastated by Kennedy's assassination. She traveled to Arlington National Cemetery the week after his death to visit his grave, and she still visits regularly each time she's in the Washington area. To Edna, Kennedy represented idealism and a motivation to learn and overcome challenge. She was not the only woman who referred to President Kennedy as a role model. Several other women in government, including State Senator Elizabeth Quinlan, were inspired to choose their careers based on their admiration for Kennedy and his call to young people to make a commitment to their nation.

Despite the fact that professors and friends were selected frequently as most important models or mentors, parents and other relatives continued to be important role models for these women even through college and graduate school. Many of the women also credited advisors and work supervisors as being inspiring, and those few successful women who didn't complete college often consciously selected models from their work and world experiences. Sports publicist Sally Sahn's first boss after college graduation was an extremely important mentor to her. He was a Yale graduate and served as editor of the small-town newspaper she worked for. Although Sally considered him to have been "a little pompous and a little sexist," she also thought he was "a great teacher and supporter." Sally's story emphasizes that women didn't have to totally accept or admire a mentor to learn from him. Many women learned to ignore the negative but nevertheless value a mentor's good qualities.

Psychologist Dr. Anne Caroles could not say enough good things about her graduate school advisor, who encouraged her every step of the way. She recalled his get-out-there-and-do-it message and his helping her fulfill her childhood dream of wanting to be Madame Curie and make a difference in her world.

It was clear that mentors weren't necessarily women, nor were they necessarily "perfect" people. Mentors inspired and believed in the women they guided and often made a positive difference without even realizing the impact they had.

POSITIVE EXPERIENCES

College classes (not parties) were most frequently selected as these women's most influential experiences (see Figure 9.3). Apparently at least some of these women wanted their "money's worth." Dr. Lisa Smith,* a chemistry professor, remembers how important classes were to her at Case Western Reserve University. She had a four-year half-tuition scholarship but had to pay the rest on her own. Her parents had always told her, "You are going to college, but you'll be paying for it on your own so that you'll appreciate it more." She calculated how much she would be spending if she cut a class. At $33 an hour (at the time it was a lot), she didn't cut a lot of classes, nor was she very happy when the college sent her report card to her parents instead of her. She was also the young woman who was quoted earlier as saying that while she was attending college she thought she had "died and gone to heaven." Perhaps personally investing in at least part of one's education does improve appreciation for it.

The next most frequently cited influences by the women were jobs they held at college. All but 6 percent worked during their college years, and more than half of the women worked at jobs related to their eventual careers.

Travel was selected again in college, as it was in elementary, middle, and high school, as having an important impact on careers. The women mainly referred to the independence and novelty of their travel experiences during their college years. Compared to any other career group,

FIGURE 9.3

College Experiences That Had Important Career Influences

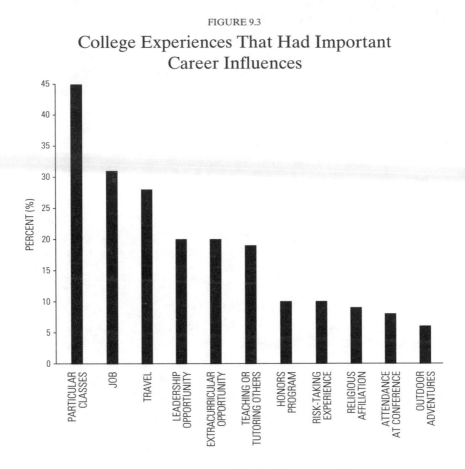

more of the artists selected travel as an important influence on their careers, and many of their trips were tied directly to the study of art in museums all over the world. Fewer of the homemakers chose either classes or travel as important influences, perhaps an early indication of their preference for the cozier world of home life compared to the broader, more complex world of a career. Leadership and extracurricular activities were next in order of importance for these women. These were selected even more frequently by women in the power-broker professions, including government, law, and business. They were apparently practicing to be movers and shakers while in undergraduate school. Teaching and tutoring others was chosen as next in order of importance; perhaps not so surprisingly, these were selected more frequently by women who became teachers as well as by musicians, who often taught music while they were in college.

RESILIENCE

Successful women typically arrived at their success by coping with challenge. Many women (62 percent) described a time or times during their education when they "hit a wall" and believed they would not be able to continue along their planned stairways to success. The difficulties they referred to came during college, graduate school, and in their careers. Percentages were similar for all careers. Many of the women reported multiple incidents when they felt they were in serious trouble. Some of the examples of "walls" for these women included difficulty in completing college courses (or actually failing them), financial problems, divorce, illness, death in the family, loss of confidence in their academic ability or loss of confidence in a more global sense, depression, anxiety, blatant sexism, transfer of husbands or boyfriends, breakup with boyfriends or significant others, and inability to cope with competition.

Figures 9.4 and 9.5 show the solutions these women used to overcome their problems. Most of the women indicated more than one problem and more than one solution. Solutions differed for the various careers. As you can see by the figures, not all the solutions were positive at the time, but perseverance won out as the most frequently mentioned positive solution. Neither anxiety nor depression permanently prevented these women from their successes; perhaps they were even powerful motivators. Resiliency or the ability to recover from misfortune was an absolutely necessary ingredient in the success of these

FIGURE 9.4

Positive Responses When Successful Women "Hit a Wall"

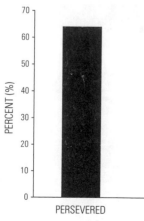

FIGURE 9.5

Negative Responses When
Successful Women "Hit a Wall"

FIGURE 9.6

When Successful Women "Hit a Wall"

Percentage That Dropped Out of College

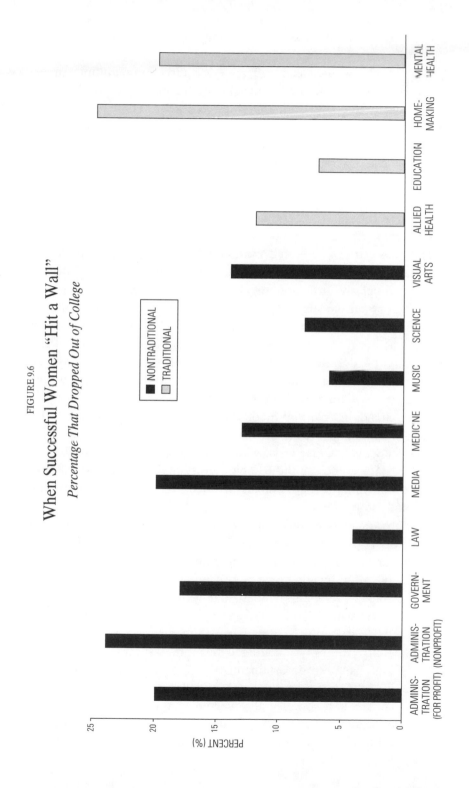

women, but creativity and flexibility played a part in that resiliency, along with perseverance.

Many of the women changed their life directions multiple times. Although most of these successful women overcame their problems (53 percent), others coped with their difficulties by temporarily under-achieving (21 percent), changing career direction (14 percent), drop-ping out of school (14 percent), changing majors (11 percent), or changing schools (10 percent).

Dropping out of college was a difficult alternative for women in some career groups (Figure 9.6). Most of the women who dropped out returned to college at a later time in life to resume their study or identi-fied alternative plans for continuing their education.

The physicians commented most frequently on the determination necessary to make it in a career that did not encourage women. Surgery was a particularly unwelcoming specialty. There were even negative comments about the surgical rotation for the women who intended to go into other specialty areas. Women were simply unwelcome. Several orthopedic surgeons recalled both their discouragement and their determination, despite the apparent impossibility of the career ahead. Dr. Ruth O'Keefe* described her experience: "In the first three weeks of college, my advisor told me not to count on medicine as a career because girls didn't get into medical schools easily, and my economics professor announced that he would not make appointments with female students because girls were only in college to find husbands; therefore, girls could see the teaching assistants if they had questions. These events had profound damaging effects on me, although nothing ever totally stopped me."

Another orthopedic surgeon, Dr. Gwen Caldwell, commented on similar sexist obstacles: "A comment in medical school by a male doctor made my drive to be a surgeon stronger than ever. On my third surgical rotation, the attending doctor, a navy captain, said, 'Back when I was a resident, ships were made of wood, men were men, giants roamed the halls, and'—here he looked directly at me—'women went into nursing.' That was 1987. The attitude of men in orthopedics was that women just did not belong! This only encouraged me more to show them they were wrong. I was absolutely determined."

Other life influences such as divorce and illness seemed to strengthen rather than weaken some of the women in their resolve. The most important influence for attorney Monica Riggs was a need to become economically self-sufficient. Her marriage was failing, and she knew she would need to support herself and her son. That same issue had encouraged artist Sandra Sheets to discontinue her media career and create a more profitable modeling school. Attorney Jennifer Harrison's major influence in deciding to go to law school was the fact that she had cancer at the age of forty-four. She was determined from that point on that nothing was going to stop her from doing what she truly wanted to do, and she wanted more than anything to become an attorney.

Television producer Denise Dennison summarized well the perspective on succeeding that represents what resilience is all about: "I always go into situations that are incredibly challenging which I'm not completely confident about, but I have a very strong drive to succeed. I have this need to prove to myself or to others that I can do this. I don't do something that I should be doing just because I have an underlying really good sense that I'm going to succeed at it. I'm always at the edge, so there are a lot of costs in pressure for me, but it keeps me going. Challenge and risk taking seem to attract me, but I also wonder why I'm not attracted to easier and more secure paths."

Part 2: Advice

You may wonder if your daughter is resilient enough to enter college if she is younger than the typical college student entrant, if she seems immature, or if she has been seriously underachieving in high school. There are many ways to test her readiness before investing in the first semester's tuition.

Advanced placement courses in high school can give you some reassurance about her academic readiness for college. There are more advanced placement courses in high schools now than ever before. Dual admission—that is, taking a college course on a college campus while still in high school—will give you a further sense of your daughter's readiness and also prepare her for what to expect when she finally attends college. Because academic and social adjustment should go hand in hand when your daughter attends college, it also helps to project whether your daughter will manage the first real separation from home. Experiences at summer camp or with independent travel can provide you with a sense of her social and emotional independence and her readiness for living on a college campus.

If your daughter has been achieving well in school but seems immature, you may consider sending her on a summer foreign exchange trip to accustom her to studying and living independently. There may be scholarship assistance available for such programs. Also, a small college may be more comfortable than a large university if she's unaccustomed to independence. Attending a college that is only a short drive from home (two hours or less) facilitates frequent visits home as she adjusts to her new environment and permits more gradual accommodation to her new environment. Sometimes young women can even live at home for a year or two if parents think they require that bridge to independence. For the most part, however, I recommend students establish their autonomy by living at college. Living away from home will encourage their self-sufficiency. A fifteen-year-old may be more mature than an eighteen-year-old, and in that case, she needs to be treated as if she's ready. It's reasonable to say that it's normal for most or perhaps all parents (and their kids) to worry quite a bit about their children's adjustment to college, and it may be that a daughter's young age could worry a parent more, but our data suggest no basis for worry. Age of entrance to college had no bearing on academic or social adjustment.

It is important to remember that most college students are unaccustomed to the challenging curriculum they find there. Nor are they used to being surrounded by quite so many intelligent, hardworking students. If your daughters' first-semester grades are lower than you or they expected, don't try to punish them into higher grades. They may be doing the best they can, or at least the best they know how to at the time. Put your coaching cap on. Recall your own college issues, if you attended college, and patiently help your daughters to understand their problems. If helping them directly seems to be beyond your skills or your relationship, encourage them to get counseling or tutoring at college. That's a small additional price to pay for their success and confidence compared to the other costs of college and to their potential income for the rest of their lives.

REVERSING UNDERACHIEVEMENT IN COLLEGE

If your daughter underachieved in high school and you worry she may not have the self-discipline to accomplish a college education, a year at a post-high-school college preparatory program or a year in the workforce may provide some maturation and a sense of what the work ethic required by colleges truly means. There is, of course, the risk that she will never attend college. If she doesn't go to college, encourage her to spend her year working at a menial job that feels like drudgery. Ask her to put half her salary aside for college, or if she lives with you, be sure she contributes to room and board. If you can manage it financially, consider saving that money for her should she decide to go to college the following year. After a semester or a year, she may hear your communication about how education will provide her with a more creative and challenging career, and she may be convinced that even study is better than her present uninspiring, unrewarding job. The risk of her not returning is increased if she finds a financially rewarding job that seems interesting to her. She will be hesitant about giving up her income for the lesser status of student.

If your daughter has underachieved in high school and wants to attend college, give her the opportunity to attempt it. It is unlikely she will automatically reverse her habits in college even when she promises you she will. Maturity and reality can reverse her pattern of underachievement, but it's a good idea to be sure she's invested in her education before you take the risk of throwing away the many thousands of dollars that colleges cost. Even if underachievers pay their own way, there is no assurance of success, but sharing in the investment does connect behavior with consequences for underachieving students, who often do not understand that link. Consider their investment to be a learning experience.

CHOOSING THE RIGHT COLLEGE

Selecting a college is a family adventure, so join your almost-adults in the exciting experience. You'll probably want to begin with a bookstore, a public library, or the Internet, where you will find considerable information to guide your search for colleges. You and your daughters can sift through their information to learn about size, location, type of campus, specialty majors, average SAT scores of college entrants, and more information than you'll ever need. Your daughters' schools will undoubtedly sponsor college fairs or college visits as well. Once you have a smattering of information about what's out there, you can begin to identify the kinds of colleges at which your daughter will thrive, as well as the kinds of colleges that will likely accept her. Unfortunately, finances will also need to be part of the discussion. Even when you do a little narrowing down, you will undoubtedly have a long list of colleges to think about or to visit.

If you and your daughter are considering a women's college, your list of colleges will be quite small. There were two very different groups of careers that had large proportions of women who attended women's colleges—the traditional careers, like teaching and nursing, and the power brokers, women in government and business. You may recall that the women in the latter group had considerable leadership opportunity in their women's colleges. Consider your daughter's interests, and, of course, her preferences in choosing. Your daughter will not adjust well to a women's college if she absolutely prefers a mixed-gender education. However, she may want to read up on some of the research on women's colleges because women's colleges have done some impressive training for leadership.

Our research suggests that the size of the college does seem to make a difference for students. For example, girls from small high schools may make a better transition to a small college where teachers are more accessible. On the other hand, a large university provides a great variety of opportunities for women who have not had the opportunity to explore many courses in a smaller high school. All colleges require women to be independent, but attending a large university will demand more autonomy, initiative, and self-confidence than going to a smaller school. Professors are readily available at all-size schools, but women at larger schools will need to be more assertive and take more initiative to locate both the help and the inspiring mentors from whom they can learn. If your daughters are interested in research-oriented careers in any field, larger universities provide many more research-related learning opportunities and jobs than do small colleges that put more emphasis on teaching.

Even in the literature and arts, your daughters may find more high-level practitioners—that is, actual artists, musicians, and authors—at larger universities than at smaller ones, but extremely talented artists, musicians, and authors may also be found at small specialty schools and conservatories. If your daughter knows exactly what her career direction is, size may have a low priority compared to the particular department and faculty within her interest area.

If your daughter is younger than the typical-age college student, a large university may be more appropriate than a small college. In general, large universities tolerate differences better than small ones, but there is considerable difference between schools of the same size. Sometimes particular colleges have specific programs for younger students that combine the intellectual stimulation they require with the consideration for difference in age.

CHOOSING A MAJOR

Although in looking back at the childhoods of the women in our study it was clear that their interests and their social propensities combined to direct them toward appropriate careers, most of the women's career choices were not obvious to them before they entered college. If your daughters aren't at all certain of where they want to direct their college education, consider that to be normal. It would be better for you to encourage them to explore a variety of courses before deciding on the direction to follow for their career.

For those who are certain of their direction and who are already passionate about their interests, you may believe your only choice is to support those interests. While most parents want to do that, it makes sense to encourage your daughters to learn more about the career before simply following their hearts. Speaking with women in the career in which they're interested is probably the best way for them to explore. Encourage your daughters to ask about the best and the worst parts of their career choice. If there are few or no women in the career they've chosen, they should talk to several men. They will need to discover if women are welcomed and recognize that if they aren't, an extreme amount of determination will be necessary to pioneer in what is primarily a man's world. You can remind your daughters that many women in our study pioneered and succeeded where women had not before, and if they wish to choose such a career for themselves, you are most willing to be supportive.

Young women will need to continue to be aware of sexist men who don't believe that women can succeed in fields that are not traditional for them. Although unconscious sexism is undoubtedly more prevalent among older men who have been raised with the traditional view of women's roles, younger men may also view women as presenting more competition in an already crowded field. It is important for your daughters to know how competitive their chosen field is, how many opportunities there are likely to be by the time they complete their education, and how they may be accepted into the particular career field. You will recall that for some women, unwelcoming men mainly provided a challenge, not a deterrent. Other women were dissuaded from pursuing careers in these fields and selected more cordial ones. Your daughters need to assess their own personal determination before they choose a pioneering career.

Although financial reward may not be on your daughters' agendas when they're eighteen because all their material needs to date have been met by their parents, ten years later they may feel frustrated by low compensation in their chosen field. It's better to get that information before investing their education in that direction. Even if low financial remuneration would not deter them, it seems wise for them to do the research. It is also not likely at this early age that they will be interested in how work and family life tend to balance out in their career choice, but it is nevertheless a good question to ask of professionals in their fields of interest.

Your young adult daughters are going to be most motivated if they love learning and the career image they've projected. They may even be likely to ignore your encouragement to investigate further practical questions. Don't let that prevent you from suggesting the questions.

Expect college and maturity to change your daughters. You may not like all the changes, and you may worry if they vacillate and modify their choice of major multiple times. It is simply part of normal decision making and of finding their identities. If you're worried that college will extend beyond the typical four years (it may if they alter their majors), you may need to negotiate about additional tuition. An extra semester or year of college is not an indication that there is something wrong with your daughter, but they certainly should cope with the reality of the extra cost. They may be able to convert their changed interest into master's or doctoral programs and even receive fellowship funding for their graduate education. Realistically, however, some especially popular majors aren't that flexible, or class selections are so limited that a change in major may delay completion of a degree.

SUPPORTING YOUR DAUGHTER'S SOCIAL/EMOTIONAL ADJUSTMENT

Although in our study the academic and social adjustment of the women were often related, that was certainly not always the case. Colleges have changed considerably and have fewer rules or even guidelines than ever before. Your daughter may be shocked by the lack of privacy in dormitories, by a roommate who continually invites her boyfriend or lesbian partner to spend the night, by alcohol and drug abuse, and by the total absence of dormitory quiet time. There are actually a variety of atmospheres at colleges to choose from, and part of your daughter's college search should include researching living arrangements that will be more comfortable and secure for her. There are quiet dorms, single-gender and coed dorms, apartments, small and large quarters, sororities, and numerous differences within each category. Your daughter may not find a happy match at first, but usually by semester's end, and sometimes even before, she can make a change. Consider that coping with an unhappy match is another component of developing resilience. It's most important to give your daughter some time and support during the adjustment period. She'll soon find a comfortable neighborhood.

If you have attended college in this country, you'll be in a better position to prepare your daughter for the differences ahead despite the many changes since your college years. If you haven't ever attended college, or if you attended college in another country, you may not be able to provide much information, and you may have some unrealistic expectations for your daughter's college social adjustment. It may also be harder for your daughter to adjust if she is the first of her generation to attend college. If she wants to get some counseling, she may need permission from you—not in the sense of having you sign a permission slip, but because she may worry that there is something wrong with her if she has to go for help. Perhaps she only needs to hear that most women seek a little counseling during college and graduate school, and some women go for almost constant therapy. Your daughter may need to hear her parents say, "Go for it if it's helpful," and she may also need to hear you say, "Quit if you think it's a waste of time." Part of growing up as a "good little girl" may be a fear of acknowledging that one has problems, and she may believe that being a "good little girl" requires that she follow a counselor's advice. Neither is mandatory for strong, independent women, but many college women are only in the process of becoming strong and independent. They are in transition, so they may need your support and that of others. Loving parents should not hesitate to call a dean's office when they are concerned for the well-being of their children.

COLLEGE FRIENDSHIPS

You can expect that your daughters will make friends among a broad group of less homogeneous adults when they go to college. It's best if you're as comfortable with the heterogeneity as they are. If their friends are serious about their education, regardless of their individual differences, you can see it as an excellent experience for your daughters. If they surround themselves with friends who are unlikely to graduate from college, you may have reason to worry. At this age there's probably little or nothing you can do about their friendships, but you do have a responsibility to express your concerns. Women who surround themselves with others who are seriously seeking an education are in a better position to get peer support for all the studying they need to do to prepare for high-level, interesting careers.

SEARCHING FOR MENTORS

You may find that you can no longer coach your daughter adequately because you don't have the specialized knowledge or experience to

guide her. Encourage her to find mentors. Willing mentors are every-
where for interested women who take initiative and are considerate of
others' time. However, successful mentors are very busy people, and
your daughters may too easily feel rejected because of their time short-
age. If they're assertive enough and flexible enough to make appointments that fit in with mentors' schedules, they can learn much to help
them direct their own careers and even their lifestyles. Consider also
that if they persevere, enthusiastic mentors can facilitate special opportunities within their careers. Many women were appreciative of facilitative mentors, and some even attributed their personal success to the
opportunities their mentors provided.

Both young women and young men learn from and are influenced by
college professors and mentors. It's more important for women to be
sensitive to a need for adopting mentors because most of them have
observed fewer professional adult female role models during their
childhoods. Although they are automatically more likely to find male
professors to mentor them in professions that are not traditional for
women, the women who become successful in those careers will be
more willing to reach out to help younger women. Unfortunately, that
is not always the case; professional women are often so busy balancing
their careers and families that they may find little time to reach out to
younger women. The smaller numbers of women who are single without families and who are older with grown families can become good
targets for young women's searches for help. Most universities and professional law schools now have associations of women professors who
include among their goals mentoring women students. Your daughter
can look for an organized mentoring system or simply search out people who exemplify the kind of professional she would like to become.
Many of the women in the study did exactly that.

Although there may be a short supply of successful women in your
daughter's career field, one mentor can inspire many women over time.
Many men, especially those with daughters of their own, are willing to
reach out to help young women.

Your daughters need to be prepared to accept criticism from mentors.
Many women admitted that they had learned to accept criticism from
their fathers and that this had prepared them to accept criticism from
professors at college or employers in their new careers. Others indicated that they found criticism discouraging and changed career direction based on a loss of confidence directly related to harsh criticism.
Science teacher Mary Sadowski was partially deterred from completing

her Ph.D. because her college education was referred to as that of a "glorified high school." Furthermore, there were no mentors who energized her at this level of her education. Those women who accepted criticism well seemed to be able to reframe that criticism and interpret it to mean that the mentor believed that their products or achievement were worth criticizing. They were able to use the strong advice, and although sometimes they may have felt discouraged, they did not entirely lose confidence in their abilities. Learning to accept criticism is a gradual process that begins early. Adult resilience is sometimes dependent on the ability to learn from mentors who often set very high expectations.

ENCOURAGING RESILIENCE IN YOUR DAUGHTER

Your daughter is away at college and she called you twice this week, or was it every day? She sounded anxious and depressed. She talked about college as not being the right place for her, and she's planning to drop a course or change her major or maybe even change colleges. It was just last week that you were wishing she'd call once in a while because you hadn't been hearing from her at all. Up to this point, college sounded like pure joy, and you were worried that she wasn't working hard enough. You may question your parenting, the high school you sent her to, the religion you did or didn't provide, the neighborhood you chose to live in, and, of course, the college you agreed she could go to. Now that you've read our research findings, you know that your daughter may be experiencing a very common phenomenon, and you needn't bother blaming yourself. Next week may be very different and more positive, or this week may be the beginning of a persistent theme.

Your daughter may need a weekend at home, a letter of support, a talk with a counselor, and, most important, a message that she's not alone. Be sure not to offer her an easy way out, although you may be tempted to feel sorry for her. Give her your message of confidence and let her know you love her. Remind her that college is ten times more difficult than high school and encourage her not to make quick decisions. If you can find a way to describe her central characteristic as "perseverance" or "determination," she may be able to take heart. If the depression or anxiety persists, psychotherapy is available, and in some cases medication may provide her with important support. Let your daughter know that you're happy to take her calls, and help her to remember that after exams there is a break.

If your daughter is too independent to call for help when she's feeling like she wants to drop out of college, or if she hasn't told you that she feels confused and directionless, it may well be time to call her. It's certainly reasonable to set up a weekly call time with your college-age daughter so that communication doesn't have to wait for emergencies.

While you're worrying, keep in mind that many successful women struggled during college, graduate, medical, or law school, and resilience is the magic word. Your daughter is not alone, and she's getting stronger. Let her know at least once a week that you believe in her.

RESILIENT AND OPTIMISTIC, SHE JUST WOULDN'T QUIT

Sandra Sheets
Visual Artist

Sandra reflects back on her early years and thinks of herself as a WASP princess—secure, loved, and wealthy, with all her needs and wants easily met. She was a beautiful and verbal child, adored by all. She has wonderful memories of how her executive engineer dad would pile the family into the car and drive to rural Pine Hollow, Pennsylvania, every weekend in the summer. They would hike the pine-covered hills, go fishing and boating, swim in the crystal-clear streams, and learn about nature from her knowledgeable father and the erudite guests he would invite along. Teachers were their favorite guests, and they always seemed so smart to Sandra. Even when they sat around the fire and told stories, the guests always seemed so special. Second to her loving dad, the visiting teachers were Sandra's greatest childhood influence, and she aspired to be like them. She had idyllic dreams of someday being one of those teachers.

There were other important and fond memories from Sandra's early childhood. Her dad would take his daughters to work with him, and they'd go right into the shop, where Sandra would see men working on cars. She wondered why girls couldn't work on those cars. Sandra's sister would hold her hands over her ears and want to leave, but Sandra was intrigued and wanted to stay and watch. She remembers, too, that her dad loved books and would read to her as well. He wanted her to become a teacher, and they bonded over their love of learning and books.

When Sandra was eight years old, her world changed dramatically. Her adored dad died suddenly, and a new, unanticipated vagabond life began. Her dad left the family a sizable inheritance, which her mother immediately began to gamble away. Sandra didn't understand at the time that her mother had both alcohol and gambling problems. They traveled from one gambling site to another. Initially they lived in elaborate hotel suites, but as circumstances grew worse, cheap hotel rooms became their temporary, constantly changing homes. As Sandra's mother searched for places to win a new fortune, she took her daughters to Las Vegas to bet on the races. Sandra describes her mother as betting on "anything that could race—dogs, horses, and even two spiders racing across the floor would do." By the time Sandra was thirteen they had gone from being wealthy to being penniless, from mixing with only upper-class Caucasian children to befriending people from every economic stratum, race, culture, and walk of life. The girls were shuffled from one school to another, never settling long enough in any city or school to make any friends. There were no books in her home, only racing forms. Schools and libraries became Sandra's shelters. She could hide away in books, and the librarians always seemed to understand that she needed shelter. They would put their arms around her as they guided her to good books, and they permitted her to read in their libraries for hours. Teachers adored her and encouraged her learning, and she felt safe as long as she surrounded herself with books and learning. When accommodations and traveling became too absurd and Sandra felt desperate, she would dream of her father for inspiration, and his memory would keep her motivated to go on.

When Sandra's mother had gambled away all of the money, she expected her daughters to go to work to support the family. By age fourteen Sandra was working full time at night, sometimes at two separate jobs to pay for rent and food for the family. She would work at clerical jobs, waitressing, or as a night clerk in a hotel. She lied about her age to get the jobs and worked very hard to keep them. She suspects her bosses always knew she wasn't telling the truth, but they pretended they didn't because they always liked her and knew she was a hard worker. Also, because she was in school, they often let her study or do homework in quiet moments. She kept her grades high, participated in no extracurricular activities, and had almost no friends. There was no time for anything but work and school.

When she was fifteen she was raped by one her mother's boyfriends. She never had the courage to tell her mother or even her sister about it, and she never reported it to the police, but she moved out and left her mother and sister to fend for themselves. She rented a small room in the hotel where her grandmother lived. In those days, Sandra said, they didn't talk about sex, but she often confided in her grandmother, and thought her grandmother understood what had happened. She recalls that every morning her grandmother would bring her a cup of tea and a warm roll, which was the first time anyone had served her any kind of meal since her dad had died. As she thinks of that time now, she still misses her grandmother. It was then that Sandra learned from her grandmother that her mother had always had gambling and drinking problems. Sandra's grandmother was embarrassed to talk about her daughter, who, even in the good days before her husband died, just sat around and played bridge and never did any work. Sandra's beautiful mom had never even graduated from high school, but her dad, who so loved learning and education and was himself a college graduate, adored her anyway.

In the second semester of her senior year, Sandra fell asleep in her favorite English class. She was working more than full time and was exhausted. However, no one knew what she did with her time. When she nodded off, the teacher gave her a zero and berated her in front of the class, making comments about her lipstick and about "having such a wild night." Because Sandra was unusually beautiful, everyone assumed that she was on a fast social track. The truth was that she had never even dated a boy at that age. She was so embarrassed by the teacher's remarks that she can to this day recall the feeling of the heat rising on her face as if it were yesterday. She got up, walked out of her class, and never returned to school. She didn't even have the courage to explain, and although she was only a few weeks from graduation, she settled for only a GED.

Sandra had destroyed her dreams of college and teaching, and she regretted that for the rest of her life. Still determined, Sandra needed to find a way to support herself and embarked on a course of learning from life. Encouraged only by her grandmother and her bosses, who seemed to believe in her, she took it one day at a time, building her confidence around her work ethic and her father's aspirations for her, which were preserved in her memories. Her religious beliefs and her optimism were also very important to her at this difficult juncture in her life.

At a party one evening a guest approached her and said his wife pointed her out as being perfect for "Miss Chicken of the Sea." Sandra modeled as the mermaid and appeared on hundreds of thousands of tuna fish cans. The man also offered her a radio program, which later led to a television program. Television opened up opportunities for more modeling jobs, and finally Sandra moved to New York City for a full career of modeling, radio, and television performances.

Sandra's mentors included a friend who ran a modeling agency and the many guests she interviewed on radio and television. She especially used to love to talk to the famous vocalist Kate Smith in her dressing room. She admired her and learned from her an incredible amount about show business.

Sandra's mother expected that Sandra would marry someone wealthy who would support her. Sandra was married briefly, but it was a bad marriage to a man who was nothing like the father she had adored. She was left a single parent.

While Sandra was in New York, she frequented the Metropolitan Museum of Art and the Museum of Modern Art and studied the art that was on display. She read every art book she could get her hands on. As she immersed herself in the study of art, she knew it was inevitable that someday, after she had raised her son, she would become an artist. That became her goal in life.

Although Sandra's New York career was going well, the city was no place to raise her son. She decided to move to Florida and use what she had learned in New York to start her own successful modeling agency. Her mother lived with her. Sandra never minded supporting her and actually enjoyed her mother's sense of humor. She never felt the bitterness toward her that her sister felt. The art career that Sandra explored in New York was placed on the back burner so she could continue to support her son and her mother. Finally, in her fifties, Sandra was able to sell her successful businesses, watch her son go out on his own, and retire to the artistic career she had always wanted. She began working with oils and immediately began selling her paintings. Shortly after, she discovered she had breast cancer. While going through chemotherapy, she found she could no longer use oil paint, so she changed her medium to watercolor. She exhibits at a great many galleries and is very successful.

Across the street from her home in Arizona, she met a bachelor whom she befriended. Interestingly, he was an engineer, like her dad. For a while they ran a small successful newspaper together. Their marriage has made for a loving and pleasant relationship during her painting days.

Sandra's optimism, perseverance, extensive reading, and life experiences provided her with further education and success. Sandra believes her sister, on the other hand, made a poor adjustment to their father's death and seemed sad and angry all of her adult life. Sandra points out that she and her sister always looked very much alike, and her sister was also especially pretty. The only difference was the curve of their lips. While Sandra smiles frequently, her sister's turned-down mouth reflects the sadness and anger that captured her life.

At sixty-nine, Sandra can't help believing that she was just "the luck-iest woman in the world to get out alive," and to have the wonderful life now that she never expected. Obstacles and poverty pervaded her life, but her optimism and resilience never let her quit.

MADAME CURIE WAS HER ROLE MODEL

Dr. Anne Caroles
Psychologist

As a young girl, Dr. Anne Caroles always wanted to be a doctor and researcher like Madame Curie. Parents and teachers alike encour-aged her academic success throughout her childhood, but when she actually decided to major in premedical education, paradoxically, she was totally discouraged by everyone. Her mother criticized her choice and told her she wasn't compassionate enough to be a doctor, and, even more important, it would prevent her from having a good marriage and a family. Her soon-to-be homemaker sister thought Anne was strange for "wanting to go to school for that long," and her friends couldn't imagine her taking on so many years of education. Furthermore, there was absolutely no one who would be able to help finance such an endeavor. Anne majored in chemistry and worked in a laboratory for a while until she was married. Her husband was the first to encourage her to go to medical school, and she was accepted into and began medical school only to discover she was pregnant. At first, Anne tried to con-tinue despite the pregnancy, but her pregnancy became difficult, and she was forced to choose between her baby and continuing her medical education. She decided to drop out of medical school.

In contrast to Anne, Anne's sister was as "smashingly beautiful" as their mother. Although Anne considers both her mother and sister to be highly intelligent and very creative, her own plain appearance set her apart from the rest of the family. Even her brother and father were very handsome. As a preadolescent and through her teen years, Anne thought of herself as ugly, although she now finally views herself as just normal-looking. Her mother would say about her daughters, "Becky has the looks and Anne has the brains." Anne interpreted this message as, "You're bright but not very attractive and people aren't going to want to be around you, so you'd better develop your intelligence." Anne believes her bright, capable sister was the more disadvantaged by the comparison. She thinks her sister is just as bright as she is, but Becky's strengths were in verbal areas, and she was a very creative and excellent writer as a child. However, because only science and math intelligence were valued during those "race in space" days, the family never considered Anne's sister to be highly intelligent. As a result, she underachieved, never attended college, and is a full-time homemaker.

Anne felt different because she was told she was "different" regularly. She never identified with either her mother or her father, and although she never felt brilliant, she had plenty of academic confidence and always did well in school. She recalls that her IQ score was 135, and she graduated from high school as valedictorian and a National Merit Scholar.

When Anne was born her dad was in the military, and her mom was a full-time homemaker but also a frustrated musician. Her dad's military service included frequent national and international moves. Anne attended both Catholic and public schools at various times during her childhood. Anne recalled that her father was an alcoholic; he would return home late from work (or a bar) and fall asleep on the couch. She also remembered with anger that he abused her sexually, but that finally stopped by middle school. Perhaps her mother knew, too, and felt trapped without a way to support the three children. It's no wonder her mother emphasized independence so much. Anne never felt very close to her mother. She thought that if she was expected to be independent, she couldn't be too close. She always felt as if she were looking in at her family from the outside, not quite a part of it, again mainly because she didn't look as pretty as they. Her dad was always easy on Anne, perhaps because he wanted sexual favors, and her mother was always strict. Maybe, Anne thought, her mother was disappointed because Anne wasn't prettier. Anne remembered a very stormy adolescence with her mother, during which her mother labeled her as "too big for her britches."

Anne had many mentors along the way, beginning with Marie Curie and Clara Barton, whose biographies she read many times. She loved their assertiveness and was excited about the idea that women could be scientists, doctors, and nurses in a world where the only real doctors she knew were men. She admits books about women were sparse; even her history books included very few women.

Anne believes the feelings of being different may have been facilitative in elementary school. Although she remembers feeling popular in first grade, it was also the last grade in which she felt completely accepted. She was very shy, and recalls that the first Catholic school she attended used harsh and abusive discipline. She was truly afraid, but she soon found she could succeed academically; to avoid getting into trouble, she began her pattern of overstudy. She worked very hard to be extremely successful. She recalls that other children might get beaten for their report cards, but she would always shine, consistently having the best report card in the class.

Anne acknowledged that her mother encouraged her to be an excellent student when Anne was younger, and it wasn't until young adulthood that she pressured Anne to become a nurse and a traditional homemaker. Anne's Girl Scout leader was ahead of her times and an inspiration. She helped Anne believe that she would be able to accomplish more than women had traditionally.

Anne's family moved to Japan when Anne entered middle school, and an entirely new world opened up for her. She was given considerable independence because it was safe for children to wander about the streets of Tokyo. Anne was allowed to get on the train and travel to downtown Tokyo to explore the city on her own. She not only developed a tremendous amount of confidence but thoroughly enjoyed the freedom.

The latitude provided by Anne's new public school, on the military base, initially trapped Anne academically. For the first time all her friends weren't from the homogeneous environment of her Catholic school. Her social life expanded, and she became interested in boys. She was excited and felt free, albeit a little too free. She did little homework and her grades plummeted. Anne's parents responded swiftly and surely with severe punishment. There were absolutely no privileges or social life; or in Anne's words, she "didn't see the light of day" until the grades were all A's again, and that happened very quickly, but surveillance by her parents never disappeared again during her school years.

Anne's schoolwork during her time in Japan continued to go well, and her family life became smoother than it had ever been. Her dad ceased both drinking and abusing her. He came home to be with his family every night right after work because he was part of a car pool whose members returned together. Anne's parents seemed happier. She remembers Japan as exciting, stimulating, peaceful, adventurous, and almost as an oasis in a childhood desert because it was so pronouncedly different from the rest of her childhood.

Anne's intellectual confidence continued in high school on an army base in the States. One time in a chemistry class when learning biochemistry, the whole class failed a test, including Anne. The teacher said she'd give them an opportunity for a retest. Anne went to the library, searched out a book that explained the material, and taught it to one of her friends. On the next test, she and her friend earned 100's, but the remaining students in the class failed again. It was that kind of intellectual experience that led Anne to believe she could learn anything she put her mind to.

Anne does recall feeling pressured in high school, especially by her parents. She was always afraid she'd get into trouble if she didn't perform. Of course, there were the memories of how her parents had come crashing down on her in middle school when her grades had slipped briefly, but it was more than that. She thinks now that much of the pressure she felt was her own and that her parents were only very proud of her achievements and that felt like pressure to her. She defined herself by her intelligence and didn't have very many other areas of confidence. Also, her rank in class and high test scores were her ticket to scholarships and freedom. With all the emphasis on the need to beat the Russians in the cold war, Anne even felt she had a personal intellectual obligation to the world. She was committed to making a contribution, mainly because she was so adept at science and math at a time in history when those very specific skills were the main definition of high intelligence.

The principal of Anne's high school was the first one who sat Anne down to tell her how capable she really was. Anne recalls, "She knew about my high SAT scores and told me that I could shine at any major top-notch university. I knew I couldn't do that because that would require total financial support, and there was absolutely none forthcoming from my parents. Nevertheless, the principal really encouraged me to be the best I could be and raised my confidence to a new height."

Anne was the first person in her extended family to go to college. Her parents then assumed that after graduation she should get a job instead of going on to medical school. They reminded her again that she wasn't compassionate enough for medicine, and it would prevent her from ever having a family. When Anne was in college she was the only woman in her science and math classes. She knew she was unique for her time. Anne now believes that her parents' first reason for her not going on to medical school was only an excuse for their underlying second reason: They wanted her to follow the more traditional woman's path. To Anne, theirs was a continuous contradictory double message.

Two chemistry professors in college tried to encourage Anne to go on to medical school, but with the emotional pressure from her parents, she was too afraid that she would be isolated and wouldn't be able to complete medical school. Eventually Anne's parents relented and encouraged her to go to graduate school. They, too, were changing. However, Anne became totally bored by her Ph.D. program in chemistry and left after one semester. She became somewhat depressed, lost confidence in herself and her intelligence, and dropped out of graduate school. She really only wanted to be a medical doctor but didn't believe she could manage it. Anne recalls wondering how she would ever become Madame Curie and make a difference if she couldn't go on with her education.

Because teaching paired well with parenting, Anne taught math and science for several years. Nineteen years after her college graduation, she returned to earn her master's degree in counseling and then continued on at the state university to finally earn her doctorate in psychology. She's worked as a school counselor and a school psychologist while continuing her lengthy education. She appreciates her husband's absolute, unqualified support and has managed to balance this education and career with raising three children. Anne wonders how much has really changed for women when she finds herself, now at age forty-three, reassuring her daughter that she can become a doctor although her daughter still believes that being a nurse would be the more reasonable path for her because she's a woman.

As Anne thinks retrospectively about her choices, she does value the family time and vacation time her temporary career in education provided. She isn't at all sure that she would have liked missing that time and leaving the child care to a nanny, as she would have had to do if she had gone into medicine.

Anne found her clinical training in psychology to be incredibly therapeutic. She has finally come to terms with her ability to be both scientific and compassionate. She, indeed, derives great joy from her clinical relationships with her clients. Although she has no regrets about the psychology career she loves, she wonders how it would have been if she could have followed the path of her childhood role model, Madame Curie. She recently looked at a picture of Marie Curie in her daughter's science book in which the French scientist was pictured leaning on a man on either side. "No," thought Anne, "our girls need to be given more independence than that. They need to be the way Marie Curie really was." As she thought about Madame Curie, her mother's emphasis on independence echoed. She wondered again about how much independence to expect her daughter to have. How much is enough to help her build her individuality and yet maintain emotional relationships with others? Anne hasn't yet clearly arrived at an answer.

CHAPTER 10

SEE JANE STOP

Glass Ceilings, Sticky Floors, and Circuitous Stairways

Part 1: Findings

Where are women now and how are they managing? Their homes have expanded into the career world, as have their talents and confidence. A home seems an appropriate metaphor for women because for so long they have been the homemakers and tradition bearers for our society. However, their routes to their new and expanded homes are not always direct and straightforward. Indeed, some women feel stuck on the bottom floor, while others see the stairway winding upward in a circuitous path, and when they arrive at the top, an invisible barrier, or "glass ceiling," keeps them from maximal achievement. Still others have emerged as relatively successful in their careers, but they remain uncertain whether the sacrifices they made in terms of family life and relationships have been worthwhile.

HOW FAR HAVE WE COME?

Women have come a long way but continue to face many challenges. It was only in the eighteenth century that Jean-Jacques Rousseau warned, "Women's entire education should be planned in relation to men; to please men, to be useful to them, to win their love and respect, to raise them as children, care for them as adults, counsel and console them, make their lives sweet and pleasant. These are women's duties in all ages; these are what they should be taught from childhood on."[1] By the early 1900s, Dr. Edward Thorndike assured women that education was not likely to "harm women's health" and that some women could even be educated toward careers, provided those careers involved nurturing roles.[2] It was thus that women were given permission by men to be teachers, nurses, and social workers as long as those careers didn't interfere with their roles as mothers and wives.

Margaret Rossiter, in her book *Women Scientists in America: Before Affirmative Action, 1940–1972,* reminded women that although World War II mobilized them into the workplace and even into laboratories, most women were forced to leave their occupations after the war.[3] Not only were they no longer recruited into universities or colleges, but they actually lost their jobs because they were supposed to be caring for their children and keeping their husbands comfortable. Dr. Mary Ainsworth,* a research psychologist, shared a picture of herself in military uniform as she recalled that the war had given her and many women unprecedented opportunities. She remained on the faculty of the University of Toronto while in the service. Very few men were left on that faculty because they had almost all been drafted into active duty. Mary was promoted to the rank of major and given a trailblazing leadership position organizing the assessments of all army personnel. After she left the army, she was one of the few women retained by the University of Toronto, perhaps because of her prestigious position in the service, or perhaps because she was not married at the time and didn't have children. She considered herself lucky that she survived in her position when most of the women entirely lost theirs.

Today more girls than boys graduate from high school. More women than men receive bachelor's degrees (54 percent).[4] However, as of 1995, more of the doctorates, 60.7 percent, are awarded to men.[5] The traditional women's careers are still dominated by women. Ninety-three percent of registered nurses are women.[6] As of 1996, women make up approximately 98 percent of the educators in preschools and kindergartens, 83 percent of those in elementary schools, and 60 percent of those in secondary schools.[7] Despite the high percentage of women in teaching, women were less than 1 percent of school superintendents until 1979. That figure increased to only 7.1 percent by 1993.

Forty-four percent of the teachers at colleges and universities were women in 1996, compared to only 36 percent in 1983.[8] A 1972 *Time* magazine article recommended, "If a woman wishes to become a college president, she is advised to become a nun." The percentage of women in college administration has also increased, albeit to a modest degree. By 1994 a study indicated that the percentage of women college presidents had indeed risen, but to only 12 percent.[9]

An area of great recent progress for women is business. By 1986 there was an extraordinary relative increase in the numbers of women majoring in business. The business share of all degrees earned by women increased tenfold, from less than 3 percent in 1970 to over 20 percent in 1986.[10] Even this apparent progress was at first balanced by a downside, because women with MBAs earned so much less than men. In 1990 statistics showed that in the first year after receiving an MBA, men earn a salary that is 12 percent higher, on average, than that of women.[11] The good news is that there have been continuous and dramatic changes in women's success in business since then. As of 1995, women MBA graduates outpaced men in starting salaries by $5,000. These women had better graduate test scores, more prior work experience, and greater participation in honorary societies than men.[12] According to an article published in the *New York Times* in 1995, most successful women believe they became successful because they consistently exceeded expectations.[13] This conclusion seemed to be consistent with what the successful women in our study expressed about their own successes. As of 1997, women held 10.6 percent of the total board seats in Fortune 500 companies, and 84 percent of Fortune 500 companies now have at least one woman on their boards.[14] However, one study found that women in business continue to prefer lower-paid jobs that are safer and allow for more flexible hours to be with their children. Only 14 percent of corporate women aspired to CEO positions, compared to 46 percent of their male counterparts.[15]

In medicine, too, there is improvement. The *New England Journal of Medicine* reported that as of 1996, women constitute 40 percent of the student body in medical schools, in contrast to less than 10 percent in the late 1960s and early 1970s. The number of women physicians has quadrupled in the past twenty years. However, neither their status nor their earnings have kept pace with those of male physicians. The salary differential was explained in the report by the number of hours worked as well as the specialty areas that women tend to select. Most women choose primary-care specialties rather than high-paying specialties such as surgery.[16] There continues to be an invisible glass-ceiling effect in medicine. There were only forty-seven women chairpersons of all clinical departments in U.S. medical schools, and in pediatrics, a field that attracts the largest number of women, there were only five chairpersons in a total of 128 U.S. medical school pediatrics departments in 1989.[17] One of those, Dr. Janet Smith, participated in our study. For the 1986–87 academic year, only 1.6 percent of all medical school deans, 9.6 percent of associate deans, and 20 percent of all assistant deans were women.[18] Four years later, in 1992, only two medical schools out of a total of 126 were led by women, and as of 1994, only 4 percent of the academic chairs were held by women.[19]

Despite the fact that almost half of medical students are women, as of 1995, eleven years after finishing medical school, only 59 percent of the women who graduated in 1984 and went into teaching were associate or full professors, compared to 83 percent of similar male graduates.[20] Twenty-three percent of the males who graduated in that year had achieved the rank of full professor, compared to only 5 percent of the females. The researchers called this a "sticky floor effect" because not only were few women given leadership roles, but most were literally "stuck" in the lower ranks of academics.[21]

Women in law and government are making slow progress. Although at least half of law school graduates are women, and women now make up 25 percent of this country's attorneys, only 6 percent had achieved partnership status as of 1994.[22] Between 1971 and 1991 the proportion of elected mayors who were women went from 1 percent to 17 percent, still far short of true representation. As of 1993 approximately 20 percent of elected state legislators were women, but only 10 percent of federal legislators were women. By 1998, five years later, that has increased to only 11 percent.[23] In government, women have a long way to go to achieve equity.

In 1966 there were virtually no baccalaureate degrees granted to women in civil, electrical, or mechanical engineering. By 1985 the figures had increased to 17, 12, and 10 percent, respectively. Instead of continued increase, however, eleven years later the percentages had decreased slightly, to 15, 8, and 7 percent.[24] Females continue to bypass engineering in their choices of majors. A study that compared women engineers to women math educators found that the challenging mathematics coursework was not what distinguished the two groups. The women in engineering expressed greater desire for prestige and leadership, while the educators tended to look for dependability and reliability of their positions.[25] As of 1990, only 4 percent of all engineers were women.[26]

We were also reminded that women have not yet established themselves in the arts; one commentator points out that "there have been no supremely great women artists. . . . There are no women equivalents for Michelangelo or Rembrandt, Delacroix or Cezanne, Picasso or Matisse."[27] Statistics for 1996 show that half of present painters, sculptors, craft artists, and print makers are women.[28] With new opportunities for women's involvement in art, perhaps more women will begin to emerge as great artists.

New statistics report that 34 percent of musicians and composers are women. However, among the major symphony orchestras, an average of only 20 percent of the orchestral members are women. When I addressed a group of women orchestral members to recruit them for our study, they indicated that, at least compared to the past, they no longer felt like pioneers. Marilyn Bergman, a violist, recalled a time when she was the only women in her symphony orchestra. She believed if it hadn't been for World War II and the need for symphonic players, she would still be teaching in elementary school. Kathy Drew, principal violist for a symphony orchestra, recalls the glass ceiling as a great problem when she joined the orchestra. She described typical orchestras in the 1960s: "When I advanced as much as the ceiling would allow, I switched my field emphasis from violin to viola to become principal violist. When I first joined the symphony, men were seated at the outside edge of the orchestra in an attempt to hide the female players, who were also required to wear their hair up at concerts."

CIRCUITOUS STAIRCASES

Although men in our society more frequently pursue a linear route and more often define themselves by their careers, the women in our study followed a variety of pathways during their careers. Not only did more women take roundabout steps, but they were often detoured by family responsibilities and delayed by pregnancy and childbearing. Some returned to school multiple times before completing their education and initiated careers years after they had planned. Their later careers were often entirely different from their original careers. This was particularly the case for many of the older women in the study whose initial career was a traditional teaching career. Other women stayed in their careers but intentionally slowed their climb upward so they could avoid the guilt and/or participate in the joy of parenting their children. More than one woman in media, business, art, medicine, and science recognized a glass ceiling in her career field. That bothered the women less than the realization that they were personally torn between their wish to pursue their careers assertively and their concern about missing out entirely on important parenting experiences. They knew they lacked the time and energy for the greater travel demands, the longer hours for grant writing or research, or the pressures that the more vertical and aggressive upward climb entailed. They were willing to pay the career penalty. "For now," they repeated continuously, "I'll settle for a lower level in my career because I don't want to miss out on my family, but I'm constantly torn between home and career." Attorney Lindsey Olsen stated it succinctly: "The feminist movement sold us a bill of goods, but there is no shape or form in which you can have it all. It's just impossible!" Many women concurred, or at least concluded that they could have it all only by sequencing their careers and family planning differently than men did.

The result of this career/family dilemma is that as of 1997, working women earned 75 cents for every dollar men earn, and this difference holds for college graduates as well as for women in careers where they outnumber men. There are millions of women now working who stayed home to raise children and who have thus been in the workforce fewer years than men in the same professions. The salaries of young women who have never had a child or older women who have never married approach equity, and in the latter case even exceed those of men. This research concluded that women's financial penalty is directly related to their investment of time in the childbearing years.[29] Not all would agree.

CAREER SATISFACTION

Of the more than 1,400 women who completed questionnaires for the study, 1,236 met the criteria for the selected career categories of being either very happy or moderately happy in their career choice. Women who indicated they were neutral, moderately unhappy, or very unhappy about their careers were eliminated from the study. However, even when they claimed happiness and satisfaction in the questionnaire, they talked about glass ceilings, family conflicts, modified plans, and the frustrations conflicting career and family goals during their interviews. They often discussed the career sacrifices they made for their relationships, particularly among those who were single or divorced. Nevertheless, most of the women, 82 percent, advised other women to pursue careers similar to theirs. Only 13 percent were ambivalent, pointing out both advantages and disadvantages, and 5 percent did not recommend their careers to women of the future, despite their own satisfaction with their chosen careers.

The main reasons for positive recommendations are worth noting. The descriptor of their careers as "challenging" was chosen most frequently, by 87 percent of the women, followed closely by "makes a contribution," "creative," and "fulfilling." Only a third of the women selected either "financially satisfying" or "prestigious" as a reason for recommending their careers.

Although there was consistency in many of the women's assessments of their careers as challenging, there were considerable differences between categories for those who believed they made a contribution and had creative and fulfilling careers. Fewer of the business executives, musicians, and artists felt they were making important contributions to society in comparison to the nonprofit business executives and the women in government and medicine. Also, more of the women in the traditional fields considered themselves to be making a contribution to society, and the group that most frequently viewed themselves as making contributions to society were the mental health professionals. "Fulfillment" was selected most frequently by the full-time homemakers and least by the business executives. Perhaps not surprisingly, the artists selected "creative" more frequently than any other group. Much more surprisingly, the women in medicine and allied health described their careers as "creative" least frequently compared to all other groups.

Women who described their careers as gratifying because they believed they were "making a contribution," "attaining personal fulfillment," or "being creative" did not necessarily perceive that they were financially satisfied. The women in business were most financially satisfied, although they infrequently selected "makes a contribution" and "fulfilling" on their questionnaires. Most of the women in government, education, and mental health believed they were making important contributions despite their lack of financial satisfaction. The artists indicated least financial satisfaction with their work, as did the homemakers. It may well be difficult to put the ideal package together for women; however, we have no evidence that the same issues would be different for men.

CAREER DISSATISFACTION

Of the small number of women who were either ambivalent or negative about recommending their career to younger women, their main complaints were that their careers were financially disappointing, took too

much time away from their families and relationships, or were too competitive (see Figures 10.1, 10.2, and 10.3).

Only 2 percent of the women in business found their careers to be
financially disappointing. However, lest you think that business is a
sure route to financial success, be reminded that the businesswomen
who participated in our study had already been selected specifically for
their success. Those who were impoverished failures or had declared
bankruptcy were not included. It's important also to realize that the
successful businesswomen in our study did not find business an easy
route. They were committed to hard work and endured great pressures.

The legendary "starving artists" were most financially disappointed,
and the very talented orchestral musicians were not very far behind in
their concerns about money. The orchestral women voiced the most
concern about competitiveness compared to any other career group,
despite the fact that these women were heavily involved in musical

FIGURE 10.1

Why Successful Women Don't Recommend
Their Careers: Percentage of Women Who Checked
"Financially Disappointing"

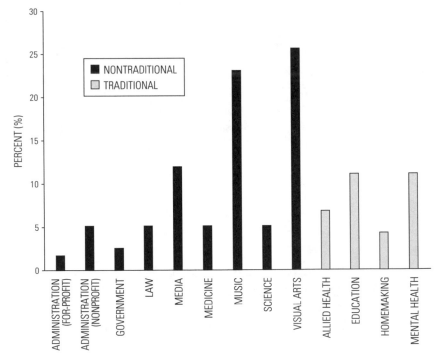

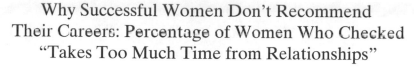

FIGURE 10.2

Why Successful Women Don't Recommend Their Careers: Percentage of Women Who Checked "Takes Too Much Time from Relationships"

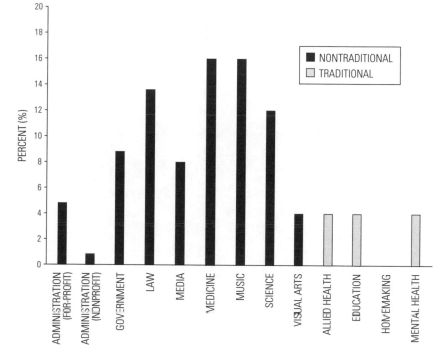

competition during their entire childhoods; many may have first encountered disappointment in competition as adults. As Figure 10.2 illustrates, the musicians, as well as the physicians, attorneys, and scientists, most frequently expressed concern that their careers took too much time away from their family and relationships. This figure makes it clear why the traditional careers were indeed traditional for women: They fit well with women's homemaking responsibilities. Only the women leaders in business complained as little about the impact on their family relationships as the women in the traditional careers.

ATTRIBUTION OF SUCCESS

Considerable research on male-female differences has indicated that males (both children and adults) tend to attribute their success to their high abilities and their failures to other people or bad luck. Research also finds that females tend to attribute their success either to hard

FIGURE 10.3

Why Successful Women Don't Recommend Their Careers: Percentage of Women Who Checked "Too Competitive"

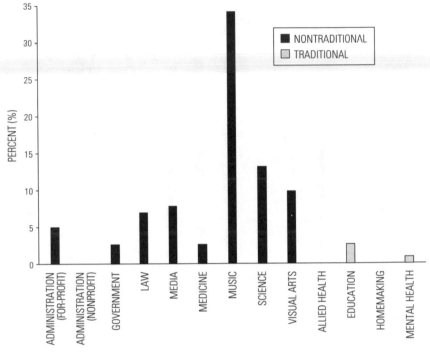

work or good luck but take personal responsibility for their failures or may not consider themselves smart enough.[30]

Here's an example of a typical man's story of his promotion to program director of a major radio station: "You know, I didn't get to this level by chance. I made smart decisions, and I know what's best for this station." And here's a typical example of a boy's explanation for a bad report card: "Mom, what do you expect? That teacher has no idea of how to teach."

In contrast, consider what most of the women in our study said about their success. Executive Susan Widham* related how she was never afraid to work hard and is not hesitant about starting before dawn. Medical researcher Dr. Alyssa Gaines, who is at least as intelligent as other researchers, claimed she wasn't "as smart" as other researchers but worked harder and was more efficient. Medical researcher Dr. Janice Douglas* described her success as serendipitous. MIT engineer Dr.

Catherine Burns described as chance her decision to major in engineering and even the choice to go to graduate school; when she received a prestigious award, she considered it a matter of luck.

Almost all the women who received good grades in school attributed those grades to many hours of study. When they received good grades with little effort, they assumed their schools provided easy curricula. Although many of the women chose "smart" or "talented" from a list when they were asked to identify words that described themselves, very few described themselves that way in their interviews. Quite a few did mention their intellectual confidence as children, but—true to the upbringing of "good little girls"—they did not brag. Instead, they minimized what they had accomplished and displayed incredible modesty. They found it surprising that they were indeed successful; some were even hesitant about completing their questionnaires in the belief that they were not sufficiently successful to qualify for the study. MIT engineer Dr. Catherine Burns substantiated this finding when she asked high-level civil engineers in a conference to participate in the study. She was astonished at their hesitation about whether they qualified for our study.

CONTENTEDNESS IN FAMILY
AND FRIENDSHIP RELATIONSHIPS

Most of the women also met the criteria for being at least moderately happy in their family and friendship relationships. Fewer than 1 percent indicated they were very unhappy, and only 3 percent acknowledged they were moderately unhappy. The research group was indeed a reasonably happy group of women.

Seventy-one percent of the women were married, 9 percent were single, 8 percent were divorced, and 5 percent indicated they were in other relationships. One percent were in lesbian relationships. The remaining women (approximately 6 percent) were not specific about their relationships.

The divorce rate for these women was indeed considerably lower than that of their parents—a little more than half of their parents' 14 percent. However, the average age of the group of women was only forty-four, so it is likely that more of them may divorce sometime in the future despite their relatively happy family lives at this time.

Figure 10.4 shows the careers in which most women categorized their family relationships as very happy. Most career categories were similar, with the exception of the homemakers. Apparently assigning a high

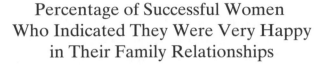

FIGURE 10.4

Percentage of Successful Women
Who Indicated They Were Very Happy
in Their Family Relationships

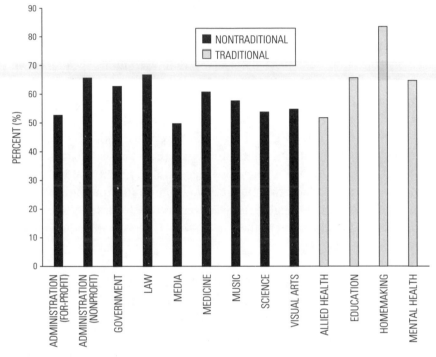

priority to homemaking brought women in this category the great family happiness they were hoping for, although there is also the possibility that they found it most satisfactory because they had no alternative career at the time, nor did they aspire to a career. Also, the average age of the homemakers was somewhat younger than the total group. Certainly the women who combined family and career were routinely pressed for time and struggled incessantly with the pressures of family and career commitments. Quite a few of the women confided that their husbands encouraged them to temporarily give up their careers or at least commit less time to them. However, they also admitted that their career was part of their definition and an important component of their fulfillment. The option of giving up a career often felt threatening to their sense of self and their independence.

Interestingly enough, although careers were self-defining for many of the women, others, even those who were renowned and remarkably successful in their careers, would often refer to their families as their central and highest priority. Even as medical researcher Dr. Alyssa Gaines shared her successful story, she pointed to the picture of her family and reminded her interviewer, "They are what life is really about. My family is really where the joy comes from."

Husbands and adult relationships were extremely critical to the success of the women in our study. Many women credited their husbands for their support and their sharing of power.

Some of the successful women were continuously supportive of their husbands and prioritized their husbands' careers above their own, whereas other couples compromised, took turns prioritizing one partner's career goals, or lived apart to accommodate the two-careers-plus-family challenge.

Environmental engineer Dr. Sandra Calvin and her husband continuously accommodated each other. At one point Sandra turned down a very promising tenure-track position to take a less prestigious postdoctoral position so that she and her husband could continue to live in the same city. Likewise, after their first child arrived, her husband turned down a comparable promising opportunity so the two of them could maintain their egalitarian family life. Between the two of them, during the ten years following graduate school, she and her husband had worked twelve different jobs combined. They took turns being the family "breadwinner," returning to school for more training, and taking care of their child.

Part 2: Advice

Dr. Erik Erikson, in describing the stages of child and adult development, proclaimed that women established their identity through the men they married.[31] He was describing what he saw in the 1950s, and afterward he acknowledged, at least informally (according to his friend Mary Catherine Bateson*), that perhaps he had been wrong and that his interpretation only reflected the times. Your daughters will be influenced strongly by the men in their lives—their fathers, their boyfriends, and eventually their husbands—but parents should raise their daughters to establish their own identities. Discovering her strengths, her interests, her essential values, her career directions, and the fit for family in her life is a very individual and individuating task of a girl's late adolescence and young adulthood. When identity is established only through marriage, it makes a woman dependent and unprepared for the contemporary world.

Observing and participating in your daughters' lives can be fraught with frustration and puzzlement, especially for parents who have lived in a very different world with regard to the status of women. Your own workplace and your home may have been very different from what your daughters' are now and will be in the future. Your daughters have many more options available to them. They may choose to have no children, may postpone a career until after they have children, may begin a promising career and suddenly decide to take time off for children, may balance a challenging career with children and child care, may choose a traditional career and postpone entering the workforce or become involved part time in a career while raising their children, may pursue a challenging full-time career while their husbands are full-time homemakers, may arrange to share careers and child care on a half-and-half basis, may bring up a family in a lesbian relationship, may choose not to marry but select a partner and continue with plans for family, may be divorced and may or may not remarry, may lose a husband to death or serious illness, or may choose to bring up children alone without benefit of another man or woman. It may be even more difficult for you to understand your daughters' workplace in our changing society than it has been for you to understand the rapid changes in your own workplace. It will always be difficult to interpret whether there are glass ceilings or sticky floors in the workplace or whether the inhospitality of your daughters' workplace is due to her own lack of skills, motivation, or simply the overwhelming busyness that comes with dividing her time between the responsibilities of careers and relationships.

SEQUENCE PATTERNS FOR MARRIED WOMEN

Figure 10.5 delineates some of the alternative patterns followed by the women in our study.

Four main sequences for married women in our study are described in the figure. There are permutations and combinations within these patterns, and family and career rewards and penalties that accompany each. Pattern 1, the "traditional" pattern, was typified by homemaker-volunteer Roberta Baldwin,* and a variation of this pattern—to return to a traditional career, such as teaching, nursing, or social work, after the children are grown—is exemplified by homemaker-teacher Nancy Collier and nurse Angela Sands. Roberta received an excellent education, married after college, and worked briefly until her first child was born. Thereafter, she parented and made significant volunteer leadership

FIGURE 10.5

Optional Sequence Patterns
for the Married Women in the Study

Pattern 1: Traditional	Pattern 2: Delayed Career	Pattern 3: Linear Career	Pattern 4: Late Bloomer
College	College	College	High School Graduation
Marriage	Brief Career	Graduate or Professional School (Optional depending on career)	Marriage (or parenting before marriage)
Wife/Parent/ Volunteer	Marriage	Early Career and Marriage	Preschool Parenting
Wife/Volunteer	Preschool Parenting	Early Career and Preschool Parenting	School-Age Parenting and College Attendance
	School-Age Parenting and Return to School or Career	Middle Career and School-Age Parenting	Early Career
	Early Career	Peak Career	Middle Career
	Middle Career		
	Peak Career		

contributions to her community. Nancy and Angela prioritized parenting, but managed to keep working in their professions, at least part time, to keep their confidence and skills up. They plan to return to their professions full time when their children are grown.

The rewards for the women in this sequence include time to concentrate on raising children and time and energy for providing psychological support to the principal breadwinner, the husband and father. The traditional relationship gave the husband and father optimal time to develop his career, and it typically gave him more power over family decisions, more status in the community, and even more status with his children. A few other important rewards came to the community in the provision of educated volunteers who made contributions to schools, hospitals, community agencies, and government. These women also provided a strong support group for each other and a stable community foundation.

The penalty for the women was often, but not always, dependency on their husbands (particularly if there was divorce, abuse by the husband, or a husband's death). The women's identities were tied directly to their husbands' and children's successes and failures. If the women returned to careers, they often remained at the lower or middle levels of those careers and did not have sufficient time remaining to reach the peaks of their career potential.

The "delayed career" pattern, pattern 2, followed by many women in the study, including State Senator Suzanne Daniels and Dr. Anne Caroles, included delay of continued education or postponement of total involvement in a career until preschool-age and sometimes elementary-school-age parenting was done, and then a gradual embrace of the challenge of continued education or a high-level career. This group of women were often frustrated at the delay necessary to develop their career direction and were overwhelmed trying to balance child rearing, education, and early careers. However, they had more time to devote to their children than women who pursued a linear career path, and they got a head start on their careers compared to traditionalists. Some were able to move through their careers toward peak accomplishment without losing the opportunity to spend time at home with their preschoolers.

The main penalties for the women who followed this pattern came in the form of frustration at the delay of their careers and the loss of confidence and skills during that period of preschool parenting. They may also have forfeited more prestigious careers or achievement of their maximal career potential. The risks in returning to school or the workplace were high for them because they had often lost academic and even general confidence. The women's movement was very encouraging and facilitative for these women. The support of their husbands was often invaluable in making this change in their life. On the other hand, sometimes their delayed career status changed family dynamics and resulted in divorce if either the husband felt threatened by the woman's success or the woman believed she had outgrown her husband.

Those who followed the "linear career" pattern, pattern 3, focused directly on establishing their careers. They were typically doctors, attorneys, business executives, orchestral musicians, and scientists. Executive Susan Widham,* Rabbi Miriam Kane, attorney Diana Doyle, medical researchers Dr. Janice Douglas* and Dr. Alyssa Gaines, engineer Dr. Catherine Burns, television anchor Donna Draves, and cardiothoracic surgeon Dr. Ana Casa were a few of the linear career women whose case stories are shared in our book. There were many more. All of the single women in the study also followed the linear pattern without the marriage and/or parenting sequences.

The great rewards for the women who followed this pattern were career benefits and the rapid development of self-confidence. They moved to the peak of their careers more swiftly compared to those in the traditional and delayed-career patterns. There were, nevertheless, penalties. They were more vulnerable to gender bias and thus did not necessarily move to the peak of their careers as quickly as men in similar careers. Furthermore, the balancing of family life during their challenging careers was often difficult and stressful. Many took little time to be with their new babies. Nannies and child-care workers provided much of the child care during their children's preschool years. The postponement of childbearing probably was the basis for the fertility problems some of these women experienced. The women in this pattern often came to a period of reappraisal in their lives as well, sometimes wondering whether they needed to reevaluate their life relationships once they had achieved success in their careers. This reappraisal stage is similar to that often found in adult male development. Sometimes, in stepping back and putting their careers in perspective, our women realized they defined themselves as much by their family and friends as by their careers. Medical researcher Dr. Alyssa Gaines and cardiothoracic surgeon Dr. Ana Casa provided examples of self-definition through family and friends despite their high-powered, successful careers.

The "late bloomers" in pattern 4 were typified by the stories of publishing figure Helen Gurley Brown,* executive Margaret Karnes, and artist Sandra Sheets. These women were thrust into the parenting or work worlds early, and only much later and very gradually did they accomplish their education and move into successful careers. They had not earlier projected success for themselves, but regrouped and found stairways upward, discovering their individual identities later in life. Although some of the women in the study who followed this pattern are happy with their accomplishments and were able to reach the peak of their careers, the postponement of education for many women who are late bloomers barely permits them to get started in a career. The balancing of child rearing and further education was certainly a heavy burden for these women. This is not a recommended career path for your daughters because there is much risk that they will not be able to overcome their late start. Many women in our society who drop out of high school or don't complete college never fulfill their potential, accepting lower-status or less interesting jobs because overwhelming parenting burdens prevent their continued education. They may never discover their capabilities. On the other hand, the success stories of the "late bloomers" in our study also reveal that it is never too late to redirect your life.

Some careers cannot be achieved with some sequences. That is, if your daughter prioritizes a sequence choice above a career choice, certain careers will not be possible. Also, consider a further analogy proposed by Mary Catherine Bateson* at the second annual Matanuska-Susitna Women's Conference in Wasilla, Alaska, in the fall of 1997. She, too, compared women's lives to a home, from the perspective of putting an addition on a home. She pointed out that when families add to their home, they not only add a room or two, but they typically change the uses of other rooms and reorganize the entire house. Mary Catherine thus maintains that with the longer life spans and healthier active lifestyles of women today, not only can their lives expand and be redesigned in a fashion to provide more time for relationships, parenting, careers, explorations, and so on, but they can also change the sequences and directions of those activities.

For women today, thirty-five or forty is not too old for beginning a career, starting a family, reappraising one's lifestyle, or initiating a new phase of life. Women are not only adding time but enhancing, changing, and restructuring the manner in which they lead their lives. Although women may not be able to accomplish all at once everything that the feminist movement encourages them to do, their remodeled lives may permit them to accomplish what they wish to accomplish in alternating sequences.

TAKING RESPONSIBILITY FOR SUCCESS

Surely some chance circumstances do play a part in the achievement of success. It is also true that efficiency and hard work are directly connected to success for both men and women. However, intelligence, creativity, and smart choices are also critical to success. Perhaps it is time for parents to teach their daughters to abandon some modesty and take appropriate credit for their accomplishments. Indeed, their denial of responsibility for their own success may steal from them their upward mobility. While modesty and humility continue to be virtues, women who announce they have done little when they have done much will not be viewed as achievers by their employers or by their children. When your daughter receives a compliment or an award, she can thank the person who compliments her, give credit to others who have contributed to her accomplishment, and acknowledge that she does feel good about what she has accomplished. For most women, that may feel like bragging, but it is simple honesty.

TEMPERING DREAMS WITH REALITY

There is continuous research in most careers on the acceptance and promotion of women in the workplace. Be open to new findings, and encourage your daughter to examine various careers and the latest research findings on women's issues. It is a disservice to women, and to everyone, to blame gender bias for a problem that is rooted in absence of merit. On the other hand, it will be helpful for your daughter to be realistic about how her career dreams match reality for women in the workplace.

Girls with above-average abilities, a reasonable work ethic, and good social skills often have realistic expectations for themselves. Because their expectations are moderate, although they may face occasional disappointments, they are delightfully surprised with the extent of their successes, particularly when they didn't anticipate them. To do better than one expects is always exhilarating. It brings confidence and delight. The wonderful stories that some of the women recalled about being just a shy average kid, and then being able to say, "Look at me now," are reassuring for parents who worry about their own daughters doing well.

Many women in our study had circuitous climbs to the top of their careers. If they had reasonable expectations for themselves, each step upward was a surprise and motivated them to climb the next steps that they believed they were capable of climbing. However, the meanderings of delayed and circuitous careers may be painfully disappointing for women who have very high expectations and very specific goals. Each landing, rejection, or postponement may cause them to believe they've failed. They may experience loss of confidence, anxiety, or depression. They may worry that the dreams of their childhood may never be fulfilled, and for some those dreams will indeed not be fulfilled. They may have to temper their dreams with reality, and as parents of these women, you may need to encourage patience and communicate your appreciation of them as they are. You may have to readjust your expectations; this may be easier for you than it is for them.

For some of your daughters, as they try to temper their dreams, it will be difficult for them to determine when perseverance and resilience are the best course or when a creative approach to changing direction is a more promising strategy. You may not agree that their choice is correct, but those decisions must be your daughters'. It's best for you to have given them some forewarning during adolescence, but even if you did, they may not have heard you, or they may have heard your urging for flexibility as an insult to their talents. It is important to encourage your daughters to be flexible while they follow their dreams, or reality will be difficult for them to accept.

THE V OF LOVE

You can never love your daughters too much, but it is helpful to view your daughters' gradual empowerment in a V shape. The V of love pairs freedom, choices, and power with responsibility and encourages loving parents to gradually empower children by increasing all four of these. Thus, when small children are at the base of the V, they have little freedom and responsibility, but by adolescence the V has spread to encompass increased freedom, power, and responsibility. There are dangers in empowering children too early and in taking away power and freedom from children who had been given more power than they could handle, because relative to the earlier power they felt, they will feel powerless, depressed, and angry. I call that an inverted V, or Λ.

There are two components of the "V of love" analogy that seem to fit with parents' positions relative to tempering their adult daughters' dreams. The first is permitting children to leave that V of love to become the adults you raised them to be. The timing of the onset of adult independence in our culture is far less specific than the endpoints of the V. The education of successful women in our society is often prolonged much beyond the start of legal adulthood. Thus, conflicts between dependence and independence may continue considerably beyond high school and college graduation. In the words of the husband and father of the authors of this book, "It may be that you don't ever stop being a parent until you die." However, once your adult daughters have made their decisions, there is room only for your support and for the adjustment of your own expectations.

There is a second concept that has relevance to this later time in your daughters' lives, and that is "dethronement." In Chapter 8 I described an enthroned prince or princess, a first or only child (and often even a first grandchild) who was so verbal and bright and positive until another sibling came along and dethroned the first child. I pointed out how this child could also be dethroned by the classroom experience of having to share power and attention. The effect of dethronement is that a formerly confident, optimistic, and positive child becomes negative, angry, or depressed, and that new persona comes to dominate the child's personality.

Although dethronement is seen more obviously in childhood and adolescence because it is simpler to see at that stage, in young adulthood dethronement is much more related to disappointment in not accomplishing very competitive career goals. Women are much more vulnerable to dethronement because of gender discrimination in so many highly competitive careers and the difficult decisions related to the timing of pregnancy, birth, and child-care commitments. Dethronement changes women's self-perceptions; for example, Dr. Anne Caroles, who wanted to be a medical scientist, must have felt dethroned for years after she dropped out of medical school, became a full-time homemaker, saw her husband become successful, and lost confidence in herself. Her return to school gradually restored her confidence.

Dethronement may take place for the women in pattern 1, the "traditional" pattern, if they were excellent students and find themselves full-time homemakers without other rewarding choices. Dethronement can take place during the delay for women who follow pattern 2, "delayed career," as they see their dreams disappearing. For those who follow pattern 3, "linear career," dethronement takes place if they are not able to accomplish their high goals after much sacrifice of their social life and relationships. For "late bloomers," early dethronement takes place sometimes in a very shattering and shocking way, but gradually these women build confidence again if they manage an education or a career.

Understanding the psychological damage caused by dethronement can help young women and their parents to identify the symptoms of the problem and understand the need for both resilience and creativity at such junctures on their road to success and happiness.

ADJUSTING TO YOUR ADULT DAUGHTERS' CHOICES

Our research has documented the importance of parents, relatives, husbands, partners, and friends as support to your daughters. Marriage, family relationships, and friendships usually play an important role in your daughters' happiness. Our women made it clear that for many, relationship building was sacrificed during difficult periods of their lives, and for some women there were serious regrets. On the other hand, there were many women in the study who attributed their success orientation to a mother who clearly stated, "Do as I say, not as I did." A significant number of women in our study had mothers who were full-time homemakers and would have preferred having professional careers, or who had lower-status careers because they sacrificed for the sake of their families. When the feminist movement voiced the importance of women's autonomy and careers, these mothers were encouraged to reinforce a message of independence to their daughters.

In giving advice to your own daughters in childhood (and certainly by adolescence) encourage them to seek friends of both genders who respect your daughters for their intelligence and their personal needs. Girls need to be taught early to understand *partnerships of power,* or they may find themselves in relationships with men where they are not given the opportunity to develop their own talents and careers. The true damage to girls' self-esteem comes from a self-evaluation that is tied only to pleasing boys.

The study of these successful women was intended to advise parents on how they could raise their daughters to take advantage of the ever-increasing opportunities available to women. It was not intended to denigrate traditional careers or disregard the role of full-time mothers and homemakers. Indeed, the data clearly show that many of the women in traditional careers are extremely happy with both their career and family choices. On the other hand, girls should be brought up with sufficient education and independence to allow them choices rather than simply placing them in the less powerful position of yesteryear, when their spouses' decisions left little room for choices of their own.

Compromises are required when partners have separate careers that don't fit in the same lifestyle or locality. As parents, you probably have not assumed that women must always follow their husbands' lead, as in the time of your parents and as in many families still today. Instead, you will have brought your sons and daughters up with enough confidence to negotiate and compromise on a plan that will meet either or both partners' career and relationship needs. For success-oriented young people, these compromises are never easy and may require sacrifices and even some meandering on the part of both their careers. If you, as parents, have done the best job you can in helping your daughters to feel smart, hardworking, and independent, and added a dose of the kindness and sensitivity that were so prevalent in the lives of the women in our study, you can pat yourself on the back for a job well done. You can enjoy observing your daughters creating further V's of love around them, whether those V's are in the family or the workplace. You will have helped to foster in them confidence, a success orientation, and a sense of balance in their lives. Although the stories of these successful women have shown us that winning is not only possible, but important, they have also communicated clearly that winning is only one component of their fulfilled lives.

NOTES

INTRODUCTION

1. American Association of University Women Educational Foundation, *The AAUW Report: How Schools Shortchange Girls* (Washington, DC: AAUW, 1992).

CHAPTER 2

1. In 1960 (the earliest date for which we were able to find statistics) less than 6 percent of the women in our country had earned college degrees. In that same year 10 percent of the males had attained at least college degrees. Source: *Statistical Abstract of the United States,* U.S. Dept. of Commerce, Economic and Statistics Administrator, Bureau of Census, Sept. 1994.

CHAPTER 3

1. Good study habits are similar for girls and boys, and my book *Dr. Sylvia Rimm's Smart Parenting* has many suggestions you can use.
2. See L. Garduque and M. Ruggiero, "Effects on Working in Adolescent Development," *Developmental Psychology* 18, 3 (1982), 385–395; L. Steinberg and S. Dornbusch, "Negative Correlates of Part-Time Employment During Adolescence: Replication and Elaboration," *Developmental Psychology* 17, 2 (1991), 304–313; L. Steinberg, S. Fegley, and S. Dornbusch, "Negative Impact of Part-Time Work on Adolescent Adjustment: Evidence from a Longitudinal Study," *Developmental Psychology* 29, 2 (1993), 171–180; J. Thomas, "Experts Take a Second Look at Virtue of Student Jobs," *The New York Times,* May 13, 1998.

CHAPTER 4

1. S. Rimm and K. J. Lovance, "The Use of Subject and Grade Skipping for the Prevention of Underachievement," *Gifted Child Quarterly* 36 (1992), 100–105.

CHAPTER 6

1. Group Achievement Identification Measure, S. B. Rimm, 1986, Educational Assessment Service, Inc., Watertown, WI 53098.

CHAPTER 10

1. L. G. Smith, "Centuries of Educational Inequities," *Educational Horizons* 60 (1981), 4–10.
2. Ibid.
3. M. Rossiter, *Women Scientists in America: Before Affirmative Action, 1940–1972* (Baltimore, MD: Johns Hopkins University Press, 1995).
4. "Almost, but Not Quite, Equal," *U.S. News & World Report,* January 13, 1997, 12.
5. U.S. National Science Foundation, *Selected Data on Science and Engineering Doctorate Awards,* Survey of Earned Doctorates, Division of Science Resources Studies, annual, 1995.
6. U.S. Department of Commerce, *The National Data Book: 117th Edition of the Statistical Abstract of the United States* (Washington, DC: GPO, 1997), 410.
7. Ibid.
8. Ibid.
9. G. A. Davis and S. B. Rimm, *Education of the Gifted and Talented,* 4th ed. (Boston: Allyn and Bacon, 1998).
10. S. E. Turner and W. G. Bowen, "The Flight from the Arts and Sciences: Trends in Degrees Conferred," *Science,* October 1990, 517–520.
11. J. Stacey, "USA Snapshots: Pay Inequity," *USA Today,* November 26, 1990, sec. B.
12. D. Kunde, "Women MBA Grads Outpace Men in Pay," *New Haven Register,* December 3, 1995, sec. D, pp. 1, 8.
13. J. H. Dobrzynski, "How to Succeed? Go to Wellesley: Its Graduates Scoff at Glass Ceilings," *The New York Times,* October 29, 1995, sec. 3, pp. 1, 9.
14. Sara Lee Corp., Fact Sheet of the 1997 Catalyst Census of Women Board Directors of the Fortune 500 Companies.
15. E. Rubenstein, "Right Data," *National Review,* October 13, 1997, 16.
16. R. L. Kirschstein, M.D., "Editorials: Women Physicians—Good News and Bad News," *New England Journal of Medicine* 334, 15 (1996), 982–983.
17. J. G. Shaller, "Commentary: The Advancement of Women in Academic Medicine," *Journal of the American Medical Association* 264 (1990), 1854–1855.
18. S. C. Martin, R. M. Parker, and R. M. Arnold, "Careers of Women Physicians: Choices and Constraints," *Western Journal of Medicine* 149 (1988), 758–760.
19. J. Bickel and G. J. Povar, "Women: Women as Health Professionals," in W. T. Reich (ed.), *Encyclopedia of Bioethics,* Revised Edition, 2585–2591 (New York: Simon & Schuster/Macmillan, 1995).
20. Davis and Rimm, *Education of the Gifted and Talented.*
21. B. J. Tesch, H. M. Wood, A. L. Helwig, and A. B. Nattinger, "Promotion of Women Physicians in Academic Medicine: Glass Ceiling or Sticky Floor?" *Journal of the American Medical Association* 273, 13 (1995), 1022–1025.

22. M. S. Hartman, "Leadership: The Agenda for Women in the 1990s," *Douglass Alumnae Bulletin* 67, 4 (1994), 11–13.

23. *World Almanac,* 1994; *Congressional Quarterly,* November 7, 1992, November 12, 1994, January 4, 1997.

24. U.S. Department of Commerce, *National Data Book.*

25. M. R. Brown, A. J. Eisenberg, and S. S. Sawilowsky, "Traditionality and the Discriminating Effect of Expectations of Occupational Success and Occupational Values for Women Within Math-Oriented Fields," *Journal of Vocational Behavior* 50 (1997), 418–431.

26. National Science Foundation, *Women and Minorities in Science and Engineering* (Washington, DC: NSF, 1990).

27. L. Nochlin, *Women, Art, and Power and Other Essays* (New York: Harper and Row, 1988), 149–150.

28. U.S. Department of Commerce, *National Data Book.*

29. Rubenstein, "Right Data."

30. K. Deaux, "Ahhh, She Was Just Lucky," *Psychology Today* 10 (1995), 70; I. H. Frieze, "Women's Expectations for and Causal Attributions of Success and Failure," in M. T. Mednick, S. S. Tangri, and L.W. Hoffman (eds.), *Women and Achievement: Social and Motivational Analysis* (New York: Halsted, 1975); R. D. Post, "Causal Explanations of Male and Female Academic Performance as a Function of Sex-Role Biases," *Sex Roles* 7 (1981), 691–698; C. M. Callahan, C. M. Cunningham, and J. A. Plucker, "Foundations for the Future: The Socio-Emotional Development of Gifted, Adolescent Women," *Roeper Review* 17 (1994), 99–105.

31. E. H. Erikson, *Identity and the Life Cycle: Selected Papers by Erik H. Erikson* (New York: International Universities Press, 1959).

ACKNOWLEDGMENTS

Considering the size of this research project and the large number of participants, it is not surprising to find so significant a list of people to acknowledge. Our only fear is that we may have unintentionally omitted a name of someone who has contributed to our work. If your name has been omitted, we wish to apologize and thank you, albeit anonymously.

We'd like to begin by thanking the many people who helped us to recruit women for our study, and it is indeed in this category of recruitment that we have probably omitted some names of people who were very helpful. Thanks go to almost the entire Rimm adult family, including Dr. Alfred Rimm, Janet Rimm, Dr. David Rimm, Allison Rimm, Dr. Eric Rimm, Dr. Joseph Madsen, Dr. Alan Rimm-Kaufman, Vivian Lopatin, and Carol Rimm. Obviously the co-authors, Dr. Sara Rimm-Kaufman and Dr. Ilonna Rimm, were also very active in recruitment. Others who assisted in this recruitment of participants included Nancibel Coe, Jean Considine, Lisa Fauvre, Robert and Karen Gary, Ann Gilbert, Elizabeth Greco, Dr. Deborah Griest, Meredith Gunlicks, Lisa Hatfield, Linda Gordon Kuzmack, Pierre Lehu, Dr. Susan Lemagie, Senator Barbara Lorman, Dr. Rene McGovern, Jean Moe, Jori Naegle, Ann Patty, Steve Ross, Janet Schiller, Jadwiga Sebrecht, Laurel Stavis, Dr. Cynthia Strieter, Terri Vicek, and Caitlin Williams.

In addition to the authors, we were fortunate to have some excellent assistants to interview many of the women in our study. Ann Gilbert, Elizabeth Greco, and Caroline Schaerfl are especially appreciated for the large number of women they interviewed as volunteers. Our great appreciation is also extended to volunteers Kathy Baldwin, Marian Carlson, Kathryn Demick, Beth Farrell, Lisa Goldman, Meredith Gunlicks, Bonnie Livingstone, Dr. Marilyn Quick, Janet Rimm, Susan Vassel, and Carol Wolf. We also appreciate Tracy Gary, Rebecca Ravas, and Terri Vicek, who also conducted interviews in their capacity as research assistants.

Thanks are also extended to MetroHealth Medical Center for providing partial costs for printing and distributing questionnaires, providing a part-time research assistant, and for funding a Chester summer scholar for research assistance.

The authors extend special appreciation to Dr. Alfred Rimm for his leadership in the analysis of the extensive data, and to Dr. Eric Rimm and Dr. Alan Rimm-Kaufman for their assistance in that analysis. Appreciation is also extended to research assistants Valerie Eppley, Lisa Fauvre, Rebecca Hawkins, Eileen Kelley-Moeller, Kathleen Quintus, Rebecca Ravas, Beth Slejko, Karen Ukleja, and Terri Vicek for their contributions in gathering and interpreting the qualitative information. Special appreciation is due also to Bonnie Livingstone for coding and entering the voluminous amount of data.

Extensive editorial and secretarial assistance was very valuably contributed by Joanne Riedl, who tackled this mammoth job with a thoroughness and dedication that was at least extraordinary. The secretarial assistance of Marilyn Knackert, Marian Carlson, Karen Ukleja, Alice Poduska, and high-school student volunteers Nathan Bedorossian and Charlene Chu were also critical to the completion of this major research project.

Additionally, we would like to thank our editor, Ann Patty, for her helpful suggestions and guidance, and Steve Ross, vice president of the Crown Publishing Group, for his assistance. As always, we appreciate the assistance of our agent, Pierre Lehu, in arranging for the publishing of our book, as well as for his excellent ideas for communicating our messages to women and to the parents of girls. Last but not least, we wish to extend a special thank-you to Janet Rimm, who almost miraculously thought of the excellent book title that everyone finally agreed upon.

Many busy and successful women from all over the country contributed their time by completing extensive questionnaires and/or participating in interviews. Some preferred that we not use their names anywhere in the book, to protect their confidentiality. Others gave us permission to use their names but preferred we not use them in the context of their life stories. We sincerely thank them all but can only acknowledge by name those who have given permission. We deeply appreciate the contribution of all who participated in the study, and sincerely hope that they know they have made a positive difference for girls and their parents and teachers. Their stories were inspiring, and we can only apologize for leaving out so many more wonderful stories than we could include. Our book would have been excessively long had we added any more of the valuable messages.

The long list of thank-yous follows: Carol Aalbers, Martha Aarons, Sandra Abda, Ruby Abrahams, Laura Abrahamsen, Rebecca Abrams, Melinda S. Ackerman, Susan Ackermann, Elisabeth Adkins, Connie Adler, Nancy Agres, Mary Ainsworth, Future Akins, Anne Albright, Anita Alexander, Joan Alker, Margaret Washburn Allison, Diane B. Allison, Linda Almy, Ruth Alsop, Gigi Amateau, Mary Ann Amato, Donna Ambroism, Barbara Andelman, Deborah Anderson, Jennifer C. Annandono, Brigid Annis, Kimberly Applegate, Ruth Negri Armato, Beth Arnold, Judith Arnold, Mary Rose Arnold, Deborah Arntz-Huleman, Amy Artes, Nadine Asin, Lisa Atkinson, Kathy Augustine, Faye C. Austin, Camille Avellano, Susan Axelrod, Diane M. Balach, Leslie Baldacci, Roberta Baldwin, Judyann Barkus-Ekhorutomwen, Nadine Barlow, Lisa Barner, Linda Barrett, Susan Bartlett, Doris Bartlett, C. Adrienne Baughman, Sandy Baxter, Rebecca Beavers, Jill Bederman, Susan MacDonald Bedinghaus, Lori Beetchenow, Eve Belfance, Kathryn A. Belfance, Hazel Belvo, Christine Belz, Roseann Bentley, Christine J. Bergman, Sharon M. Berliner, Margaret High Bernard,

Mary Kaye Bernardo, Nichole Bernier, Laurei Raleigh Bieze, Barbara Billingsley, Sheila M. Birch, Tamara Kay Bixler, Betty Blair, Ellen Abrams Blankenship, Julie Blum, Lyz Bly, Sally E. Blyttle-Grizer, Ann Bochnick, Effie Lee Boggess, Corinne L. Bomba, Nicolette K. Bonnstetter, Frances E. Bostwick, Karla Bourland, Mireille Boutry, Anita Bowser, MaryAnn Boysen, Ann Bracale, Nancy Q. Brady, Katherine Diane Brandt, Rodene Brchan, Sally Brechbill, Penny Anderson Brill, Karen Brocco-Kish, Margo E. Broehl, Mary M. Brogan, Mary Brooner, Terri L. Brosch, Cindy Brown, Denise Walsh Brown, Helen Gurley Brown, Donna L. Bucher, Joanie Budzileni, Elizabeth Buechler, Mary Ellen Behmer, Sarah Bullen, Sandra Bullen, Lee Ann Buras, Ellen Stein Burbach, M. Burch, Claire Burger, Mary Jane Burger, Cecelia Burnett, Jane Burnside, Diana Bush, Diane A. Butler, Keri Butler, Katherine Button, Happie Byers, Elaine L. Byrd, Judy Byrns, Carolyn P. Cacho, Barbara Cady, Elizabeth Cagan, Ruth Cahn, Linda Cain, Bobbi Aker Campbell, Katherine Campbell, Kay Carlson, Muriel Carmen, Teresa Carns, Gayle J. Carson, Pat Caruso, Yvonne Caruthers, Mary Rose Cassa, Norma Castaneda, Evelynn S. Caterson, Patricia Milligan Causis, Phylles Smith Cayse, Mary M. Chadbourner, Paula Irene Chambers, Alice Chalifoux, Judy Charlick, Altagracia M. Chavez, Janice M. Chebra, Terry M. Cheplowitz, Jan Chirchirillo, P. Dian Christian, M. Jane Christyson, Dona Cipkus, Elaine Cipriano, Diane E. Citrino, Diane M. Clare, Syd Clayton-Seeber, Nancy Clem, Joyce Clements, Jennifer Cline, LaVerne C. Clouden, Lynn K. Coalmer, Jane Cochran, Janet Coggins, Jane Cohen, Sara-Jane Cohen, Suzette F. Cohen, Joanna M. Coin, Jan Arvin Combs, Lynn M. Congos, C. Ellen Connally, Barbara Conroy, Barbara S. Cornett, Faith Corrigan, Shelly Coss, Hope Coulter, Katherine Covich, Christine Cowan-Gascoigne, JoAnn Cox, Marilyn Coyne, Kathryn Cramer, Melissa Crespy, Maxine Crespy, Judith A. Cross, Alice Crume, Frances M. Culbertson, Patricia Cullen, Virginia L. Culver, Carole Cupps, Judith Curr, Carol L. Curtis, Rita Cydulka, Pat D'Amore, Elizabeth M. Dabrowski, Deanna L. Dahl-Grove, Linda Daichendt, Theodora P. Dakin, L. Karen Darrer, Holly Darus, Holly Davenport, JoDee Davis, Victoria Davis, Carrie Davis, Deborah V. Dawson, Anne Day, Wendy DeBow, Susan DeChiara, Debbie DeJoseph, Helen Deluno, Michelle Demarsh, Beth DeMauro, Louise P. Dempsey, Hilda Green Demsky, Joanne D. Denko, Debra Dennett, Gloria J. DePasquale, Maureen DeVito, Elizabeth J. Deucher, Lorna Cooke DeVaron, Valerie T. DiMaria, Brenda Dipman, Karen M. Dirks, Susan L. Dolin, Catherine Domann, Mary Patricia Donahue, Aralee Dorough, Chantel Dothey, Eileen Doughty, Janice G. Douglas, Lorraine Doyle, Claire Draucker, Elizabeth J. Dreyfuss, Betty Del Duca, Holly Duck, Ann Duff, Lydia A. Eastbum, Anne Eddis, Diane Eden, Mary Lou Edgar, Beth Embrescia, Nancy Louise Engelhardt-Moore, Miriam Erick, Heather R. Ettinger, Diane Evans, Nikki Evans, Denise L. Evert, LaVerne Ewart, Muriel Fahrion, Vera Fajtova, Lisa Fannin, Amy Fasnacht, Judith Fay-Gruber, Terri Fayer, Mary Lou Ferbert, Karen Ferrick-Roman, Linda Ferris, Maureen McGlynn Flanagan, Mary Jo Florio Flanagan, Donna Congeni Flanigan, Wanda Filer, Janet Fitzgerald, Louise Foerster, Bev Footer, Tracy Ford, Sharon Forte, Mary Foust, Arlene Frank, Ingrid Franse, Bonnie R. Fraser, Dorothy Freed, Jeanne Freeman, Ruth A. Freeman, Beebe Freitas, Janet French, Susan Freras, Carmela Freund, Betsy Friedman, Molly Friedrich, Donna Fromberg, Kathy Fronheiser, Vickie Fruehauf, Alsion Peters Fujito, Beth Fuller, Erin Furbee, Polly Furey, Carol Gabler, Carolyn Gadill-Warner, Marilee Gallagher, Julia A. Gallaugher, Linda Gandee, Wendy M. Garcia, Robin Garland, Judy Garner, Bailey Gartner, Debra Gatton, Susan Gavazzi, Wendy Geaney, Sara M. Gear, Dee Geisert, Susan Gerard, Laura Geuther, Eunice Gibson, Ann Gilbert, Sue Gilbert, Kathleen M. Gill, Phyllis Gilmore,

Freda Gimpel, Jill Ginsberg, Gina Ginsberg-Riggs, Judith McGlincky Giovanetti, Sally Ann Glenn, Kathy Goettl, Linda G. Gordon, Marion Gordon, Lesley Gouradian, Jennifer A. Gozdan, Kathy Grall, Irene Breslaw Grapel, Sharon Grebanir, Elizabeth Greco, Marjorie Greenfield, Nancy Gregory, Carolyn K. Grenfell, Debra Griest, Donna Sue Groves, Betty Grundberg, Daisy Gomes Gualberto, Binnie R. Gun, Karen Habblitz, Kirsten Hadden, Kathy Hafner, Amy Hager, Germaine Hahnel, Alison Hall, Brynda Hall, Mary Hamilton, Mary Hammann, Robyn Hannigan, Jo A. Hannifin, Amy Axt Hanson, Alice Harpel, Sue Harper, Stacey Harper, Paula Hartman-Stein, Katie Hartsell, Lisa Hatfield, Linda C. Hays, Karen J. Hayt Marcus, Linda Headrick, Mavis Heatherington, Barbara A. Heenan, Linda J. Heffner, Kathi Heim, Alice Heiman, Patricia Hemann, Julie Henry, Christine E. S. Hensley, Henrietta Herbert, Alice Herman, Susan Sara Herman, Sylvia Susan Hernandez-Curtis, Barbara Hershey, M. Christine Hetrick, Marcia Hill, Sharyn Hinman, Nadine K. Hinton, Maureen Corr Hite, Caryn Holbrook, Pat Holcomb, Patricia Hollingsworth, Earlene A. Horne, K. M. Horoszewski, Deena Horst, Mary L. Houser, Mary M. Howe, Deborah Hrabinski, Christine Huddleson, Peggy Huppert, Paula Hurwitz, Michelle Husted, Holly Hyman, MaryAnn U. Ihejirika, Patricia L. Inman, Nancy Ireland, Sarah Isto, Heidi Trevor Itashiki, JoAnn Jackson, Donna E. Jacobson, Karny Jacoby, Wendy James, Dana A. Jamison, Carol A. Janda, Sara L. Janlonicz, Sue Janssen, Susan Steves Jaros, Stephanuie B. Jarrett, Lucille Jennings, Patricia P. Jennings, Kathryn P. Jensen, Kerri Jewell, Nancy K. Johnson, Pam Johnson, Candice Johnson, Katherine M. Johnston, Pam Johnston, Peggy Jones, Elayne Jones, Gretchen Jones, Cynthia Jones-Nosacelo, Sharon Lackey Jones, Diana Jordan, Ellen S. Jordan, Jennie R. Jordan, Evelyn Kaden, Monica Kaforey, Chrys Kahn-Egan, Mary Kaldunski, Joan Kalhorn, Susann Kalnay-Brady, Anne DeVroome Kamerling, Carolyn Kanasek-Needles, Gail Rose Kane, Patricia Karcher, Cheryl Karner, Andrea Kay, Elizabeth S. Kaufman, Marlene Keene, Carolyn S. Kehler, Pauleete M. Kelch, Karla Kellenberger, Loreen M. Keller, Katherine Ann Kelley, Mary Agnes Kendre, Eleanor Kennedy, P. C. Kenschaft, Leanne Kerschner, Annamarie Kersten, Sandra A. Key, Virginia S. Kharasch, Lynn Kiaer, Kathy Kienzle, Marie Foley Kijewski, Jane Elizabeth Kilby, Sandra Killy, Rosemary Basile King, Diana L. King, Kathy King, Karen Kitzmiller, Shawn Ida Klasek, Patricia Ann Kleri, Carol Ward Knox, Sandra Koenig, Paula Konvolinka, Donna D. Kostyn, Rosemary Kovacs, Rachel Kramer, Paula S. Krauser, Elaine Kraut, Cathann Kress, Margaret Krolikowski, Johanna Krontiris-Litowitz, Holly Krys, Jan Kunz, Barbara Kurtz, Linda Gordon Kuzmack, Lisa-Beth Lambert, Pamela S. Langford, Kim Langley, Rebecca Langford, Colleen Lanning, Karen Larson, Adrienne Galler Lastra, Ivonne Lastrz, Sharon Latkovich, Bonnie D. Lau, Claude Laurent, Annette Lawrence, Joan W. Lawrence, Sally Ledgerwood, Eva Lee, Charlotte Lees, Laura Leff, Sally Anne Legarth, Stephanie Legnist, Margaret Lehrman, Joanne Seminara Lehu, Susan Lemagie, Kay Leonard, S. Leonard-Schneck, Marcy LePique, Randi Letar, Margaret Lewin, Marcia Lewis, Carolyn Lewis, Mirca Liberti, Lynne M. Lieberth, Constance Harding Liejio, Jean Lifter, Betty A. Liggins-Lane, Ann Lillya, Denise Lindholme, Bobbi Lineweaver, Beth Lino, Paulette Lisy, Sharon Litton, A. Lorraine Livingston, Britt-Marie Ljung, Nancy Ller, Mary Loeken, Dawn R. Lombard, Kimberly A. Long, Nina Jo Look, Kristine Loosley, Paulette Lisy, Barbara Lorman, Liz Ludlow, Mary A. Lundby, Debra J. Lusk, Rita Lydulka, Kathy Maas, Marieta A. MacIsaac, Deirdre Madden, Diana Maddock, Michelle Maguire, Julie Mailey, Gail Majcher, Diana Majeski, Virginia Maksymowicz, Linda Malicki, M. Joan Mallcik, Susan E. Mandel, Martha Mann, Barb Maple, Neela Marnell, Catherine B. Martineau, Amber Martines,

Alice Martinson, Karen Marx, Bernadette Mast, Kathryn Mansfield Matera, Ann Michelle Matheny, Diane Mather, Carol Lee May, Virginia Shea McCormick, Marilyn McCollar, Catherine McGinn, Susan McGinn, Rene McGovern, Nancy McHugh, Patricia McKay, Robin Elise McKee, Patricia McKiernan, Nancy McKinley, Irene McLaughlin, Rhine Lana McLin, Eileen McShea, Doris McVay, Priscilla Mead, Patricia S. Mearns, Bonnie Medinger, Lisa Meek, Catharina Meints, Nadine Meints, Linda Lee Meixner, Rosemary Taft Melby, Laurie H. Mental, Ann Mercer-Watler, Mary Merle, Ilka Meruis, Helen Meta, Carolyn Meyer, Paula Michaud, Leslie Lyles Middleton, Priscilla Midkiff, Virginia Miles, Betty Miller, Nicolette Miller, Kathy Miller, Marianne Miller, Lorie J. Miller, Patricia D. Miller, Ellen G. Miller, Michele E. Mills, Erica Miner, Sara Minkoff, Bea Mitchell, Julie Mitchell, Judy Montfort, Denise Montisano, Marilyn Moore, Margaret Morino, Linda M. Morley-Torok, Carol J. Moser, Dawn Mosley, Helen Moss, Martha Mott-Gale, Michelle Moyer, Mary Kay Mueller, Nancy Mueller, Kathleen A. Muja, Margaret Mulley, Theresa Mulraeny, Mary Murphy, Jean Murray, Karen K. Murray, Susan E. Murray, Rosalyn Muskovitz, Lisa Najavits, Marie Michaela Nastasia, Patricia March Natali, Nancy B. Nathan, Charlotte M. Nealeigh, Linda Nelson, Neli R. Nelz, Mary Neuhauser, Judy Nicely, Maureen Niese, Marnie Baker Niver, Luanne Norris, Carol L. Nowka, Mary O'Brien, Mary O'Connor, K. O'Hare, Ruth Ann O'Keefe, Louise O'Knight, Kathleen McDonald O'Malley, Leah Oates, Kim R. Oberholtzer, Kathleen Olds, Levona W. Olmsted, Barbara Onekan, Pamela R. Openshaw, Sharon Oshin, Elizabeth Anne Ouellette, Sunshine Janda Overkamp, Elizabeth D. Owens, Donna M. Pacchioni, Katherine Pacovsky, Paula Page, Elizabeth Panox, Judy Ayotte Paradis, Mary M. Parnell, Susan M. Paschke, Barbara Patterson, D. Helaine Patterson, Sue Patterson, Ann Patty, Shirley I. Paulsrud, Pamela Peck, Susan Pedone, Georgia Peeples, Janey L. Perry, Cheryl Petro, Alice Petrullis, Kitty Piercy, Damaris Peters Pike, Ann Pilarczyk, Carol Pineau, Susan Polakoff Shaw, Nihc Pollock, Fern Pomerantz, Frederique Popitz-Bergez, Rita Porfiris, Libby B. Portnoy, Martha Posner, Jeannette M. Potts, Linda Potts, Geralyn M. Presti, Barbara C. Pringle, Sara Purcell, Leslie Quandt-Walle, Marilyn Quick, Mary Quinn, Marilyn Rackoff, Rosemary Rader, June Rader, Annette P. Radick, Patricia Radigan, Kate Raftney, Susan Rakow, Betty Ramey, Lynn Ramsey, Kathleen Rand, Teresa Randall, Joan Raskin, Lynn Rasko, F. Ellen Rathjen, Karen Ray, Carolyn Ray, Janice Reash, Bonnie Reeser-Solorzano, Judy Reeves, Susan Reeves, Barbara Rego, Susan Rehm, Diane Rehor, Lisa Amato Reid, Shirley Reynolds, Teresa M. Rhodes, Carol Rhymer, Sherrie D. Richey, Tracie Richey, Vanessa Richmond, Susan Riddle, Deborah L. Rice, Sally Ries, Aleida Garza Rior, Norma Rist, Karen Rizk, Lisa Roach, Shari Roan, Trina Robbins, Julia Link Roberts, Heidi Gorovitz Robertson, Bonnie Robinson, Carol Robinson, Debra Roby, Ieda Weber Rodrigues, Maureen Rogan, Margaret Rejdak Rohlik, Lorraine S. Rojek, Sharon Roman, Dorothy L. Rosenthal, Liliana Castaneda Rossmann, Judith Roth, Susan L. Rotman, Barbara G. Rowane, Vicky Emig Ruble, Lori Ruff, Lynn Rush, Mary Doria Russell, Marjorie Bell Sachs, S. Strickland Saffoys, Marilyn Sagrillo, Mindy Salisbury, Wilma Salisbury, Natalie D. Sallee, Helen Salz, Leona Samson, Kathleen Sandman, Teri Sanor, M. C. Santana, Jan Michelle Santerre, Flordelys Santiano, Madelyn R. Satz, Laura Wallens Savren, Jane W. Saxl, Susan Scarponi, Katherine S. Schendt, Susan Scherl, Anne M. Schillaci, Bunny Schiller, Janet Schiller, Ralph Schiller, Jane Schindenolf, Karen Lankton Schmidt, Divinna S. Schmitt, Amy Schnapper, Laura Schoen, Betty Rebecca Schoenberg, Debby Scholl, Susan S. Schommer, Sharon Schroeder, Donna Schuele, Phyllis L. Schwahn, Pamela Schwartz, Sheila M. Schwartz, Karen Scott, Jennifer Scott-Wasilk,

Jean Seaton, Jean M. Seaver, Jadwiga Sebrecht, Lynnette K. Sefcik, Hanna Lacuert Segal, Brenda Selinger, Kim Sells, Phyllis Seltzer, Coleen Seng, Marty Senterfit, Beth Ann Sersig, Marie Setzer, Klara Sever, Judy Shabert, Linda Shambarger, Janet Schwartz Shapiro, Gail Naomi Sharpe, Rebecca D. Shaw, Nancy Shaw, Debra M. Shaws, Ginny Shea, Lisa Sheehan, Lynn Shesser, Naomi Shields, Kathleen M. Shilling, Karen Shriver, Amy Shuman, Joan Seigal, Jane M. Seigel, Stephanie Sierra, Betty Sima, Doris Simonis, Patricia A. Simon, Theresa Sinclair, Deborah Wilder Singer, Virginia Skinner-Linnenberg, Tracy Skripac, Kathleen Slamka, Jean Slane, Jan Slater, Sharon Slettebaugh, Angela Smith, Barbara A. Smith, Julie B. Smith, Karen Smith, Lisa Smith, Susan K. Smith, Susan Marie Smith, Meredith Snow, Bettie V. Sogor, Cheryl Spahr, Andrea Spencer-Linzie, Cindy Spitz, Cynthia Stadler, Margaret Morey Stager, Faye Stahl, Claire Stamper, Esther Stanard, Deborah M. Stankovich, Heidi J. Stauber, Darlene Stedman, Kristy Steeves, Lynda Steiner, Nancy G. Stevens, Lisa Stilling, Julie Stolzer, Jan Storck, Leocadia V. Storey, Susan B. Strauss, Linda Striefsky, Nancy Strnad-Novak, Linda Strong, Laura Strychaiski, Laurie A. Stuart, Melissa Bichl Sturgis, Janie Sullivan, Mary M. Sullivan, Charmaine Szanyi-Hrusch, Deborah Tylor Tate, Ione L. Taylor, Ann E. Taylor, Marilyn Terrill, Kathi D. Tetley, Regina Thibideau, Julie Thomas, Lois Thome, Ruth Thompson, Margot K. Timbel, Lynn C. Toler, Dixie Tollkes, Anne Tomins, Jeanne Toomey, Linda Toote, Margaret Toth, Dorothy E. Touvell, Irene Treppler, Alexandra N. Turk, Peggy Ann Turner, Sue Tyler, Phyllis Uchtman, Helen Cerra Ulan, Frances Unger, Helen Unterleitner, Penelope Valentik, Nancy M. Valentine, Linda J. Van Manter, Petra Vandermark, Liz VanLeeuwen, Ann Van Heest, Donna Vecchione, Mary Vermeulen, Kathryn Wachob, Virginia Wachtel, Imogene Waddle, Andrea Wagoner, Susan Waisbren, Joyce Walker, Kathy Walker, Patricia Walunis, Katharine Warmerdam, Helen Washburn, Jill Harrison Vassar, Joyce M. Vazquez, Zorraine M. Waguespack, Carolyn Warner, Virginia Guild Watkin, Judith Waxman, Sylvia A. Weber, Karen Weiland, June Weisberger, Linda Weise, Marilyn Weitzel, Coco A. Wellington, Sarah Wells, Stella Welsh, Eve Welts, Michele Warholic Wertherald, Karen Westall, Cheryl Wetzstein, Lisa Lorraine Whiting, Kim Whetstone, Diana Whittlesey, Susan Widham, Juliann Willey, Dawn Williams, Courtenay Willis, Barbara Wilson, Evelyn L. Wilson, Nila Wilson, Margaret Witecki, Deborah Witman, Becky Rogers Witsell, Andrea Wood, Barbara Woodburn, Carol Woods, H. Dawn Wrant, Dayle K. Wright, Nancy Wunderlich, Pamela N. Wurster, Susie Wyse, Barbara Yahr, Barbara Friedman Yaksic, Carolyn Yanda, Leslie Yerkes, Peggy Zabicki, Marlene Zeitz, Suzanne Zimmerman, Patricia L. Zobel, and Sandy Zurkey.

INDEX

About the Authors

DR. SYLVIA RIMM is the author of *Why Bright Kids Get Poor Grades, How to Parent So Children Will Learn,* and *Raising Preschoolers.* A clinical professor at Case Western Reserve University School of Medicine, she is also the director of the Family Achievement Clinic at Metro-Health Medical Center in Cleveland and a contributing correspondent for the *Today* show. DR. SARA RIMM-KAUFMAN is a research psychologist at the University of Virginia and lives in Charlottesville, Virginia. DR. ILONNA RIMM is a pediatric oncology researcher who lives in Boston.